5\

RAINBOW'S END

THE JUDY GARLAND SHOW

RAINBOW'S END

THE JUDY GARLAND SHOW

COYNE STEVEN SANDERS

WILLIAM MORROW
AND COMPANY, INC.
NEW YORK

Library of Congress Cataloging-in-Publication Data

Sanders, Coyne Steven.
Rainbow's end : the Judy Garland Show / Coyne Steven Sanders.
p.   cm.
ISBN 0-688-09088-5
1. Judy Garland Show (Television program)   I. Title.
PN1992.77.J833S26   1990
791.45'72—dc20   90-6450
                                                             CIP

Printed in the United States of America
First Edition
1 2 3 4 5 6 7 8 9 10
BOOK DESIGN BY BERNARD SCHLEIFER

For Judy

INTRODUCTION

From the moment *The Judy Garland Show* was created as a concept in December of 1962, it unleashed a storm of controversy that has not ceased in more than twenty-five years.

By March 1963, less than three months after the project had become a reality through a multimillion-dollar deal entered into between the Columbia Broadcasting System and Judy Garland's production company, Kingsrow Enterprises, it was already pegged as a failure by television-industry insiders and the show-business trade papers (*Variety* and *The Hollywood Reporter*) alike.

As the series entered into its preproduction phase throughout the first half of 1963, Garland herself was a target of attack. The gossip columns predicted that she wouldn't last through the first taping, she wouldn't show up on time, she couldn't possibly sustain the grind. But when Garland's premiere episode was a great success, such reports of doom were revised to suggest that the temperamental, "undependable" superstar couldn't possibly last through half a season, let alone a full thirty-two-week season.

"Just wait and see her fail" was the prevailing attitude. Garland was under a microscope the likes of which she had never known, not even during her days at Metro-Goldwyn-Mayer under patriarchal despot Louis B. Mayer.

Yet throughout 1963 and 1964, Garland continued to surprise

everyone with her grit and determination to make her weekly series a hit—and in the process, astounded her critics, her production staff, and even CBS. For despite the ominous forecasts of certain disaster, the singer lasted on the air long after the doomsayers predicted.

In fact, Judy Garland gave some of her greatest performances on her series, and in turn gave television some of its finest hours. And had the forces swirling around her been more benevolent, the run might have been considerably longer.

The ramifications of attempting weekly television profoundly affected the remainder of Judy Garland's life until her death five years later, in 1969, at the age of forty-seven. In her difficult last days, she suffered from declining health and duplicitous business advisors, resulting in a crippling financial state that placed her nearly half a million dollars in debt and forced her to work when rest was indicated.

Her tumultuous final days for a time risked permanently dimming the star of Garland's greatness. Disturbing headlines, it seemed, proved more potent than the more than thirty years of magnificent performances that she lavished upon the public— the hundreds of stage appearances, dozens of movies, television programs, radio broadcasts, and record albums.

But history has a way of putting things in perspective. Now, more than twenty years after her death, Judy Garland seems to be more appreciated with each passing year—her sincerity, her artistry, her talent, untouched by changing tastes in music and performing styles. Tony Bennett, for one, recently deemed Judy Garland "the greatest singer of the twentieth century."

There is no better example of this phenomenal rebirth of popularity and respect for Judy Garland than *The Judy Garland Show*. In 1985, the Public Broadcasting System presented *Judy Garland: The Concert Years*. The title of the *Great Performances* production was actually a misnomer, the ninety-minute documentary relying primarily on more than three dozen clips from Judy's weekly television series rather than (unfortunately nonexistent) "live" concert footage. Garland's magnificent performances on these programs were unanimously praised and "rediscovered" by a new generation.

John J. O'Connor in *The New York Times* described the total effect as "an uncommon abundance of thrilling moments," adding, "Time has hardly dimmed the emotional impact of a Garland performance. She remains the special kind of theatrical force that exposes itself completely. . . . She croons, she belts, she flirts outrageously with her audiences . . . but always there are the voice and inimitable hand gestures, wrapping themselves around the familiar favorites—'Over the Rainbow' and 'The Man That Got Away'—and brilliantly tackling the unexpected—'Old Man River,' 'The Battle Hymn of the Republic.' " O'Connor concluded, "Any opportunity to watch her again has to be special, and . . . *The Concert Years* is certainly that."

The controversy surrounding the series erupted again in 1970, only a year after Judy's accidental death in London the previous June. Singer-songwriter Mel Tormé (who wrote special musical material for Garland's series) published his memoirs, offering his version of an ill-tempered, undisciplined, impossible star, as well as the whole that was *The Judy Garland Show*.

The Other Side of the Rainbow with Judy Garland on the Dawn Patrol, as it was cumbersomely titled, happened to be the first book published upon Garland's passing. The book—and the timing of its release—sparked a tremendous outcry among Garland's supporters, fans, and coworkers who felt Tormé was exploiting her death and defaming the Garland legend.

"The thing about Garland is that she was so special," declares Judy's first executive producer, George Schlatter. "She was so much bigger than life in so many ways that everybody tended to put themselves in the middle of a Garland experience, even if their participation was on the periphery. I don't care what anybody has heard or what anybody has said. She was great. Garland was a very important, wonderful, terrible, frightening, hysterically funny, funny event."

As Frank Peppiatt, one of her writers on the series, noted in 1989 with more than a bit of scorn, "Everybody benefited from *The Judy Garland Show* except for one person—Judy Garland."

Garland, who had an extraordinary sense of humor, likely would appreciate the irony that, more than twenty-five years after she took her final bow on Stage 43 at CBS Television City in Hollywood, *The Judy Garland Show*—once dismissed as the singer's greatest failure of her adult career—has since become her most important, and respected, body of work. Future generations have been given an enormous legacy of Judy Garland at her peak, with the added pleasure of seeing the incomparable Judy working with some of the greatest talents in show business, preserved forever on film and videotape.

The on-camera and behind-the scenes cast of characters of *The Judy Garland Show* is extraordinary: Mickey Rooney, Liza Minnelli, Barbra Streisand, George Schlatter, Norman Jewison, Gary Smith, Ethel Merman, Mort Lindsey, Ray Aghayan, Bob Mackie, Vic Damone, Peggy Lee, Jack Jones, Sid Luft, Lorna Luft, Joe Luft, David Begelman, Freddie Fields, Alan Ladd, Jr., Guy McElwaine, Count Basie, Lena Horne, June Allyson, Donald O'Connor, Jane Powell, Jerry Van Dyke, Steve Allen, Mel Tormé, Bobby Darin, Bob Newhart, Shelley Berman, Martha Raye, Diahann Carroll, Bill Colleran, Frank Peppiatt, John Aylesworth, Johnny Bradford, James Aubrey, Jr., Hunt Stromberg, Jr., Michael Dann, William S. Paley, Bill Hobin, Dean Whitmore, and Edith Head, among many others.

This is the story of a series that might have been, should have been, one of television's—and one of Judy Garland's—greatest triumphs. Instead, it was quickly dubbed at the time "the *Cleopatra* of TV," referring to the gigantic motion-picture debacle of 1963 starring Elizabeth Taylor and Richard Burton.

Yet critics heaped praise upon Garland and her series, and were uncommonly vocal in their objections when CBS canceled it. Letters of protest poured in to the network, to television newspaper columns, to *TV Guide*. A "Save Judy" campaign was vigorously launched—all to no avail.

Most of all, this is a celebration of a great artist who left behind performances that remain timeless and unequaled. Few others have been as generous in leaving behind such an enormous legacy as Judy Garland's—even if the price she paid to do so was higher than she ever could have imagined.

The story of *The Judy Garland Show* is even more astounding than its cast.

This is that story.

—Coyne Steven Sanders

"My year on television was very enlightening—and funny. It was instant disaster. Sometimes instant success. It was that way every week, one way or the other . . . but I did prove to everybody that I was reliable. They said I'd never answer the bell for the second round. But we turned out twenty-six shows. And some of them damned good, too."

—Judy Garland

1

"I'm a great TV fan—I watch it from 7 a.m. clear through Jackson Wheeler at night. Soapers are my favorite. I saw the clip of me singing 'Dear Mr. Gable' on 'MGM Parade' and I was so embarrassed at seeing me when I was 12. I was funny looking, fat, and vulgarly young!"

—Judy Garland, 1956

In the fall of 1953, Judy Garland was far more interested in making her motion-picture comeback than she was in embarking on an entirely new career in television. Realizing a dream many years in the making, Judy was about to star in a musical adaptation of *A Star Is Born*, her first film after departing Metro-Goldwyn-Mayer in 1950.

Garland, along with Sid Luft, her husband and producer of the film, had formed their own company to produce *A Star Is Born* in association with Warner Bros., giving Judy a degree of creative control she had never known in her days as a contract player.

The tour-de-force vehicle was a stunning showcase for Garland's talents, and she was eager, at the age of thirty-one, to play her first on-screen adult role. The already twice-filmed tale of a young actress who reaches the pinnacle of success as her matinee-idol husband succumbs to alcohol and suicide had for years been coveted as a screen property by Garland, who had first performed the role of hopeful Esther Blodgett on radio in 1942.

Garland's screen comeback had attracted some of Hollywood's finest talent, including leading man James Mason, director George Cukor, screenwriter Moss Hart, Judy's MGM musical mentor Roger Edens, choreographer Richard Barstow, and the composing team of Harold Arlen and Ira Gershwin.

The year before, Judy deflected her rather conspicuous absence from television by cautiously remarking, "I'll wait until more improvements are made in the medium, particularly the lighting." She added, somewhat obligingly, "But don't think I dislike TV. It's wonderful to watch."

Just as production was to commence on *A Star Is Born,* Judy declared to *TV Guide* that she "wanted no part of TV for the time being." Reflecting, no doubt, her active participation in virtually every element of the making of *A Star Is Born,* Judy noted that she would venture into television strictly on her own terms: "Every facet of any television show I might do would have to fit perfectly—story, network, time on the air, how many per year, and everything else."

Judy's criticisms of the embryonic medium that was television in the first few years of the decade were certainly not without merit; she was as much a skilled technician as she was a gifted artist. The primary factor keeping Judy away from television was not poor production values (although such criticisms had validity), but rather her deeply ingrained insecurities about her physical appearance.

Despite her overwhelming feelings to the contrary, Judy Garland was a uniquely beautiful woman far removed from the often-calculated artifice of such pinup girls as Lana Turner, Rita Hayworth, and Ava Gardner. Since her break from MGM, however, her appearance had changed dramatically. Away from films for several years, Garland had little motivation to diet, and rebelled against years of being admonished by MGM to appear slim before the cameras. While gaining weight gave Judy control of her body and destiny, it also made her increasingly insecure about her plumpness. A natural propensity to put on weight combined with the birth of two children had saddled Judy, barely thirty years old, with a decidedly matronly appearance.

To a woman as sensitive as Judy Garland, the possibility of poor lighting, bad camera work, and a distorted photographic image made television a most terrifying proposition indeed. Forced to subject herself to crash dieting in order to step before the cameras for *A Star Is Born,* she briefly won the battle against weight, only to find herself pregnant with her third child just as the picture neared completion.

In 1954, after completion of *A Star Is Born*, Judy was approached by the producers of *Lux Video Theatre* (the television spin-off of the radio hit that featured one-hour adaptations of popular films) to appear in *The Heiress* with *Star Is Born* costar James Mason. So terrified was she of television that Judy declined the offer, which would have netted her the extraordinary sum of fifty thousand dollars. And scheduled to appear on *The Ed Sullivan Show* to sing the lovely ballad "It's a New World" (from *A Star Is Born*) with the song's composer, Harold Arlen, accompanying her at the piano, Judy, at the last minute, backed out, leaving Arlen to perform the song alone.

By 1955, nearly every major performing talent from Hollywood, Broadway, or the world of pop music—including Bing Crosby, Bob Hope, Red Skelton, Jack Benny, Frank Sinatra, George Burns and Gracie Allen, Perry Como, and Dinah Shore, to name but a few—as well as many lesser lights who, overnight, clicked on the new medium—such as Milton Berle, Sid Caesar and Imogene Coca, Wally Cox, Steve Allen, Joan Davis, Betty White, and Kukla, Fran, and Ollie—had jumped aboard the bandwagon, and were firmly established, regular television celebrities. It seemed everyone was on TV except Judy, so self-conscious was she about her appearance. Most of them were also laughing all the way to the bank, a phrase first coined by Liberace, who amassed a considerable fortune from his own syndicated series that decade.

Top-line entertainers in Garland's league could command anywhere from $30,000 to $100,000 for only a half or full hour's performance on a special. It would, more often than not, be the stagggering performance fees offered to artists that influenced this decision.

And it would be money that would finally lure Judy Garland onto television.

While Judy's greatly heralded movie comeback in *A Star Is Born* had been, for the most part, a highly prestigious critical success, it had been such a long time a-borning, running so alarmingly over budget and then proving to be such a box-office disappointment, that plans for other films at Warner Bros. were canceled. This left her not quite knowing where she was to go professionally. If her big-screen return was, for many practical purposes, a fizzle, and she wasn't willing to meet the home-screen challenge, that left very few options indeed. As she invariably did when all else failed, she decided to return to the stage.

But following the birth of her son, Joe, Judy was not in the best of shape. Her third cesarean, it had been an extremely difficult birth, and Joe, a premature baby, had been given only a fifty-fifty chance of survival. While he was soon a robust, healthy baby, Judy had a somewhat shakier time of it. She lapsed into the severe postpartum depression she always suffered after giving birth, and was plagued by her usual doubts and fears, exacerbated by the crushing blow of losing the 1954 Academy Award for Best Actress to Grace Kelly. In a bind, knowing he was sitting on a potential powder keg, Sid Luft realized he had to act quickly, not only to ensure the family's financial security, but to keep his wife from spiraling off into one of her emotional tailspins.

His plan was to book Judy into a prestigious, first-class multicity tour for the fall of 1955, including Chicago's Orchestra Hall and the Los Angeles Shrine Auditorium, winding up with a two-month run on Broadway at the Winter Garden. But because many of the theaters would not post the requested guaranteed per-nightly fee against an agreed percentage of the house, the Lufts' plans hit an unexpected snag. The overriding production expenses of such a tour required such guarantees; without them, the entire plan was economically unfeasable. Everything seemed about to fall apart.

In a quandary, Sid turned to Judy's agent at MCA, Jule Stein, who told him that he felt certain he could get Judy and Sid a contract to do a ninety-minute TV show. The offer was from CBS to headline *Ford Star Jubilee*, with CBS vice president of programming Hubbell Robinson in charge of the deal on the network side. Discussions had actually begun that July to acquire Garland, with Robinson credited with creating the "basic premise" for the special. The Garland offering not only launched the once-monthly, big-budget *Ford Star Jubilee* series, the event was pegged as the network's first full-scale color telecast. And the TV special allowed the Lufts contractual release from their financially risky multicity tour.

When Sid told Judy of the CBS offer, her reaction was not excitement but fear. Sid reassured her by saying, "All Ford is buying is the same show you've been doing night after night.

And it would be one night, not twenty." Judy immediately asked, "Do you think I'm too heavy?" Still recovering from Joe's birth a few months earlier, she would have to diet, although rehearsals would help get her into shape.

Garland's first television special was to be closely fashioned upon Judy's 1951 Palace "vaudeville" act, and would include a production number replicating "Get Happy" (from her last MGM picture, *Summer Stock*), the donning of the tramp costume from *Easter Parade* for "A Couple of Swells"—leading into the climax of the show, "Over the Rainbow"—and such Garland trademarks as "The Boy Next Door," "The Trolley Song," "Rock-a-Bye Your Baby (With a Dixie Melody)," "You Made Me Love You," and "Swanee." ("The Man That Got Away," the Oscar-nominated song from *A Star Is Born*, was dropped prior to showtime.) Other songs from Judy's first Capitol LP, *Miss Show Business*, issued concurrently, were also to be included, as well as Roger Edens's lengthy "Judy at the Palace" routine, comprised of signature tunes by past luminaries who played the venerable theater.

The program was budgeted at $300,000. Judy's salary was in the neighborhood of $100,000, with Sid netting $10,000 for producing the special. Signed to act as master of ceremonies was David Wayne of *Teahouse of the August Moon* Broadway fame. Other acts to appear included the novelty comedy act the Goofers, the Escorts dance team, and twelve-year-old Japanese singer Mitsuko Sawamura.

Judy joked about her apprehension at facing the TV cameras: "Well, I'll just walk out there, faint dead away and then where will I go to make a comeback?" She added, "In movies, I know about the key lights and where the camera is. In television, there is a camera with four eyes. I don't know which to look into. There is a man with earphones and a mouthpiece, and I don't know what he is saying. There is lots to learn before getting the show on the air. Sid, my husband, finds out, and I learn because I have to know."

Invariably, the issue of her weight, and how she would photograph on television, was brought up during interviews to promote the program. "I'm not going to worry about being plump," said Judy defensively. "I have had three children, and I am concentrating on singing."

Fall 1955 advance publicity shot of Judy "in front of the cameras" on *Ford Star Jubilee*
COURTESY OF STEPHEN COX COLLECTION

Her fears, phobias, and anxiety grew every day closer to broadcast. Her tensions were reflected in a large sign outside the CBS stage during final rehearsals for the show that read, NO VISITORS. THIS IS POSITIVELY A CLOSED SET. NO EXCEPTIONS.

The day before the live telecast, Hollywood columnist James Bacon reported that Judy was "nursing laryngitis." CBS, he said, might be worried, but Judy wasn't. "I always get laryngitis as opening night nears. Just nerves. That's all it is. No germs involved," Judy assured him, although it seemed an attempt to convince herself as much as anyone else. "It'll go away as soon as I get in front of the audience, I hope. If not, I'll just sing over it. I'm not going to worry about it. I'll just work my head off, get good and sick thirty minutes before airtime, and by Sunday morning we'll know whether or not I've laid an egg."

By midafternoon Saturday, the egg was beginning to hatch. It was uncertain whether Judy would be able to do the show that night. Her "nerves, not germs" laryngitis was brought on by sheer panic and exhaustion as the live show drew nearer. Unable to rest for days, Judy resorted to too many sleeping pills near dawn the morning of the telecast, hoping to get a glimpse of sleep. Sid attempted vainly to revive her, carrying her into an ice-cold shower and walking her back and forth in her bedroom. He then phoned her doctor to prescribe a stimulant.

Within a few hours, Sid had gotten the prescription for Judy and taken her to the CBS studios. Judy's throat doctor advised Sid to call out for an order of Chinese food and a large amount of iced tea. The food would reduce the impact of the sleeping pills, and the tea would act as a diuretic to flush out at least some of the medication. Sid explained Judy's inability to sing at dress rehearsal as being more or less normal procedure to save her voice for the telecast. Although the CBS executives and the audience were nonplussed, Judy walked through all of the dress rehearsal. By showtime, she was in far better shape, but her voice was still husky, the vibrato slow and wide.

Although she shook off the effects of the medication as the show progressed, her laryngitis remained. Only in the last number (following "Swells" with David Wayne as her foil) was Judy's magic undiluted, with her magnificent performance of "Over the Rainbow" standing not only as one of the greatest moments in television history, but as one of the most brilliant of her career. After the show, when Judy and Sid were in her dressing room, he noticed that the insides of her wrists were bleeding. "I had to dig for those last notes in 'Rainbow,' " she explained to him, "and I didn't realize it, I had my hands behind me, and I just dug my nails into my wrists. Oh, I had to dig for those notes, but I didn't know it." (She was also superstitious about the tramp outfit, saying, "Please, don't touch it," to a wardrobe woman who started to comb out the dishelved wig before the show.)

Janet Kern of the *Chicago American* stated, "There is something painfully pathetic in watching a talented star, still young and able, wallowing in reminiscence, never permitted to turn from wistful backward glances to hint that there is still a present and a future in her horoscope. The material and treatment of this *Star Jubilee* would have been great . . . had the program been *This Is Your Life* with Sophie Tucker. But this was a Saturday night musical revue which called itself a 'Jubilee' and the nostalgic star was thirty-three!"

Despite the backstage melodrama, *Ford Star Jubilee* was a ratings smash, winning the Nielsen Trendex ratings contest with a

34.8 ratings average over fifteen cities tallied. By contrast, the next *Ford Star Jubilee* production—the critically acclaimed pairing of Noël Coward and Mary Martin in *Together with Music*—could not touch Judy's ratings success, averaging a total ratings number of only 19.8, little more than half the audience that Garland pulled in the month before. Garland's television debut attracted the largest audience to date ever to have watched a "spectacular."

Interestingly, CBS and the Lufts had not entered into a joint contract at the time of the Ford show, but instead viewed the production as a nonexclusive, testing-the-waters arrangement. It was not until mid-December that Judy signed a production deal with CBS. The exclusive contract, involving approximately $300,000, was a three-year pact, with options calling for one appearance a year in a color special. Sid Luft would produce, with the first Garland showcase a live 1956 presentation still in development.

The concept for this special, announced during negotiations that January, was a most tantalizing one: Judy Garland in concert, backed by Leonard Bernstein and the New York Philharmonic Orchestra in a live, thirty-minute all-music production. Such a prestigious teaming of two musical giants would be a landmark event.

The ambitious plans for Garland's second network special fell through not long before rehearsals were to begin, leaving an entirely new format to be devised—not a good omen for a program resting on the shoulders of a star already burdened with insecurity. Instead of relying on sentiment and nostalgia, this time Judy would be presented in a surrealistic, stylized atmosphere, with famed photographer Richard Avedon providing simple settings and backdrops and Broadway dancer Peter Gennaro choreographing. Producer Luft chose veteran director Ralph Nelson to take on those same chores for the G.E. half hour. Classical pianist Leonard Pennario was signed to accompany Judy as well as to perform a solo piece. With Nelson Riddle as musical director, the original rundown included "I Feel a Song Comin' On," "Maybe I'll Come Back," "When the World Was Young," "Life Is Just a Bowl of Cherries," "Dirty Hands, Dirty Face," "Come Rain or Come Shine," and, closing the show, "I'll Be Seeing You." The Garland special was slated to air live on April 8 as a special installment of the thirty-minute *General Electric Theatre* anthology series hosted by Ronald Reagan.

Far removed from the head-on Garland-Bernstein "event" production, the revamped show would be arch, offbeat, avant-garde. No full sets, no curtain, no variety acts would be in evidence, all staples of standard variety programming of the day.

In the middle of rehearsals, as the air date drew near, Judy injured her foot. "When I got to her house, she had a cast on her ankle," recalls Peter Gennaro of his first meeting with Judy. "The show was in two weeks, and she said, 'You just do the stepping in front of me, and I'll learn it.' That's the way we rehearsed, and when the time came, the cast came off and we went to work. I couldn't believe it, but there it all was. She was a wonderful musician and had such a great feeling for jazz, blues and all kinds of music. She could have been one of the great dancers ever."

Then, at the last minute, classical pianist Leonard Pennario was replaced by jazz pianist Joe Buskin. Pennario was slated to play a portion of Ravel's "Bolero," but when he was told his number had to be cut by a minute to allow for commercials, he

Judy and Leonard Pennario rehearsing for *General Electric Theatre* on April 6, 1956
JOHN GRAHAM COLLECTION

insisted that it could not be abridged without damaging the content of the piece. Although Buskin performed, Pennario received full pay for his services.

The rundown of songs was then modified, but after the original choices had been sent out by CBS for publication. Gone were "When the World Was Young" and "I'll Be Seeing You," replaced by "Last Night When We Were Young" and, closing the show, "April Showers." Judy, by all reports, was in fine voice during rehearsals up to the day of broadcast, but then, once again, panic seized her. Again, as with the Ford show, laryngitis resulted. (Even the prerecorded numbers revealed Garland in poor voice.)

In a spotlight on a bare stage, Judy opened the show with a prerecorded "I Feel a Song Comin' On," followed by "Maybe I'll Come Back"—again lip-synched, but peculiarly rendered, with Judy twirling a cane as a fan blew up her skirt as she danced. The rich ballad "Last Night When We Were Young" (which had been included in and then cut from her MGM film *In the Good Old Summertime*) was next, perhaps the most effective moment of the program; the ensuing "Life Is Just a Bowl of Cherries" was forceful but rough. "Dirty Hands, Dirty Face"—sung to a prerecorded track in a dressing-room setting—was a picture of misdirected intensity as she sang to a photograph of her infant son, Joe. Rarely did Judy's instincts err in performing a song, but here she was overwrought and overemotional to an uncomfortable degree.

The centerpiece production number of the show—"Come Rain or Come Shine"—was a rather arch counterpoint to "Get Happy" in both costume design and execution, and both failed to meet the high ideals of the concept. Sung to a group of "musicians" accompanying her around a piano, Judy darted from one to the next in a seductive but playful manner during the number, dusting herself off as she finished, walking off-camera. If Judy had been up to it, it might have succeeded, but it was a failure. The close of the show, "April Showers," was performed on a winding staircase that Judy walked up backward as she sang, disappearing from view as the credits rolled.

"Judy Garland wasn't at her singing best Sunday night. Not even determination and hard work, of which she gave plenty, could bring this half-hour up to the standards of her full capability," stated *Variety*.

Harriet Van Horne of the *New York World Telegram* mused, "There was something amiss last night. Her usual control and discipline were lacking. The notes that tremble so gloriously in that rich throat trembled a little too long. There was too much anguish in the sad songs and there was just too much wild glee— for my taste—in the production number that had Miss G. ruffling the hair of all the boys in the band. Every gesture, every emotion, was a little bigger than life."

Barely recovered from the debacle, one week after the live broadcast Judy and Sid saw a *Daily Variety* banner on page one: GE STOPS JUDY GARLAND KINE, NOW HELD TOO RISQUE FOR TV VIEWING. The paper reported that General Electric was ordering the withdrawal of the kinescope of the live Garland special from fourteen television stations scheduled to play the show one week later, due to "protests against Miss Garland flaunting her legs in the half-hour musical."

The absurd incident served as nothing more than a sublimely ridiculous footnote to an endeavor that sputtered out almost before it began.

Judy was obviously jinxed when it came to television. And the next chain of events pitting her against the small tube were even more dramatic and even more preposterous, causing her to flee television for years to come.

2

"I'll never do a show a week in television."

—Judy Garland, 1955

The first week of 1957, CBS submitted to the Lufts a proposed format for her next special, which was a cross between Judy's 1956 Palace and Las Vegas acts. The network, without waiting for Garland's approval of the concept, had already signed Buick and L&M Filters as cosponsors.

Judy surprised the network when she deemed the show outline unacceptable, arguing that she had already done her original Palace act on the 1955 *Ford Star Jubilee* program. And she did not want to use her current concert material, claiming that it would seem stale and therefore unusable on a "live" tour after national television exposure. She also felt that, in effect, CBS was asking her to use a package she already owned.

A substitute format was submitted to Judy by her agent—Freddie Fields, then of MCA—that would have her accompanied by different orchestras, including a jazz group and a symphony orchestra (obviously a throwback to the aborted Leonard Bernstein idea). Judy rejected this the following day, saying that it was unsuitable as a ninety-minute television show. With Garland and CBS at an impasse, the network took the position that the agreement had been terminated by her. Her contract stated that while CBS had "sole discretion" of format nature and content, it did give the singer "right of prior approval"—"which she shall not unreasonably withhold"—over script, choice of producer, director, stand-in, wardrobe mistress, makeup man, and hairdresser.

To CBS, the reference in her contract to a script meant a finished script, and with the producer and director, the procedure allowed the network to furnish a list of three possible producers and three possible directors. If she did not find anyone suitable, she was able to submit a similar list to CBS, which the network could reject, ultimately staffing the show with its own final choices. The Luft camp held the view that CBS violated the contract, with the network submitting a four-page outline, and not a finished script or a list of personnel required. Garland did not feel she "disapproved," since the submissions required in the deal on the network side were never made; thus, she did not "unreasonably withhold" her approval as the network contended.

The network would not comment further except to reiterate that the pact was terminated, due to Judy's failure to perform. As a result, Judy and CBS parted company two years before her contract expired. Sid Luft said that it was likely legal action would soon be taken against the network. "We feel CBS has certainly breached our contract," he stated.

Judy's reluctance to do a third variety program did not begin with her rejection of the network's concept for her 1957 special. More than a year earlier—when another *Ford Star* spectacular was scheduled to follow the G.E. program—Judy said that she wanted to do a light play, or a comedy with music, "something like *Meet Me in St. Louis.* I can't do another variety show—once is it. Any others like the first would have to be repetitious. I don't care for big production numbers, and I think it would be wise next time to try to use music in the most intimate way—because you are singing to people in their homes.

"I'll never do a TV series," Judy stated. "I don't want to be in a lot of homes every week. I just want to do something good once a year on TV." She added, "We haven't come to a decision on whether my shows will be filmed. I personally would like to film them. You feel more secure, and the photography can be more flattering. I don't know if Ford or CBS will agree with me, however. If we have to do them live, I'll do what Noël Coward did on *Blithe Spirit* and have a kine made first, so that we can check it before the telecast."

Because of the resounding failure of the 1956 special and the fact that the next special never got off the ground, the break with CBS seemed inevitable. On March 15, 1957, two months after the contract dispute was announced, Judy sued CBS for $1,393,333, charging that the network broke her contract.

In the federal-court action, she further stated that CBS on January 9 authorized and induced publication of "false and deflamatory matter" concerning her. That complaint stemmed from an article by *New York Herald Tribune* television columnist Marie Torre, who wrote on January 10 that an unnamed CBS executive stated that Garland "is known for a highly developed inferiority complex" and did not "want to work because something is bothering her," adding, "I don't know what that is, but I wouldn't be surprised if it's because she thinks she's terribly fat." The suit sought $1 million for libel and an additional $393,333 for breach of contract. Garland's suit stated that the CBS deal, originally announced as a three-year pact, was in fact for five years. Under that agreement, she was to receive $83,333 for each of the programs during the first three years, $90,000 for the fourth year, and $95,000 for the fifth year.

While Garland's attorney sought to confirm the identity of the CBS executive quoted by Torre, the reporter refused to comply despite an order to do so by Federal District Judge Sylvester J. Ryan. "I can't give it," Torre insisted, referring to the executive's identity. "It is that just working in a business like this so long, you don't give the name." The judge, feeling the question posed by Garland's attorney was a proper one, gave Torre the chance to reconsider. She again refused, and the judge told her that she could face thirty days in jail for contempt. The judge ultimately gave Torre a ten-day sentence, saying, "I sympathize with you, but your position is improperly taken and you have no judicial support." He added that "the process of the court must be obeyed, notwithstanding the high motives which have prompted you to act as you have."

The highly publicized incident unfortunately did Garland little good, with members of the press and public opinion standing behind Torre. One judge even went so far as to dub Torre "the Joan of Arc of her profession" in this landmark "freedom of the press" case.

The irony, of course, is that the remarks made by the "unnamed CBS executive" were, in large part, true, however ungallant and stinging. The experience was so painful that it gave Judy the excuse to escape television for the rest of the decade, although it was hotly rumored a few years later that Judy and Mickey Rooney were to reunite for a television adaptation of *The Letter*—a *Manhattan Tower*–type musical following the romance of a New York couple written by Gordon Jenkins—which she had recorded as an album for Capitol Records in 1959. A one-hour television adaptation of *Born in a Trunk* and talk in 1960 of a weekly series were rumored. None of the projects ever went past the discussion stage. She even avoided films, rejecting such diverse properties as *The Helen Morgan Story*, *The Three Faces of Eve*, and *Butterfield 8*; hopes of her starring in *South Pacific* or *Carousel* (with Frank Sinatra, although he ultimately withdrew from the film himself) remained unfulfilled.

Judy's ever-growing insecurities, manifesting in ill health and weight gain, had, by 1959, bloated her four-foot, eleven-inch frame to an almost unrecognizable 185 pounds. Normally mobile during performance, Judy would often do little more than stand in front of the microphone and gesture. Hospitalized in December 1959 with a diseased liver—announced as hepatitis, but treated as cirrhosis—she would not survive, doctors first predicted, underestimating her almost superhuman recuperative powers. In twenty days, more than twenty quarts of fluid were drained from her body. She was told that she would remain a semi-invalid for the rest of her life and certainly would never perform again.

Miraculously, Judy recovered, was released from Doctors Hospital in New York on January 5, 1960, and returned to California to rest. In July, she moved to London, with Sid and the children joining her soon after. Her strength and voice returning, Judy wanted to sing again, and Sid booked her for a return to the London Palladium in August and then a second appearance the following week—her first one-woman concerts. A complete triumph, Judy had bounced back, stronger, healthier, and in better voice than ever. The renaissance of Judy Garland had begun, leading into the greatest comeback of her career.

Sid Luft, by the end of 1960, had decided to turn the management of Judy Garland's career over to Freddie Fields, who at that time was vice president of the Music Corporation of America. Fields was planning to quit MCA and open his own agency. His initial clients would be his wife, Polly Bergen, comedian Phil Silvers, and Peter Sellers. Sid, who wanted more time to devote to outside interests, convinced Judy to sign with Fields. Later, Fields would bring in as his partner David Begelman, and the two would form CMA, Creative Management Associates. Fields handled West Coast operations, and Begelman was based in New York. (Eventually, Garland formed her own company, Kingsrow Enterprises, with Fields and Begelman installed as partners.)

Unlike Judy, Freddie Fields did not underestimate the importance of television to the resurrection of her career, which was now in full swing as she returned to America on December 31, 1960. Only weeks after signing Judy as his client, Fields initiated negotiations with CBS to clear the still-unsettled legal battles— dormant since 1957—between the star and the network. Discussions between Fields and CBS were fruitful, and on January 9 it was announced that Judy had dropped her suit. At the same time, the network withdrew a counterclaim against Garland.

The dividends to both parties resulting from the newly restored relationship were equally great: CBS had first option on Judy's services in the near future, with Fields at the same time hammering out a deal with CBS network president James Aubrey for Garland to headline a television special to air that fall; concert dates and film work delayed her large-scale return to the small screen until early 1962. For her "comeback" special, Frank Sinatra and Dean Martin were signed as guests. (The original title, *Miss Show Business*, was later changed to *The Judy Garland Show*.)

The magnitude of Judy's newfound popularity was mirrored by the Capitol Records release of Garland's April 23 historic concert at Carnegie Hall. Issued that summer, the two-record set held the number-one position on Billboard's Top 40 chart for thirteen weeks, remaining in the Top 40 for an incredible seventy-three weeks. *Judy at Carnegie Hall* won five Grammy Awards, including Best Female Vocalist for Judy and Album of the Year. Carnegie Hall was by no means an isolated event, however, and Judy repeated, if not exceeded, that performance dozens of times that year. Judy Garland was back, better than ever, and was at the very peak of her popularity, already regarded in her lifetime as "a living legend."

"Something wonderful takes place between me and all the

people out there," said Judy in late 1961. "It's like a marvelous love affair. All you have to do is never cheat and work your best and work your hardest, and they'll respond to you. Such satisfaction can't apply to many other things in life."

Fields and Begelman courted producer-director Norman Jewison to orchestrate Judy's television comeback. Jewison describes his first meeting with Garland after one concert during the 1961 tour: "I explained to her that the special would be a challenge, maybe the most exciting, brilliant concert ever staged on American television. And if we were going to do something with elegance and style, it needed tremendous concentration and effort on her part. She said, 'I know all that, kid. I've done enough movies to know that.'"

Kay Thompson (possibly Judy's greatest musical influence after Roger Edens) was signed as creative consultant, and Norman joined Kay, Garland's musical director, Mort Lindsey, Judy and her children at their rented home in Scarsdale for many memorable evenings. Recalls Norman: "We got together at Judy's house around the piano with Mort, and that's where I met Liza, Lorna, and Joe. Liza was about fourteen at the time. One time, she and her mother surprised me with a rendition of 'Two Ladies in the Shade of the Banana Tree.' They had hats and a little routine, and it was a Bob Fosse scene right out of *All That Jazz*."

Sinatra phoned him after hearing Jewison was scheduling several nights of rehearsal before the January 5–9 taping sessions. "He said, 'What's this about rehearsing in Burbank?' I said, 'You know, Frank, Judy has a few problems sleeping and is not at her best during the day, so we decided to have rehearsals in the evening. I would deeply appreciate it if you would come. I know that the fifty-five thousand dollars we're paying you is not the highest price,' but at that time, it was fairly substantial. He said, 'All right, kid. I'll come.' I said, 'Bring Dean with you!' And he laughed. They both drove onto the lot at six P.M. Judy and I decided that since Romanoff's was Sinatra's favorite restaurant, we called the boss and told them to send over a waiter, and we had a bar set up with a waiter from Romanoff's, fully catered. When Frank walked in, he laughed. There was his Jack Daniel's, he sat down, and worked at the piano with Dean, Judy, and Kay, and he was fantastic. They worked until eleven at night, worked out all the routines."

The television triumph was not without its backstage prob-

Dean Martin, Judy, and Frank Sinatra at dress rehearsal in January 1962
JOHN GRAHAM COLLECTION

lems, ranging from the small ("at one point, we were picking up a taxi radio on her wireless microphone," states Norman of the climactic concert sequence) to the more serious. "CBS was furious at me because I wouldn't work in 'the Russian tire factory,' " remarks the producer-director about his choosing the Burbank NBC studios over CBS Television City.

The special aired on February 25, 1962, to overwhelmingly glowing reviews. *The Hollywood Reporter* summed up what most critics felt about the show: "Sunday night, she was perfect—nary the slightest vocal flaw nor quaver, and her delivery was such that few setsiders will quarrel with the wild cheering by the live audience after her every tune. . . . There were no elaborate sets, no vocal and dance ensembles—nor were any needed." *The New York Times* added, "Judy Garland held television in the palm of her hand last night."

Said Kay Thompson of Garland's work on the program, "Most people still think Judy is helpless, with people waiting on her and doing things for her." She added that Judy conceived and selected her concert program, helped design her wardrobe, had input in musical arrangements, and supervised the lighting. "She has an executive's mind. She goes in, gets the thing done, and leaves."

Tom Cooper, a young singer who had attended many of Judy's concerts throughout the 1950s and who became an acquaintance of Garland's and friend to daughter Liza, remembers Judy's exacting methods during taping of the show. For the opening segment, in which she sang "Just in Time" and "When You're Smiling" in front of giant bulbs that spelled out her first name, Cooper remembers, "She had a little monitor off-camera, and she was watching it when she made her entrance. She was actually directing. She was doing the camera direction."

Judy dismissed such praise, remarking, "If I didn't know how to do these things, I'd be pretty dumb after all these years. It's a protection for me to have technical knowledge."

The program had the highest rating in its time period, beating the NBC western series *Bonanza*, the second-highest rated program on the air that season, and was also reported to be CBS's highest-rated special to date. (Garland and her program won four Emmy nominations.)

Garland was quite heavy as she embarked on her 1961 comeback but began to slim down by the end of the year for the filming of *A Child Is Waiting*. It was not until the middle of 1962—when she was in England completing what was to be her last film, *I Could Go On Singing*—that she made any serious attempts at dieting.

When Judy returned to the States in August, she accepted a booking arranged by her managers, Fields and Begelman, to appear at Las Vegas's Sahara Hotel for a reported forty thousand dollars per week. Prior to the Sahara engagement, she vacationed for a month in Lake Tahoe, where she had moved to establish residency to divorce Sid Luft.

She had still not completely won her battle against weight. It was time to retire the Norman Norell mandarin jackets (which, as Judy quipped, were designed to "hide a multitude of sins") and shapeless black dresses and exchange them for a contemporary, glamorous wardrobe—and a contemporary, glamorous Judy. It was also a symbolic shedding of the stagnant, bloated last years of the previous decade in exchange for a bright, optimistic, future offering new challenges, new worlds to conquer, and, as her marriage to Sid tottered, new relationships.

Judy—being Judy—could not, and would not, be satisfied with gradual weight loss. Characteristically doing nothing halfway, she devised an effective but quite drastic, and dangerous, method of dieting: two cups of tea a day—no cream or sugar—and nothing else. No food, no juice, no vitamins. Just tea. And it worked.

By mid-September, Judy had slimmed down to one hundred pounds, trim and streamlined. But four days before she was set to open at the Sahara for the four-week engagement, she paid the price for her thirty-day bout of radical fasting and was stricken with an excruciating kidney attack. ("Having children is a pleasure compared to it," Judy later remarked.) According to her physician, Dr. Richard Grundy, Judy suffered from acute pyelonephritis in the right kidney, which produces a severe pain similar to kidney stones. The press, thinking the kidney condition was a smokescreen, hinted at a pill overdose, which her physician flatly denied.

Within forty-eight hours, Judy had recovered, checked herself out of the hospital, and won three standing ovations on the Sahara stage opening night. JUDY AT SPARKLING BEST IN NEW LAS VEGAS OPENING: TRIUMPHS OVER STAY IN HOSPITAL, was the headline of the *Los Angeles Herald-Examiner* on September 19. "It was the best show to hit the strip in a long, long time," said UPI.

Judy, in peak form that night, did not indicate the clouds that were hovering over her personal life. The divorce battle with Sid escalated while she was preparing for the Sahara show. And just as she was stricken with the kidney attack, seventeen-year-old Liza (who had flown in from school in Paris to be with her mother for her opening) had to be hospitalized for food poisoning. ("They've been knocking us over like tenpins," said Judy to a reporter following her opening-night show.) Her opening night resulted in extraordinary reviews, which were carried nationally by both the Associated Press and United Press International newspaper wire services. Further sweetening the Sahara triumph for Judy, virtually every review of her opening-night show pointed out her new, trim figure in a most complimentary, if overtly surprised, tone.

After the four-week engagement, Judy was held over for an additional two weeks for an unprecedented 2:30 A.M. show, the first time in Las Vegas history that such a contract had been made with a performer. For her first 2:30 A.M. show, Garland played to a capacity crowd of 812, with 1,400 people turned away; the entire engagement was a complete sellout. The Sahara stint, reported show-business columnist Hedda Hopper on October 17, was also memorable for another reason: "Her nine-year-old daughter, Lorna, debuted on stage last week singing 'Swanee' and 7-year-old Joey got into the act, too. He stood there and hummed."

By the end of September, a follow-up special was in the works. Norman Jewison was to produce and direct, but by November he had to bow out due to a prior commitment to direct a Broadway show. Judy denied reports that she wanted Jackie Gleason to guest on the special but did reveal that she was intent on snaring another show-business legend: Elvis Presley! (Reportedly, Judy's top guest fee of fifty thousand dollars was too low, and the once-in-a-lifetime pairing of Judy and Elvis unfortunately never materialized.)

In November, Judy traveled to Chicago for a twofold purpose. A concert at the Arie Crown Theatre was scheduled for the seventh, followed by a personal appearance two days later for the world premiere of her new film, the full-length animated feature *Gay Purr-ee* at the State-Lake Theatre. As the *Chicago Tribune*'s Herb Lyon noted: "Chicago's press lads and lassies were overwhelmed at the magic transformation in Judy Garland. . . . Judy again has the slender alive face she had during her teenage MGM movie days. Her vivacity, honesty, and wit entranced the gathering. 'I've finally learned,' declared Judy, 'who I am and how to enjoy life!' It's beautiful to behold."

The star's new look was so remarkable that one viewer noted of her Arie Crown concert, "Judy, understandably, couldn't resist showing off her new slim figure (she looked elegant) and strutted slowly across the stage, pushing back her jacket by putting her left hand on her hip. The men in the audience whistled, and Judy grinned and winked at them."

Amid a flurry of professional activity closing the year, a milestone in Judy Garland's career was announced during the third week of November. To promote *Gay Purr-ee*, Judy (and costar Robert Goulet) were booked to appear on Jack Paar's prime-time program on December 7. The appearance was an unveiling of sorts: It marked the first time that Judy—a newly trim and tanned Judy—would be interviewed at length on television, and have the opportunity to display her considerable skills as a storyteller and raconteur. "We talked more than she sang, and this was a

The "new" Judy with Lorna and Joey at the Sahara, November 13, 1962
JOHN FRICKE COLLECTION

side of her which was my discovery," wrote the talk-show host in his book, *P.S. Jack Paar*. His assessment, though, was only partially correct. Most everyone in show business knew of Garland's legendary sense of humor, her sharp wit and intelligence; Paar can be credited with revealing Judy, the real Judy, to the general public.

She rose to the challenge magnificently. In top form, the "new" Judy Garland had stunningly emerged, winning her some of the best notices of her career. Said *Variety*, "This session displayed a Judy Garland who was a picture of mental and physical health. She had slimmed down noticeably and appeared to be affable and eager to reestablish herself in the graces of a public which had been patient with her shenanigans. . . . Miss Garland told stories, entertained with songs from 'Gay Purr-ee' and related highly personal bits about her touring days in vaudeville with her sisters and mother as the Gumm Sisters. . . . Also of great interest was her description of the Metro school for its moppet stars with fellow students, which included Deanna Durbin, Mickey Rooney, Lana Turner and Elizabeth Taylor, among others. . . . It was a highly rewarding and gratifying display." (Counting off her MGM cohorts, Judy quipped, "Have you seen us since we've come out? We were a very peculiar group!," which caused Paar to double over in laughter.)

John Horn of the *New York Herald Tribune* was equally captivated. He found Judy "seldom looking or sounding better" and added that "she revealed herself an engaging raconteur with an irrepressible urge to act out her stories, a gift for a telling phrase, and a large store of show business yarns. . . . In her performance, much of the child she was still glowed in the older woman."

Of the Paar program, Judy herself admitted, "I liked myself for the first time on television." Indeed, during rehearsals for the Paar show, not only did she make a point to meet each of the musicians in the orchestra—expanded that night only for her appearance—she also met with the camera and lighting men to suggest how she wished to be photographed and what angles she favored.

The Jack Paar guest shot was of tantamount importance for workings going on behind the scenes. Fields and Begelman had convinced Judy that the time was right to venture into weekly television. She had never been hotter than she was at the moment, and had never been presented in better form on television than in the Paar appearance. The logical next step, the culmination of the biggest comeback of her career, would be to star in a big-budget variety series showcasing her storytelling abilities as well as her singing; the Paar show, freshly imprinted on the minds of network executives, made this the ideal moment to negotiate a deal.

"David Begelman told me there was no reason I shouldn't have a steady home with my children, be very rich, and do a weekly show—that I should have been rich a long time ago, like Bob Hope or [Perry] Como," revealed Judy a year later. If Judy took the plunge into television on a weekly basis, she could make in the neighborhood of $20 million, she was advised, giving her the freedom to never work again, if she chose. Judy was now convinced, and her managers had only to pitch the concept to the three networks. Interest, not surprisingly, came immediately, and not only from CBS—where she was under contract for specials—but from NBC and ABC as well.

On December 19, only two weeks after the Paar appearance, *Variety* revealed that Garland was "being peddled by her manager, Freddie Fields, for a 60-minute weekly showcase for the '63–'64 season which the star will front. Hottest contender for the Garland package (it's reportedly being projected as a $5,000,000 deal) is ABC-TV, although NBC is also said to be in the running." (Unable to match the offers of the two giants, ABC—the distant third of the networks at the time—dropped out of the bidding war the last week of December.)

While Fields recalls that interest came from all three networks, "the conversation focused right in with [CBS president James] Aubrey until the deal was done. Jim was very aggressive about it." A meeting between Judy and Aubrey, arranged by Fields, was successful, with Judy "doing a little charm number on him." *Variety*, however, noted that Fields's asking price for Garland was at first too expensive for CBS, leaving the initial battle between NBC and ABC. The specter of rival NBC grabbing Garland was quite present, according to Sal Iannucci, then in charge of business affairs for CBS. "Freddie and David . . . were about to put together a deal over at NBC for her . . . and they were able to convince Aubrey, through [senior vice president of programs] Hubbell Robinson, to buy a series starring Judy Garland. We stole her away from NBC."

Iannucci, who handled the deal for CBS, notes that no particular format was discussed as part of Garland signing. "Once you have a major star, you know that you have a vehicle. It didn't have to go into development. We could commit to a major star knowing that creative elements would be brought in and get the show on the air." Garland would be CBS's biggest catch of the 1963–64 season, joining already-signed headliners Danny Kaye, Carol Burnett (for a series of specials), Phil Silvers in a new half-hour situation comedy, and George C. Scott in the gritty, realistic drama *East Side, West Side*.

The Judy Garland Show budget for each hour installment was first estimated at $150,000, but eventually climbed to more than $165,000. Judy, she was told, would net about twenty-five thousand dollars per week, with her production company, Kingsrow

Enterprises, owning the show. CBS paid Kingsrow to produce it and Judy's company was, in turn, responsible for salaries and production costs. CMA's fee was 10 percent of the original $150,000 weekly budget.

Fields and Begelman negotiated such an extraordinary deal that *Variety* deemed it "perhaps the strongest contract ever elicited by a TV performer." The pact uniquely allowed Garland the power to cancel after the first thirteen-week cycle; the network, amazingly, did not have the same right. The network defended giving the star such one-sided control by speculating that Judy would logically prefer to walk away from the series if it wasn't a smash, which would relieve the sponsors of the show from putting further advertising dollars into a ratings loser. That part of the contract, concurs Iannucci, "broke all the rules."

The Garland package represented a $6 million outlay by the network, with the contract extending over a four-year period, options to be exercised at the expiration of each year; the total deal represented at least $24 million. It was anticipated that Judy would headline thirty-two original episodes, followed by eight repeats and twelve weeks of a summer-replacement program, which, it was bandied about, might star Liza Minnelli.

With no advance publicity, Judy Garland, David Begelman, Hubbell Robinson, and Sal Iannucci—and other key CBS executives—gathered at the St. Moritz Hotel in New York on December 28, 1962, to witness Garland signing a contract to star in a weekly television series premiering the next September. Judy, rested and fit, looked dazzling. "She came out of her bedroom, smiled a lot, the way Judy was, and she was pleasant, but she was frightened, fearful of someone striking out or lashing out at her," recalls Iannucci. "We signed, she signed, we toasted, Hubbell said a few words, I said a few words and that was the launching of her deal."

Yet Judy, according to Fields, still harbored "very mixed emotions" about it all, and the corridors at CBS buzzed with speculation about whether the unpredictable, unreliable Garland would be able to hold up to the rigors of a weekly television series.

"We all hoped she was going to do it," recalls Iannucci. "She was a major star, but we didn't know if she had the strength, both emotionally and physically, to withstand the weekly grind

December 28, 1962: A beaming Judy at the signing of her CBS contract with Sal Iannucci, Hubbell Robinson, and David Begelman
CBS INC.

of putting on a variety show. . . . No one in management believed she was going to do it," reveals Iannucci. "No one ever thought that she was really going to survive the rigors of week-to-week television due to political structure of the company at the time, the personalities involved and the need for programs, and Freddie and David's need for a television series. . . . The feeling that we all had was that it was only short-term. Maybe it was not enunciated or articulated in our meetings, but everyone knew."

Everyone, it seemed, except Judy Garland.

3

Even by her extraordinary standards, 1963 promised to be a most
challenging and unusual year for Judy Garland. In January alone,
she would reconcile with estranged husband Sid Luft, begin preproduction meetings for her upcoming special, meet with CBS
brass in huddles about the series, and prepare for an engagement at Harrah's resort in Lake Tahoe beginning in February. In
addition, Judy had agreed to fly to London in March for the
world premiere of *I Could Go On Singing* and, while there, appear on the British variety program *Sunday Night at the Palladium*.

In the preceeding year and a half, Garland had worked on
three motion pictures—*Gay Purr-ee*, *A Child Is Waiting*, and *I Could
Go On Singing* (the latter starting only days after *Child* had finished)—done over forty one-woman concerts coast-to-coast, appeared on the Paar show, stumped through Chicago and greater
New York to promote *Purr-ee*, headlined one television special,
and was steeped in preparations for another while at the same
time she was embroiled in meetings with top-echelon CBS executives about her weekly series.

Such pressures could only endanger Judy's mental and physical health, and would likely at the same time increase her dependency on stimulants and barbiturates. Getting back on the
debilitating roller coaster of excessive medication (prescribed
stimulants and barbituates taken not for recreational use, but

simply so as to function at the level expected of her) might get Judy through a performance or a film or a television show, but the long-term effects put her at tremendous risk. Her managers certainly were aware of the consequences.

Judy, in her zealous quest for financial security and a permanent home for her family, continued to work at a breakneck pace, despite warnings from Sid Luft to both her and her managers. From their point of view, Judy was at her peak now, and needed to extract whatever earnings she could draw at the moment. Everyone was simply capitalizing on the momentum of her career renaissance.

And the burgeoning CMA agency needed Garland's revenue as much as it relied on her prestigious name at the top of its client list to enlarge its operations. The company was expanding in terms of employees and clients and fast becoming an influential, powerful force in the entertainment industry. Freddie Fields and David Begelman, two extraordinarily dynamic, driven, and intelligent men, created in CMA a multimillion-dollar enterprise. And the CBS-Garland pact, the most lucrative deal of Judy Garland's career, represented the apex of the CMA success story.

Sweetening it all the more, Garland's upcoming special would itself be a most profitable venture. Although Elvis Presley, Mary Martin, Ethel Merman, and Frank Sinatra were rumored to be in the running, Robert Goulet and Phil Silvers—both CMA clients— were signed as Garland's guests on the special.

The show was scheduled to be taped in Los Angeles, although Judy at first briefly considered shooting it in Las Vegas. By the end of the year, it was determined that the special would be done in New York the first week of February, conveniently allowing Judy to be available for meetings with East Coast CBS executives about the series. By January, Silvers and Goulet were set. With Norman Jewison unavailable, Burt Shevelove was signed to produce, Charles S. Dubin to direct, and Larry Gelbart to write the special; Gelbart and Shevelove had already partnered on the recent Broadway hit *A Funny Thing Happened on the Way to the Forum*. Mort Lindsey and arranger Saul Chaplin, who had worked together for *I Could Go On Singing*, handled music responsibilities. All the elements in place, the show took on the rather long-winded title *Judy Garland and Her Guests Phil Silvers and Robert Goulet*.

While Frank Sinatra, the top-billed guest of her previous special, outclassed Goulet and Silvers in name value, the teaming here nonetheless would take advantage of her long friendship with comedian Silvers (a friend since the early 1940s and a costar in *Summer Stock* in 1950), and her chemistry with *Camelot* star Robert Goulet, displayed so successfully on the Paar program.

The special, serving as the prototype and pilot for the series, was expressly designed to display a different, more contemporary Judy Garland. For the first time on television, Judy would be allowed to be sophisticated and take on a more glamorous image but at the same time indulge in sketches, physical comedy, and dance routines. The strong emphasis on dialogue and comedy—virtually nonexistent in her past three specials—was underscored by the signing of the witty Gelbart and funnyman Silvers. Judy, furthermore, would not dip into her trunk of reliable standards for this outing and would instead perform new material.

Producer Shevelove deemed the special "the first of the new Judy shows," remarking that "rather than looking backward, as previous Garland specials have, this one looks forward. We felt it was time to break away from nostalgia, from the long parade of classics identified with Judy." Writer Gelbart concurred, dubbing the show "The Beginning of the Judy of Tomorrow." Adding considerably to the fresh, contemporary approach was set designer Jac Venza, who created simple backdrops; he called his approach "electronic vaudeville." Hollywood designer Edith Head, who had costumed Garland for *I Could Go On Singing*, was brought in to create a wardrobe showcasing the newly streamlined star.

The hour was originally conceived as a five-act presentation. In the first segment, Judy and Silvers were to pay tribute to New York in a comedy sketch, beginning with a Garland solo of the seldom-performed Cole Porter song "I Happen to Like New York." Act Two had Judy teaming with Goulet for a medley of love songs, followed by a third act comprised of three Garland solos: "As Long as He Needs Me"; her concert medley of "Almost Like Being in Love" and "This Can't Be Love"; and "By Myself," showcasing the highly charged, powerhouse arrangement featured in *I Could Go On Singing*. Silvers was to reteam with Judy for the fourth act, designed to have the two reminisce about some of the more outrageous aspects of their careers, both

Robert Goulet, Judy, and Phil Silvers in a publicity shot for *Judy and Her* *Guests*
JOHN GRAHAM COLLECTION

onstage and behind the scenes. For the final act, Garland, Goulet, and Silvers were to perform another comedy sketch, featuring bits of songs and quick costume changes.

The taping spanned five nights the first week of February, all marked by late starts and late finishes. And while Judy looked quite well, she was still at the point of exhaustion. Her voice reflected this and temporarily took on a slightly husky quality. Judy's vocal condition, more often than not, largely reflected the amount of rest—and the amount of medication—she had experienced. Also, in the past year, as she had reached her fortieth birthday, Judy's voice had deepened somewhat, and her lower register had expanded and taken on a richer quality. When in good shape, her upper register did not suffer perceptibly, and neither her tremendous vocal power, nor her ability to sing with great purity, was affected. The Garland voice, if anything, had taken on even more dramatic urgency than before.

Saul Chaplin commented on Judy's legendary reputation as a quick study: "To work with her was indescribable. Like a Xerox machine. You played something to her, and she sang it right back the way you did it. She ate up music like a vacuum cleaner."

The final rundown of the show varied considerably from the initial concept. Judy opened the show in a single spotlight against a dark backdrop singing "Hello, Bluebird" (from *I Could Go On Singing*), which she reprised immediately with her two guests. The comedy sketch saluting Manhattan followed, which prompted an amusing incident never seen by the television audience. While Head chose to dress Garland primarily in dark colors throughout the show, she wore a light-colored dress for the taping of the comedy sketch. Always conscious of her appearance, Judy remarked to the audience, "Now I'm going to watch the tape so they can yell at me and say, 'What are we going to do with your stomach? What *are* we going to do with your stomach?' " (The sketch was then redone with Garland in a dark dress.)

The "Manhattan" sketch, sharp and very funny, had Judy playing a singing hopeful (in a deliberately awful performance of "Can't Help Lovin' That Man"), a lady wrestler, a Salvation Army worker vainly attempting to sell a raffle ticket to a hard-boiled Silvers, a woman "mashed" in Central Park, and a world-weary society matron. With Silvers as her foil, she seemed delighted at the opportunity to dig into good comedy material. Despite her considerable skills as a comedienne, she had not performed in a comedy sketch since her appearances on Bing Crosby's radio series a decade earlier.

Following Goulet's solo, "Love Walked In," the baritone joined Judy for the lengthy medley of romantic songs that included "Here I'll Stay," "If Ever I Would Leave You," "Don't Let It Get You Down," and Judy's favorite song, the Vincent Youmans ballad "Through the Years." The chemistry between the two was unmistakably at full boil, so erotic and full of such interplay that it led one critic to quip that the duet was as "friendly as an Italian movie!"

The trio of Garland solos was next, although "As Long as He Needs Me" had been replaced by "Get Happy." The medley of "Almost Like Being in Love" and "This Can't Be Love" followed, sung with gusto if not with sheer vocal perfection. The third number, "By Myself," the most challenging song of the hour, displayed Judy in near-peak form; she had channeled what spare energy she held in reserve for this number. All three songs were most effectively staged, with Judy in dark clothes on a stage bathed in spotlights.

For the final portion of the show, Judy, Goulet, and Silvers engaged in a number of quick costume changes made possible by stop-action photography, centered around the song "I'm Following You." Blessed by the able choreography of Marc Breaux and Dee Dee Wood, the trio paraded in military outfits (shades of *Sergeant Bilko*), as a beatnik folk group (singing "If I Had a Hammer"), the Three Musketeers, Revolutionary War patriots, and—displaying the broad physical comedy that she loved—with Judy as an inept ballet dancer mangling *Swan Lake*. The highlight of the routine was Judy singing "Where or When," complete with her typical gestures, mannerisms, and hand-wringing—backed by Silvers and Goulet, dressed identically as Garland, imitating every movement down to copying her demure walk off-camera, Silvers tripping in his high-heeled shoes. Closing the hour was Garland belting the title song from *I Could Go On Singing*.

While Judy, as usual, was charming and warm with the studio audience—many of them loyal fans with whom she was acquainted—during the nights of taping, it was clear to everyone she was exhausted. One observer recalls that when Judy wasn't "sparkling" before the cameras, she appeared "rather tired," particularly the final night the closing sketch was taped, which required many quick costume changes. On that last evening, as Judy walked to her dressing room, obviously drained, she nevertheless stopped for a moment to speak to a fan who said good night, thanking her for the performance. "Good night and thank *you*," replied Judy. "Thank you for coming and staying so late." A depleted Judy, still in the Revolutionary War costume, trudged on to her dressing room.

It was perhaps inevitable that rumors flew accusing Judy of tantrums and bursts of temperament. Director Charles Dubin came to her defense, saying that the basis for the rumors stemmed from the final taping night that went on until 5:25 A.M. "The session started around two in the afternoon, and we completed the segments with Silvers and Goulet by midnight. Judy was exhausted and asked for a break. We all agreed that she had a pretty rough day, so we suspended while she rested. Fortunately, we didn't have too big a crew, so the overtimes were kept to a minimum, and we let Judy call the shots on when to start taping again." Mort Lindsey, who was musical director, concurs, remembering that everyone was told that Judy, completely spent, had fallen asleep in her dressing room; Dee Dee Wood also remembers the wait, but recalls no outbursts of temperament by Judy, either at rehearsals or during the taping.

When asked whether he thought Judy would be able to handle the rigors of a weekly series, Dubin deftly sidestepped the question: "I think her manager has learned something from producing the special. The exhaustion at the tapings was caused by excessive costume changes." An explanation, perhaps, but hardly the complete truth. He did say that he was quite open to working with Garland on her weekly series, quipping that she could do the show "in her rehearsal clothes" if she wanted, as a means of avoiding tiring costume changes. "With a talent like that," he concluded, "who cares?"

The weeks of rehearsing and taping the television special only further strained her health. Not helping matters was Judy's commitment (made in the fall of 1962) to perform for three weeks at Harrah's at Lake Tahoe—with opening night scheduled for Thursday, February 7, only a few days after the taping of the television show.

Judy was a smash at her opening, despite her fatigue. Her voice, however, began to give out toward the end of the show, even with her performance time reduced from her usual ninety minutes to about an hour. Judy's potency was no less diminished, though, and her reviews were excellent.

On the following Monday, Judy canceled her show due to an illness diagnosed as the flu. She bounced back sufficiently to return to Harrah's and perform the following night but was again stricken on Wednesday, collapsing in her dressing room just as she was about to go onstage. Her doctors now diagnosed her ailment as exhaustion, not the flu, and ordered her to rest. The next morning, she was taken to a hospital in Carson City via ambulance, experiencing slight paralysis of her left side and partial lack of sensation. (When word leaked out about Judy's illness and whereabouts, the hospital was so deluged with calls wishing her well that an extra switchboard operator had to be brought in.) Tests were scheduled to determine more about her condition.

As unpredictable as ever, she made a surprise visit to the hospital administrator's office on Thursday afternoon and declared that she felt fine and was immediately returning to Lake Tahoe. This rather remarkable patient was released from the hospital, saying she was looking forward to a "quiet Valentine's Day party" with her children.

While the results of Judy's tests—which came in after she left the hospital—were not disclosed, they were sufficiently serious for Harrah's management to allow her to break her contract, saying only the singer was "too tired" to continue the engagement. Trying to squelch rumors that her health was on the downside, it was announced from Judy's camp that it was a simple Asian flu that had temporarily stricken the singer and optimistically noted that she was now "coming along nicely." When she had originally been admitted to the Carson City hospital, however, the same spokesperson admitted that the cause was "complete exhaustion."

Although she declared the next day that she was feeling "much better," her old friend Mickey Rooney was called upon to complete her Harrah's three-week stint.

Judy promptly phoned Hollywood gossip columnist Louella Parsons from Lake Tahoe to announce that her condition had much improved. She acknowledged, though, that she would have to "recuperate in New York for three weeks," having to be there anyway for CBS meetings about the series. "I've been working too hard and let myself run down—but I won't do that again," she vowed. She further revealed to Parsons that Sid was with her, although she was quick to point out that they were, in Louella's words, "not occupying the same residence." The headlines resulting from Judy's collapse had completely overshadowed the fact that Judy and Sid had, most unexpectedly, reconciled.

This news was surprising in light of the bitter, protracted battle between the two begun the preceding September, when Judy temporarily resided in Nevada to obtain a divorce. Her divorce suit was followed promptly by a countersuit filed by her estranged husband, with both of them hurling accusations at each other. So heated was the fight—involving alimony, property, assets, and, standing as the largest issue, custody of Lorna and Joey—that every development filled newspaper columns steadily for the last four months of the year. Before she was unexpectedly forced by the courts to delay divorce proceedings, Judy, in fact, had fully planned to be legally free from Sid by the close of 1962.

Since her divorce action, and his resulting countersuit, had been stalled, Judy and Sid dropped legal proceedings, and simply kissed and made up. The Associated Press quickly picked up the story, snapping a photograph of the two dining cozily at the Dunes Hotel in Las Vegas. The fact was that Sid, always most protective of Judy, had never been out of the picture entirely.

Louella Parsons's archrival Hedda Hopper took a dim view of the Luft reconciliation in her column filed on February 14: "What's this? Judy Garland and Sid Luft back together. Oh, no! Well, Valentine's Day always did strange things to people!"

From a less romantic point of view, it could also be speculated that the reconciliation of the Lufts was a masterful stroke of good timing. Much was riding on the CBS deal, and Judy was particularly vulnerable to bad press, as she hoped to ingratiate herself into the homes of Middle America week after week beginning in September. Aside from a very real desire to be happily married and provide her children with a permanent, loving home, it was vital from a public-relations point of view to have her appear stable, married, and as a most dedicated mother (which she was), playing down her more tumultuous, mercurial image. Whether by chance or design, the divorce action—and public feuding between the Lufts—ceased immediately as the CBS deal was being finalized. This reconciliation, similarly, came about just as the special was being aired, just as the network was pursuing sponsors to bankroll the high-priced Garland series.

The first week of March, Judy flew to London for the premiere of *I Could Go On Singing*. The musical drama had her playing a world-renowned but troubled singer—rather like its star—who attempts to meet the illegitimate son she gave up for adoption at birth. Her efforts meet with resistance by the boy's father, played by Dirk Bogarde. Judy—already armed upon arrival with a junket of key American press members in tow—was major news, with thousands turning out for the event. "If the

Judy who once stole Andy Hardy's heart is gone somewhere over a rainbow of hard knocks and sleeping pills," *Time* magazine summed up, "Garland the actress seems here to stay."

On March 10, Judy made an appearance on the live British television program *Sunday Night at the Palladium*. Looking exceptionally good, dressed in a sparkling black top and white skirt, she sang four numbers on the show: the "Almost Like Being in Love" "This Can't Be Love" medley; "Smile," written by Charles Chaplin and new to her repertoire; "Comes Once in a Lifetime," complete with a few false starts that had Judy quip, "Come on! Let's stop! We can even stop on television!"; and ending with "I Could Go On Singing." Still experiencing a bit of laryngitis aggravated by damp, drizzling London weather, Judy rose above it completely for "Smile," so moving and beautifully sung that it stands for many as the quintessential Garland performance of this era. She astounded the British, who, in all of her personal appearances there, had never seen Judy Garland slender since the days of her post–World War II MGM films.

The Palladium television guest shot was an important building block as Garland prepared for the weekly series. It was the first time she effectively performed live on the medium and without benefit of script. Her mastery of TV was all the more remarkable considering that she had developed it in only two years. "Smile" and "Singing" were to air the following month on Ed Sullivan's CBS Sunday night variety series, and it would be another tantalizing glimpse of the Judy Garland who soon would appear on her own television show. It also would be her last television appearance before the premiere of her series in September. Her performance was well received on both sides of the Atlantic, with virtually all reviewers commenting on her new appearance, one calling her "a new-look Judy who seems to have shed as many years as she has pounds." Another remarked, "Judy Garland—her plumpness gone, double chin vanished—left the Palladium stage to the biggest applause of the season."

The Silvers-Goulet special aired nine days after the Palladium show, to generally favorable reviews. The *Detroit Free Press* said, "It's too much to expect this kind of perfection in a show which will turn up every week next season when Judy starts her new CBS-TV series. But if she and the people behind her can come close, it will eclipse anything on view now." The *Philadelphia In-*

quirer offered, "Miss Garland, looking youthful, vibrant and strikingly slender, opened strong and closed the same way, and if some of the intervening segments lagged, they didn't seriously vitiate the program's tremendous overall impact."

Variety gave both star and show a glowing notice: "Taking her special last Tuesday as a sample of what may be in store when Judy Garland has her own weekly series on CBS-TV next fall, it's going to be welcome fare indeed . . . slimmed down to svelte proportions, she again has unlimited costuming possibilities that allow her the maximum range to show off a song. . . . More important, her singing last Tuesday projected over the cathode tube almost as though over the footlights, with an immediacy and an impact that is rarely achieved in video. . . . The series will have a star who is steeped in the knowhow and who vocally is far from past her prime. . . . Where CBS is concerned, the timing of the special couldn't have been better. If this performance doesn't bring in the final sponsor for next season's series, probably nothing will."

Three days prior to the telecast, though, a disturbing incident occurred that revealed how deeply Judy's state of near-exhaustion was affecting her emotional and physical well-being.

The day following the Palladium show, Judy flew back to New York and checked into a suite at the St. Regis Hotel. On Thursday evening, a few days later, she took an overdose of sleeping pills. With her at the time was her hairdresser, Orval Paine, with whom Judy had formed a close friendship since he had begun working for her during the Sahara engagement the previous September. Although a doctor was summoned, Judy was treated in her suite and not taken to a hospital; Sid Luft, however, immediately flew from Los Angeles to Manhattan to be with her when he received word of the incident.

A unnamed "close friend," who was not present, recounted the incident to New York–based columnist Earl Wilson. Wilson's source theorized that the overdose came about following a "week of tremendous professional activity," referring to her London trip, return to New York, and a party she gave for Liza, who was in rehearsal for an off-Broadway revival of *Best Foot Forward*. Then, speculated the columnist's source, "suddenly it all stopped. There was nobody around. There was nothing to do. And Judy is a girl who likes to keep going until dawn."

Sitting and chatting with Orval in her suite for a time, she went into the next room and made a phone call; the conversation upset Judy to the point of tears. Orval heard her crying, became concerned, and went into her room. She told him she was lonely, and he offered to stay in the next room all night to keep her company. "The next thing he knew," continued Wilson's source, "she had swallowed some pills and was in a deep sleep that alarmed him." Orval immediately called for a doctor.

Apparently, Judy had been in an agitated state upon arriving at the St. Regis. The phone call in question was her breaking point. Hotel employees noted that she had been "upset noticeably" during the week, one claiming knowledge of a "loud rumpus" in her suite, and added that they had noticed a nurse there. Sid took charge when he arrived, and was able to calm Judy down. No similar incidents followed, with the St. Regis episode standing as virtually the only negative publicity surrounding her personal life that would surface in print for almost a full year from this point. There was no other time after leaving MGM in 1950 that this was so.

The overdose at the St. Regis is telling, regardless of Judy's motivations. On the surface, she finally had everything. She was united with her husband and children. New bills and old debts were being paid. For the first time in years, she felt a sense of financial security. She had never looked better. She more often than not proclaimed during this time that, after years of troubles, she had finally attained personal satisfaction and a newfound sense of purpose and direction. She had never been busier or more in demand. After all, at the time of the overdose, she had just triumphed at the premiere of her new film, had a television special airing in a matter of days, and was in discussions about her multimillion-dollar series, produced by her own company.

Judy Garland was a woman of remarkable intelligence and strength. In the last three years alone, she had faced death and won when all the odds were against her. She had weathered, since 1941, three marriages, bad health, bad luck, pill addiction, and nervous breakdowns. She not only survived but was at the zenith of her career. The fact remained, however, that Judy simply was not indestructible, and the enormous workload and pressures put upon her during 1961 and 1962 were too much for

her to handle. Her two collapses within a six-month period—
prior to the Sahara engagement in September 1962, and at Harrah's in February—were, by themselves, clear warning signs.

The St. Regis overdose attempt, most likely, was an impul-
sive, reckless bid for attention by a highly strung woman under
great strain and at the point of exhaustion. Far less probable was
that it was a genuine, serious act to end her life. But whatever
the motives, such an act was a signal of trouble ahead.

4

"You really want to know why I'm tackling a weekly television series? Because CBS is letting me be myself—letting me be a whole, total, complete person."

—Judy Garland, 1963

With the success of the Silvers-Goulet special serving as a solid bargaining chip to lure advertisers, CBS began a determined, aggressive campaign to launch *The Judy Garland Show*. Not only were advertisers necessary, of course, to underwrite the series, sponsorship was key to the network's need to promote Garland as being ready, able, and bankable, week after week.

Snaring the sponsors, however, was only one of the matters at hand for CBS involving *The Judy Garland Show*. When the contract announcement was made, it was not specified which of the two available time slots the Garland show and Danny Kaye's variety series would occupy.

A Sunday night slot, following Ed Sullivan, was the more prestigious of the two. Sunday was considered the premium night of television, with more sets tuned in then than on any other evening. However, the Sunday night slot at nine (EST) had one major drawback; it faced the most formidable competition television had to offer—NBC's western series *Bonanza*, the fourth highest-rated show on the air of the 1962–63 season. (The highest-rated program on television that same season, according to the A. C. Nielsen Company, was the CBS situation comedy *The Beverly Hillbillies*.) *Bonanza* had the advantage of an already established and huge audience, and unlike the Garland hour, it was aired in color, first a novelty but now a key competitive factor as color television sales soared in 1963.

52

Westerns enjoyed great popularity on the tube, as did such unsophisticated rural comedies as *The Beverly Hillbillies* and *The Andy Griffith Show*. Still, *The Real McCoys* (another corn-fed comedy) was a distant second to *Bonanza* the year before. Aubrey—who bought *McCoys* from ABC expressly to go against *Bonanza*—canceled it at the end of the 1962–63 season. At the same time, the CBS president also dropped *True Theatre*, an anthology series sponsored by General Electric that ran in the second half hour competing against *Bonanza*. (*The Real McCoys* in January of 1963 posted a quite respectable 21.0 Nielsen rating. "By any standards, that's a hit," noted *Variety*, but in the prime Sunday nighttime slot opposite *Bonanza*, the rural comedy's numbers were not acceptable to Aubrey.)

As far as CBS was concerned, the one-hour time period opposite *Bonanza* was a graveyard for whatever they placed there. Even the venerable Jack Benny (pitted against *Bonanza* in the 1961–62 season) withered on the vine and was moved to a safe Tuesday night berth between Red Skelton and Garry Moore the next year.

Widely regarded as the "Tiffany of the networks," CBS, in the 1962–63 season, had an extraordinary sixteen of the top twenty shows, and nineteen out of the top twenty-five. Much of the credit for the current wave of CBS's success went not to founder and chairman William Paley, but rather to network president James Aubrey, a complex, driven, highly controversial figure deemed so ruthless and cunning by his detractors that he was dubbed "The Smiling Cobra." (He had also made CBS tremendous profits. In 1962, CBS set a profit and sales record, with a record $29,053,734 net income, a 33 percent increase over the previous year.)

Aubrey also had open a Wednesday night berth on the 1963–64 CBS prime-time schedule, far less prestigious but far safer than the Sunday slot following the Sullivan show. Kaye, at first, was placed opposite the popular but not unbeatable NBC *Dr. Kildare* series, but when it was learned that CBS had positioned Kaye on Wednesdays from 10:00 to 11:00 P.M. (EST), NBC immediately moved *Kildare* to another night to avoid the competition. Thus, Danny Kaye was given an even greater chance to survive—uniquely due to the efforts of CBS *and* NBC.

CBS decided that Judy would take the prime Sunday night position. The network attempted to bolster her confidence by publicly declaring that only she, and not Danny Kaye, could trample the NBC western—as her 1962 special had done. It was true that CBS was betting millions that Garland would trounce *Bonanza*. Largely ignored was the fact that the same network was also betting virtually the same amount of money that *The Danny Kaye Show* would beat such instantly forgettable competition as *Channing* on ABC and *Eleventh Hour* on NBC on Wednesday nights.

CBS head of programming Michael Dann remembers that Kaye and his manager flatly refused the Sunday night spot when it was first offered to them, both realizing that they had little chance for Sunday night survival opposite *Bonanza*. Dann states, "Ted Ashley [Kaye's representative] told me in no uncertain terms that Danny would not take the Sunday night time slot. . . . David Begelman was very gifted about the handling of talent, but he was not as gifted in knowing it's where a program is, not what the content is. Ninety percent of a program's success is where it's scheduled."

Interestingly, Judy's management company, CMA, also represented David Dortort—producer and creator of *Bonanza*.

Further undermining Judy's position at the network was Kaye's status as Aubrey's "personal favorite" (according to *The Hollywood Reporter*) and a star he aggressively pursued for his network with great determination. Kaye also had the advantage of a powerhouse lead-in factor, following the top-rated show on the air, *The Beverly Hillbillies,* and the critically acclaimed situation comedy, *The Dick Van Dyke Show,* the ninth highest-rated program of the 1962–63 season. *The Danny Kaye Show*, in addition, benefited from following similar, but not exact, programs (situation comedies), which would be complimented by the Kaye hour. Judy had a less desirable lead-in, *The Ed Sullivan Show.* While Sullivan was a strong ratings performer (fourteenth place among all shows in the 1962–63 season), Garland following the stone-faced host meant two hours of variety programming, back-to-back, which some experienced observers felt might be too much of the same genre.

Whether Garland could succeed was one question raised early on by *Variety*: "It's hardly betraying a secret that the multi-million dollar investment in Judy Garland represents a calculated risk—since there's no guarantee of a full-season lock-in on her services. Depending upon any number of reasons, Miss Garland, some feel, might suddenly decide to blow the whole thing." However vague such reports might attempt to be, it was clear that her checkered reputation had come around to haunt her.

The time-slot question having been answered, with a sponsor for the show still being pursued, the next order of business for CBS was to hire a producer who would in turn be responsible for assembling the production staff.

The network's first choice was television veteran Bob Banner, who presently was producing Garry Moore's New York–based variety series. In December, Banner had turned down CBS's offer to produce the upcoming Kaye series because he would not relocate to California from the East Coast. The Garland series was to be taped in Manhattan, and although Banner was interested, he and CBS ultimately could not come to terms.

In late February, Bob Finkel—former Dinah Shore producer, who currently held the same post for Andy Williams's NBC program—was approached to produce the Garland series. CBS was eager to sign Finkel. *The Judy Garland Show,* still in need of a sponsor, keenly required a producer to alert advertisers that the still-questionable series was indeed on track. CBS offered Finkel not only the Garland producer credit "for a handsome salary," the network offered his production company, Teram Corporation, financial participation in *The Judy Garland Show.* Although he called it "the most attractive offer I have ever received in my 16 years in radio and TV," Finkel would not relocate to New York for Judy's series.

Next, Bill Hobin, a highly respected veteran television producer and director (who currently was helming the *Sing Along with Mitch* series on NBC starring Mitch Miller), was approached to produce and direct *The Judy Garland Show.* His track record was impressive, and Hobin had won Peabody and Emmy awards for directing the classic Sid Caesar *Your Show of Shows* program from 1951–54; other credits included directing *Your Hit Parade* for two years, producing and directing Pat Boone's *Chevy Showroom* series in the late 1950s (where he worked with Judy's musical director, Mort Lindsey) and serving as producer and director of the critically acclaimed *Bell Telephone Hour* series.

Having already decided to leave the Miller program, Hobin, a solid, extremely gifted craftsman who admired Garland's talents tremendously, jumped at the opportunity. And unlike Finkel, he was already based on the East Coast. With Hobin on board wearing two hats, the Garland series had found not only its producer, but its director as well.

East Coast–based Hobin was completely unaware that West Coast–based George Schlatter was also intent on becoming Garland's producer. In a record period of time, the outgoing, confident Schlatter had gone from being a bouncer at the famed Ciro's Sunset Strip nightclub to agenting at MCA, then producing shows in Las Vegas before launching a career in television. He began his broadcasting career as an NBC program executive and then became a producer, most recently for Dinah Shore's NBC series of specials. When Dinah opted to forgo weekly television at the close of the 1962–63 season, Schlatter decided to very aggressively pursue the producer post of *The Judy Garland Show*. An ex-college football player, he was a brash and imposing figure, armed with an abundance of salty humor. Admittedly "street-wise" and still in his early thirties, Schlatter thought he would be perfect for Judy's series.

"I really wanted to do the Garland show," confesses Schlatter, "because I was a real fan. She was the last of the real superstars. [CBS head of programming] Mike Dann would stay at the Beverly Hills Hotel, and I'd chase him down the street yelling out of a convertible, 'I have to do that show!' I was fascinated by her reputation because I had worked at Ciro's, I'd been an agent at MCA, I'd book talent and produce shows at the Frontier and Silver Slipper in Vegas. I had heard the reputation of Sophie Tucker, Maurice Chevalier, Pearl Bailey, Martin and Lewis, and I've really gotten along very well with them because most of those people are not really difficult—they are exacting and demanding, because they demand the same kind of perfection out of others that they expect out of themselves."

Schlatter was as unaware that Hobin had already been promised the job as Hobin was that Schlatter had been lobbying for it. Although the deal was set for Hobin to produce and direct the Garland show based on his negotiations with CBS in New York, Schlatter was so determined in his efforts to get the job that he, almost simultaneously, was signed by the network—on the West Coast—to be producer.

Hobin and Schlatter were also, unwittingly, caught in a rather one-sided power play between network president Jim Aubrey and Hubbell Robinson, CBS senior vice president of programs. It was Robinson who sought Hobin out to produce and direct the Garland series and in turn hired him, but when the network executive was abruptly fired by Aubrey—reportedly at a scheduling meeting for the upcoming season—gone, too, was Robinson's edict to hire Hobin for both posts. The contracts, recalls Hobin, were, in fact, being drawn up when Robinson was dismissed.

Robinson had been with the network since 1949 (moving steadily up the corporate ladder from radio and television vice president in charge of network programs to executive vice president overseeing all programming ten years later). He felt himself to be the logical successor to network president Louis Cowan, who was dismissed in December 1959 and was furious when James Aubrey was given that position instead.

Aubrey began his career in broadcasting in 1948, selling advertising time for CBS radio and television stations in Los Angeles. He, too, moved quickly up the CBS ranks, and by 1956 was managing the network's Hollywood programming. Discontented at his limited power base at CBS, he was wooed away by ABC where he was given the title vice president for programs and talent at thirty-five thousand dollars per year. In charge of filmed series for the third-place network, he shrewdly created great success for the network with such programs as the offbeat western *Maverick* with James Garner and *The Rifleman* with Chuck Connors, the slick detective series *77 Sunset Strip*, the rural comedy *The Real McCoys*, and the long-running family situation comedy *The Donna Reed Show*.

His reign at ABC had such impact that he was soon romanced by CBS founder Bill Paley and president Dr. Frank Stanton and rejoined the company in April of 1958 as a vice president. By June 1959, Aubrey was named executive vice president, and when he became Cowan's successor, Robinson—credited as a pioneer of landmark television dramas and such programs as the renowned *Playhouse 90*—bitterly departed the network and tried his hand at independent production.

At the other extreme, Aubrey would change the look of CBS, and all of television, with such lowbrow but extremely popular and profitable programs as *The Beverly Hillbillies, The Andy Grif-*

fith Show, Mr. Ed, Gomer Pyle U.S.M.C., Petticoat Junction, and
Green Acres. (As a result, CBS net profits nearly doubled in five
years, jumping from $25 million a year in 1959 to $49 million
by 1964.)

Aubrey, who quickly set his administrative pattern of auton-
omous management, brought in Hunt Stromberg, Jr., as a West
Coast–based vice president. Known as Aubrey's confidant and
right-hand man, Stromberg (whose father was a noted film producer in Hollywood's golden age) was almost as controversial
and disliked as the network president himself.

In early 1962, Paley decided to bring Robinson back into the
CBS fold, and Aubrey, knowing the ramifications of disobeying
an edict from the very top, agreed. The move by Paley to reinstate Robinson was seen as a means to splinter Aubrey's power
and raise the quality of CBS's programming. Concurs Mike Dann,
"We were being criticized as 'The Hillbilly Network.' We wanted
a touch of class and excitement which only Kaye and Garland
could provide."

Robinson rejoined the network, but the hierarchy was quite
different from what he had known there before. Aubrey paid
little attention to Robinson's programming and hiring suggestions, evidenced by Aubrey's purposeful disregard of Bill Hobin's pact with Robinson to produce and direct *The Judy Garland
Show.* As *Variety* summed up when reporting his departure, "It
was evident almost from the day Robinson returned to the network that prexy Jim Aubrey would be calling all the program
shots, as he has subsequently done."

When Robinson left CBS for the second time—when Aubrey
told him, "You're through" at the scheduling meeting—his most
recent tenure was exactly one day short of one year, from March
12, 1962, to March 11, 1963. In turn, Judy lost a strong ally at
CBS. Robinson had represented CBS in the ceremonial signing
of the weekly series contract and represented the show in CBS
press materials. Now, suddenly, he was gone.

With Paley having no visible presence near Garland or *The
Judy Garland Show,* Judy would face instead "Smiling Cobra" Aubrey, the cunning Stromberg, and Mike Dann, who attempted
to hold his own ground against the all-powerful Aubrey. "Hubbell Robinson had bought Judy Garland," confirms George
Schlatter. "It was not a Hunt Stromberg buy, but Hunt wanted
into the show."

Alan Courtney (second in command under Robinson until he resigned in protest over Robinson's dismissal) says of Aubrey's CBS, "I never found a better-operating machine than CBS, but it was like being in a concentration camp. Everybody was scared to death of what they said, where they moved, and all the time it was pervaded by the intense Aubrey charm." According to Courtney, James Aubrey was "one of the brightest men I've ever known, one of the most decisive and dramatic men in the business. On one side, he was probably the most charming, gracious, delightful guy in the world, and, on the other, he was just lethal."

Hunt Stromberg, assesses Courtney, "was a really repulsive human being. He ran the West Coast with an iron hand. The destruction of Hubbell Robinson was one of the most awful things I'd ever seen—it was like watching a snake swallowing a bird." CBS was a hotbed of political intrigue, rife with back-stabbing and egos inflated to gigantic proportions. Increasingly aware of this situation, Hobin accepted the reduced role of director without contest or rancor, dismissing the matter as "a political thing."

The confusion over the dual signings resolved, Schlatter's hiring was announced first, with no mention of Hobin already having been set to direct. Meanwhile, George had been signed to produce *The Judy Garland Show* without having met the superstar. Finally, and unexpectedly, the meeting between the two came about when George was in New York in the beginning stages of preproduction.

"Mike Dann called and asked, 'Can you come down to my office for a minute?,' and I was a mess," recalls George. "I go downstairs, and in walks Judy Garland. I was first amazed that she was so small, because the aura of Judy Garland was a woman who was nine feet tall. And this little person walked in. I couldn't think of what to say, because I was not prepared to meet her. So I said to her, 'I don't care what you may have heard, there's no truth to the rumor that I'm difficult!' Well, she started to laugh, hysterical, and said, 'Why don't we get out of here and have a drink,' and we did. Twenty minutes later, we were drinking Blue Nun and laughing hysterically. I was stunned, because this woman was bawdy and funny and intense." Schlatter, despite the conviviality of it all, remained a bit cautious. "I also was aware that all of those stories about her weren't fairy tales."

In *Variety* later that same week, reporter George Rosen dourly predicted, "Even if Judy Garland survives her initial season of weekly Sunday night hours (and they're placing bets on this one) the chances are indeed remote that she'll want to try again in '64–'65"—echoing the words of CBS executive Sal Iannucci that all concerned (except Garland) viewed Judy's series as "short-term." The deal was barely three months old, and the series was already blanketed with certain doom.

In the midst of all of this, Judy, Sid, and the children escaped on a long-overdue vacation, a two-week excursion to the Caribbean. The trip was meant to strengthen the reconciliation between the two and give Judy a rest before jumping into work. From the beginning, Sid believed it was a mistake for Judy to tackle a weekly television series and told her so—she was too large for the small tube and risked overexposure.

If she was entering into the weekly series with mixed emotions, even aware of its negative aura, she now was determined to do *The Judy Garland Show*.

The arguments Judy presented to Sid were undoubtedly similar to those she presented only two weeks earlier to a New York–based reporter: "It was a big decision, but a wonderful decision. I don't think of it as so formidable. I'm going to be a female Perry Como. I'm going to take it easy, and have wonderful guests, and share the spotlight. I'm not going to try and carry the show every week all by myself."

Remembering her earlier television productions, Judy stated, "A weekly show isn't anything like a special. On a special, you feel so pushed, so responsible. You only have one chance. It's concentrated chaos. Everything depends on it. If you're on every week, you can relax. If you are not absolutely great one Sunday, there's another Sunday coming right up. I want to keep the show simple," she wisely noted. "In television, you are in a room, not on a stage, so you don't get too fancy."

George Schlatter at another point of the globe was working to assemble *The Judy Garland Show* production team. With director Hobin set, Schlatter still had to find writers, a choreographer, and a key musical figure to augment the work of Mort Lindsey, who, of course, would be musical director for the series, as he had been for two of Garland's recent films, television specials, and almost every concert engagement since early 1961.

Peter Gennaro, who had worked well with Judy on the ill-fated 1956 *G.E. Theatre* special, was recruited to take on chore-ography chores. Schlatter also hired the writing team of brothers Frank and Tom Waldman, although he first brought in television veteran Johnny Bradford as head writer to script *The Judy Garland Show*. Bradford also happened to be the brother of Bob Wells, who cowrote the classic holiday tune "The Christmas Song" with Mel Tormé. Schlatter, coincidentally or not, had also decided to actively pursue noted singer-composer-arranger Tormé to write special material for both Judy and her guests on a weekly basis.

In early April, Schlatter tracked Mel Tormé down in Miami Beach. Tormé had met Schlatter only once, briefly, during George's days at Ciro's. Tormé's immediate reaction was that Schlatter felt his singing career was on the downslide and that he might consider, instead, using his time "making other people look and sound good." Schlatter doggedly pursued Tormé, call-ing him twice the next day in attempting to break down Mel's resistance. Mel did not want to "suddenly subordinate my own singing status and chain myself to a piano for someone else."

He still vacillated, until George sweetened the proposition by offering him two guest spots among the first thirteen programs. Not only would Tormé write for Judy and other talented singer-guests, but he would also sing solos and duets with her and write whatever material they would do together. Tormé agreed to the improved terms, and a three-thousand-dollar weekly sal-ary, and joined *The Judy Garland Show* team.

Schlatter viewed Gary Smith as a natural for the Garland se-ries after his highly successful art-direction showcasing of the star in the 1962 special with Frank Sinatra. Highly gifted, in-spired, and armed with an abundance of sophisticated good taste, Smith was responsible for the unique "Judy bulbs" (as they were nicknamed) and the lighted runway, which would be an integral part of the stylish, theatrical look of the Garland series. Schlat-ter, Smith, and the others were so determined to create a show well above the norm that George, from the onset, dubbed the Garland hours "a weekly series of specials," a phrase picked up in short order by the CBS publicity department.

"We were able to put together an absolutely super group of people for the show, because *everybody* wanted to work with Garland," says Schlatter.

The hunt for sponsors for *The Judy Garland Show*—whether it was to be a weekly series or "weekly series of specials"—continued. *The Danny Kaye Show* had already bagged the Armstrong Cork Corporation, which had been offered sponsorship first by CBS because it had sponsored *Armstrong Circle Theatre*, which the network had dropped in favor of the Kaye show (airing in the same time period for the 1963–64 season). American Motors and the Ralston-Purina Company picked up the remaining tab for Danny's series. But unlike Kaye's series, the Sunday night Garland slot held no sponsor loyalty from years past, with only canceled, low-rated shows in its graveyard. The Ford Motor Company had expressed interest in sponsoring the series (as it did her Goulet-Silvers special, and, of course, the 1955 *Ford Star Jubilee* spectacular) but had to bow out when Garland was given the Sunday night spot. Ford declared it would have fully sponsored the entire Garland show every week but could not because company policy dictated that Ford could not sponsor a show opposite a major competitor; Chevrolet happened to sponsor *Bonanza*.

General Mills, however, in a move to advertise on "adult" programs, bid for *The Judy Garland Show*, and bought an alternate half-hour block. American Tobacco and the Menley & James pharmaceutical company (to promote, among other products, its new cold remedy, Contac) signed next, with Proctor & Gamble, after some time, jumping in to fill the last open quarter of sponsorship.

The commercial-time prices asked by CBS for both the Garland and Kaye series set a new record and created concern that the network, although it was firmly in first place, might price itself out of the market. While popular programs headlined by Ed Sullivan and Garry Moore represented an estimated $12 million annual total advertising revenue brought to CBS by each series, the two new CBS variety shows (and Jackie Gleason's continuing program) had upped the ante to $15 million per season, per program, setting an unheard of price of fifty thousand dollars for a one-minute commercial, which translated itself into $2.5 million advertising revenue generated from each series (combining all participating sponsors for each program) in one year.

While Kaye and Garland were matched in show budget and advertiser support, Judy Garland clearly was the main attraction at CBS's annual two-day affiliates meeting held at New York's Waldorf-Astoria Hotel on Thursday and Friday, May 9–10. Buoyed by a recent Emmy nomination for *Judy and Her Guests* as best musical program of the year, Garland headlined thirty-seven CBS network stars, including Lucille Ball, Vivian Vance, Burt Reynolds, Phil Silvers, Danny Kaye, the cast of *The Beverly Hillbillies*, Ed Sullivan, Clint Eastwood, and Rose Marie, Morey Amsterdam, Richard Deacon, and Mary Tyler Moore of *The Dick Van Dyke Show*.

The convention, which included more than one thousand employees from CBS stations around the country, began and continued on a high note, with CBS winning a stunning seven-night rating sweep. According to an April report from A. C. Nielsen, CBS had fourteen of the top twenty shows, ten out of the top ten daytime shows and thirty-one out of the top fifty prime-time half-hour programs on the air. CBS stations made 200 percent more profit than their rival affiliate stations. Aubrey was at his zenith, enjoying peak earnings for the network as well as incomparable ratings for his hand-picked programs. "We're talking now about a network whose profits for the year amounted to more than all the major Hollywood film studios combined," Aubrey boasted to his delegation, who had named him "the new Mister Television."

"Television," said Aubrey to the affiliates, "has come of age in 1963," commanding the best talent of motion pictures and the theater, becoming the "true entertainment medium." In reciting some names on the CBS roster of talent, Aubrey emphasized to the delegates, "When you can commit to weekly shows with such personalities as Danny Kaye and Judy Garland . . . you know you've got something big going for you."

While a parade of CBS stars appeared during the evening ceremonies onstage and were seated among the affiliates from table to table, Judy and Danny Kaye were scheduled to be the primary entertainment events. On Thursday, affiliates would see Danny Kaye's one-man show, which had opened April 10, at the Ziegfeld Theatre.

Friday night's entertainment would be held at the Waldorf-Astoria, featuring the cast of *The Beverly Hillbillies* and Phil Silvers. Capping it all would be Judy Garland in concert, with Mort Lindsey conducting. There could be no greater finish, and certainly none more logical, yet George Schlatter faced problems with the network on how to showcase her. It seemed that, although CBS was prepared to shell out perhaps $25 million for her services, it seemed to have little understanding of the greatest single talent it had under contract.

"We're putting together the show, and I get a call from Hunt Stromberg," recalls Schlatter, "telling me that Judy had to go to New York to do the affiliates dinner. He was afraid to talk to her directly. He didn't want to pet the panther, so he told me to talk to her about appearing in front of the CBS affiliates." Her immediate reaction about having to face the station representatives was fear. "She was terrified," recalls Schlatter. "She didn't know what to say to them." Although she would do a one-hour concert backed by Mort Lindsey and a full orchestra, as she boarded a plane to New York with George, Gary Smith, Bill Hobin, and Johnny Bradford, Judy was still concerned about the audience of wall-to-wall CBS station delegates she would face the following night.

"What am I going to do?" Judy asked George.

"You've been in front of millions of people," he reassured her.

"But these," said Judy, with great logic, "are *affiliates*! How am I going to tell them not to worry that I'll be there each week?"

"Out of the blue," remembers George, "we start singing, 'Call Me Irresponsible.' So we get the idea on the plane and put this thing together." But that was not the end of Schlatter's CBS troubles. "We get to New York, and Hunt calls up and says, We want her to come out with the *Parade of Stars*. I said, She *can't* come out with a *Parade of Stars* and then come back later for a moment. I'll deliver her once, but you can't have her twice. They said, You're being difficult. I said, I'm not being difficult, the woman is an event! You don't do it twice. Fireworks go off once, they don't come back and set them up again. Big argument at that point with CBS. *The Parade of Stars* came out *without* Judy Garland. That was the first time they said they were going to fire me," Schlatter wryly notes, "which they said with more and more frequency as time went on."

Judy did, however, attend Danny Kaye's show at the Ziegfeld. Aubrey, recalls CBS executive Oscar Katz, wanted to escape the crowded postperformance party. He told Oscar to hail a cab and meet the group outside in ten minutes, during which time Aubrey collected about eight or nine people, including his teenaged daughter Susan, Katz and his wife, and Judy. Aubrey was determined to have an informal, impromptu, less crowded party of his own and chose a favorite bar of his near the United Nations Building as the location for his private party.

"It was an Italian place," remembers Katz. "There was a very good black piano player whose eyes popped out when he saw Judy. We ordered drinks, and she sang for an hour or two." Aubrey had a request. "He asked Judy to sing 'Over the Rainbow,' which she didn't like to sing. He said it was for his daughter. Judy said, 'Have her come and sit next to me.' Aubrey's daughter sat next to her, and she sang it, looking at her the whole time, singing it to her. The kid, then sixteen or seventeen, couldn't believe it." The experience of Judy singing—to perhaps a dozen people at most—remains for Katz "one of the great nights in show business."

Judy's performance, in front of a packed assembly of CBS station brass the following night, was equally effective. "The orchestra played her overture," as Schlatter recounts, "and this little woman walks out into the spotlight, now confident that she knew what she was going to do—and got her heel caught in the stage and couldn't move. Her heel found the *only* crack in the stage of the Waldorf, which is unbelievable, but she was accident-prone. And then she started to laugh. She took off her shoes, walked down to the footlights, and the ovation finally stopped."

Looking squarely into the assembled CBS eye, Judy launched into the Garland-Schlatter-Bradford parody of "Call Me Irresponsible," which, roughly, went:

> Call me irresponsible.
> Call me unreliable
> Throw in undependable, too.
> Do my foolish alibis bore you?
> Are you worried
> I might not show up for you?
> Call me unpredictable.
> Say that I'm impractical.
> Rainbows I'm inclined to pursue . . .
> But it's undeniably true—
> But I'm irrevocably signed to you!

Judy, sans shoes, wins over
the CBS affiliates at the Waldorf-Astoria.
CBS INC.

Below, Judy in concert at the
affiliates meeting
CBS INC.

"The place went crazy," remembers Schlatter. "She had them in the palm of her hand," concurs Katz. "The song was addressed right to their worries."

"Judy," recalls George, "could have *owned* the network at this point. And then she proceeds to pulverize everyone with a concert!"

It seemed that Garland had won over CBS. Lucille Ball took the overall network crown, but Judy Garland, if reaction from this hard-boiled group of station people was any indication, was the new musical queen of the network. Finally, *The Judy Garland Show* was on track, in production, and sure to be a great success. Despite a slow start, a dubious reputation, and an unpredictable star, Garland would win out.

"The hottest contest of the upcoming season," predicted *Variety*, would be Garland versus the men of the Ponderosa. While the trade paper offered, "You can collect bets on either side," the conclusion was less hopeful: "The feeling prevails that *Bonanza*, particularly in view of its tremendous small town and rural appeal, should squeak out ahead."

Perhaps, as CBS had done in wanting to sprinkle her among the other network stars, critics were underestimating her as well. All George Schlatter had to do was maintain (and, at the same time, dispel) the myth of "The Legend" that was Judy Garland, keep her tremendous appeal intact (but somehow distill it for weekly television), make her an event on a weekly basis that would, at the same time, not overexpose her tremendous larger-then-life personality that had to conform to all of America coast-to-coast—while still remaining unique.

Although Judy Garland admitted to the CBS affiliates that she was inclined to pursue rainbows, George Schlatter seemed to be chasing quite a few of his own.

5

George Schlatter had little time to bask in the glory of the CBS affiliates triumph. The rest of the production staff had to be hired, the specific concept, approach, and look of the series all had to be determined. Also, CBS was pushing Schlatter to find Judy a supporting player, someone to be her second banana. Guests— befitting Garland's stature and the best in the business—had to be booked.

Months before the series went into actual production, it was announced that the husband and wife team of Gordon and Sheila MacRae was set to appear; Judy, typical of her healthy sense of humor about herself, actually encouraged the idea of Sheila doing her wicked impression of Garland face-to-face on the show. Nat "King" Cole had also been announced as a guest, as were singers Vic Damone and Tony Martin, the latter having appeared with Judy in *Pigskin Parade* in 1936 and *Ziegfeld Girl* in 1941.

In late May, Judy attended the SHARE tenth anniversary party, the show business philanthropic organization's benefit for the Exceptional Children's Foundation. Raising money for charity, Judy put herself on the auction block, taking song requests from the highest bidders. Judy sang "San Francisco," "Shine On, Harvest Moon" (in a duet with Sammy Davis, Jr.), "Up a Lazy River" in a medley with composer Johnny Mercer, and "For Me and My Gal" with Gene Kelly. The event sparked several booking ideas in the minds of Judy and her producer; Schlatter expressed interest in booking the SHARE chorus line for the Garland show. Judy's old friend Sammy Davis was a natural guest possibility, and Gene Kelly confirmed several weeks later that he would appear with Judy on her series. Judy even planned to ask John Wayne to warble with her on one of her hours; the idea came to her after she sat next to "The Duke" during the SHARE benefit.

Donald O'Connor, who had known Judy and her family since their days in vaudeville together, was set very early on to appear on *The Judy Garland Show*. Judy and the talented hoofer had remained close friends through their days at MGM to the present, and she held his talent in high regard, second only to that of Mickey Rooney.

The two were such old friends that Donald, during his act at the Cocoanut Grove that March, quipped to the audience that he was so naive as a youth, "I didn't know Judy Garland was a girl until Mickey Rooney explained things to me!" The following month, Donald invited Judy onstage during his show at New York's Americana Hotel. Liza, who was with her mother, was then brought up to join them onstage, and the trio launched into an impromptu, spirited performance, much to the delight of the surprised audience.

However, there was no better guest for the premiere episode of *The Judy Garland Show* than her most cherished friend, Mickey Rooney. Companions since first meeting in 1933 at a children's theatrical school (long before their years of movie stardom), Judy and Mickey were also among Hollywood's most beloved screen teams during their years at MGM. In the thirty years they had known each other, Garland and Rooney's friendship had never wavered. No one had a better champion than Mickey had in Judy; for her part, she made her feelings clear when she once described Rooney as "the world's greatest talent."

Now, in 1963, the scales were not equal. Mickey, still a man of incomparable talent, had fallen on hard times. He had even declared bankruptcy the year before. Judy Garland, on the other hand, was once again at the very top, about to embark on a multimillion-dollar weekly television series.

If the scramble to book "A-List" guests for the show was not enough of a headache for Schlatter, decisions considered final by the network were now suddenly being reversed on almost a daily basis.

Live television, although on the decline by 1963, was still in practice, and Judy's series (as well as Danny Kaye's) was envisioned by CBS to continue that tradition. Jerry Lewis was banking heavily on the unpredictable aspect of live television to attract viewers on his upcoming two-hour Saturday night ABC variety series. Then CBS recanted and announced that both the Garland and Kaye series would be shot "live-on-tape."

For a time, that about-face by CBS was almost revised again. Since Judy and her Kingsrow Enterprises retained 100 percent ownership of the show, the idea of filming it (an unusual practice) was considered, primarily to make it more appealing to prospective foreign buyers. Shooting the series on high-quality 35mm stock and distributing the shows in either 35mm or less expensive 16mm versions would appeal to foreign stations who did not have videotape facilities. Film was therefore more practical and more expeditious in securing deals with other countries. It was also far more durable than videotape, better able to withstand shipping, temperature changes, and repeated showings—and, unlike videotape, film, if properly maintained, could last decades, while tape disintegrated within a matter of years. In the end, videotape won out over film. Its deficiencies were somewhat balanced by the fact that tape would provide an immediacy, an unmistakable impact, a feeling of live television and live performance, that film could not offer.

CBS then made a decision that completely altered the original master plan of *The Judy Garland Show*. From the beginning, the series was set to originate from New York. Mirroring the demise of film over videotaped programming, Hollywood was gaining favor over Manhattan in terms of television production; *The Danny Kaye Show*, at the insistence of its star, was considered a West Coast product from the very beginning. Suddenly Garland's series was moved from Manhattan to Hollywood.

There were several reasons for the East Coast to West Coast switch. At the time, it was assumed that Judy alone was responsible for the decision. While she disliked California, Judy felt that living there would benefit Lorna and Joe. The weather and the environment certainly were much nicer. She also believed the children would get a better education in Los Angeles than they would in New York. And now that she was back again with Sid, Los Angeles seemed the right place to live together as a family. (Liza had already moved to New York, appearing in the off-Broadway revival of *Best Foot Forward*, which had opened in April.)

Reflecting her belief that the series represented family stability, Judy remarked to a reporter several weeks before, "You know how I look on this series? As a secure way of living. I can get up in the morning and go to work and come home at night to things that are familiar to me. I'm so tired of being on the road. The concerts have been marvelous to me, but I've been living in hotels now for the last three years and I've had it. To look around a hotel room, night after night, and not even see a picture on the wall that belongs to you, is terrible. I want my children to have their own rooms to come home to." Judy was clearly optimistic about television, determinedly so. "Things are better now," she said firmly. "They get better every year."

Orval Paine, Judy's hairdresser, suggests that he might have played some part in her decision to move the show to California as well. Devoted, very protective, and fiercely loyal, Orval immediately became a confidant and a friend to Judy. "The first time I met her was when I got a call from Harrah's and some girl asked me if I'd be willing to go over to Judy Garland's house and do her hair. I said sure. I went over, and Judy asked me at the door, 'Are you going to do my hair the way I want it done, or are you going to *tell* me how to do it?' I said, 'You pay me to do your hair, that's the way I'm going to do it. If you want your head *shaved*, I'll shave it!' " Judy laughed, opened the door for him, and said, "We're going to get along great!"

Orval often became Judy's escort and was quickly exposed to her irrepressible sense of humor. Once, when they were in New York having dinner during work on the taping of the Silvers-Goulet special in February, an aquaintance of Judy's spotted her and rushed over to their table. "She introduced me as Orval, some sultan from some unknown place, and my mouth dropped open." With a perfectly straight face, Judy added that Orval was her fiancé. After the friend left, Judy turned to Orval and deadpanned, "You didn't *mind*, did you?"

Judy, naturally, wanted the skilled Paine to do her hair for the series. When he told her that he was unable to relocate to New York for that length of time, George Schlatter intervened and called him. "George carried on for quite a while," recalls Orval, "because Judy told him with great finality, 'If they can't get him to do my hair, there will be no show!' "

Personal factors aside, CBS likely played a hand in the decision as well. Approximately 40 percent of all CBS programming—including many game shows and soap operas, virtually the network's entire daytime rundown—originated from the East Coast. The network for some time had been experiencing a severe shortage of both studio and dressing room availability in New York. Responding to the crisis in 1962, CBS's Mike Dann announced a $15 million renovation for the Fifty-seventh Street facility that would add four new studios. The massive project, though, was not anticipated to be completed until sometime during the 1963–64 season.

Taking a completely different approach only a few months later in the spring of 1963, Dann began extolling the virtues of CBS's Hollywood production facilities. Soon after, *The Hollywood Reporter* announced that Los Angeles, and not New York, would be the site of her first taping, now set for a July start-up date. Confusion still reigned at the network, with *Variety* reporting only three weeks later that Garland's series would begin taping in June—in New York.

By May, CBS officially announced that *The Judy Garland Show* would be a West Coast production, with the network saying the decision was dictated by Judy's "personal wishes." To many observers, the switch to Hollywood marked the beginning of Aubrey's disfavor with both Garland and *The Judy Garland Show*.

With the exception of Tormé and Schlatter (who had agreed to relocate to New York from California), everyone else was based in New York and signed for the show on the assumption it would be produced there. While the staff was enthused at the prospect of working with Garland and agreed to uproot themselves (most of them with their families), it was nevertheless an expensive, time-consuming decision. This also put the show further behind schedule, a factor that would put more pressure on Garland and the producers; CBS expected ten completed episodes by September.

Bill Hobin later candidly acknowledged, "I wouldn't have accepted it if I'd known they would change the original plan of New York originations to Hollywood." (He hastened to add, as production began, though, "I couldn't have asked to work with a more talented and cooperative producer than George Schlatter, and Judy is a dream to direct. I have never seen a performer work so hard, and she's always early—not late, as I've been led to believe—for every rehearsal and taping call.") Hobin revealed why the offer to direct the show was irresistible to him: "The Garland series appeared to be the challenge of the decade."

When it was announced that the show was to be based on the West Coast, it was assumed it would be taped at CBS's Hollywood-adjacent Television City facility. The truth was that George Schlatter and his staff fought from the beginning to tape anywhere *but* Television City, trying to find a larger, more suitable home. The ceilings in the Television City studios were so low that none allowed for scenery to be raised or lowered, requiring everything to be manually moved in and out, which could cause lengthy, expensive setup delays between segments.

Exploring other options, Schlatter approached NBC. The rival network aggressively bid to lease CBS studio space in Burbank. Taping the show at the large, fully equipped, and more sophisticated NBC studios was certainly an attractive proposition, but CBS refused to allow the show to be taped at the competing network. Schlatter then considered the Samuel Goldwyn Studios in Hollywood, which offered an enormous stage and an audience capacity of seven hundred. CBS vetoed the idea, and it was announced at the end of May that Television City at the corner of Beverly and Fairfax avenues would indeed be the home of the Garland series.

The switch to Hollywood forced Peter Gennaro to drop out of *The Judy Garland Show.* "When the series came up," remembers the choreographer, "I was very excited because it was right in New York and right up my alley. When things changed, I just couldn't go to the Coast. I had two young kids, I was working whenever I wanted, and I didn't want to disrupt everything."

Schlatter thought of another respected choreographer, Danny Daniels (who had recently worked with Liza Minnelli in *Best Foot Forward*), but was momentarily deterred when Daniels could not join the show immediately. Daniels had signed to dance at Lincoln Center with the New York Philharmonic and could not be on the West Coast for preproduction and tapings of the first two Garland episodes. Daniels, however, struck a multi-episode deal

George Schlatter takes Judy (with David Begelman) on her first tour of Studio 43.

with Schlatter that would begin with Danny's working on the third show—which, by happy coincidence, would have Liza Minnelli as a guest.

George then turned to Nick Castle to choreograph the first two programs until Daniels was able to take over. Castle had the unique advantage of having worked with Judy during her MGM years. She and the veteran choreographer got along well, as did Castle and Schlatter; the two had teamed for some earlier Dinah Shore shows. Nick helped to get the dance department on track and assembled a core group of talented dancers in the process.

Dance-music arranger Jack Elliott approached Mort Lindsey at the time of the CBS affiliates meeting and mentioned that he was interested in working on the Garland series. Mort offered to let him play piano for Judy during her concert performance, which also would give them a chance to meet. He also met Schlatter and Johnny Bradford. When Gennaro dropped out and Castle was temporarily signed, Elliott renewed his efforts to join the

Garland team. With CBS willing to pick up his relocation costs to move from New York, Jack was hired by Schlatter as music coordinator; he would write dance arrangements as well as play the rehearsal piano.

With Los Angeles confirmed as the site of the Garland series, Schlatter finalized the remainder of his production staff. It was decided that Gary Smith would not only be art director but associate producer as well, relieving Schlatter of finding someone for the latter position. Schlatter also hired Bill Brown as choral director, Maggie Banks as assistant choreographer, Gene McAvoy as assistant designer, and Jerry Leshay as associate director. CBS's George Sunga was named production supervisor.

Edith Head was signed to create Garland's wardrobe. Ray Aghayan, who had worked with George on the Shore programs, would handle costume design for everyone else appearing on the show; his young assistant preferred to be called "Robert," but later chose to be billed less formally as Bob Mackie. Gene Hibbs, who had been Judy's makeup artist for her two recent specials, was signed. Esteemed CBS lighting director Leard Davis was also brought in.

Schlatter also secured Bob Wynn to be production consultant. Although only in his late twenties, Wynn was extremely bright, very observant, and possessed an abundance of both business and common sense. Judy sparked to him immediately. Wynn would work on behalf of Kingsrow Enterprises; he would deal with financial matters and was authorized to issue checks on the company account.

"When she came out here from New York," remembers Bob Wynn, "I was only twenty-eight. The only company car we had for the first few weeks was my beat-up station wagon. We would be out at some fancy restaurant somewhere, and when we were ready to leave, the valet would bring this ramshackle piece of junk to us. He sees Garland and falls all over himself, apologizing, saying he must have made a mistake. Very casually, Judy assures him, 'No, it's my car,' as she regally climbs into the broken-down station wagon, bedecked in a glittering evening gown."

With personnel for the show locked in, George Schlatter then had to deal with CBS's insistence that Judy Garland be surrounded by "a television family." Garland's prototype, according to CBS, was *The Garry Moore Show*, which featured diversely talented supporting players, including at various times Carol Burnett, Dorothy Loudon, and Marion Lorne; Allen Funt and Durward Kirby's *Candid Camera* weekly segment was part of the Moore show as well.

CBS knew vaguely but exactly what was needed: one supporting character or two of them to play off each other or three second bananas—maybe more. CBS could not have been more, or less, specific. CBS *was* resolute that Garland was not to be showcased as a larger-than-life show-business legend but should be remolded into television's new "girl next door."

Schlatter balked at this, but the network remained adamant that Garland needed a supporting player. More than a dozen candidates were considered, with Ann B. Davis ("Shultzy" on Bob Cummings's 1950s situation comedy series and later the housekeeper on *The Brady Bunch*), Jonathan Winters, and new comedian Jerry Van Dyke the front-runners.

Van Dyke was signed first, which would free Judy from serving as "femcee" (as *The Hollywood Reporter* dubbed it), giving him his own comedy spots while also serving as a "bumbling host, i.e., one who malaprops name intros and announcements in the chatter segues with Judy." The same item in early June noted that this search for humorous backup performers indicated the Garland series would "lean heavily on informal comedy." While comedian Winters was not mentioned by name in that report, he was actively courted behind the scenes. Davis, however, was cited as a possibility for character roles in comedy sketches.

Only a day later, Davis confirmed that she had been offered a continuing role on the Garland show but added that she was also being wooed by *The Danny Kaye Show*. While her roles on either series would be much the same, the comedienne revealed she was leaning to Judy because Kaye offered alternate-week employment, and Garland would use her on every program. (In the end, Ann B. Davis was signed for neither.) Winters—a gifted and often brilliant performer with a rapid-fire, free-association form of comedy—also lost his bid to be a regular on the Garland series. Of the three candidates, Winters clearly was the most inspired casting idea. But Schlatter was forced to abandon the plan when CBS pressured him to hire Van Dyke, a not-untalented but relatively new stand-up comic. Hunt Stromberg, Jr., exerted further pressure on the producer to have Van Dyke as Judy's *only* regular on the series, an about-face from the "family of regulars" that occurred only two weeks before the first episode was taped.

It appeared to many that Jerry Van Dyke was thrown into *The Judy Garland Show* to capitalize on the success of his older brother Dick, then starring in his own critically acclaimed situation comedy on CBS. *The Dick Van Dyke Show* was not a favorite of network president Jim Aubrey, who believed the show was "too inside" in its depiction of the life of a television-comedy writer; according to costar Rose Marie, Aubrey wanted creator Carl Reiner to make the Van Dyke character an insurance salesman instead. Reiner adamantly refused. Aubrey put the show on the air but placed it opposite the very popular Perry Como *Kraft Music Hall* program—ensuring that it would have little chance to succeed.

At the end of its first season, Aubrey canceled the Van Dyke show and only relented when Proctor & Gamble told the network it would cancel its daytime advertising if CBS did not reinstate it. The sophisticated, multiple Emmy Award–winning series found its audience in its second season and became a genuine television classic as well as an unqualified hit. Aubrey, unwilling to admit his mistake, dismissed its ratings triumph as the single result of it following *The Beverly Hillbillies*.

Jerry Van Dyke had, in fact, launched his television career on *The Dick Van Dyke Show*, in a March 1962 two-part episode that had him play the brother to Dick's television character Rob Petrie. CBS, or more specifically Hunt Stromberg, had high hopes for Jerry, who had come to the attention of the CBS executive after Stromberg's secretary saw him on his brother's show and told her boss that she was impressed with his performance. Stromberg arranged a private screening and, that August, signed Van Dyke to a five-year contract for a reported fifty thousand dollars annually. "Jerry Van Dyke," declared Stromberg of the thirty-two-year-old banjo-playing comedian, "is a marvelously fresh talent, who, with seasoning, will be a big star." He announced that Jerry would star in his own series within a year.

Stromberg felt much the same way about a redheaded comedienne named Cara Williams, whom he believed would be the network's new Lucille Ball. As a result, Williams—a marginally talented low-rent Lucy—was pushed into numerous guest appearances on CBS variety shows and was given two of her own situation comedies by Stromberg, both of which were failures. At the end of 1962, Stromberg even wanted to cast Jerry Van Dyke as Cara Williams's costar. Jerry refused, wanting his own situation comedy.

By his own account, Jerry's concerns about his "bumbling host" role began at the very beginning. "I didn't know what I was doing," confesses Van Dyke. "CBS signed me to a contract for five hundred dollars a week, and I was just out of playing strip joints where I was making three hundred dollars a week for working five shows a night." When Schlatter met with Jerry, alarm bells went off in his head. "I'll never forget, he said, 'I don't know what we're going to do with you, but it's going to be great.' I thought he'd seen me [perform], but he hadn't."

Ethel Winant, an esteemed veteran CBS casting director, today underscores Hunt Stromberg's great influence at the network. "Aubrey depended to a great extent on Hunt's judgment about talent. They just decided that Jerry was an up-and-coming star." Winant disagreed. "I thought he was a very poor choice for Judy. She needed someone stronger, certainly more interesting. She didn't need someone funny as much as she needed someone that gave her a great sense of security when she walked on that stage. Instead, you had this real second banana. I thought she needed to have a leading man."

Although Stromberg was Jerry's mentor, the comic found the network executive abrasive. ("He was a screamer.") Virtually all who came in contact with Stromberg—with the single exception, perhaps, of Jim Aubrey—felt that he was a ruthless, cunning, odd figure. Stromberg had, more often than not, a pet monkey in his company during business hours. (One CBS executive who worked with Stromberg said, half-jokingly, that his tenure "was rather like Caligula running the network." George Schlatter, upon hearing the remark, quipped, "I think I should protest the comparison on behalf of *Caligula!*") Stromberg, sums up Schlatter with more than a small note of lingering bitterness, "added new meaning to the words 'network participation.' "

Aubrey, remembers Jerry Van Dyke, was liked little more than Stromberg. "Everybody hated him, because he could break people—and he did."

Stromberg, in his zealous efforts to make Jerry Van Dyke a CBS star, cast him as the host of *Picture This*, a short-lived sum-

mer-replacement quiz show airing in Jack Benny's usual Tuesday night time slot—at the exact time he was required to begin
work on the Garland series. *Picture This* originated from New
York. Van Dyke would thus be required to fly coast-to-coast every
weekend from June through September. This certainly was not
to the benefit of *The Judy Garland Show*. Stromberg, however,
wanted to get his money's worth out of the comic and to prove
correct his own judgment of potential television superstardom;
it would be as accurate in the case of Jerry Van Dyke as it would
be for Cara Williams.

Interestingly, when the network confirmed that Jerry Van Dyke
would be a regular on Judy's show, CBS also stated that the
comic would star in his own filmed situation comedy for the
1964–65 season. Did that simply indicate Garland would pick up
a new supporting player for the next television year, or did it
mean that *The Judy Garland Show* was indeed considered only a
single-season venture by CBS from the very beginning?

Having resigned themselves to CBS Television City as their
home, Schlatter and his staff set out to transform the CBS studio
into something remotely suitable. George and Bob Wynn made
their ambitious, large-scale plans for Garland evident to production supervisor George Sunga at their very first meeting. "George
and Bob said, 'We're going to work here, but we have to work
like they do at the big place'—meaning NBC in Burbank. Bob
even invited me to NBC to see how they were doing the work
so that I could compare. Bob Wynn executed all the things for
George and, in turn, would turn to me to get everything executed on the CBS side."

Studio 43 had been selected for *The Judy Garland Show*. Although it was large, it still required substantial refurbishing. To
circumvent Studio 43's inability to raise and lower scenery, a
unique turntable was devised that would hide a new set, in place
and ready, to be spun around when required. This would ingeniously avoid delays in transporting and constructing sets between takes. It also allowed Judy to be hidden in shadow and
make an effective entrance on-camera. Assistant designer Gene
McAvoy remembers, "It gave CBS quite a heart attack to build
the turntable, which cost about a couple of hundred thousand
dollars at that point."

Gary Smith hit upon the deceptively simple look that was to

mark *The Judy Garland Show*. The set was white-on-white with a stylized, crisp, theatrical "backstage" set of stage lights, adjacent dressing-room doors (one identified for Garland and the other for the primary guest that week), and a stairway leading to an imaginary second level. Both the floor and the backdrop were high-gloss white, giving the sense of unlimited horizon. The total effect was a particularly elegant, clean look that made the Garland series incomparable to anything of the day and most programs for years to come. Furthermore, the stage had been raised more than two-and-one-half feet off the floor, with a light-bulb-lined runway that extended down the center of the audience section. (The bulbs were orange; they would photograph as white.) About three hundred orange-and-black chairs had been installed—adequate seating, but far less than that offered by NBC or the Goldwyn studios. Still, largely due to Smith's inspired designs, Studio 43 in its new form was spectacular.

The studio was located on ground level; the Garland suite of production offices was situated on the third floor. On one occasion, when George Schlatter was notified that Garland was about to step off the elevator for a preproduction conference early in the preproduction of the series, he hatched a plan to make her visit one she would not soon forget. The entire staff purposely ignored Judy upon her arrival and the star was left to stand in silence for several moments. She then backed out of the doorway and pointedly read *The Judy Garland Show* sign out loud. "Oh, thank *Christ* I'm in the right place," she deadpanned. "For a minute I thought I'd wandered into the Gale Storm offices!"

The Judy Garland Show was finally ready to roll tape—blessed with a happy, optimistic star, an enthusiastic, talented production team, a new studio, production offices, and Judy's close friend Mickey Rooney as its first guest. And, on June 24, Garland and Rooney would step together before the cameras again for the first time in fifteen years.

LEIGH WIENER

6

Underscoring her belief that weekly television would provide her
with both a long-running hit series and financial independence,
Judy decided to buy a home for the newly united Luft family.
Although it was quite a distance from CBS Television City in
Hollywood, she chose one complete with pool and a guest house
on South Rockingham Drive in the Brentwood section of West
Los Angeles.

With the first taping of *The Judy Garland Show* only two weeks
away, Judy and Sid gave a housewarming party. The celebration
fell on the weekend of Judy's forty-first birthday, marking as
well the Lufts' eleventh wedding anniversary. The guests were
pals of long standing (some harking back to her days at MGM),
various business associates, and more than a few members of
The Judy Garland Show production family.

The Rockingham house party made for a sparkling, unforgettable evening. As veteran Hollywood reporter Army Archerd
noted, "The bash was one for the book [with] the Metro alumni
association putting on a show which should have been taped—
it may be—for one of Garland's TV'ers. Producer George Schlatter, director Bill Hobin, Nick Castle, and scribes all took notes."
(Donald O'Connor, June Allyson, and Roddy McDowall were at
least a few of the guests Schlatter cornered at the party who
agreed to appear on early episodes of *The Judy Garland Show*.)

Studio 43 saw more of Judy Garland than did Rockingham Drive as she became steeped in preparations for the all-important first program. So enthusiastic, involved, and dedicated was she that even her most loyal supporters within the Garland series group were themselves surprised at her energy and hard work. "She was happy. She was sleeping. Part of it was making her feel that somebody cared and was letting her have fun," remembers Schlatter.

The producer drew upon that axiom to solve a perplexing, most unexpected problem facing him.

While there was not the overwhelming studio and production office-space shortage there was at CBS in New York, the network had another, even greater crisis at CBS in Hollywood: the battle for dressing-room supremacy among CBS's three variety-series stars. Ego-bruising and displays of temperament were feared among CBS veteran Red Skelton, Danny Kaye (who was new to the network but who had, after all, chosen Hollywood for his show from the beginning), and Garland. Kaye's producer, Perry Lafferty, had secured for his star a lavish penthouse-suite dressing room.

A small dressing area directly offstage was reserved for Judy, but it was far from lavish. Schlatter hit upon a way to create something that was even better than Danny Kaye's penthouse suite: He convinced CBS to provide Judy with a quite roomy, fully accommodated house trailer, situated close to Studio 43. The forty-by-ten-foot house trailer was hoisted to a second-floor ramp. A canvas structure in candy red-and-white stripes (resembling a maharani's tent) was erected around the doorway. Schlatter ordered the trailer be outfitted with wall-to-wall carpeting, antique marble tables, a makeup room, a kitchen, a bar, a bed, and an office–living room area, all shaded in indirect pink lighting. Schlatter also had a *Wizard of Oz*–like yellow brick road painted to lead from her trailer, winding down the hall and right into the studio. Artificial grass and trees were installed in front of the trailer. As an added touch, near the kissing Cupids door knocker, George had a sign placed on the trailer door inscribed, simply, THE LEGEND. No other identification was necessary.

Now, not only did she have a new, lavish house on the best block in Brentwood, she had a second home at CBS—furnished much like her Rockingham Drive residence. Judy, remembers

Judy proudly stands in front of her lavish trailer at CBS Television City during the taping of the first episode.
CBS INC.

everyone, instantly fell in love with her luxurious accommodations. At the same time, they irritated other longtime CBS stars. *House Party* series-host Art Linkletter—himself an eighteen-year veteran on the network—said that he wanted CBS to provide him with a heliport. That way, he sniffed, "I can get to my shows on time." While Danny Kaye kept publicly silent, he was rather upset at Garland's one-upmanship, according to Jack Elliott. He also remembers Red Skelton's reply when he was asked about Garland's and Kaye's lavish dressing-room suites: "Listen," he shot back, "I'll be here long after they're gone." (Judy Garland certainly was being pampered, but no more than other top-name television stars: Jack Benny had his own stage named after him at the Revue Studios, Arthur Godfrey had his own plane, and Garry Moore a yacht.)

Schlatter had won his victory. While Kaye's penthouse cost the network $75,000, Mike Dann estimates that the Garland trailer cost in the area of $150,000. "She loved that trailer," Dann says, remembering that Judy once remarked to him, "You know, you come back from doing a show and let's say you walk into the biggest suite in the Waldorf Towers. And you were alone and there were eight rooms." The trailer, in contrast, gave her a place to unwind after taping a show—with her own belongings and photographs surrounding her. Her CBS home instantly became a source of refuge for Judy, as much as it would serve as the social hub for Garland's invited staff members and guests. The trailer gave Judy a constancy in her workplace and a sense of belonging she had not known since her days at MGM.

However enamored she was of her private accommodations, Garland quickly took on most everyone else's dislike of CBS Television City's mid-1950s design. "It must have been built by the same guys who designed the fun house," she would joke later. "I could never find anything in that building. I had to get there forty-five minutes early every day so I could get lost for a while. I went on the sight-seeing tour with the crowds three different times just to find out where my office was!"

If Television City was not problematic enough, the newly refurbished Studio 43 still posed serious obstacles. Because of the turntable, there was no room onstage for the musicians, so an offstage enclosed cube had to be built for Mort Lindsey and his nearly forty-piece orchestra. Although speakers were placed on the set, Judy (and everyone else) had a natural tendency to listen to the live music rather than to the speakers, which carried it a split second behind. This could cause an annoying staggered effect between the singer and the orchestra. Bill Hobin speculates the speakers also did not give Judy the needed "drive" of the live orchestra. "The audio mix wasn't right from the beginning," says the director. "They were still searching. It was a whole new audio setup. The balances were bad. It wasn't an ideal setup for her show."

The director remembers that the audio situation was the single circumstance that brought on a flash of the legendary Garland temper as the series got underway. "She took direction beautifully. I never had a problem. The only thing she had problems with was the audio, and rightfully so. She wanted it right for her. But as far as anything else—staging, blocking her moves—she was never a problem."

The audio deficiencies were offset somewhat by CBS's purchase of four very expensive brand-new Marconi cameras for *The Judy Garland Show.* According to lighting director Leard Davis, these cameras were far superior to the then-prevalent RCA cameras, due to their ability to register a complete range of tones, from pure black to pure white along with every shade of gray

Bill Hobin, Mickey, Mort Lindsey, and Judy early in the week of rehearsals
COURTESY BILL HOBIN

in-between; the RCA cameras, by contrast, could register only perhaps 85 percent of those tones and, as Davis appraises, "would flatten out."

While the Marconi cameras were largely heralded to have the mysterious ability to eliminate wrinkles without softening the picture image—something of keen interest to most any performer with the possible exceptions of Lassie and Walter Brennan—Hobin assesses that the so-called magic came simply from a series of filters made for the camera, which were numbered according to how much they diffused the picture image.

Hobin ingeniously positioned his four cameras in strategic places: a crane-mounted camera for center and runway shots; the second in the pit adjacent to the center ramp; the third on a dolly, and the fourth on a pedestal to the left. (Hobin followed Judy's instructions that the cameras shoot her primarily from the left, which she considered her better side.) "The pit camera was the one that gave a wonderful dramatic look," recalls Hobin. "I loved what Gary Smith did with the stage. He built the elevated stage with the turntable with an infinite horizon so we could get great dance shots as well."

"Judy knew what lighting and sound [were], I'll tell you that," says Johnny Bradford. "Nobody could tell her anything about those areas. She knew what was good for Judy, when she looked good and when she sounded good."

Hobin and Schlatter each remember contributing to make Garland look spectacular. Hobin credits lighting director Leard Davis ("If she found her mark, she looked beautiful") but also used a softening filter "just to take the edge off. She was a woman starting to show the lines." The filters softened the image, but, recalls Hobin, "not enough to make it obvious." For his part, Schlatter states that when Judy came in for her first makeup, lighting, and camera tests on June 18, "I found that I could turn the camera about an eighth of an inch out of focus, which did what gauze would do for a film camera. It gave her a wonderful softness around her face."

Whatever disparate factors were involved, it was clear that all were united in unveiling an elegant, beautiful, and sophisticated Garland. While not underestimating the substantial contributions of all concerned, it must be said that Judy at this time was uncommonly lovely, rested, and fresh-looking. As George Schlatter observes, "It was a magical moment of her career. She wanted to work. She was thin. She was back with Sid. She had Freddie and David. Liza was doing well in her career. Judy was comfortable in her new home. Lorna and Joey were happy. And she was happy, because she was floating on a very creative support group."

While the final draft of the Rooney script was being completed, it was decided that the first program would open with an overture, patterned closely on the electrifying, incomparable arrangement of Garland signature tunes that had opened all of her concerts of the last few years. Judy would then make her entrance and launch into her first number, "Sunny Side Up." Lindsey put together a spectacularly effective, inspired mix of other Garland trademark songs—including "You Made Me Love You," "Rock-a-bye Your Baby (With a Dixie Melody)," "Swanee," "I Can't Give You Anything but Love," "San Francisco," and "By Myself."

"We spent quite a bit of time laying out that overture. We

mapped it out on paper and then laid out every shot and shot it live, with no editing at all," says Hobin. "That was the first time I ever got any reaction from Judy. We'd been in the rehearsal hall together, but not much because this was done before we actually rehearsed the first show. Unbenownst to me, George called Judy in while I was shooting the tape. She stood behind me, but I didn't know it. So I finished, and I'm standing up, and I feel these arms around me and she says, 'You're my man.' And I said, 'Oh, my God!,' because I always had sort of a boyish crush on her. For her to say that was a great compliment." Hobin adds, "We had a good rapport. We never had any problems, the two of us. She listened, she took direction. I had such respect for her talent, like everybody did."

As rehearsals got under way, Schlatter also further refined how Garland would be presented. "We blocked every shot so we gave her a little height, because she was so short. We shot up on her a little bit. Everything else was eye level. We also put colors in the spotlights. The spotlights were pink, which gave her a feeling of theater and also gave her a softness."

Writers Johnny Bradford and Tom and Frank Waldman also revealed their own softness, in attempting to focus on the character of Jerry Van Dyke as the final taping draft of the Rooney show script was completed. Far from unskilled, the three were nevertheless as unsure as CBS how to showcase Van Dyke and his "bumbling host" character. "I don't know where Jerry Van Dyke came from," laments Bradford. "I'd never even heard of him. He had one funny routine, a pantomime to an old *Lone Ranger* radio broadcast. That was it." Bill Hobin notes that Van Dyke "was one of George's mistakes. It was a shame, because he has his own talent."

"I met Judy at CBS," remembers Jerry. "She was coming out of the building by herself. I didn't recognize her right off. I didn't know her. She stopped *me* and said, 'I'm Judy Garland. It's a pleasure to have you on the show!' "

Wanting to extend Van Dyke's role beyond that of a "bumbling host," the writers compounded the problem by creating a spectacularly unfunny sketch for Jerry and Mickey Rooney to perform. The leaden material had Rooney play a mad scientist and Van Dyke a television repairman; Mickey calls Jerry when a stuffed bear with a TV set in its stomach (broadcasting Garland

singing "Exactly Like You") goes out of order. According to Van
Dyke, no one was more aghast at the dreadful material than the
two actors. "I didn't know what it was about," says Jerry. "Mickey
came to me and said, 'What is this, we can't do this.' Mickey
raised hell. He said, 'This is the worst thing I've ever read.' "
Van Dyke remembers asking Rooney to suggest substituting an
old routine of his, a takeoff on *Candid Camera*; Mickey agreed
on the condition that he be paid for the material. When the request was refused, Mickey and Jerry had no choice but to do the
sketch. Van Dyke was also saddled with such "bumbling host"
dialogue as:

> JERRY: (FORCED JOVIALITY) Good evening, jadies and len-
> tlemen! This is Derry Van Jyke welcoming you to
> the Gudy Jarland Show! . . . Steady, Jerry, baby.
> After all, what is it? Just another show. And . . .
> Good evening, Germans and Ladlemen! (GROANS)
> Oh, boy!

"That material couldn't work," says Jerry Van Dyke. "I don't
care who was doing it. In retrospect, the day George Schlatter
said, 'We don't know what we're going to do with you' was the
day I should have said, 'Well, then, you're not going to do anything with me.' "

The unfunny comedy dialogue was, thankfully, largely offset
by the charming, natural scripted banter between Judy and
Mickey. Far removed from forced one-liners, the script allowed
them a lengthy, comfortable exchange of humor and memories
as the two sat on director's chairs, viewing old stills of their MGM
films together. As George Schlatter notes, "The moments between Mickey and Judy were lovely, because they sat and talked
and reminisced and they touched. Remember, this was 1963. This
was much closer to a natural man-and-woman discussion than
was usually seen on television."

The writers had used the Rockingham housewarming party
as a base to write dialogue for Garland that would ring true. "It
was all scripted after conversations with her. A lot of it was based
on her experiences. And she told it so wittily. We just listened
to her and got out of her way, so to speak," says Johnny Bradford.

Judy early on displayed a healthy sense of humor about herself to staff members. As Frank Waldman remembers: "We had

a meeting at CBS just as we were to start on the first show. Freddie and David were there, George Schlatter, Gary Smith, my brother, Tom, John Bradford, and several other production people. Freddie launched into quite a serious talk to the assembled group, saying, in effect, this is very important to Judy. It's really her last chance, because of the way she's been up and down and being a success on tour, and being a flop, and really, this is her last chance of chances. He continued that while it's been fun up to now, from now on it's really going to be serious work. He just built and built on that theme. And the door opens at that precise moment, and Judy walks into the room wearing a striped convict's outfit, like the convicts wore in the South in the chain gangs. 'Can anyone spare a dime for a girl who's down on her luck?' she asked, and absolutely broke everyone up. It was all a put-on, and David and Freddie played straight and did a marvelous job."

Schlatter and the writers determined that the final segment of every program would showcase Garland in a "Born in a Trunk" segment. Its black background and twin strips of lighted bulbs gave the illusion that Garland was on the actual lighted runway, when in fact she was facing it. (Originally, it was planned to have several white trunks placed horizontally and vertically around Judy so that she could sit on one, or stand alongside another, but it was ultimately decided that only one trunk, placed vertically, would be present. And, while the single trunk was purported to be Judy's own, it was actually nothing more than a random one located by head propmaster Earl Carlson. "The trunk represented her, her life of living out of a trunk," says Schlatter. "Judy was comfortable with the trunk because she put things of her own inside of it."

"Too Late Now" was selected to be the first number for the "Trunk" spot. The beautiful ballad was an ironic choice, for it had been written for Judy before she was replaced by Jane Powell in the MGM musical *Royal Wedding*. Now, thirteen years later on her own multimillion-dollar television series, Judy Garland pointedly chose to take "Too Late Now" and make it her own. The second number scheduled was "Island in the West Indies," a throwback to her vacation with Sid months earlier. The climax would be Judy singing "Old Man River," her first public performance of the showstopping number from *Show Boat*.

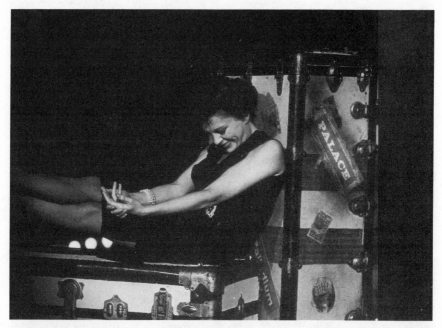

Judy at the close of the dress rehearsal for the Rooney show. By the taping the following evening, only the upright trunk would remain.
LEIGH WIENER

"She usually made the suggestions on her own songs," reveals Mort Lindsey. "Nobody came up to her and said, 'Hey, you ought to sing this song.' She knew enough songs, stuff that she hadn't recorded and hadn't orchestrated. She always did that. She came up with 'Old Man River.' "

Schlatter remembers, "Garland came in one day and asked if she could sing 'Old Man River.' I asked her if she was asking me if I would let her, or if I thought she could do it. I said, 'I've never seen a woman sing 'Old Man River.' " The producer concurs that Judy was involved musically from the onset. "I didn't decide numbers. We had some of the best musical people in the world. I wanted to stretch her musically into other areas, and she would try anything. She certainly did have input."

But Schlatter remembers that her choice did not please CBS. "It bothered them, because they wanted her to close with 'Over the Rainbow.' 'She wants to sing 'Old Man River,' ' I told them, 'so we'll leave her alone.' And they said, 'Why doesn't she sing "The Trolley Song," and this song and that song,' and I said,

Rehearsing "Old Man River"
LEIGH WIENER

'She will, she will. You already have the Garland fans, why not get the ones who are not already Garland fans?' "

Judy took great pleasure in having this newfound musical freedom. "I can sing anything I want to sing," she crowed to a TV critic. " 'Old Man River'—I've never sung that song before. I don't think any woman has. But I'll sing it in one of our shows."

Schlatter remembers that the network then wanted Judy to end each show with a few bars of "Over the Rainbow." "They wanted her to do some kind of typical kiss-ass closing," says the producer. "I said, 'Judy, boy, that sounds like such crap to me.' She said, 'Well, listen, my daddy taught me a song called "Maybe I'll Come Back." ' The words were so shitty and arrogant. So I said to her, 'That's it!' The first time CBS heard the song, they had a heart attack! Hunt Stromberg said, 'How can you take this major network commitment and allow her to do this?' I said, 'Allow her, shit, I didn't allow her—I *asked* her!' That was always a boner with the network." (CBS was perhaps wondering if the unpredictable Garland *would* come back week after week.)

"Maybe I'll Come Back"—a short, snappy, but very obscure novelty tune (written in 1911)—was certainly far removed from Dinah Shore's trademark "smooch" send-off, Jimmy Durante's "Good night, Mrs. Calabash, wherever you are," Liberace's "I'll Be Seeing You," or other similarly sentimental television partings:

> I will come back
> when the elephants roost in the trees.
> I will come back
> when the birds make love to the bees.
> I will come back
> when the sun refuses to shine—
> and [President Coolidge] is a cousin of mine.
> I will come back
> when the fish walk around on two feet
> and promenade up and down on Washington Street.
> When the snow has turned from white to blue,
> then maybe I will come back to you!

The tune—however disliked by Stromberg—allowed Judy a wonderful way to spoof her own unreliable image. Each week, Schlatter planned for the show credits to roll over the orchestral vamping of the melody, while Judy would dance, mug, or talk with the audience. (A new name would be substituted for "President Coolidge" at the end of each show.)

Although CBS backed down when Judy adamantly refused to close the first show with "Over the Rainbow," staff members, much to her astonishment, suggested doing a comedy bit centered around her trademark song. "You've all got to be kidding," Judy said sternly. "There will be no jokes of any kind about 'Over the Rainbow.' It's kind of—sacred. I don't want anybody anywhere to lose the thing they have about Dorothy or that song!" When asked if she might consent to sing it on a later show, she pondered, "I don't know. Maybe not. If I do, it will have to be for a very good reason." ("Over the Rainbow" would not be sung until the fifteenth episode.) Judy's respect for the song remained indelible in Mel Tormé's mind. As he wrote in *The Other Side of the Rainbow*, "To her, 'Over the Rainbow' was nothing short of holy, and she regarded it with gratitude and awe."

After the battles over "Old Man River" and "Maybe I'll Come

Back," Schlatter had another run-in with CBS when he suggested they throw a big party after the taping of the first show for Garland's friends, network stars, and all-important members of the press. The idea was an inspired one, sure to get tremendous newspaper and gossip-column coverage, reflecting Schlatter's years of public-relations savvy. The network balked at the suggestion. CBS, recalls Schlatter, rather inanely argued, " 'Well, if she doesn't show up, how are you going to keep that a secret with everyone there for the party?' I said, 'The woman shows up all the time. She's been here every day. I can't say, "Judy, we can't have the press, we can't have your friends, because you may not show up." This was about the third time already that CBS said they were going to fire me.' " Undaunted, George Schlatter overruled the network, and CBS indeed agreed to sponsor the post-taping bash.

From the days of preproduction through the actual days of rehearsal leading up to the taping (Friday the twenty-first through Monday, June 24), it was clear to everyone present that the extraordinary rapport between Judy and Mickey had not diminished and, in fact, had only deepened with the passing years. "It was such magic," says George Sunga. "Mickey, during the dress rehearsal, said to us, 'You guys have got to do everything you can to make her look good, make her feel comfortable.' The fact that he showed his concern for her welfare to all of us was very special." Sunga notes that everyone followed Schlatter's lead. "George treated the show like it was a major special, and it *was* a major special."

Bill Hobin recalls the week of rehearsals with great fondness. "The first reading wasn't a reading. We just sat there while they reminisced. And it was wonderful. It was one of those great moments. I wish we had recorded it. The one thing I remember out of it more than anything, amidst all of this reminiscing, was Mickey saying to her, 'You know, we should have married each other, we'd both be better off!' I don't know how much truth there was to that, but I remember him saying it. They were talking about doing three pictures at once, being worked to death. Sent out on publicity tours. How Louis B. Mayer would force them to take pills and stuff. But it was a wonderful reunion just sitting there, listening to them talk about all the things that happened in the Metro days. You could tell they had a genuine love for each other."

"The rehearsals were the biggest joy in the world," concurs Gary Smith. "Everybody felt they were working on an event. We could have rehearsed that show for a month. She was in every day. She learned her steps, her choreography was great. Everybody felt it was something special. No problems. Smooth sailing. It was perfect, and Mickey was adorable." Frank Waldman remembers Rooney as someone "loud, who would do anything for a laugh. He wrote something on a cue card that was absolutely filthy, and it absolutely broke Judy up. She was obviously nervous about the whole thing, and he was the ideal guest to keep her happy and loose and laughing."

Renowned photographer Leigh Wiener (who had photographed Judy at various times over the years) was assigned by *Life* to cover the rehearsal and taping for a pictorial magazine feature. As an outsider, he had a slightly different perspective on the proceedings. "When things got taut—there may have been one director, but in reality there were ten—Mickey was the one that she went to. She was getting it from all sides. The only refuge she had was Mickey. Everyone was trying to please Judy, but the one thing you don't want is twenty-seven people telling you what to do. I don't think anyone was trying to be malicious. But when everyone is trying to be the savior, you have chaos. There was a lot of horsing around. They had a lot of people breaking in with, 'I think we should do it this way.' Most of the chaos that I perceived was not from Rooney or generated by Garland.

"All during the day, Judy would go off to a corner by herself when Rooney was doing his thing. When he wasn't available for Judy, she'd go over and find a piece of isolation and try to sort things out. She knew what everyone else knew—the show was riding on her and her alone. If there were any problems, I didn't see any caused by Judy."

Wiener glimpsed the enormous pressure Garland was under when he approached her for a photograph as she was preparing for the dress rehearsal. "I said to Judy, 'I know you're tired, but can I get a shot of you and Mickey?' And Mickey was about ten feet away. And she blew up—not at me, but at the circumstances. She said, 'Look, I'm sorry. I'm nervous. Not now, later.' Well, there's no 'later' in my business. Rooney came over, and he knew it, too, and he took Judy by the arm and said, 'No, this guy's been working all day harder than you have.' He turned to me and said, 'What do you want?' What I really wanted was for them to move sixty-five feet away for some decent lighting, but I knew if I made that request, I would have lost the picture. I said, 'I just want to get a picture now.' " Judy immediately calmed down, and the photographer got his shot.

Wiener remembers a tense moment during the dress rehearsal on June 23, one day before the taping of the final broadcast version. "Everything was all set to go. The first shot was Judy singing with the number-one camera coming down the runway in a long shot. The key shot was that camera coming down the runway, moving in for a closeup. Someone screwed up, and the camera really got jammed, a big mix-up with the cables. The director called cut, and Judy went to pieces. She was really distressed. The audience stayed there. The director was going to come out of the booth, and I heard him talking to some other people who were thinking about excusing the audience. Mickey Rooney said no. He went over to the water fountain offstage, got his hair good and wet, and went to the stage director, borrowed his headphones and put them on backward. He turned to the audience and said, Look at me, listen to me, I am your favorite Martian! Under the pretense of entertaining the audience, what he really was doing was calming Judy. Judy sat there, smoking a cigarette, and puffing like a chimney. She just sat there, watching Rooney. And all of a sudden, Judy Garland was back with us. She was calm. They repaired whatever it was. I think very highly of Mickey Rooney and especially the relationship he had with Garland."

While Rooney's friendship with Garland only blossomed in the heat of their television reunion, Judy's marriage to Sid was again in trouble. Perhaps not unexpectedly (in light of the overwhelming pressures now upon her), the Lufts' reconciliation did not hold, and Sid moved out of the Rockingham house.

The battle between the diametrically opposed twin powers of Sid Luft and Fields and Begelman had been brewing for some time, and in fact it had been leaked in May that Judy was close to divorcing her managers, not her husband. One column item that month tellingly stated, "Judy Garland is moving rapidly to end her relationship with agents Freddie Fields and David Begelman, who were very much responsible for the upsurge in her career. Showbiz insiders, aware of the friction between her agents

Judy intently listens to George Schlatter moments before showtime.
LEIGH WIENER

and her husband, Sid Luft, expected the move as soon as Judy announced that she and Sid had reconciled. Her first move was to ask that all her tax records be turned over to Sid's lawyer, Guy Ward."

Judy, particularly vulnerable at this critical time, had an open ear to most anyone who professed to have her best interests at heart. Certainly, it is not impossible that Fields and Begelman—surely put out by Judy's reconciliation with Sid, much less her announced plans to dump them—may have had a hand in pulling the two apart to protect their own interests. As Bob Wynn notes, "Judy had to be directed in a very positive way. If you decided to direct Judy negatively, and you had her confidence, you could take her down the wrong side of the tracks, and a lot of people did just that." And so, less than two weeks after the idyllic housewarming and anniversary party, the Lufts were irrevocably estranged. (This would be their last attempt at saving their marriage before finally divorcing in 1965.)

Schlatter remembers that the final taping on June 24 (scheduled from 8:00 to 9:30 P.M.) went without a hitch. "We taped in an hour and five minutes, an hour and ten minutes, tops. I had her convinced it was like doing theater. No stops and starts. And we rehearsed it like a stage show. There were no cue cards. She rehearsed it, she learned it, and, *bam*, she did it."

Dozens of network executives and stars began filing into Studio 43 for the taping at 7:30 P.M. Celebrities present included Lucille Ball (with husband Gary Morton), Jack Benny, Natalie Wood, Hedda Hopper with her son William Hopper (of *Perry Mason*), Louella Parsons with songwriter Jimmy McHugh ("I Can't Give You Anything but Love"), Clint Eastwood, Cara Williams, Dick Van Dyke, Carl Reiner, cast members of *The Dick Van Dyke Show*, Van Heflin (Judy's costar in MGM's 1943 film *Presenting Lily Mars*), and Sheldon Leonard, among many others.

Jerry Van Dyke came out to warm up the audience, opening with, "Asking me to introduce Judy Garland is like asking Pinky Lee to introduce the Pope!" He then explained that, due to the restrictions of the stage, the "stuffed bear" comedy sketch would have to be shot first, out of sequence with the rest of the show. (Taping the Van Dyke-Rooney comedy routine first had another, if not anticipated, purpose—it would, hopefully, be long forgotten by the stellar studio audience, erased by the memories of the inspired musical portions of the show to follow.) Judy's dialogue and song setting up the sketch ("Exactly Like You") were pretaped, wisely not taking the edge off of her bona-fide grand entrance a few minutes later.

The stage was then cleared, save for the enormous klieg light standing at the back of the set. The pre-taped overture segment was played to the studio audience, and at its conclusion Judy walked out from the back left of the stage toward the camera.

She launched into "Keep Your Sunny Side Up," quickly running her tongue along her teeth before singing, either to make sure her slip-on caps for her teeth were in place or, more likely, conscious of lipstick smeared on her teeth sure to be picked up in closeup shots. Judy was touched by the enthusiastic, prolonged audience applause. Ebullient but quite obviously nervous, she bit into Mel Tormé's special arrangement of "Sunny Side Up"—with Mel, out of camera range, coaching Judy on his tricky arrangement of the old standard to give her encourage-

"Sunny Side Up"
LEIGH WIENER

ment. Keyed up, on edge, Judy was somewhat constricted vocally by her nervousness although she was vibrant and electric.

However nervous at the outset, Judy had clearly won over the audience, warming up as the song drew to its close. The applause (over the show's beautiful theme, "A Song for Judy," written by Mort Lindsey) continued well after the cameras had stopped. Judy, beginning to relax, popped out from stageside, which caused the applause to swell and continue. When a spotlight caught her, Judy darted out of view.

After his solo of "All I Need Is the Girl," Mickey joined Judy onstage for the first time during the taping. The two ad-libbed their exchanges:

> MICKEY: How is my girl?
> JUDY: Am I your girl?
> MICKEY: You're my girl. You've been my girl for so many years. You know, this is an occasion tonight. We haven't worked together for, I'd say, about, oh, too many years.
> JUDY: Yeah, too many to *mention*!

(A FLORAL HORSESHOE WITH A CARD SAYING, "MICKEY LOVES JUDY—STILL" IS BROUGHT ON STAGE. JUDY BEGINS TO EXIT TO HER ON-STAGE "DRESSING ROOM," AND AD-LIBS:)

JUDY: Come on into the dressing room with me while I
         powder my nose.
MICKEY: You remember the time when I used to have hair?
JUDY: I remember *everything*!

Judy (still somewhat on edge herself) joined Jerry for a duet
on "I Believe in You." Mickey's "Thank Heaven for Little Girls"
production number was next. Judy scored well with "When the
Sun Comes Out," her throat finally opening up when she attacked the final bars of the song with full-voiced belting power.
(After singing the torch song, Judy ran across the stage, grabbed
the wardrobe mistress, raced back with her across the set, yelling out, "Wardrobe! Wardrobe!")

Before a Mickey-Judy "You're So Right for Me" routine, Garland stood at the front of the stage with George Schlatter and
made a point of introducing him to the audience—inadvertently
nearly falling over backward when she mockingly leaned back
to show him that her throat was still in fine shape. In the spirit
of the moment, Lucille Ball noticed Judy's very full chiffon skirt
(with many splits around it, enabling her to dance) and playfully
puffed it up for comic effect. In turn, Judy and Mickey then focused their attention on Lucy, trying—unsuccessfully—to get her
to join them onstage.

The "You're So Right for Me" segment was a delight, with a
great feeling of spontaneity. Judy and Mickey, never missing a
beat, freely improvised their dialogue throughout. While glancing at a MGM publicity still of a young Judy placing a long-
stemmed flower within a large arrangement, they ad-libbed:

MICKEY: These are the flowers they gave you as a bonus,
         remember?
JUDY: Yeah. One flower a year—
MICKEY: For every picture you made—
JUDY: A *bud*!

The "Trunk" segment ended the taping in grand style. "Too
Late Now" was sung to perfection by Judy, beautifully performed to the solo piano accompaniment of Mort Lindsey. The
middle "Trunk" number, "Island in the West Indies" had been
cut, replaced at dress rehearsal by another tropical tune, "Two
Ladies in the Shade of the Banana Tree," but it, too, was dropped

Jerry, Judy, and Mickey kick up their heels during "Maybe I'll Come Back."
LEIGH WIENER

at the last minute. Ultimately, "Who Cares?" was substituted. "Old Man River" was Garland in peak form (aided by Hobin's brilliant direction and Leard Davis's equally stunning lighting), as she effortlessly held the last incredible notes for what seemed like an eternity ("he just keeps rolling—along!"), powerfully sending them well past the very last row of seats in Studio 43.

Garland's performance was so spectacular that Mickey Rooney impulsively rushed onstage after the cameras stopped, asking the audience of show-business professionals and network executives, "Have you ever heard 'Old Man River' sung like that before? I've heard it nine times at rehearsals, and each time better!"

The final segment had Judy joined first by Mickey and then Jerry Van Dyke for a rousing, spirited song-and-dance performance of "Maybe I'll Come Back." Mickey prompted Judy to return to the stage as the orchestra vamped the closing theme, signaling the end of the show.

The great emotion of the evening was perhaps best expressed by Mickey Rooney, when he remarked to the audience after the taping was completed, "Without being corny, we've had a wonderful seven days together here." ("Let's do it again," Judy broke in.) Mickey continued, "This is not only tradition, this is the love of my life. My wife knows this." He added, after a beat, "My *wives* know this." (The audience, and Judy, roared.) "It always has been because there never will be, there aren't adjectives enough to express in the world how the one-and-only Judy *is* Judy." Overcome with emotion, Judy led Mickey offstage.

Thus, on a very high note, the taping of the first episode of *The Judy Garland Show* was not only complete but a bona-fide success. The taping took less than the ninety minutes it had been allotted, and the notoriously unpredictable Garland had required not a second take on any number. The taping could not have gone more smoothly.

The post-show party was a glittering affair attended by dozens of celebrities and CBS executives, a roster including Aubrey, Stromberg, Mike Dann, and Bob Lewine. Judy appeared early on—glowing, and in understandably great spirits—flanked by her managers Fields and Begelman. (She, inexplicably, wore none of the Edith Head creations designed for her but chose instead to wear the striped summer dress she had worn earlier in the week at rehearsals!) CBS, as Bob Wynn remembers, loved the show;

Freddie Fields, Judy, and David Begelman make their entrance at the posttaping bash.
CBS INC.

Judy delights CBS network president James Aubrey, Lucille Ball, and Lucy's husband, Gary Morton.
CBS INC.

indeed, Judy spent a good deal of the party locked in spirited, anecdote-swapping conversation with Aubrey, Lucille Ball, and Gary Morton.

Jerry Van Dyke recalls that network executives loved the Garland-Rooney hour and made their feelings known at the post-taping gala. "They were ecstatic," the comic states. "They kept saying, '*Bonanza* is through, it's on its last legs,' telling me that we were going to kill off *Bonanza* bad."

Aubrey, however, cornered by an inquisitive reporter at the party, was rather reserved when asked whether the show would be a hit: "Who can tell? We can only hope for the best."

If CBS doubted for a moment that the party was not an inspired idea and one sure to get tremendous press, the network executives only had to read *The Hollywood Reporter* two days later: "Practically all of CBS-TV's primetime stars studded the audience for taping of the first Judy Garland show on Monday night at CBS TV City, and the party tossed by the [network] after the show was such a gas, they had to douse the lights on Stage 43 after midnight to get the guests to leave."

The *Los Angeles Times* also raved about the show. "Judy, almost paper-thin, stood on her spike heels, feet wide apart in that way of hers, rolled those wide, haunted eyes at the lights above and sang her heart out. The audience was with her all the way. . . . Judy seemed so assured, so self-possessed, so happy in her work that it sounds good for the shows."

Army Archerd in *Variety* reported, "Judy Garland taped her initial CBS show Monday p.m. before an audience featuring the web's top stars—and brass. The turnout was well-rewarded. . . . Mickey Rooney, anxious to start the session, urged, 'Let's get going before the whole show gets attached—I'm due in court in 15 minutes!' (He has just gone bankrupt.) Miss G. lived night and day in her fancy CBS trailer during the rehearsal days for the show. She seemed to enjoy every minute of the taping, and, without exaggeration, Judy never looked or sounded better."

"The relationship between Judy and George Schlatter was terrific," says George Sunga, adding, "It seemed like they were life partners. They just seemed to understand each other."

As if underscoring this, Garland spotted Schlatter just as she was to make her grand entrance at the after-show party and rushed over to him. Bubbling with excitement, she flashed him a dazzling smile and asked him, "What time do you want me in tomorrow morning?"

7

"Singing with Count Basie is like having a shotgun at your back!"

—Judy Garland, 1963

"The talk of the television industry out here is *The Judy Garland Show*," wrote Hollywood-based critic Tom Mackin the week following the taping of the first episode. "Stars, producers and directors at NBC and ABC, as well as at CBS . . . are betting the controversial, troubled singer will not make it through the entire season."

George Schlatter immediately jumped to Judy's defense. "In all my years in television, I've never met anyone as cooperative and dedicated as Judy, and I've handled more than a few difficult ones," he insisted. "She knows this is her most challenging year in show business, and she's determined to make the most of it."

Addressing reports of temperament and tardiness on Garland's part, George shot back, "I've been late for rehearsals three times more than she has. What you're talking about is her magnetism. Look, television needs her more than she needs television. When it comes down to it, I'd rather have a great performer than a dependable one."

Mort Lindsey was baffled by the flurry of reports speculating that Garland would be unable to get through a television season intact: "I don't know why people are saying Judy won't finish this series. I've been with her for two-and-a-half years, including forty concerts, two movies, and two TV specials, and we've never even had an argument."

Another kind of difference of opinion occurred between George Schlatter and Judy's wardrobe designer, Edith Head, immediately after the first show had been taped. The Academy Award-winning costumer had a definite approach to outfitting Garland for the series: "Judy has lost a great deal of weight, and her figure is marvelous. I have conceived her gowns as a background. They won't overpower her. When the show is over, you'll remember she was well dressed, but you won't remember what she wore. No, that won't give me a pang. That was our grand design, you might say." Only a few days after expressing these remarks, Edith Head was summarily fired from *The Judy Garland Show*.

Designer Ray Aghayan and his assistant Bob Mackie were creating wardrobe for the rest of the cast. According to Ray, Schlatter was unhappy with Edith Head, disliking not only the gowns she created for Garland but her work methods and full-time duties at Paramount Studios.

"Edith Head insisted on putting Judy all in browns and blacks," says Bob Wynn. "George was responsible for getting her out of those godawful things and brought in glamour."

Schlatter asked Aghayan and Mackie to sketch some costume ideas for Garland, and Judy instantly fell in love with the high-fashion image that Ray and Bob had in mind for her. "After that first set of sketches, it just became a matter of absolute trust between us. Half the time, she never even saw what it would look like until she put it on to go on."

Aghayan, in designing for Garland, followed his old axiom: "Every woman has some things that are not as good as other things, so I covered those, and exposed the good ones. It was all a matter of proportion. Her bosom was not big. The thing that made the clothes really work was that Judy had such long legs, proportionately, and you could do a lot of things with her that you couldn't do with a lot of people. Everybody always talks about how wonderful I made her look, but they forget that I also got her at a wonderful time. Judy had lost an enormous amount of weight, and she looked terrific."

During the time design duties shifted from Edith Head to Aghayan and Mackie, the staff juggled a change in guests for the next program. It had been announced that Liza Minnelli was scheduled for show number two (to be taped July 1), but her appearance was moved to the third episode. Subsequent reports that June Allyson and Mel Tormé were to be the guests for show number two were partially correct; in rather quick fulfillment of his agreement with Schlatter that guaranteed him two guest appearances within the first thirteen programs, Tormé was set to appear—not with June, but with renowned bandleader Count Basie.

Also signed as a guest on the Basie-Tormé hour was Judy Henske, a rather nondescript Joan Baez imitator. The gangly, instantly famous and instantly forgettable Henske was curiously announced early on to join Jerry Van Dyke as a regular on *The Judy Garland Show*, a rather obvious stab at attracting a wider-based audience and, specifically, younger viewers. Although the idea was quickly dropped, she, confusingly, was still listed as a regular in newspaper television listings for the show's premiere at the end of September.

Concurrently, rumors circulated that Mickey Rooney was also being wooed to be a regular, or semiregular, on the Garland series. The matter was soon dropped, and CBS ceased all mention of Mickey joining the series until, curiously, the end of July, when reports surfaced that CBS was again pursuing Mickey for multiple guest shots, if not signing him as a regular. Nothing materialized.

Meanwhile, it was decided that, beginning with the second program, the dress rehearsal would be taped along with the final performance following. This wise decision allowed some of the "one chance only" pressure to be taken off of Judy's shoulders; it also provided the freedom to pick and choose the better performance of the two for the final air tape. (While it became standard practice that an equal mix of dress-rehearsal and final-taping footage would be seen on Garland shows—often interchanging from one segment to the next—the edited final product, infrequently but deftly, even cut back and forth within the same segment.)

The Garland show took a one-week break before embarking on rehearsals for the Basie program, giving all concerned a much-deserved respite after grueling months of preproduction. The revised schedule had rehearsals set for July 4, further polishing and prerecording the following day, the taping of the dress rehearsal on July 6, and the final performance on Sunday, July 7.

Although the layoff ideally gave everyone the chance to reflect on the first program's strengths and weaknesses and do whatever fine-tuning was deemed necessary, the script for the second show would mirror both the positive and the negative elements of the first. While the musical material was first-rate, well selected, and impeccably arranged, the strained attempts at humor, if anything, were even more dismal than before. As a result, Jerry Van Dyke was left with neither an appealing, well-defined character nor decent material to overcome that obstacle. As writer Frank Waldman frankly now admits, "Obviously, we didn't have a grasp on the second-banana character that he was supposed to play. He was feeling his way, and we were, too."

George Schlatter was hard-pressed when asked by a television critic why Jerry Van Dyke had been chosen for the Garland show. Unable to tell the real reason for hiring him (pressure from Stromberg), the usually fast-on-his-feet Schlatter could only offer, "Jerry's a nice guy. He likes to be helpful to everyone around him." Then, with remarkable candor, he admitted, "Sometimes this turns out to be funny. Sometimes it's disastrous." Perhaps realizing the bluntness of his remark, George quickly added, "But we want him to let it happen, and we want to let the viewers see Judy's reaction to him."

The week off from taping was far from restful for Judy. Although Sid Luft had moved out of the Rockingham house, he was still very much in the picture. His concern for his wife's welfare was matched by his distrust of Freddie Fields and David Begelman.

As Luft remarked in 1978 to Jeanie Kasindorf, contributing editor to *New West* magazine, "I was the father, the sweetheart, the lover, everything. And now I'm relieved. I'm being replaced." He added, "I was the villain. I stole all of her money according to them. She was childlike about business. You can't run a company and sing your songs and do your bookkeeping and be an executive. They set her up." (Kasindorf interviewed Luft after it was said that Begelman had misappropriated $61,008 in corporate funds and $23,000 in expenses while serving as president of Columbia Pictures in addition to forging actor Cliff Robertson's name on a Columbia payroll check in the amount of $10,000 and cashing the check himself. After a brief hiatus, Begelman, however, was reinstated as Columbia Pictures president in December 1977.)

In the escalating war between Luft and the two CMA partners, Judy Garland was squarely in the middle. Luft continued
to press Judy about her finances. In Sid's view, with hundreds
of thousands of dollars pouring into her managers' hands, it was
imperative that she be alerted to what he considered were matters requiring her immediate attention. When the Lufts reconciled the previous February, Judy authorized Sid's attorney, Guy
Ward, to examine her financial records. Ward then gave the files
(spanning January 1961 to April 1963) to Beverly Hills accountant
Oscar Steinberg. Three days after the Rooney show was taped,
Steinberg issued an ominous report, which, he advised Luft,
contained "certain items requiring additional explanation." Sid
approached Judy with this information the first week of July,
just as rehearsals began for the Basie show.

According to Kasindorf's *New West* article, Steinberg's report
included not just one alleged misappropriation of Garland's funds,
but several possible incidents. From May to October of 1962,
Steinberg noted that Begelman had written thirteen checks to
"Cash" on Kingsrow's account, for a total of $35,714. Ranging
from $500 to $6,000 each, the checks were cashed by Begelman
at the Sahara and the Dunes Hotel in Las Vegas. The amount of
these checks was itemized in the Kingsrow bookkeeping ledger
as part of Garland's salary, spent for "protection."

After Garland's managers advised her that a picture existed
of her having her stomach pumped during an overdose in London the previous year, Judy (frightened at losing the CBS deal,
which was just about to be finalized) agreed to pay fifty thousand dollars to have the negative and all existing copies of the
damaging photo returned to her; a bank transfer in that amount
was made from Garland's Chase Manhattan Bank account in
London to Chase Manhattan on Park Avenue in New York in
December of the previous year. Although a letter of instruction
transferring the funds had Garland's signature, it also ordered
the bank to deposit $24,355 of the $50,000 to the "Executive Producer Account, Special" for David Begelman, who was the sole
signatory on the account. The letter also instructed Chase to deposit $3,245 from the $50,000 to the account of "201 East 62nd
Street Building Company, Inc." Begelman and his then-wife, Lee
Reynolds, subsequently relocated to a cooperative apartment at
that same address—which was in the process of being built when
the check was deposited.

Steinberg also noted a ten-thousand-dollar check that had been written on the Kingsrow Chase Manhattan account itemized on Kingsrow's files as "bank transfers." Steinberg was told that the same check was deposited into an account in the name of "David Begelman in trust for Judy Garland," with the ten thousand dollars ultimately being placed into an account bearing Begelman's name only before the entire sum was withdrawn from the account. (In her 1965 divorce deposition against Luft, she testified that she knew nothing about the transfer.) The accountant also questioned five checks (each in the amount of $490.33) written on the Kingsrow account as payment to CMA for "TV Production Supervisors" for the Silvers-Goulet special; the "employees," according to Steinberg, were never noted in the Kingsrow books, and all of the checks had been written by David Begelman.

Steinberg also discovered that a $750 check had been issued from Kingsrow to CMA, representing an agent's commission for Judy's Jack Paar appearance the past December—although Steinberg concluded that the commission "apparently" had already been paid to CMA out of the fee from Paar's own production company. The Kingsrow check for $750, representing Judy being billed for a double commission, was written by Begelman. Luft himself discovered that part of her fee for appearing on the Paar show was a new 1963 Cadillac convertible, which he states Judy knew nothing about. (Bob Wynn's recollection about Judy not having a car when she moved to Los Angeles from New York when the series began backs up this claim.) The 1965 registration of the same car was in the name of David Begelman, according to Luft.

Armed with the report, Sid was amazingly thwarted by Judy, who refused to take action. Luft recalls her rationalization: "Look, suppose he did steal two hundred thousand dollars to three hundred thousand dollars," he remembers her telling him. "Sweep it under the rug now. I'm going to make twenty million on these television shows. What is three hundred thousand?"

So determined was she to succeed with the series, to look ahead, Judy could not and would not investigate further. Wanting to bury the matter but with it haunting her still, she attempted (with almost superhuman endurance) to be at her best while under enormous pressure from all sides. Garland had to juggle CBS, the producers and staff members of her show, the exhausting hours of meetings and rehearsals, the business responsibilities of Kingsrow, and, in spite of everything, provide a good home for her children while being squarely in the middle of the charges and countercharges flying back and forth between Luft and Fields and Begelman.

Judy's future career depended largely on the success of her television series, and she, understandably, resisted the idea of an open confrontation with her managers. Not only would such adverse publicity likely jeopardize her relationship with CBS but her prospects of being accepted by America's television audience as well. Furthermore, Fields and Begelman held the upper hand. While Kingsrow held documentation of possible financial wrongdoing on the part of her managers, Judy's emotional problems, chemical dependency, and erratic behavior over the years were certain to be rehashed at great length during any legal proceedings. In effect, Judy's fear rendered her impotent, completely unable and unwilling to do battle; she chose to take the path of denial.

The money recovered, whatever the sum, if any, found to be due, could not mend the irreparable damage such testimony would have on her reputation, her future career, and any prospect she would have to be granted custody of her two younger children as she and Sid prepared for their divorce action. Judy was trapped; she knew it, Sid knew it, and, likely, CMA did as well. Evidence of this is the fact that in May came the news that Judy was planning to break away from Fields and Begelman; in a swift but complete turnabout, *The Hollywood Reporter* on July 24 stated that Garland (and Kingsrow) had signed a new three-year contract with Creative Management Associates, exactly one month after Sid and Judy had separated and, more pointedly, only three weeks after Luft presented Judy with Steinberg's disturbing audit.

Orval Paine, who became deeply involved in both Garland's personal and professional life, was aware of the turmoil between Luft and Fields and Begelman. "Sid always had her interests at heart," Orval states. "I don't feel that any of it was from a selfish standpoint, or for what he would gain from it."

While Judy struck a happy, upbeat public stance as rehearsals for the Basie program got under way, the debilitating effects of these backstage battles manifested in late-night calls to, among

Judy rehearsing "Memories of You"

others, Schlatter, Johnny Bradford, and Bob Wynn, and, occasionally, Mel Tormé, CBS executives Bob Lewine and Mike Dann as well as such friends as Roddy McDowall and Rock Hudson. Garland here began the practice of making rounds of frequent nocturnal telephone calls, which sometimes resulted in a brusque response or, more often, reassuring words, and, in some cases, late-night visits to the Rockingham house. Once there, visitors would attempt to reassure her, calm her fears, or just listen to her until she was finally able to fall asleep.

Frank Waldman describes the late-night visits as mostly centering around Judy's penchant for playing cards. "She loved to play poker and loved to talk. She was a marvelous talker, so entertaining. The thing that I appreciated about her was her sense of humor about herself, which was so sensational. She never felt sorry for herself, or dwelled on her problems." The long nights spent with Garland on Rockingham Drive could, nevertheless, be taxing. "We were aware of Bradford and Schlatter saying, We were there until four o'clock this morning, and we finally had to leave to meet with you guys." Mike Dann, on more than a few occasions, "would take her to dinner at La Scala about midnight and sit talking until two-thirty or three, and then take her back, and then she would panic about being left alone and, about four-thirty or five, would make her nightly call to David Begelman," before finally falling to sleep.

"She was a very lonely girl," says Bob Lewine. "She wanted to talk to someone, have people around. You'd get there, and Judy would say, 'Let's make some coffee and eggs.' " Lewine was aware of Judy's concerns about her financial affairs. "I don't think the relationship between Judy and Freddie and David was that good at that time. I think Judy was getting ready to sue them for taking some of her money. Ultimately, that whole suit was set aside." Lewine also noted Judy's nocturnal calls to Begelman, saying, "It was rumored that David had a romantic relationship with Judy at that time." (Sid Luft also believed that Begelman entered into an "affair" with a vulnerable Judy, a claim he made in a sworn deposition in a lawsuit Luft filed against the CMA partner in 1968.)

(In 1989, David Begelman declined to be interviewed for this book, saying only, "My relationship with Miss Garland was a long and complicated business relationship. I deem it ancient history, and I'm not prepared to talk about it for publication." When asked to answer a single query, Begelman snapped, "If you want to ask me one question, I assume the question is how do I spell my name or something, and I'll be happy to answer that.")

Bob Wynn was present for a rather harrowing experience at the Rockingham house, triggered by Begelman's failure to visit Judy as she had expected late one night: "Begelman was supposed to come out. Guards are outside the house, she and I are inside the house. The calls keep coming, he's going to be late, then maybe later, and, finally, that he's probably not going to come." The news, according to Wynn, caused Judy to become extremely distraught, and she began crying. "She grabbed something that looked like pills to me, and said, 'You don't think I'll do it, do you?' I said, 'Yeah, I think you'll do it.' She took them. I leaped over the couch, put my knee on her throat and began to pull the stuff out. She was crying hysterically. I hit her. Time went on, and it was obvious that Begelman was not coming. It got to be about two or three, and she wanted a doctor for her back. I said, 'We'll get a doctor, but we'd better go to CBS and get a doctor to come down there.' The next day was tape day. If the doctor put her asleep in her house, I knew we'd never get her on the stage. I got her into CBS about three or four in the morning. I called George about six and said, 'George, get your ass down here, I'm fading fast.' I got her downstairs in the basement. By this time, everything had kicked in and she was gone." The incident did have a trace of humor: "I put her on a film cart and pushed her through the halls of CBS. A watchman looked down at her, looked up at me, and just kept on walking, shaking his head."

The seemingly indestructible Garland bounced back within a matter of only a few hours to tape the Basie show. "George came over, and by God, she was on stage that day, singing her ass off." (Still, although she was occasionally tardy for rehearsal calls at this point, Wynn stresses, "She was always there." Frank Waldman adds, "She was really pretty regular. I can remember her being an hour late to rehearsal, but, listen, we used to call her 'The Legend' to her face. It went with the territory.")

George Schlatter dismisses the more melodramatic elements of Judy's late-night calls by noting, "She'd call me up and say, 'I'm alone.' I'd say, 'I'm with my wife and my daughter.' She'd say. 'It's all great for you guys. We rehearse, you get me all cranked up, and I go out and sing and everybody applauds, laughs, and cries. And you go home to your families and have a lovely evening. What do I do? What happens to me?' I'd say, 'I'll come over and talk to you.' That was the whole thing. She got so high [from performing], and then there was the emptiness that followed it. Everybody made their money, everybody had a good time. And there she was at home, alone. Judy was right. She'd walk out onto a stage, perform for hours and make you laugh, make you cry, make you love her, and make you stand up and cheer. That was the end of your evening. That was the beginning of Judy Garland's evening. When you're up with that kind of adrenaline, that kind of energy, and the rest of the world has been entertained, we expect Judy Garland to be a quiet little girl, go home, have some milk and cookies, and quietly go to bed until we prop her up again to go out and do that magic.

"We demand heroes. We make them," Schlatter says with

great emotion. "We love them. We adore them. And once we make them a hero, we are just as eager to tear them down. We build them into something they can never perpetuate, and then we're surprised when they don't measure up to all of the things we expect of them. Judy was sometimes exasperating, but she was wonderful. It was all worth what you got. She loved to laugh. She loved people. She was funny. She was very special. My relationship with her was very special. She gave to us more than she took. And she took a lot."

George was, of course, keenly aware of Judy's mounting pressures, including a complex web of financial problems reaching back many years into the past. "She did get nervous about it. She did owe people money. There was always somebody [wanting money], people sending wires, telegrams. At night, those people were waiting there for her." (As only one example, that same month Judy was sued by a London hotel for a three-thousand-dollar long-distance telephone bill run up while she was in London during the filming of *I Could Go On Singing*; reporters hounded her at CBS Television City for comment, which she declined to provide.)

Judy's escalating personal troubles were known only to a very few members of *The Judy Garland Show* staff. Garland was in top form and high spirits from rehearsals through the final taping of the second episode, relaxed and confident, appearing even more beautiful and dazzling than she had on the Rooney show. And her voice was full-bodied and in complete control.

The dress rehearsal on Saturday, July 6, went without a hitch, starting a bit past 7:30 P.M., and wrapping up only ninety minutes later. In keeping with George Schlatter's "weekly series of specials" vision, the Basie hour had a quite different approach than the first show. The Rooney production was warm, appropriately bathed in loving nostalgia, featuring seemingly unrehearsed, spontaneous reminiscence. The Basie-Tormé program, in contrast to the overture and grand entrance leading into "Keep Your Sunny Side Up," opened quietly (the audience was asked not to applaud as Judy made her appearance) and very effectively, with Judy singing the first few bars of "I Hear Music" while members of the Basie band took their positions on the darkened stage. The striking mixture of clusters of highback chairs in semicircles and suspended Tiffany lamps in contrast to streams of floor cables and microphone stands instantly established that the hour promised to be a stylish, sophisticated musical event. A poised and confident Garland then launched into high gear with "The Sweetest Sounds." The end of Tormé's highly effective arrangement had her sing, "Count Basie (instead of "Hey, leader") . . . strike up the band," punctuated by Garland slamming her hand on Basie's white grand piano for emphasis as she soared with the final note.

And, while the first show had Garland command attention with such blockbusters as "When the Sun Comes Out" and "Old Man River," here she conquered the more subtle and offbeat ("A Cottage for Sale," "The Sweetest Sounds," and "Memories of You"), a relatively new Broadway tune ("Hey, Look Me Over" from *Wildcat*, starring Lucille Ball) and "I've Got My Love to Keep Me Warm," an old standard made fresh by a sparkling arrangement and Garland's spirited delivery. Pegged to be little more than a brisk throwaway number, Judy's playful working of the song and her hitting every high note without effort made it memorable.

By contrast, Tormé's following solo, "Don't Dream of Anybody but Me" was mannered and devoid of spontaneity, he determinedly working the television camera head-on for effect. Still, he most ably performd his jazz-influenced arrangement of "Fascinating Rhythm," and displayed not only a good sense of comedy timing during a Judy-Jerry running gag (about Van Dyke wanting "to join Basie's band") but also a comfortable, affectionate rapport with Garland. Their "April in Paris" duet was infused with wonderful interplay and, for her part, Judy seemed delighted to be singing with Tormé. Frank Waldman describes both their on-camera and behind-the-scenes relationship as "ideal and marvelous," adding, "He and Judy meshed perfectly."

Not in harmony were Basie's band and Studio 43. The soundstage's severe audio problems and limitations forced the large Basie band to prerecord their orchestral tracks for the show; Garland and Tormé would sing live. (The prerecorded music was more or less successfully mimed by Basie's band, although the Count could be seen hitting a note on the piano out of synchronization to the playback, causing a bit of the spontaneous feel of the performance to be taken away.)

Smith's theatrical backstage set was nicely showcased, and

Count Basie (at the piano), Mel Tormé, and Judy perform "April in Paris" at dress rehearsal.

the revolving turntable was well utilized for Judy's beautiful rendering of the Eubie Blake standard "Memories of You." Bill Hobin's direction was impeccable, from his sweeping shots of Basie's band to stunning close-up profiles of Garland in the "Trunk" finale.

The musical segment featuring the two Basie band solos and the Garland-Tormé numbers had already been taped, to be played to the dress-rehearsal and final-taping audiences at the time it was to be slotted in the final rundown of the show. At the dress rehearsal (which was still a bit more relaxed than the final version recorded the following night), Judy sat down on the edge of the stage next to Lorna and Joe, who were at the corner of the stage in what would become their customary seats in the front row of the audience. Judy kissed Lorna's hand while she intently watched herself singing on the monitor, clapping enthusiastically at the end of her number, which, of course, got a big laugh from the studio audience. During Mel's solo of "Don't Dream of Anybody but Me," Judy playfully danced with any willing crew member. When the tape came to "April in Paris" Judy surprised Mel by dragging him onstage to sing the duet for the live audience with each other on the monitor, giving the delighted audience the most unusual sight of two Judy Garlands and two Mel Tormés.

When she joined Nick Castle's dancers for "Soul Bossa Nova," Judy's obvious delight at displaying her new knockout figure as well as having the chance to shimmy and be playfully seductive (all in a deceptively tongue-in-cheek manner) made the routine one of the hour's highlights. "She hadn't danced in years, and we had her dancing with Nick," Schlatter notes with pride. "We let her have some room. Her instincts were very good about what was good for her." Sharon Shore (an accomplished dancer first brought in by Nick Castle and who remained for the entire run of the show) concurs: "She had wonderful instincts. She was a very quick study. Nick had a great sense of humor, as did she, and he'd give her a clue as to what the routine was to be, and she would pick it up right away and know exactly what he wanted."

During the "Trunk" dress rehearsal (so good that it was used in the final broadcast version), Judy humorously fluffed some of her song lyrics to "Hey, Look Me Over!" Although the mistakes were minor, and she recovered beautifully—stuttering twice but instantly reworking the next line, "just in case you need more proof," to "just in case you think I'll goof!"—Judy went around the audience, apologizing for the gaffes and thanking the group for their support when they had spontaneously burst into a second round of applause after the cameras had stopped taping. (ABC technician and longtime Garland fan Richard Connolly impulsively shouted out, "Thank you!" in recognition of her fine performance as Judy turned her back to leave the stage. Hearing him, Judy spun around and spotted who had made the remark, and then walked the length of the stage, bending down past the footlights of the runway. Taking his hand, she looked him straight in the eye and, with great sincerity, said, "No, thank *you*.")

The final taping, boasted Schlatter, "set a pre-taping record," completed in exactly eighty-four minutes. Frank Waldman remembers, "Basie said he enjoyed doing the show because if he

Judy sings a swinging "Witchcraft," cut from the final broadcast version.

wasn't on-camera playing, he was being talked about all through the show, and he liked that. And the Count wasn't the most comfortable man with lines. What a dear man he was." Basie, not surprisingly, admired Garland's talents greatly and relished the opportunity to work with her; their interplay together is warm and relaxed, with Judy reaching over to him to clasp his hand at the conclusion of both "Strike Up the Band" and "Memories of You." Bob Wynn clearly recalls the "tremendous rapport" that existed between Judy and the Count, and Gary Smith holds the Basie hour as one of Garland's favorites, primarily because of how much she delighted in working with him.

The second entry of *The Judy Garland Show* is a high-gloss, expensive-looking, and sophisticated production, one that displays a happy, confident, and beautiful Garland who gamely and successfully tackled new, challenging material. As a whole, however, the production falls short of being a great show, due to the periodic nosedives it takes as the script weaves in and out of a Jerry Van Dyke "wanting to play in Basie's band" running gag. Also, the inexplicable booking of Henske, whose out-of-sync performing style coupled with an amateurish and embarrassing "Peter, Paul and Irving" comedy sketch with Henske, Tormé, and Van Dyke that brought the show to a dead halt. (None of them was even able to hit the final note of their routine, hitting clinkers instead.)

The excellent musical moments of the show contrasted with Henske's appearance, and the flat comedy material gave the program a wildly uneven, almost schizophrenic quality—from great to good to terrible, and then nearly redeeming itself with later moments of sheer brilliance.

Happily, the third show in the series—only one week away—would be the best one yet. Judy Garland and Liza Minnelli, in their first television appearance together, deserved nothing less.

8

"I remember being thoroughly surprised that she wanted me as a guest on her show," reveals Liza Minnelli. "Because, remember, at that point, I hadn't done anything. I was in *Best Foot Forward,* and that was it. She said, 'That's good enough—go read your reviews again and call me back!' I said, 'Yeah, but Mama, that's just in *New York.*' Then she got slightly annoyed with me, because she thought for a minute that I thought she was patronizing me. She said, 'I'm too talented, too impatient, too *old,* too nice, to patronize you, and have too little time to patronize *anybody'* " Judy, of course, got her way. Saving her trump card for last, she asked, with irrefutable logic, "What, *Ed Sullivan* gets to have you and *I* can't have you?"

Although by the summer of 1963, Liza Minnelli's most prominent credit was the off-Broadway revival of the 1941 hit musical *Best Foot Forward* (winning her rave reviews), it by no means represented the sum total of her career.

Liza had made her stage debut during Judy's second engagement at the Palace Theatre in 1956, dancing as her mother belted "Swanee." At the age of thirteen, Liza made her television debut on a Gene Kelly special, performing *For Me and My Gal;* two years later, in 1961, she successfully auditioned for enrollment in the High School of Performing Arts. ("She's practically a pro already," Judy remarked not long after, adding that her daughter was "very hip to show business.")

While Judy and the family spent the summer of 1961 in Hyannis Port, Massachusetts, Liza apprenticed at the Cape Cod Melody Tent and soon was cast as a dancer in the chorus of a production of *Wish You Were Here,* which Judy attended with her old friend (and Liza's godmother) Kay Thompson. Later that year, while Liza was enrolled at Scarsdale High School, she was cast as the lead in *The Diary of Anne Frank* and gave a sensitive, luminous performance. So impressed was "Mama" with Liza's dramatic stage debut, Judy exclaimed backstage, "My God, I've got an *annuity!*" Liza then signed to provide the speaking and singing voice of "Dorothy" for an animated theatrical feature film, *Return to the Land of Oz,* which also starred the voices of Ethel Merman, Danny Thomas, Peter Lawford, and Margaret Hamilton, Judy's "Wicked Witch of the West" from *The Wizard of Oz.*

It was during Judy's engagement at the Sahara Hotel in Las Vegas during the fall of 1962 that Liza "officially" told her mother that she had decided to pursue a career in show business. The year before, Judy seemed wary at the thought of any of her children embarking on a show-business career by saying, "I think it robs a youngster of too many things. It's too competitive. I don't think children should be thrown into that at all. They should have proms and football games and all of the fun of growing up. I was onstage from the age of two. I don't regret it, I learned a lot, and I've been successful. But I do think I've missed a lot." She added, "I have no ambitions for my children except for them to be happy and well adjusted. I don't want to push."

The protective mother, of course, relented and gave Liza her blessing. "She thought I was too young for show business," said the seventeen-year-old in the summer of 1963, one year after she broke the news to Judy. " 'Are you really ready?' she asked. We talked awhile. Suddenly, she leaned over, kissed me, and said, 'You know what?—you *are* ready!' Mama didn't have to tell me about the business. I had seen it all from childhood—the heartache and the happiness."

In early 1963, Liza was cast in *Best Foot Forward* by the show's director-choreographer Danny Daniels. During the night of the first run-through, Liza caught her foot on a broken floorboard and broke a bone. (Judy was horrified at the news, which came in a transatlantic call from Liza just as Judy left the stage after her *Sunday Night at the Palladium* television appearance in March.)

Judy missed Liza's April 2, 1963, opening night "professional debut" because the Lufts (just returning from their Caribbean vacation) missed a plane connection in Florida; Judy, Sid, Lorna, and Joe went the following evening instead. "In a sense, we are delighted that we weren't there in view of all the excitement stirred up about this," Sid said at the time. "We wanted Liza to have her own big night without any distraction." And big it was. *Look* magazine raved, "[A] new star was born. Liza brought the house down. She has everything—a big voice with the faintly mournful catch, and a wealth of musical-comedy talent that is more unique than reminiscent."

By now, Judy had fully embraced Liza's decision to enter show business. "If she weren't talented, I'd be miserable about it," Judy said a few months before, "but she's a good singer and a good dancer and a good little actress. I staved it off as long as I could, to keep her out of the competition while she was still a child, but now she's seventeen years old. She wants to go to work, so what can I do? What I'm happiest about is that she's a lovely person."

Television beckoned to Liza Minnelli; she was booked on Ed Sullivan's variety series several times and also made an appearance on Jack Paar's program. On June 3, she was a guest on *The Tonight Show*, with Arthur Godfrey as the substitute host. Judy was so excited about Liza appearing on the late-night talk show that she scooped up June Allyson, Aaron Spelling, and his then-wife, actress Carolyn Jones, from LaScala's restaurant in Beverly Hills, and took them down the street to Sid's office where they waited until 12:45 A.M. for Liza to appear on screen. One review said, "Judy Garland's wonderfully unaffected daughter . . . sang, resembling her mother in style and showing more knowledge of what lyrics are all about than singers triple her age." Liza followed that up with an appearance a month later on the CBS summer-replacement series *Celebrity Talent Scouts*, hosted by Merv Griffin. And by summer of 1963, she had recorded the cast album for *Best Foot Forward*, cut a Cadence Records single of "You Are for Loving" (a song interpolated into the revival expressly for her), and signed a contract with Capitol Records.

Liza Minnelli was far from a stranger to television—despite her protestations of modesty to the contrary—when her mother invited her to guest on her show. Indeed, Frank Waldman remembers not a bit of protest from CBS or any staff member at

Liza's full-fledged guest-star status on the Garland series. Liza temporarily left her play and flew to California a week before Judy's show was to be shot, attending rehearsals and tapings of the Count Basie show. (Liza's arrival from New York gave George Schlatter the chance to try his hand at home decorating: "Judy called me the day before Liza was coming out from New York and said, 'Liza's coming and I haven't done her room!' I said, 'She gets here *tomorrow!*' " The resourceful Schlatter met the challenge. "We got lots of rattan furniture and did Liza's room in one day," he laughs.)

It was clear to everyone that Judy was thrilled to have Liza guest on the show. "How she doted on Liza," says Jerry Van Dyke. And Liza was far from immune to Judy's mesmerizing talent. "Liza was awestruck when her mother performed," recalls dancer Bea Busch.

Liza remembers not being anxious at the thought of working with her mother. "I was fearless," she laughs, "because I was very comfortable with her, and she was so much fun to work with. I liked George very much, and it was wonderful to work with Mel because, musically, he was terrific. And of course I knew Danny Daniels from *Best Foot Forward*, so it all was working in my favor."

Indeed it was. Not only was the musical material first-rate, (as it had been for the two previous shows), Bradford and the Waldmans devised a well-paced, focused script virtually devoid of the peaks and valleys of the previous episodes, with Van Dyke's "bumbling host" dialogue and the comedy moments vastly improved. The musical and comedic elements of the script blended perfectly, due to what Frank Waldman describes as "a very harmonious show, and everybody came up with suggestions."

Both Judy and Liza, of course, were much involved in choosing their material. Liza remembers that Judy phoned her and asked what song she wanted to do, and the idea of "Put On a Happy Face" came up. Judy was certainly not surprised at the choice. "She knew my favorite show was *Bye Bye Birdie*," explains Liza. Indeed, so enamored was she of the hit musical when she first saw it in 1961 that it clinched her decision to go into show business.

Mother and daughter also chose the program's closing production number, "Two Lost Souls" from *Damn Yankees*. "We both loved that song," says Liza, adding, "She had seen me do her part for the tramp number in rehearsals for one of her concerts or something, and it made her laugh so hard that she wanted to do something like that." As a result, "Two Lost Souls" was to be fashioned in exactly that way, both appearing (to great effect) in tramp costumes (similar to Judy's "Couple of Swells" getup, but in new ones created by Aghayan and Mackie), with a dance routine created by Danny Daniels.

It was also decided that Judy and Liza would do a medley together, opening with a portion of "We Could Make Such Beautiful Music Together," leading into "The Best Is Yet to Come" and "Bye Bye, Baby" (accompanied by a soft-shoe routine), ending with an old family favorite, the lightening-quick, purposely nonsensical novelty tune, "Bob White (Whatcha Gonna Swing Tonight). Liza again credits Judy with selecting their material. "She thought it up. She worked with Mel and said, 'These are some of the songs we'd like to sing, make a medley of it.' That's what she usually did." Liza remembers her mother's strong musical influence in the series, noting, "She was totally involved."

Another song they chose to perform in duet was "Together (Wherever We Go)," a most logical choice with *Gypsy* a favorite musical of Judy and her children. (When Joey was only five years old, Judy took him to see *Gypsy*; he sat on her lap in a front-row seat. Joey and Lorna had taken to singing the entire score of *Gypsy* relentlessly, day after day, and in his little baby voice he began singing along with Ethel Merman, who was belting "Some People." His voice kept growing as Merman reached the end of the number, and by the climax, Joe's *"but not Wose!"* could be heard right along with Merman's.)

Judy would open the show with the beautiful Gershwin song "Liza," and then solo on two blockbuster numbers, "Come Rain or Come Shine" and "As Long as He Needs Me"; Liza chose "You Are for Loving" for her spot. The Brothers Castro (rather like The Lettermen singing group with castinets) were to perform "Malaguena" and, with a number of girl dancers, "You Make Me Feel So Young." Jerry Van Dyke and guest Soupy Sales were to perform a comedy bit in which fanatical Garland fan Soupy anxiously waits to meet his idol, with Jerry reassuring him by singing "I'm Calm"; the desired effect finally comes, and Soupy is relaxed—until Judy crosses the set and cheerily says, "Hi, fellas!" causing both to collapse.

Perhaps the most remembered (and cleverest) bit of dialogue in the script, says Waldman, was not an inspiration of the writers, but from Judy and Liza. "There was a line in the show that came quite naturally. The first day of blocking, one of them said, 'Imagine calling Judy Garland "Mama," ' and the other said, 'Imagine calling Mama "Judy Garland"!' That happened so naturally that my brother [Tom] and I were quick to write it down":

The exchange came at the beginning of the program:

LIZA: Hi, Jerry. Where's Mama?
JERRY: You mean Judy?
LIZA: Yeah, Mama.
JERRY: Imagine calling Judy Garland "Mama."
LIZA: (MATTER OF FACTLY) Imagine calling Mama "Judy Garland."
JERRY: I guess it's the same with me and Dick.
LIZA: Oh, Dick Van Dyke is your father?
JERRY: (PAUSE, BRIGHTLY) Yeah!

Waldman, with rather surprising candor, credits Garland with improving the script by making suggestions during rehearsals, or simply by paraphrasing or ad-libbing on the spot during tapings. "She'd come up with a better line than was written, or something in the script would remind her of a story or an anecdote, out of which would come a better line. Or, after she told us, we, as writers, kind of put them in written form."

As Liza explains, "Mama was wonderful at giving people their due. She could make other people think it was their idea. She'd bring something up in a conversation—I'd watch her do it all the time—and say, 'Well, maybe that's not a good idea, but what about this?' And pretty soon, they'd be saying, 'Listen, you know when you were talking about that first thing? What if . . .' And she'd say, 'Oh, that's a great idea!' She was a master at letting people keep their self-esteem and their self-respect, and guiding them. She wanted everybody to look good. It's a great sense of her self-esteem, and her knowing who she was, that she was so strong that she was able to be generous. You can't be generous if you're screwed up. You just can't be. That says other great things about the woman herself."

Judy, remembers Liza, often would take another approach, but with the same result: "The television series was elegant and classy, just like she was, and she insisted it stay that way. In television at that point, every other show had a bit of hokum, and she resisted, without ever throwing a fit. She'd say, 'Yeah, that's a good idea—let me think about it.' That was one of her great lines. And then the subject would be dropped. Or if somebody called her on it and said, 'What about that thing with the banana peel when you fall down?' She'd then say, 'I really wouldn't feel comfortable doing that, and I'm sure somebody else could do it better.' She got around it without hurting anybody's feelings."

Adds Waldman, "She was completely happy, or she appeared to be completely happy in what we were giving her. In private, she might have been saying, 'Jesus, get rid of the writers!' " Jerry Van Dyke recalls, "I remember sitting in the script readings, and the laughs came when Judy would tell stories. The script wasn't being read. I guess they figured they'd get a lot of material from her. George would say, 'Do that, do that!' and she'd say, 'Do what?' She wouldn't remember what she'd said."

As Liza analyzes, "Even when she was stuck with skits and bits like that, she was wonderful. Everything that was not great about the series shows how talented she is. If a skit didn't have a strong punch line, she'd think of a take. She'd do *something*. Even the phony television dialogue always seemed extremely real. It showed, again, her strength and her femininity. There was nothing weak about the woman, believe it or not. She was totally a woman, in control, and knew exactly what she was doing, and what she wanted.

"How comfortable she made other people, how close she was to her family, how important details were to her," stresses Liza. "She knew everything, but she didn't tell the person how to do it. If it was right she'd say, 'This is great, thank you very much.' If it was wrong, she'd say, 'You know, I didn't sleep well, and I've got a little circle under my eyes, maybe you could protect me by moving the key light over.' She'd find a way to do it without being bossy, or unfeminine, or a ball-buster, making them feel good because they are doing it. Many times, I'd say, 'Gee, Mama, that looks funny, the hem is wrong, or there's a shadow on your face,' and she'd say, 'They'll figure it out. They know.' She was a true artist, and a true artist at living, too."

Soupy Sales found the set of *The Judy Garland Show* to be a

**Rehearsing "We Could Make Such
Beautiful Music Together"** . . .
CBS INC.

. . . **and then before the cameras**
CBS INC.

most happy, harmonious one. "It was really a team," remembers the comedian. "It was like a big family. She got along so great with George and the Waldmans, because it was a team effort and they had fun doing it. I was thrilled to do the show. I just loved her, and she was so nice to me. Judy was very happy, was wonderful to work with, and really came in to work and to do it. She was drinking just a little Liebfraumilch, nothing more, and she looked wonderful."

Although Liza's presence at home and on the show was tremendously uplifting, with Judy adopting a happy, upbeat public pose, there were private moments that indicated that all was not quite well. Soupy remembers, "A couple of times she got depressed, and they'd say, 'Why don't you drop by her trailer and see her.' So I'd drop in there, we'd sit and have a couple of glasses of wine. I'd tell her a few jokes, and she'd break up laughing, and that would be it. She'd be fine and back in great spirits again."

Waldman observes, "George was a master at putting people up to anything to break Judy up and keep her in a good mood. Soupy was marvelous because he had the ability to make her laugh like Mickey did. George and everyone else really tried to keep her happy and laughing and in a good mood."

"George got along famously with Judy," notes Jerry Van Dyke, "as everybody did. Judy was always nice. I didn't ever see her go crazy, or tell anybody off, or scream."

"Once you made her laugh, everything was okay," according to Schlatter. "She had moments when she would get very tight, but I found if you could make her laugh, you released that spring. The first time she got uptight onstage, I played a tape that we'd made of machine guns, bazookas, explosions, bombs, and sirens—loud. It just scared her to death. She said, 'What the *fuck* was *that?*' And I said, 'Don't fool with *me*, lady, I've got an *army!*' So many times she'd present a problem just to see how I'd deal with it. The next time she got upset with me onstage, I played a tape of fart jokes. Well, she loved flatulation jokes more than anybody. She had a collection of the best fart jokes I ever heard in my entire life, and could do two hours of them that could put you on the floor. And of course they were favorite jokes of mine as well, too, so we shared that. She heard the tape and got hysterical."

George raised the stakes the next time around. "Then one day she really started to get uptight, and I said,'Okay, we've got to stop this.' So, I started to sing 'Over the Rainbow.' She turned to me and said, 'What are you doing?' I told her, 'I thought if you were going to produce, I'd sing!' At that point, she went into her trailer, and I thought maybe I'd gone too far this time. So I followed her into her trailer with a matchbook, and when I held it under the sprinklers, she yelled, 'What are you doing?' I said, 'If you don't apologize, I'll drown you!' She didn't want to have the trailer ruined, so she said, 'All right—I'm sorry!' And I said, 'See that it doesn't happen again!' I went out the door, and she chased me down the hall with a lamp! We went back onstage."

While Judy thoroughly enjoyed and responded to Schlatter's pranks, Frank Waldman adds, "She had a marvelous laugh and really cracked up so easily and enjoyed laughing both at herself and other situations. She had a great sense of humor about her position as a legend. The fact that we were calling her 'The Legend' to her face would make her laugh or giggle."

"She was just a joy," says Johnny Bradford of these days. "We played all sorts of tricks on each other. She was like a sister to George, and me, and everybody else." (Mel Tormé, reported Hedda Hopper, was no more exempt than anyone else from being the subject of a practical joke: "Mel's famous for never carrying a penny, so the company fixed him a few days ago when they went to lunch with him and managed to sneak out, leaving Mel sitting there with the check. He had a heck of a time convincing the waitress [he was good for the check]. . . . Finally, he had to sing a song to prove he was Mel Tormé!")

Schlatter pegs "incompetence" of those around her not doing their jobs properly and "nerves" as the two factors that would aggravate and agitate Judy. "She would take little lifters. Little capsules. I had the secretary empty the capsules out, and we put sugar in them. And she got a natural lift from performing, anyhow. She didn't know there was sugar in the pills. I also found out that Judy was a toucher, and would grab at me. I discovered that if you just reached out and touched her, that's what she needed, that contact. It took a couple of weeks to find this compulsion."

A common thread in the recollections among most behind-the-scenes people involved in the series was Judy's kindness, in addition to her unassuming, warm manner—often at odds with the image they had envisioned about the superstar. "I remember sitting on the ramp during an orchestra run-through," recounts George Sunga, "and if it happened to be Judy's number, it would not be uncommon for her to come down, sit next to me, and maybe grab my arm and sing her song, pat me on the head, and then go on with business. In that sense, she was a very warm lady."

Assistant set designer Gene McAvoy offers, "She seemed like you could have a personal relationship with her, if you wanted to. Some people make you feel at home that way. You always felt that you were part of seeing her working for perfection, trying to do better and better. The beauty of Judy was that she was normal, and yet not normal. There wasn't a category to put her in. She was a very special person for one hundred different reasons. I don't think that you could find one person, whether it was someone onstage with her, or a grip, or a lighting person, or anybody, that didn't have that kind of feeling for her. Even though I wasn't really close to her, I felt very personal about her. And it wasn't that she was overly gracious to them—it was just that people had a feeling for her that you didn't have for anyone else."

McAvoy's first real encounter with Judy occurred during the third show. "She never really knew who I was. I was there, but nobody had formally introduced us. I had just bought a new shirt and came onstage. She turned around and introduced herself to me and wanted to know who I was and what I did. Then she commented that she liked my shirt. She had noticed that. I had been frightened of this superstar. Judy would seek out people on the stage and say, 'Hello, who are you?' And she wouldn't forget your name. She did it with everybody."

Earl Carlson was put on the show by CBS, working alternately as propman, set decorator, and Judy's stage manager. "I rehearsed lines with her. When she came onstage, I held her cigarette, or held her Liebfraumilch and her script. Her entourage would leave, and often she was left there by herself, and she would say, 'I pay these people big money to tell me how great I am, and now where are they?' She needed someone to lean on and help her along. She was quite insecure. I can't say that we became really close. I don't think she allowed that. She'd been burned so many times by so many people, she was always wary of how people were going to treat her. But she knew I was there to help her. One time during a show, I was right by the crane camera giving her some movement directions, and the camera came down and grazed me and stunned me for a second. She saw it and stopped the show. I was very embarrassed about it, but she wanted it that way."

The final day for general rehearsals of show three was Sunday, July 14, with prerecording taking place later that evening. Monday was the day of the dress-rehearsal taping, with the final taping set for Tuesday, July 16. "Judy was wonderful with Liza," says dancer Bea Busch. "She rehearsed very, very hard with her and made sure she was comfortable." Choreographer Danny Daniels (who had met Judy for the first time at the second night performance of *Best Foot Forward*) adds, "Judy had a good background, having worked with all the best choreographers in the Hollywood years. She'd had good training. She was very responsive. She was not prone to want to rehearse anything that was physically exhausting for her. It was a big load, she was doing the whole damn show, so you didn't get her for a great deal of time. But she was Judy, and Judy was incredible." Bill Hobin remembers, "Judy was really 'Mama' on that show, helping Liza through everything. It was very special for her."

Daniels says of Liza, "I staged 'Put On a Happy Face' and worked with Liza very extensively. We had a very close and warm relationship. She was a very talented newcomer who I realized was going to make a big splash on the scene. Because Liza was fast, she picked everything up, and when Judy couldn't remember, Liza would say, 'No, Mama, *left* foot.' "

After Liza and Judy rehearsed their medley together for an orchestra run-through, Liza came offstage and remarked, "I know I sound like Mother when I sing, but I don't intend to do it. It just happens. Sometimes when I hear my voice on a record or something, I'm really surprised at how much it resembles hers. It's kind of, well, spooky." She further noted, "I'm staying with Mother out here until this show is completed. But Mother's more like an older sister or a good friend than a mother. It's more fun that way. Yet, when I need her advice or help—Mother's always there."

Garland's fans, on the other hand, were not always present at the show tapings. "It was very much the 'in' thing to get into that audience," remembers Tom Cooper, who adds, "Judy was a little upset that most of the fans could not get in. She wanted to have more fans in the audience. They'd wait in long lines for hours before the tapings, and they couldn't get in. Maybe twenty or twenty-five, out of hundreds of them, could get in. The studio audience was mainly made up of network executives, agents, their wives, and their associates."

The opening had Judy tenderly sing "Liza" surrounded by huge blowups of her daughter from infancy to age seventeen, with Liza coming out from behind one of the photos at the end of the song to embrace Judy. Effectively and beautifully done, the in-person effect was described by Cooper as "pure magic." It was no less moving for Judy and Liza; during a run-through of the opening number, Judy cried while singing the number, and Liza rushed to Judy at the end of the song, also crying, and the two embraced.

The show continued with the "Imagine calling 'Mama' Judy Garland" bit, which led into Garland tearing full throttle into "Come Rain or Come Shine." So powerful and sustained was her last note, it caught her by momentary surprise, mouthing the words "Oh, my goodness!" after her overhead microphone had been cut off. The beginning of the song, however, was further evidence of Studio 43's audio deficiencies, with the bongos that began the arrangement overriding Judy's vocal until bars into the songs. "They had the mike so far away from her," criticizes Cooper. "Had they had it down closer, they might have gotten better presence on her voice. It doesn't quite do it justice. Live, that voice was incredible, and sometimes, because of the audio problems, it lost something in the tapings."

Liza joined Judy for a delightful duet of "Together," and the seventeen-year-old displayed her skills as a dancer, making "Put On a Happy Face" memorable. The Soupy-Jerry banter leading into their duet was next, the least successful, but still not altogether bad, segment of the entire hour. The Garland-Minnelli medley was a display of genuine talent and genuine affection between mother and daughter—Judy looking at Liza adoringly, Liza hitting a high note and Judy's proud reaction, Liza watching her mother in awe as she sings—that stands as one of the

Judy's rafter-ringing last note of "Come Rain or Come Shine"
CBS INC.

highlights of the entire series. As they were about to turn their backs to the camera during the soft-shoe dance to "Bye Bye, Baby" they ad-libbed:

> LIZA: (LAUGHING) The other side. Turn around!
> JUDY: You've really been practicing. Where did you learn this?
> LIZA: (LAUGHS) You taught it to me!
> JUDY: I *did*?

The next segment was Liza's poignant rendering of "You Are for Loving," beautifully and tenderly sung in pure, clear tones. Hitting just the right note of wistfulness, Minnelli revealed much of her blossoming talents as an actress as well as a singer.

In a bit of a departure, Judy's "Trunk" segment was in this show the second-to-the-last segment. Judy finally had the opportunity to sing "As Long as He Needs Me" (dropped twice before, on the Goulet special and on the Basie show), having introduced the hit song from the Lionel Bart musical *Oliver!* only a few months earlier at the Harrah's engagement in Lake Tahoe. Composer Bart has stated on several occasions that every song he has ever written—including the entire score from *Oliver!*—was written expressly with Judy Garland's voice as his inspiration, and Judy's alternately high-voltage and exquisitely tender interpretation ranks as one of her greatest performances. Building slowly to a thunderous climax, Judy, without erring for a moment, knew exactly when, and when not, to play directly to the camera, and Hobin's exciting, dramatic camera work created an indelible image. (Judy, in accordance with network standards, was to sing a reworked lyric, "you know, I've got my pride" instead of the objectionable original "the hell, I've got my pride." Deciding on-camera to sing the song the way it was written despite the CBS edict, Judy for a second pointedly looks into the camera, then looks away before singing "the hell . . ." Judy won. The network aired it anyway.)

The hour ended with the "Two Lost Souls" tramp-outfitted song-and-dance routine. The charming number remains a delight. Immediately launching into "Maybe I'll Come Back," Judy quickly halted the orchestra when she realized that Liza had missed her own entrance to the number. Garland, taking the blame herself, said, "Let's start once more. I must have missed it." She then quipped, "We don't want to pretend this is *taped!*" And, although "Baby Face Nelson" was scripted to get the weekly honors in "Maybe I'll Come Back," Judy, of course, changed the line to, "*Liza Minnelli* is a cousin of mine!"

Mel wrote special lyrics for Liza to sing in counterpoint to Judy's standard version of "Maybe I'll Come Back," with both of them joining in for the final "Then *maybe* I will come back to you!," hugging each other, Judy telling Liza, "You're *marvelous!*" The ovation from the audience continued well after the music had stopped and the cameras finished taping. Judy, breathlessly, acknowledged the applause, and, always the mother, instructed her daughter, "Say thank you, Liza!" before excitedly telling her, "I'll see you backstage!"

The perfect ending to the evening came when the brilliant, incomparably talented director Vincente Minnelli approached George Schlatter after watching much of the program from the control booth. "Vincente loved the show, because it was more than anything else patterned after Vincente's vision of Judy Garland than it was after CBS's. Vincente was thrilled, because we were going for the same kind of magic out of Judy that Vincente Minnelli saw." Adds Liza, "He loved the show, he just loved it, and Mama was so pleased that he was there."

"Vincente told me, 'You made Judy look like a star,' " recalls George Schlatter with enormous pride. "That meant a great deal to me."

9

"I'll bet before the series . . .
a lot of people had no idea
that I could carry on a conversation without having someone write the script!"

—Judy Garland, 1963

With the demand for top-name guest stars at its peak among the
many variety shows on the air, George Schlatter relied on the
irresistible appeal of working with Garland as his magnet. His
instincts were correct, for he was able to book Lena Horne and
British comedian Terry-Thomas for the fourth show. Tony Bennett and offbeat comedian Dick Shawn were signed for the fifth
episode. Scheduled as guests for the sixth Garland outing were
Nat "King" Cole and comedian Jack Carter.

During this time, among those (incorrectly) rumored as guests
on the Garland series were Carol Channing (Judy and Carol each
to do their "wicked" impressions of the other); Broadway singing star Robert Horton; Betty Grable and Dan Dailey, in a joint
appearance; comic Shelley Berman; and trumpet player Pete
Fountain. George Maharis (who earlier in the year departed the
CBS *Route 66* series due to health problems) was signed by
Schlatter to display his singing talents, as was Robert Goulet's
new bride, Carol Lawrence. Also expected to guest with Garland
were singer-dancers Van Johnson (Judy's costar in the 1949 MGM
musical *In the Good Old Summertime*) and Cyd Charisse. (Cyd's
husband, Tony Martin, had earlier been rumored as a guest and
even had been pegged to appear on the premiere episode.) *The
Hollywood Reporter* stated Frank Sinatra was eager to guest with
Judy; he simply was waiting to be asked. Ironically, the only two
of the entire group who actually would appear with Garland on

the series were comedian Berman and dramatic actor Maharis. Schlatter also hoped to snare Rock Hudson, Marlon Brando, Peter Sellers, Charlton Heston, Bobby Darin, and Steve Allen.

It was at this moment that CBS—in the person of Hunt Stromberg, Jr.—decided to become actively involved with *The Judy Garland Show*. Offers Schlatter, "Nobody came around the first few weeks, because they thought it was going to be explosive, that she wasn't going to show up, and that it would just go away. When they realized that she was going to show up and she'd gotten such great reaction to the first taping and the show with Liza, at that point Hunt Stromberg—who had been on the periphery up to then—said, 'I've got to get involved in that show.' And that's when Hunt started to lean on us as far as telling us that she shouldn't touch people."

While Schlatter deliberately avoided telling Judy about Stromberg's criticism (not wanting to alarm her, and feeling the entire matter was not worthy of discussion anyway), many others on the show recall that Judy likely heard of the network's disapproval and insistence that she become more "approachable."

Evidence of this is her ad-libbing during the "Trunk" segment of the fifth program, "They keep telling me to talk because you people at home have to get to know me," adding, "It might be disastrous!" During the dress rehearsal of the preceding episode, Judy had said, even more pointedly, "They have decided that I should talk more. I'm forty-one years old, and suddenly they realize I can *talk*."

Schlatter's answer to CBS was inaugurating "Tea for Two," a weekly segment showcasing Judy in ad-libbed conversation with another celebrity. Johnny Bradford championed the idea, wanting to showcase Judy's wit and sense of humor. "It would be very easy to say that we put every word into her mouth. That would be far from the truth. We just shaped it, edited it, and suggested things. I wanted her to be able to ad-lib. Aubrey hated that. But I knew how she was—a very bright, very witty person. By just letting her react to people that she respected, I knew we could get something good out of her."

Stromberg's wanting to spotlight Garland in witty conversation with her guests was certainly not a bad idea; she had, after all, been signed for the series largely due to her success on Jack Paar's talk show. The negative aura around Stromberg's edict, in Judy's eyes, was that it came along with the first hint that CBS was less than thrilled with the shows to date.

Judy and George, stung by CBS criticism, apparently avoided Television City for most of the week during rehearsals for the Lena Horne hour. Bill Hobin remembers, "We had a rehearsal, and George wasn't there, Gary, nobody. Lena and I were old friends. I kept making excuses about Judy. Lena's pretty sharp, saying, 'Come on, don't bullshit me.' I was trying to be sympathetic to Judy because the thing that was surprising about her was that she would miss rehearsals and come in, spend an hour with the rehearsal pianist, and have it down cold. She'd come out and perform just great."

Mort Lindsey, however, contends it was Schlatter—and not Garland—who created the problem. "She showed up when she was supposed to," he insists. "She was in Vegas with the producer. She figured she was with the producer, what could happen? Judy was really a very nice person who took orders. She figured, I can't be wrong. But George was wrong." Adds Orval, "Judy enjoyed the shows and wanted to do them, but there were periods of time that she would get very tired and wanted to take a break."

Jack Elliott states that Lena was irritated that quick-study Judy preferred to rehearse minimally to preserve spontaneity: "Judy would come in and do it, and that was the end of it. Lena wanted to work more, but Judy was not inclined."

Adds Schlatter, "These two women were apprehensive about each other. She and Lena had a bit of a standoff. It got competitive." (The following year, Johnny Bradford wrote a British television special for Horne, and when the subject of Garland came up, Lena expressed only positive feelings about working with her.)

The "Tea" segment with Terry-Thomas—the first and best of all of them—was a complete success, charming and spontaneous. The dress-rehearsal version did not air, probably due to an unexpected noise during the taping as well as a rather interesting reference to Aubrey's favorite, Danny Kaye:

(A VOICE FROM HALL BLARES THROUGH)

> T-T: How about that?
> JUDY: A train went through the building. . . .

Terry-Thomas displays his "talent to amuse" Judy at rehearsal.

(APPLAUSE AND LAUGHTER)

JUDY: Oh, *dear!* . . .

T-T: It's Danny Kaye. He's *very* jealous.

JUDY: Is it? Is he?

T-T: Yes.

JUDY: Was he jealous, really? I *hope* so!

And edited out of the broadcast version was her reminiscence about her overweight periods of the 1950s, and early 1960s:

JUDY: There was a fat lady's jacket maker. The jacket sort of covered up all kinds of *chins* that you might have, and if you wore a hat down to *here* and tucked everything up *here*, the jacket with a mandarin collar down to *here* covered up all kinds of things that people knew about *anyway*. There were a lot of photographers, and at one point somebody said, "Look

> over here!" and I didn't *dare*, [and said] "No, you
> come over *here*!" But I *did* drop a menu or something,
> and everything [showed] and they got *that* one!

Gary Smith's huge board of lights (reminiscent of the 1962 Sinatra-Martin special) framed Judy as she immediately launched into a brisk, spirited "Day In, Day Out" to begin the hour. After her chorus, the lightboard swung around to reveal Lena, as Judy disappeared from view. Wearing an outfit nearly identical to Judy's, Lena reprised the number (in a cool, rather mannered style) before Garland joined her to finish the number in duet. Lena, rather noticeably, avoided any eye contact with Judy well into the number, until she finally gave in and put her arm around Garland. To cement this sudden display of goodwill, Garland shrewdly gave Lena prominence at the end of the number by standing behind her, then taking her hand and gesturing the waves of the applause away from herself and to Lena alone. (The line "Not bad for a couple of MGM rejects!" followed the duet, but was dropped for the final taping.)

Judy and Lena then introduced Terry-Thomas (with Lena stumbling over one of her lines and then laughing over it), who delivered a lengthy, if only moderately amusing, monologue in his clipped British accent. Lena's three solo numbers were next, and, although they were well sung, seldom has the stunningly beautiful Horne been more or distant, almost arrogant. Perhaps influenced by the events that week, Lena was most cool and removed, not at all addressing the camera during her second number, "Where Is Love?"

Judy and Lena ad-libbed much of their dialogue leading into their medley where each sang some of the other's signature songs:

> JUDY: I know why I love to work with you. You open your
> mouth and sing louder than any other girl singer
> besides me in the *world!*
>
> LENA: I know it, I know it. (BEAT) And I hate it!
>
> (JUDY BREAKS COMPLETELY UP AT THIS AD-LIB)
>
> LENA: Unless you just open your mouth and get a big
> breath—
>
> JUDY: (GOING ALONG WITH IT) Yeah?
>
> LENA: You can't last as long as some of these arrange-
> ments we seem to have!

The "Judy Sings Lena Sings Judy" medley

After a bit more dialogue, Judy launched into a few offhand bars of "Honeysuckle Rose," with Lena then tearing into "Meet Me in St. Louis," sung in such an exaggerated come-hither delivery that it caused a greatly amused, obviously surprised Judy to laugh, "I didn't know it was a sexy song!" (The whole medley, in fact, has a wonderful aura of spontaneity; the show did not suffer as a result.) Judy counters with a good-natured, but deadly, impression of Horne while singing " 'Deed I Do," which Lena responds to with great amusement—and surprise. Duets on "The Trolley Song" and "Love" (a hit for both of them) follow, with Lena attacking the song so vigorously and defiantly (growling the lyrics, with her fists clenched all the while) that it causes Judy, for a moment, to recoil and grimace as she looks upon Lena with mock bewilderment.

"Mad Dogs and Englishmen" was a complete misfire, not helped by the gimmick of Garland and Horne dressed in Victorian-era costumes (complete with parasols) and African white hunters' hats, with Terry-Thomas garbed in a pith helmet and old-fashioned seersucker suit. Judy steadfastly avoided learning the number, with her instincts correctly pegging the production number as a total dud. Displaying her apathy, Judy even wore her Ben Franklin-type "little old lady" reading glasses (she was outfitted in a glamorous white gown, creating a most unusual effect!) during the dress rehearsal to read the still-unlearned lyrics on the cue cards. Lena and Terry-Thomas appeared no more delighted in attempting to pull it off than did Judy.

While Judy looked terrific on the show (although not quite as dazzling as on the Liza program), it is only at the "Trunk" segment that she appears stunningly beautiful. Again, in accordance with Hunt Stromberg's order, Garland has the opportunity to display her remarkable storytelling abilities. With great charm and ingenuousness, Judy relates the story of losing the Oscar in 1955 for *A Star Is Born* to Grace Kelly while in the hospital following the birth of son Joe. Judy wryly recalled how, immediately prior to the telecast of the Academy Awards, a television crew burst into her hospital room to quickly set up transmitting equipment for Judy to make her acceptance speech on the live broadcast in the event that she won the Oscar. Although Judy was not so certain she would be named Best Actress, she remembered the technicians assuring her that she and Grace Kelly were "neck in neck," which was, cracked Garland, "a *terrible thought*, you know!" Judy's confidence built as the crew set up multiple cameras and television monitors to transmit her acceptance speech ("I've got to win it, or they wouldn't go to all that trouble. . . ."), but her hopes were dashed when Grace Kelly was announced as the winner. The crew, she laughed, was so disgruntled by Judy losing—after all their work in transforming her hospital room into a broadcast studio—that "nobody said good *night*, even, they were so *mad* at me!" Proud Mama Judy ended her story by warmly noting that she left the hospital with something "*much* more important than the Oscar"—her son, Joe. She then took a photo of a beaming Joe out of the trunk, and kissed it tenderly.

After noting the song she is about to sing is from *A Star Is Born* (mentioning also its composer, Harold Arlen), Judy, in an instant, shifts mood and effortlessly begins "The Man That Got Away." Garland, for perhaps the only time ever, approaches the song in a subtle, more introspective, but no less powerful interpretation. (Hugh Martin quit as vocal arranger of *A Star Is Born* when Judy refused to perform the song in a less intense, driving manner; now, ten years later, Garland tried it his way, at least initially, to spectacular success.) In wonderful voice, aided by

Bill Hobin's deft direction and Leard Davis's wonderful lighting, Garland's magic transformed a nearly excellent program into a memorable one.

Nonetheless, conflicts among the staff were beginning to rise to the surface. Mel Tormé, according to several observers, was becoming increasingly unhappy in his continuing role as Judy's off-camera music prompter. Never secure with having to depend on the speakers to convey the sound of the distant orchestra, Judy had asked Mel early on to "conduct" her so that she would come in on the proper cue. Mel confronted George and told him he would no longer perform in this unofficial function; the producer convinced him to continue helping Judy off-camera. Still, the seeds of discord were beginning to fester among the once tightly knit, unwaveringly supportive group.

Mort Lindsey became a target of attack as well. The musician made well known his complaints about the poor scripts and inferior comedy material foisted upon Garland. Predictably, Judy's "new television family" did not take kindly to Lindsey's criticisms of the scripts, reflected in Johnny Bradford's comment, "Mort was always the nonlaugher in the group. He resented us, but we didn't understand him, or want to. Maybe we were unfair to him, I don't know."

"I think it was a good idea for her to do the series," counters Lindsey, "I just didn't think they got the right people. Schlatter approached it wrong, and I told him so. They kept calling these meetings. I'd get all restless. I would disagree with everything. They never had a group of writers in a way. You can't have situation-comedy or gag writers write for Judy. And there weren't enough writers. If you're going to do comedy, you've got to have a lot of writers. Jerry Van Dyke was a nice guy, but nobody could believe the premise of his character. About the comedy things, I would say, 'That's not her.' Finally, I didn't want to go to the meetings, and that's when Mel Tormé said, 'You're a great musician but a giant pain in the ass.' Because I never agreed with anything. I just felt that I knew her a lot better than they did. Nobody knew her, really," says Lindsey, shaking his head. "They didn't know her."

Mort Lindsey's complaint about the lack of a topflight battery of writers is not without merit. Garland had Johnny Bradford along with Tom and Frank Waldman. *The Danny Kaye Show*, on the other hand, claimed a stellar collection of some of television's finest comedy writers, including Larry Gelbart, Herb Baker, Ernie Chambers, Saul Ilson, Sheldon Keller, Mel Tolkin, Paul Mazursky, and Larry Tucker.

The fifth Garland episode, guest-starring Tony Bennett and Dick Shawn, scheduled the dress-rehearsal taping for Monday, July 29, and the final performance the following evening. The script (rewritten more than any other to date and until the very last minute) was mediocre, with Garland and the musical portions of the show burdened, once again, with the task of having to carry the entire hour.

Judy's opening number changed three times. First, Noël Coward's "Sail Away" was selected, replaced by "Comes Once in a Lifetime." Deciding against those two upbeat tunes, Judy elected to try the unusual by starting the show with one of her favorite songs, the bittersweet Coward ballad "If Love Were All." A production number of the lively "Yes, Indeed" with Judy and her guests followed. Brief scripted chitchat with Judy, Jerry, and Dick Shawn (never aired) served to set up another attempt at comedy, with Van Dyke asking the gyrating star to teach him his tricks to attract women, halting any momentum the show had generated and leading into an ill-advised duet between the two of the *Bye Bye Birdie* song "Honestly Sincere."

A medley teaming Judy and Tony Bennett (with his solo spot, curiously, slotted later in the hour) followed. The routine opened with Tony's "Lullaby of Broadway"; also included was "Carolina in the Morning" (Judy); "Kansas City" (Tony); "When the Midnight Choo-Choo Leaves for Alabam' " (Judy); "Big D" (both Judy and Tony, but later eliminated); and Tony's hit "I Left My Heart in San Francisco" (in which he was joined by Judy for a reprise following Bennett's solo). Roddy McDowall was to be the "Tea for Two" guest. Tony's solo spot of "True Blue Lou" and "Moment of Truth" (later changed to "Keep Smiling at Trouble") led into Dick Shawn's segment. First scheduled to solo on "When the World Was Young" and then go into a comedy spot with Judy, he ultimately sang "My Buddy" with Judy. He then launched into a solo routine only briefly featuring Garland. The "Trunk" closer was originally to have Judy sing the ballad "Alone Together"; it was switched to "Stormy Weather" by the final draft.

The ever-changing, confusing status of the script for show number five would accurately mirror a tumultuous week that would, more than any other, profoundly affect the present, future, and ultimate survival of *The Judy Garland Show*.

It began well enough. *Variety*'s veteran television reporter Dave Kaufman gave the series a great boost within industry circles by interviewing George Schlatter for an in-depth feature to run on Tuesday, July 30, the day of the final taping of the fifth program. Schlatter was as enthusiastic and optimistic as ever. "I'd rather be opposite *Bonanza* than opposite Garland," he boasted, adding that Judy "is one of the few remaining greats. What female performers are there today that have the excitement, the mystique, the electricity that Garland has? I have read some nonsense about my taming a tiger. We have put a frame around Judy in which she's comfortable and can play. We have just let Judy be Judy.

"In much of TV, everybody is warm and folksy and they play down to the people in the Midwest. I'm from the Midwest, and I don't feel they have to be played down to. . . . Also in TV, they say, 'Are you going to have anything for the kids?' I don't really know what that means. I believe kids like good entertainment and interesting subjects discussed. We shouldn't play down to them." Schlatter concluded, "I don't know whether I'll hold up, but Judy has held up fine. She's happy, healthy, secure, singing better than she ever has. She wants this thing to be a success."

Another good omen was Tony Bennett, who, surprisingly, had never before crossed paths with Garland. Upon meeting, the two became close, devoted friends. Tony remembers their immediate and private kinship: "She kind of kept me away from everybody. She said, 'Let's just you and I do this together.' We didn't have difficult material to memorize. She wanted both of us to relax and sing songs that we liked."

Bennett recalls that their friendship was sealed when they realized they shared a similar sense of humor. The set featured railroad-crossing signals, destination signs, and pieces of simulated railroad track. During a rehearsal of their duet, dancers (dressed as engineers) pushed Judy and Tony on a wheeled platform across the stage. "We had these two chorus boys on this little vehicle," recalls Tony. "We were going to sing 'I Left My Heart in San Francisco' and have these two chorus boys make us go around on these tracks. At rehearsal, they got so excited, they went too fast, and we fell off the tracks right into the audience! We just laughed for about an hour, and we really hit it off." The choreography was, of course, modified. Judy and Tony were unmistakably warm and affectionate on-screen, plainly delighted to be in each other's company and having a great deal of fun working together.

Judy's impact on Tony Bennett cannot be overestimated. "Judy was one of the most phenomenal artists that ever lived. She's the best singer I've ever heard. And the best performer. I learned something from watching Judy Garland. I learned the secret that a performer is nothing but a reflection of the audience. You give to an audience, that's what the audience will give back. She did it better than anyone else. No one ever received as much love from an audience as Judy."

Judy held Tony Bennett in equally high regard, saying less than a year before her death, "His sound gets into your ear and your heart. . . . Tony's feeling for a lyric sometimes will make his voice tremble just a tiny bit, and it's from pure masculine emotion. I adore that man. I adore his talent, and I adore him as a person. . . . I've always thought of Tony Bennett as a thoroughly professional entertainer."

"She was a genius at what she did. And what a great person, too," says Tony of Judy. "She was a lot of fun and very misunderstood. She just loved people, and she understood them. Everybody adored her, and I think she had a very troubled life because of that. What happens, you diminish everybody's ego. Everyone thinks they're great until someone like that walks into a room."

Tony was one of the few who stood loyally by Judy until her death in 1969. "I regret the fact that she's gone, because, in my personal life, I never had more fun. She was so intelligent. She was so funny. That's what I miss. I don't remember anyone who enjoyed herself so much. People look at her like she was Billie Holiday or Edith Piaf, but she really loved life, loved people, and that's what was so interesting about her. You could see how she just enjoyed the moment." He adds, "The last time I saw her, and I'll never forget, she saw me perform with Count Basie at the London Palladium. She came backstage. As she walked away, she said, 'You know, you're a pretty good singer.' That's the last time she ever spoke to me."

But in July 1963, before meeting Judy, Bennett remembers

being most impressed in seeing the Garland series operating at
full throttle. "The show was big time, in a way I'd never seen.
She had this fantastic trailer for a home right by the set, a big,
huge studio and a whole army of people waiting at her command to put the show on, as if she were Queen Elizabeth. It
was top-of-the-line."

Garland's spirits were noticeably improved from the week
before, and the dress-rehearsal taping on July 28 went smoothly,
no doubt due to Tony's presence. "Judy was like a racehorse,"
says Schlatter. "We timed Judy like you would time a fighter.
She was in training in what she ate, what she did." While he
remembers that Dick Shawn "was not a calming influence," Tony
had a soothing, magical effect on Judy.

Johnny Bradford remembers that Tony was "very nervous"
about working with Garland, whom he unabashedly adored. "He
was so in awe of her that he had to have a belt of brandy before
he could go on with her!" (Perhaps in indication of this, Tony
startles himself during "True Blue Lou" by hiccuping in the middle
of a note. He flashed a smile and continued with the song.) "He's
a very shy guy, but very talented," adds Bradford. "Most of her
efforts on that show were to make him comfortable."

The calm was shattered the very next day. Directly before the
final taping of the show, Hunt Stromberg, Jr., arranged to have
a luncheon meeting with Judy and George. The event remains
indelible in Schlatter's memory: "Hunt said, 'Judy, I've got some
ideas. We have to talk.' Judy said, 'What do you mean, we have
to talk?' Because she'd been isolated from the network people
until this point. He said, 'We know what to do to fix the show.'
This is right before she went on. . . . She said, 'What's broken,
why do we have to fix anything?' He said, 'No, *Judes,* I only
have a few minutes, I'll tell you what, babe, what you need is a
family.' He kept calling her 'Judes,' which really annoyed her.
And I watched this woman that I'd worked with for months start
to go. She said, 'What kind of family?' He said, 'Bob Denver,
Marion Lorne, Cara Williams, and Ken Murray.' I said, 'Hunt,
not now, not now.' I said, 'Judy, you tell me these people don't
have a sense of humor,' and I gave him a little shove."

Bob Wynn vividly recalls Judy being so outraged at Stromberg at one point that she pushed a cake into the stunned CBS
executive's face, saying, "Fuck you, Hunt!"

The meeting might have been over, but the effect that it would

The unaired version of the Judy Garland–Tony Bennett duet
CBS INC.

have on Judy and on her series had just begun. While the meeting was concluding, the doors to Studio 43 were opened. Lorna and Joe were the first to arrive, with several celebrities filing in later, including Arlene Dahl, Steve Allen and his wife, Jayne Meadows, and actress-model Suzy Parker.

Two people who attended this taping had the distinct feeling that something was amiss with Judy, having no clue as to the cause. "I didn't feel Judy was quite as on top as the other shows," said one, with Tom Cooper noting, "I wasn't feeling the magic in that one. She seemed a little edgy. Tony was wonderful and gave his all, but Judy seemed ragged, not quite together." (She still was as enthusiastic about her guests as ever. During Tony's solo of "Keep Smiling at Trouble," Judy, utterly caught up in his performance of the swinging number, accidentally clapped a couple of times during the taping; Tony can be seen looking away from the camera, smiling at Judy off-camera, plainly as delighted with her reactions as she is with his singing). Framed in a past-closing-time nightclub setting, Bennett is most effective, charming and in fine voice. Dick Shawn, however, contributed little to the hour; his only successful moment is "My Buddy," sung gently and sweetly with Judy. (Interestingly, at the first taping, Garland wore a glittering black-sequined costume that was as spectacular as it was revealing; airing instead was the version taped the following evening, with Judy conservatively wearing a white top and matching Capri pants.)

Perhaps not coincidentally, virtually half of the material taped that night would either never be seen at all or be rejected in favor of the dress-rehearsal footage. "If Love Were All" (with Judy in a glittering black gown, draped with a feather boa) was particularly well, and movingly, sung. It was never aired, however, likely due to feathers in the boa covering Judy's mouth at the start of the number, causing her to turn her back to the camera to remove them. Also not used was this night's performance of the Garland-Bennett medley, with the dress rehearsal aired instead (Judy wearing a black-and-white dress in place of the white top and slacks), further suggesting that Judy was, understandably, in better shape the night before the Stromberg encounter.

The "Tea" segment was never broadcast. Judy had expected Roddy McDowall as her guest. The script called for her to hold up some of his renowned photographic work. She would then rummage through the stack of pictures and display one of a very young Roddy from *Lassie, Come Home*. This business served as a setup for Roddy to come onstage from the audience. While the script indicated that the remainder of the segment would be entirely ad-libbed, Schlatter also had to ad-lib a guest. Roddy, at the last minute, bowed out, and George decided to use the opportunity to surprise Judy. "I went out into the hall and dragged in Steve Allen, whom I had worked with at NBC, saying, 'Would you come in and talk to Judy?' He said, 'About *what*?' I said, 'I don't give a shit, just talk to her!' "

Walking onstage, Judy expected to spot Roddy and instead found Steve; she was completely stunned and delighted to see him, repeatedly insisting to the audience that her surprise was genuine. Their obvious chemistry and shared wit was so potent that they fell victim to their own success; so good were they together that Steve was booked to be a full-fledged guest, with this initial teaming never seen so that it would not take the edge off his bona-fide later appearance. Garland and the multitalented Allen were absolutely delightful together:

JUDY: I didn't know you were here!

STEVE: I wasn't so sure myself. . . .

JUDY: I wish I'd known you were going to be here, I'd have known the proper questions. . . .

STEVE: I'll ask you questions, then.

JUDY: All right. I'll wait till you swallow your cookie so I can think of some answers. . . .

STEVE: I've been wanting, Judy, to get over here anyway to tell you how seriously magnificent your show is. . . . One way I can tell this is probably the most successful show of its kind this year in TV is that, not only is this real tea . . . this is real silver. On the average show, they have fake stuff, because who would know the difference?

JUDY: Is it really?

STEVE: I think so.

JUDY: Then I'm going to take it *home* with me! . . .

STEVE: Remember the days when you used to get paid in cash?

JUDY: No. Oh, no, I never saw any money. Everybody always said, don't worry about it, *honey* . . . we'll pick up your paycheck. . . .

STEVE: I think every performer should get paid once in a while in cash, because, otherwise, you just read about it in the papers how much you make.

JUDY: Yeah. Or how much you've gone *through*. . . .

The "Trunk" segment featured another ad-libbed Garland anecdote, this one centered around her summertime 1957 engagement at the outdoor Greek Theatre in Los Angeles. Judy very amusingly related how a moth flew into her mouth during "Over The Rainbow," explaining that the bug wasn't big enough for the *audience* to have noticed it ("they wouldn't know what I was *doing* if I made a fuss . . ."). Not wanting to break the spell of the plaintive ballad by spitting it out mid-song, her only recourse, she bemusedly remarked, was to "park him" in her cheek as she sang, where the moth fluttered around in her cheek for most of the song. "I had a faster vibrato than ever that night," she joked.

Steve Allen joins Judy for "Tea for Two."
COURTESY RICHARD CONNOLLY

Changing the mood in an instant, Judy mesmerized with "Stormy Weather," her exquisitely shaded, fully realized interpretation, alternately expressing not merely despair in the present but optimism for the future. The effect of seeing Garland's genius here, her purity and power in full bloom, is simply breathtaking.

Judy's choice of "Stormy Weather" over "Alone Together" to wrap up show number five was unwittingly, and imminently, prophetic. The chain of events about to occur at lightning speed over the next few days were to propel Judy Garland into the eye of a CBS cyclone that perhaps not even Dorothy Gale could survive.

10

"All in all, the show was a good thing to have happened to me. I learned a great deal. But if I had known what I was in for, I would never have tried a weekly series. Not ever."

—Judy Garland, 1964

The Waldmans and Johnny Bradford had begun work on the script for the sixth program during the taping days of the Bennett-Shawn hour. The first draft was completed on Friday, August 2, the same day Nat "King" Cole and Jack Carter were to report to CBS Television City for a read-through. The taped dress rehearsal was set for Tuesday, August 6, and the final taping the next night.

The rotating light wall was to reveal Judy, immediately tearing into a rollicking "Sing, You Sinners" to open the hour. Midway into the song, Nat and then Jack were to join her. Following her cue, the audience would clap along (the effect nothing short of a jubilant revival meeting), with Jerry Van Dyke jumping in. The stars would then go into the audience—an enormously effective touch—Nat shouting to the audience, "Everybody on my side, give out!" with Judy then asking only the women in the audience to applaud. Nat, Jack, and Jerry then instructed only the men to clap. As the orchestra played a musical bridge, the four were to ask everyone to join in (returning to the stage) as the dancers swung into their routine. Judy, Nat, and Jack would reappear, Garland ending the number by belting, "You can shoot the devil down in flames, if you'll sing, sing, sing!"

Some Judy-Jerry chitchat led into Jack Carter's stand-up monologue. Judy's solo spot, undecided until the end, was to be perhaps her only performance of Cole Porter's richly melodic "In the Still of the Night." Then Judy and Nat would jump into their medley of several of his signature tunes. The rundown included "Straighten Up and Fly Right" (Nat); "Sweet Lorraine" (Nat); "It's Only a Paper Moon" (Judy alone, then joined by Nat); "The Christmas Song" (Nat); "Nature Boy" (Judy and Nat); "Mona Lisa" (Nat); "Too Young" (Judy and Nat); "Put 'Em in a Box, Tie 'Em with a Ribbon (and Throw 'Em in the Deep Blue Sea)" (Judy and Nat); and Judy and Nat wrapping it up with "Orange-Colored Sky."

The program would be further enriched by Gene Kelly, who would join Judy for the "Tea" spot and perhaps coax her into an impromptu song-and-dance routine of "For Me and My Gal," recreating the memorable moment from the 1942 picture of the same name—patterned after their recent smash performance of the number at the SHARE benefit in May. Frank Waldman, who knew Kelly from their days at MGM, remembers a "marvelous half day at his house," enthusiastically discussing topics, anecdotes, and the "Gal" routine for the "Tea" segment.

Following "Tea for Two" was a Carter-Van Dyke duet of "The Company Way." Judy's "Trunk" closing featured "How About Me?" After "Maybe I'll Come Back," the show would attempt something completely different, with Nat and Jack joining her at the close of the show for a reprise of "Sing, You Sinners."

While the writers completed the final draft, Garland and Schlatter flew to Las Vegas to relax, with George also scouting for potential guests. "I took her to see a group called The Continentals, a totally outrageous, high-class musical act, hip and funny. They'd been together *fifty* years and didn't even *speak* to each other, and it was so funny. I wanted to put them on the show and have Judy do a number with them, put her in the band playing cymbals or something. She got so hysterical at seeing their act that she had to get up and leave the table. She almost fainted with laughter."

The laughter would have abruptly ceased if Schlatter had even had a clue that CBS was patiently waiting his return to set its own covert plans spinning into operation.

Rehearsals had begun by the time George and Judy flew in from Vegas. He immediately headed to Television City. "I walk in and see Freddie and David in the hall. They said, 'George,

we have to talk to you.' I said, 'Not now, I have to get to rehearsal,' and they said, 'No, you don't.' "

A meeting, he was then told, had been scheduled for that
afternoon with Jim Aubrey at his suite at the Bel-Air Hotel. Once
there, it was immediately made clear to the producer that CBS
planned to completely overhaul *The Judy Garland Show*. Schlatter
recounts, "They said, 'She needs a family, she needs regulars,
she needs recurring things, what's wrong with Ken Murray, Bob
Denver, and Cara Williams?' I said, 'Those people don't belong
with Garland!' I said, 'Lena Horne, Tony Bennett, Liza Minnelli,
and Barbra Streisand belong with Garland, not Bob Denver, Cara
Williams, and Ken Murray!' Aubrey said, 'You're being difficult.'
I said, 'I'm being *impossible*! I live with this woman fourteen hours
a day, she calls me in the middle of the night, I go to the house.
This has been a very close thing for a couple of months, and I'm
telling you, don't scare her.' They kept saying, 'The shows are
too special'—they wanted her to be the girl next door."

Bob Lewine says of that fateful meeting, "I was appointed as
the hatchet man. Aubrey was in the room as I made my speech.
I said, 'George, we're not happy with the show. We're going to
change producers,' " further telling him the Garland series would
"be new everything. New writers. Except Bill Hobin." The session, he recalls, "lasted about fifteen minutes. It was quick and
painless. I must say George took it like a soldier."

Adding a double dose of injury to the insult of being uncer-
emoniously dumped, George was told that Norman Jewison was
already being courted to be the new executive producer of *The
Judy Garland Show*—all this happening with the ink barely dry on
the issue of *Variety* quoting Schlatter detailing his ambitious plans
for the program's future.

CBS was aware of some disturbing conclusions drawn from
a national random sampling of audiences asked to view the episodes taped to date. The tests were commissioned by the network without Schlatter's knowledge. Audiences recorded their
impressions of Garland on electronic-reaction devices and on
written comment cards. According to one observer, "They judged
what they were reading about Garland in the newspapers. On
the cards, they commented on what they knew, not what they
saw. They said things like, 'I don't like her, she's nervous,' 'She
seems unhappy,' or 'She drinks.' They felt she was hiding her
real self."

Schlatter and Garland see eye to eye during rehearsals for the Lena Horne hour.
COURTESY GEORGE SCHLATTER

Schlatter's demise, it seemed, was predestined when he not only refused to take Stromberg's advice but deliberately insulted him in the process. "I told Hunt to go play in traffic, that his mother dressed him funny, and to sleep until he felt better!" As George notes, with a bit of pride, "I would think I'd been offensive enough that he probably was the one that got me fired."

Schlatter's unshakable belief in what he held was right with the Garland series was a certain factor in his termination. Conflict, sooner or later, was bound to erupt into war. Confirming this was an unnamed CBS insider who revealed at the time, "He stubbornly resisted our efforts to help improve the show. He would listen to none of our suggestions and insisted, he, as the producer, would do it his way. We had more to lose than he did, so we decided to make a change." (Another network source told *TV Guide* that Schlatter had let production "get out of hand physically and financially.")

Hedda Hopper reported another incident happening that day: "Judy Garland's TV show hit a snag, and it's not her fault. As I get it, producer George Schlatter wanted to put a mold around Judy; CBS wanted to cram her into the same old variety show. Result: George got his walking papers. Judy was low as a snake. Years ago, when MGM fired her after she'd started *Annie Get Your Gun*, she was all done up in an Indian costume, and kept running around the studio saying, 'You can't fire an Indian—I don't even have a reservation!' When George got the ax, he found an Indian warbonnet at CBS and ran into her dressing room yelling, 'I refuse to be fired!' They all had a good laugh." Hopper optimistically, but incorrectly, offered the footnote, "Don't worry. They'll be working together again."

Schlatter also dealt with the disgruntled guest stars with humor. "Nat said, 'Well, they canceled the show because I'm *black*,' and Jack Carter said, 'No, they canceled the show because I'm *Jewish*.' And I said, 'No, they canceled it because I'm *difficult*!' " The guests were as oblivious to the turmoil as everyone else. "We were in George's office discussing what Nat was going to do," says Bill Hobin. "The music was set, the sets were being made, Nat knew what he was going to do with Judy. We were all set to go." The guests, apparently, were dropped as quickly and as unexpectedly as Schlatter. When Nat was offered a subsequent booking with Garland for December, he retorted, "Well, I'll just take my sweet time about deciding on that one!" (His bitterness over the experience caused him to decline the offer.)

CBS vice president Stromberg dismissed the tumultuous immediate state of the Garland series, instead focusing on its future. "Any weekly show has to be formatted," he stated. "There have to be standard compartments that audiences look forward to, like Garry Moore's 'That Wonderful Year.' " CBS also planned to take Judy Garland off her superstar pedestal, according to Stromberg: "It's important that the audience should not be afraid to like the star. Judy is too unreachable." The already-sacked Schlatter retorted, "Since Garland is one of the giants, I felt her show required a different kind of television. I couldn't do a show with tracing paper."

Barely absorbing this initial shock, the staff soon learned that

Schlatter was not the only one on the CBS chopping block. As Lewine had told Schlatter at the Bel-Air Hotel, also dismissed were the three writers, Tom Waldman, Frank Waldman, and Johnny Bradford, along with choreographer Danny Daniels.

Daniels remains bitter about his firing: "I was rehearsing a number with Nat that first day of production. Then I went back to the house and got a call that evening from some secretary who said, 'You don't have to come in tomorrow morning.' I said, 'What do you mean, I haven't finished the number, I haven't finished my work.' She said, 'I was just told to tell you that you don't have to come in tomorrow.' And that's how I was told. I was friendly with Johnny [Bradford], and I gave him a call. I said, 'Johnny, what the hell is happening with the show?' He said, 'I know, I was fired, too.' I went in the next day to pick up my gear, and I passed the Waldman brothers, and they were very cold to me. I thought, Jesus, they didn't even say anything to me. I didn't realize they were fired, too. None of us knew. I think everybody thought that they were the only ones who got fired until the word got around several days later that the whole show had been changed over. It was a high-level decision, and handled very, very shabbily."

Waldman tells a similar story: "We went to work and worked a full day. John Bradford called my house around ten at night and said, 'We've been fired.' I couldn't believe it." Adds Johnny Bradford, "We were on a big emotional high. We thought we had the hit of the century. It was such a bolt from the blue when we were all fired."

CBS, curiously, refrained from disclosing that others had been fired at the same time, the story not surfacing until a few days later. The move backfired, however, resulting in two separate, equally prominent stories that only further ingrained within the press and public alike the sense of desperate chaos swirling about *The Judy Garland Show*.

Not long after, Judy described her feelings about the Schlatter purge: "Everybody went. I thought I was going, too. They swept out a whole bunch of people, and whoever got caught up in that whisk of a broom was out. I wish somebody would have warned me in advance—maybe I could have avoided anyone's being decapitated. I was stunned and bewildered. It came as such a shock." CBS executive Lewine dismisses the notion that Garland played a role in Schlatter's demise. "Judy did what she was told. She was as confused as anybody on that show."

There was also considerable dissension among Garland's production staff in concluding whether it was CBS—or Judy—who ordered Schlatter's termination. A pivotal scene in *The Other Side of the Rainbow* recounts a conversation between Mel Tormé and an embattled Orval Paine. Mel quotes Judy's hairdresser as saying, "Aubrey didn't fire Schlatter. Garland fired him! I was there, with her, in the room, when she gave the orders to can him. She got CBS to take the rap, because she didn't want to be the heavy; but take my word, it was all Judy's idea!"

Orval insists that the entire conversation was fabricated by Tormé, stating adamantly, "What he wrote is a lie. I never made any kind of statement like that to Mel or anyone else. I never at any time felt that way about Judy. It was not my place to make statements to anyone about Judy or about what she might, or might not, do if she didn't like something or somebody."

Bill Hobin was as mystified as everyone else on staff. "She was really swinging with it, and we were all swinging together." The director further explains, "There was no disharmony on the staff, and everything was going smoothly. We all got along, and we were proud of it, and it was exciting."

Hobin and his wife were at home entertaining out-of-town friends when Bob Lewine's secretary phoned, telling him that the CBS executive wanted to see him at Television City at once. "I walked down the hall on the third floor, and here's George standing by a coffee machine, white as a sheet, in real shock, holding his cup of coffee. He said, 'I guess you're one of the ones that didn't get fired.' " Schlatter explained that Bradford and the Waldmans had been axed as well. "I asked him why. He said, 'I don't know.' "

Gary Smith and Mel Tormé were in Lewine's office. Hobin continues, "Lewine explained, 'Well, Aubrey decided they wanted to make changes, but they wanted to keep us. They loved our work, and we were the three to stay on.' He said, 'Take two weeks off and come back and we'll get started again.' I didn't know whether George being fired would revert back to them asking me to produce or not. Meanwhile, Gary had gotten associate-producer credit and was eager, I could tell. As Mel and I left, Bob said, 'Gary, can you stay a minute.' Gary called me at home and said, 'They offered me the job as producer. Do you think I ought to take it?' I said, 'Do you want it?,' and he said, 'Yeah, I really do.' He asked, 'It wouldn't upset you?' and I said no, and good luck."

The CBS overhaul caused Hobin to leave after his contracted thirteen episodes. "There was a different feeling. I went home that evening, and my wife and I talked it over. I said, 'Don't plan on coming back, so pack everything.' " When things looked bright for the future of the series, Bill had put his new Scarsdale home up for sale; he now took it off the market. Hobin's disenchantment had actually begun when the series was moved from New York to Los Angeles; he learned of the switch just after buying a home in Scarsdale. "First I was told it would be done in New York, then they said the first show would be done in Hollywood because Judy wants to do them in Hollywood. I said, 'Okay, I'll go to California for a while,' and later we all would come back and do the show from New York. After I heard about this, I called my manager and said, Look, I want a stipulation in my contract that if it doesn't come back to New York, I want out after thirteen weeks. CBS agreed to it." (CBS, however, kept the lid on Hobin's departure until several months later, giving the mistaken, but widely held, impression that Garland's temperament caused him to walk after thirteen shows.)

News of the Garland-show upset broke two days later on Monday, August 5, leading one TV critic to say, "The singer's series may be the most awaited program of the autumn. It certainly has stirred up the most excitement."

CBS attempted to deal with its dismissal of Schlatter as diplomatically as possible, Bob Lewine issuing the official CBS statement: "We are delighted with the five shows that have been produced by Mr. Schlatter and deeply regret the differences of opinion as to the course of future production on the show. The network will continue production . . . as scheduled. We expect to name the new producer in the immediate future." *Variety*'s report of Schlatter's ousting carried the headline WE LOVE YOU, BUT YOU'RE FIRED!, which was, noted the paper, "the current gag around Hollywood."

Lewine also released Garland's rather terse official comment: "I am deeply sorry that CBS and Mr. Schlatter could not reconcile their differences."

The *Saturday Evening Post*'s Richard Warren Lewis later wrote of the happy Schlatter days: "When her guest stars were before the cameras, Judy encouraged them like a carefree schoolgirl, bouncing around out of camera range and leading the audience's applause. Often, blasé technicians, stagehands and control-room occupants would break into unabashed cheers after one of Judy's own numbers."

It remained uncertain if, and when, Nat "King" Cole and Jack Carter were to appear on the show later. Suspended for the moment were guests already booked by the Schlatter team, including upcoming appearances by Wayne Newton, comedian Shelley Berman, Steve Lawrence and his wife, Eydie Gorme, Betty Grable, and Dan Dailey (scheduled on the same show to be taped the end of August), and the Wiere Brothers, who were to report to CBS on August 12. Other signed guests caught in the shuffle were Phil Harris and wife Alice Faye, along with comedian Bob Newhart.

In spite of the uncertainty of it all, *The Judy Garland Show*, said CBS, would resume production in three weeks.

George refused to comment on the termination of his thirteen-week contract at first, later abridging the chain of events by saying, "Nobody at CBS even talked to me, even though Bob Lewine made the announcement. I was stopped in the hall by Dave Begelman and Freddie Fields . . . and told I was through." He absolved Judy of playing any part in his dismissal, gallantly noting, "I never worked with a more cooperative star, and she was always on the set before I got there. It was fun working with her, and that I'm going to miss. A finer performer it has never been my pleasure to work with."

The Hollywood Reporter on August 6 ran a curious squib that Judy was "after George Schlatter to head up her Kingsrow Productions." While the item might have been nothing more than an effort to stress that Garland had nothing to do with Schlatter being fired, if it held even a grain of truth, it is no less interesting. Just before the problems with CBS came to full boil, Judy (and Kingsrow) signed a new three-year pact with CMA on July 24. Pressure from Aubrey as well as from her managers to dump Schlatter gave her no choice but to comply. If the report was accurate, it certainly indicates Judy trusted George completely. It also perhaps suggests—in spite of her re-signing with CMA only days before—that the specter of Sid Luft's warnings about

Fields and Begelman as well as the disturbing possibilities raised by the Steinberg audit still weighed heavily on Judy's mind. Schlatter taking over Kingsrow would mean that Fields and Begelman would be under his scrutiny. (Only three days before the item appeared, accountant Steinberg filed suit in Superior Court against Kingsrow for $12,312 to recover unpaid fees for services rendered from April 9—when Judy, on Sid's advice, turned over to Steinberg her financial records—through July.)

Schlatter, understandably, chose not to relinquish his highly creative role as television producer to scrutinize Garland's business affairs; he announced a few days later that he was leaving town briefly to get "straightened out" where the climate was more "salubrious."

Schlatter had sweet vindication when CBS, much to its surprise, came under fire from the powerful advertising agencies that represented Garland's four sponsors. Said *Variety*, "All four ad agencies representing sponsors of [the series] were in a state of bewilderment this week as to the reasons behind the firing. . . . Bespeaking sentiments of the others, Jack McQueen, TV head of Foote, Cone & Belding, said, 'I've seen all five shows and they are all very excellent. We are highly pleased. They must have serious internal problems.' . . . Other agency reps who have viewed tapes of all or most of the five completed shows agreed with McQueen and so advised their clients."

Speculation that Norman Jewison was already being wooed for Garland's show came immediately on the heels of Schlatter's termination. While still negotiating with the producer-director, CBS went so far as to project that, if Jewison accepted, Smith would retain his new title of producer. Furthermore, Smith was the front-runner should Jewison decline the CBS bid, as well as being in line to succeed Jewison upon his departure after completing the thirteenth episode.

The choice to pursue Norman Jewison for Garland was hardly a surprise. He had produced and directed her universally acclaimed comeback special. Equally important, Norman worked well with Judy and had maintained a friendship with her. Although it was reported at the time that Garland unsuccessfully pursued Jewison to produce and direct her 1963 special, not publicly revealed was the fact that Jewison was Garland's first choice to produce and direct her series.

However, in mid-February, Judy somehow located Norman

deep in the woods of Canada "in a cabin on the lake and totally inaccessible. A man came in a motorboat with a telegram. The telegram said, 'Call immediately. We need you. We're at the Fairmont Hotel in San Francisco,' signed, Judy, David, and Freddie. I drove twenty miles to a phone booth and called them. Judy answered the phone. They had made the deal with Aubrey for Judy to do a weekly series, which I had pleaded with Freddie and David not to ask Judy to do. I suggested that, after the success of the special, she do four specials a year, and between those specials, do concerts. I felt, in that way, the legend would be preserved, and it would not demand that much. I said, 'You can't do it every week.' I didn't think Judy was the type of personality able to handle that kind of a grind. My friend Danny Kaye was also doing a weekly show, and he was the kind of personality who could do it. But Judy wasn't."

"I told her not to do it," Jewison states. "I tried to convince her not to. I felt they were wrong in doing [a series] because I felt it would be a disaster in trying to do too much. When you're on the air every week, you become too accessible."

Jewison's advice, however valid, was ignored. It was too late. The deal with CBS had already been made. It became clear to Norman that money was the prime motivating factor. "Freddie shook his head and said, 'This is her chance, and she needs the money,' " Jewison recalls. "The weekly show was budgeted at about a hundred-fifty-thousand dollars a week. The decision, I think, was an economic one. There was a lot of money involved."

And even if Jewison had wanted to be part of Garland's series, prior commitments (including a feature film and a Broadway show) made his participation in a projected thirty-two episodes impossible.

Now, in July 1963, Garland, Fields, and Begelman zealously went after him again. With Jewison representing perhaps the very survival of the series, they were prepared to do whatever necessary to get him—Judy's boundless optimism of only one month earlier inexorably erased by sheer panic.

"I got this frantic phone call," reveals Jewison, "and I said, 'What's this about?' Freddie and David said they'd done four shows and 'We need you and we're in trouble,' because Aubrey was disenchanted." Jewison was available at the moment (having just withdrawn from *Here's Love,* a new Broadway-bound musical by Meredith Willson of *Music Man* fame), but his participation in the Garland series would have to cease at the end of November, when he had to report to Universal for the Doris Day picture *Send Me No Flowers.*

Norman agreed to consider temporarily coming on board to revamp the show to CBS's satisfaction. To a shaken, confused Judy, those early pleas begging her not to attempt a weekly series had become chillingly prophetic—but, conversely, the same wisdom might be the very answer to making the series a hit.

The network turned its focus on finding a new writing group for Garland. Television veteran Cy Howard was the first writer to be approached by CBS. On Monday, August 12, *The New York Times* (erroneously) reported that Howard had been signed to write "special comedy material" but would not be part of the regular writing staff. The paper also noted that Gary Smith had left New York the day before (where Judy and Gary, among others, had been in meetings at CBS) for Hollywood, where he was to interview writers for the new staff.

CBS executive Oscar Katz recalls a memorable moment with Garland during this time in New York: "Judy wanted to thank the people in the East who had been of help in launching the show. She sat in my office and, one by one, I called up the vice presidents, and she thanked them individually. They were all bowled over."

New York–based Bob Wells flew to Hollywood, where he was offered the position of head writer. He reportedly declined the job, having been under the impression that he would be coproducer with Gary Smith as well; another factor was said to be that he was uncomfortable assuming the very same job from which his brother, Johnny Bradford, had been fired. In any event, Wells, in short order, returned to New York. CBS then unsuccessfully pursued the writing team of Robert E. Lee and Jerome Lawrence (who had the stage hit *Auntie Mame* among their credits) to head Garland's writing staff.

As the search for writers intensified, so did the efforts to secure Norman Jewison. "I went to New York, and my agent said Aubrey wanted to see me," recounts Jewison. "Aubrey said, 'I want you to come right in and do this.' My agents asked for a lot of money, and he said no problem. He was tough. He was,

I thought, very abusive about the show and about the talent he was dealing with. I didn't think he had enough respect for the talent, but I had been all through this before with network executives and studio heads. I didn't get along with him very well. I suggested at one point that if he knew so much about it, why didn't he produce the show. So he cooled off. He gave me a mandate that I had total control. I came out to Hollywood."

Although Bob Lewine remembers Jewison already having committed to Garland at the time Schlatter was fired, newspaper and trade press reports dutifully charted the progress of the CBS-Jewison talks over a period of several weeks. CBS and Jewison did not come to mutual agreement until the third week of the month, and the deal was reportedly not finalized until August 22. The week before, when CBS learned that the still-unsigned Jewison was available for only eight episodes, Bob Lewine promptly announced the network's new plan: "If all goes well after thirteen weeks of shows, Gary Smith would take over in the next cycle."

Norman Jewison did not come without a hefty price tag. His astounding, unheard-of salary of $12,500 per episode sent shock waves through the industry. The pressures on Garland from CBS only worsened as the show's weekly budget jumped from $160,000 to more than $200,000—absorbing the costs of Jewison's salary, settling contracts of terminated staff members for shows not produced, and additional wages for new production personnel. The Garland series undoubtedly would more than ever be scrutinized—and criticized—by the network.

Underscoring Stromberg's influence over Aubrey, Jerry Van Dyke—the weakest visible link of the series—was passed along to Norman Jewison without contest.

Immediately upon his signing, Jewison became aware of the clash of egos among those involved in the Garland series. States Jewison, "The pressure from Aubrey was incredible, especially behind Freddie's back, David's back, and Judy's back, because he would talk to me differently than he talked to anyone else. Aubrey was totally perverse. He would come down, put his arms around Judy, paint yellow brick roads for her, and all of this stuff, and then turn around and come into a production meeting and stab everybody in the back and say the most awful things about Judy and the show."

Ernie Flatt joined the Garland show as choreographer. Writers Arne Sultan and Marvin Worth signed as the new head writers (at ten thousand dollars per week); Canadian writer-producer Bernie Rothman (formerly of the Canadian Broadcasting Company) and William Nichols (*The Bell Telephone Hour*) were subsequently hired to complete the writing staff.

Sultan indicated he was prepared to fly in direct opposition to the foundation laid by George Schlatter. "Television is a habit. You can't be an event every week. If you do five shows that are each different, you are dead. There's got to be some sameness. If we had that, maybe we'd win some of the Art Linkletter–type fans. That's what keeps you on the air."

Norman Jewison said at the time, "People don't really know Judy Garland. On television, you go into millions of homes and actually expose yourself as a personality. That's how we got to know Jack Paar and Perry Como. . . . We have to do the same thing with Judy. The first thing I said to her was, 'Let's be honest, absolutely honest. I love it when you say, "Yeah, I used to be fat." Are you supposed to hide that?' Many people have a weight problem. I thought Judy should be allowed to express herself."

Norman Jewison now reveals the more important topic that was part of that first conversation: "I sat in the trailer. It was the two of us, alone. I explained to her that there were certain problems, and I would take care of those problems and she no longer had to worry about anything except the next week's show. I said, 'It's got to be like it was when we worked before. Nobody goes out to the house. You can't get in, okay, stay at home, don't worry about it. That's not where shows are done. We've got to get a show on the air every week, we're here, and it's taking fifteen hours a day, six days a week.' She came around. She said, 'Don't worry, I'll come down.'

"I took both of her hands in mine, looked her in the eye, and made her a promise. I said, 'I will get you renewed. That's what I'm here for. Don't worry about it. We're going to knock their socks off.' She [responded to] my enthusiasm, my positiveness, and my faith, my constant faith, in her talents. And she knew I would never tell her a lie. I always told her straight what was happening. There were certain things I wouldn't tell her, that Aubrey had said, or someone had said, but I would never lie to her."

When Norman assured Judy he would take care of "certain

problems," one of them, in his eyes, was Mel Tormé. "Mel is a brilliant musicologist as well as a brilliant singer. He was very concerned about his [guest] spots on the show. I thought he was a little more concerned with himself than with the show, so I tried to bring him around to where he was contributing more to the overall production of the show. Not allowing him to use the show as a vehicle of his own. I guess he didn't like that, but I felt it was essential."

Norman even approached Kay Thompson to replace Mel. "Judy adored Kay. Kay was better with her than Mel was. I wanted Kay desperately, but she said, 'I can't. We did a wonderful show [the 1962 special], let's not spoil something that was so wonderful.' "

At this time, one of Stromberg's projected members for Garland's "television family," Marion Lorne (the befuddled character actress of *Mr. Peepers* television fame), was said to be in the running to join the series as a regular along with onetime candidate Jonathan Winters. (Neither Lorne nor Winters was ultimately signed.)

Throughout this period of rampant instability, Judy steadfastly maintained an unperturbed public stance, even joking, "Thousands of dollars were bet in Las Vegas that I wouldn't even do the first three shows—they thought I wasn't going to finish a performance or even show up!" Yet Judy entered Cedars of Lebanon Hospital on August 26 for what was described as her "routine annual check-up."

To Jewison, the hospital stay was not unexpected. He was alarmed at the "enormous" change in Judy since they had worked together on the Sinatra special when she was in far more robust emotional and physical condition. "I thought she was being drained of every bit of energy she had, and every bit of talent she had," Jewison reveals. "She was being asked to carry a show every week, and I didn't think it was right. I tried desperately to help her and distribute some of that weight."

The Cedars stay forced Garland to cancel a quick London and Paris trip, along with plans to attend a nationally televised civil rights march on Washington on August 28; she would have participated along with thirty-five other top stars, including Marlon Brando, Burt Lancaster, Jack Benny, and Kirk Douglas. Although Judy left Cedars after only two days (joking that she got "an A-plus on all my tests"), she had to immediately plunge into meetings at the Beverly Hills Hotel with Aubrey, Dann, and Jewison, among others, about the "new look" of her series.

According to Garland biographer Gerold Frank, the Lufts had an emotional telephone conversation that same night. She told him, "I still want a divorce, Sid. I still need a divorce. I need your respect," but added, "I still think you're a hell of a wonderful son of a bitch." The matter of the fifty-thousand-dollar blackmail paid by Judy also came up, with Sid insisting that the photo of her getting her stomach pumped never existed. She countered that she had seen it, remarking, "It was so ugly. . . . It put me through agony to have to pay, but it would have been worse agony for it to be shown." The evening ended in an affectionate truce of sorts.

The following afternoon, August 30, Judy videotaped an interview with *Variety* columnist Army Archerd that would first be made available to television editors. After a two-week exclusivity period, local CBS stations were allowed to edit the tape for use in promotional spots. (Archerd, in early September, taped similar interviews with Phil Silvers and Danny Kaye.) Although Archerd recalls Garland being tardy for the taping—and a bit distracted—he found her to be quite charming.

In her effort to shed a most positive light around her upcoming series, Judy failed to tell him that she had just filed an injunction against her estranged husband to keep him away from her home after he allegedly scaled a high-wire fence at eight-thirty that morning. It is no wonder, then, that Garland was preoccupied with other thoughts during the Archerd interview.

In the legal complaint, Judy stated Sid had climbed the fence to obtain entry to the Rockingham house, whereupon he "terrorized" the servants and "removed personal possessions." Such actions caused Judy and the children, she said in her complaint, to live in a "constant state of apprehension and terror." Guards, it was noted, were on twenty-four-hour duty patrol to keep Sid away from her home. The legal complaint was likely a misdirected attempt to exert some sort of control over her life, increasingly chaotic since she was powerless against the forces of CBS and CMA, and unable to control the destiny of the television series bearing her name.

The Hollywood Reporter that same month certainly added to

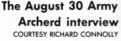

The August 30 Army
Archerd interview
COURTESY RICHARD CONNOLLY

Judy's mounting insecurities with the item "CBS-TV topper Jim Aubrey won't deny he tunes to NBC every Thursday night to study Vic Damone on his [summer-replacement series] *The Lively Ones*. We hear Damone's virtually set to warm the bench as a mid-season replacement for any CBS live show that drops dead." And in another report in the trade paper that same month: "It must be somewhat nerve-wracking for stars of new series to know that their webs already are lining up mid-season replacements before even the ax of public rejection is sharpened." Steve Lawrence and Eydie Gorme, the paper stated, were waiting in the wings with *Song-a-Minute* for a January premiere "if a certain new live-on-tape hour show peters out."

Also alarming Judy was the news that the producers of Garland's last film, *I Could Go On Singing*, were considering writing a "tell-all" book about the problem-laden production, which coincided with a particularly intense child-custody battle between Judy and Sid.

The stirring up of these painful, bitter fights perhaps helped trigger this new vendetta against Sid, further exacerbated by their emotional discussion and talk of divorce the night before. Whatever the motives, a restraining order was issued, and Luft was to appear in court on September 5 to answer the charges against him; at that time, Judy was awarded custody of Joe and Lorna, and Sid was granted visitation rights.

Ironically, Judy learned that Steve Lawrence and Eydie Gorme—whom Aubrey had ready to replace Garland if she failed—had been booked for separate guest appearances on her show. And in yet another twist of fate, Steve Lawrence was set as the guest for the very first Jewison-produced hour. (June Allyson would also appear on that show.) The notion that his success on her series might well trigger Aubrey's decision to dump Garland in Lawrence's favor could hardly have been an amusing one to Judy. (Eydie was first announced for a September 11 tape date, but in the end the singer would never appear on Garland's series.)

Judy tasted a bit of sweet revenge in 1965 when Steve Lawrence finally got his chance to headline a weekly variety series on CBS. The network seemingly had not learned much from the Garland experience—the singer was flanked by comedian Charles Nelson Reilly as *his* second banana. The series lasted only four months.

September began with the announcements that comedians Jonathan Winters and Dick Shawn were set for a minimum of two guest spots each with Garland. Norman Jewison (in the wings of the Greek Theatre) negotiated a deal with Harry Belafonte as the latter took bows after a performance on the basis that Belafonte would have his own twenty-minute solo spot. These announcements were to prove as unreliable as reports that Judy likely would tape one or two shows in New York during Christmas.

Judy also attended a rather unusual social gathering the first weekend of the month. Debbie Reynolds and her husband Harry Karl hosted an informal gathering for The Reverend Billy Graham. The low-key reception began late in the evening after the conclusion of Graham's "Los Angeles Crusade" spiritual services. Invited to the Karls' Beverly Hills home were Judy, Edie Adams, Jack Lemmon and his wife, Felicia Farr, opera singer Mary Costa, renowned hairstylist Sydney Guilaroff, and Glenn Ford, accompanied by his mother. Offered coffee and cookies instead of alcohol, the guests were assembled in the den when the minister and an assistant, former actress Joan Winmill Brown, arrived. Judy had not yet appeared.

When someone asked the Reverend Graham, "What is sin?," his response was followed by Judy opening the door. She stood there for a moment and hesitated, thinking she had interrupted Billy's response. Judy quietly moved to the sofa and sat next to the minister's assistant. When Billy asked Joan to speak of the events in her life that led to her strong religious convictions, Judy, she recalled, "looked at me and smiled that beautiful smile, as if in encouragement." Joan then candidly told the group of the painful events that had led her to contemplate suicide before finding peace with renewed spiritual beliefs. Her emotional outpouring was greeted with uncomfortable silence.

Sensing her discomfort, Judy put her hand on Joan's arm saying, "That was beautiful, darling. But you see, you had a need. I don't have any need." Rendered speechless by this remark, Joan was stunned as much by the strength of Judy's conviction as she was by what she perceived as a most heightened case of denial.

Yet within forty-eight hours of Judy's encounter with Billy Graham, a miracle—at least it seemed within the television industry—occurred. George Schlatter and CBS executive Mike Dann were spotted in deep discussions ("just talking," they said) poolside at the posh Beverly Hills Hotel. The talks were the direct result of Judy's quiet demand to CBS that Schlatter be reinstated, after Jewison's exit, as the new executive producer. Finally, it seemed that the network was listening to Judy Garland.

And the show was back on track. Armed with a new producer, new writers, and a new format, *The Judy Garland Show* would tape its first Jewison-produced hour on September 13— Friday the thirteenth.

11

The night after Sid Luft was awarded visitation rights to see Lorna and Joey, he and his estranged wife had another stormy confrontation. At the Rockingham house following Sid's dinner with his children, Judy appeared and, most unexpectedly, asked him to stay for a drink. As Luft related in Gerold Frank's biography, *Judy*, she told him, "I owe you a great deal, I really do" and wrote him a check in the amount of ten thousand dollars.

After mixing drinks, Judy's mood abruptly darkened. She told him, "I'm so fucking mad at you—to think that we could be so good, so right together, but you're insisting on digging up all our past financial troubles. I want to forget it, darling." He warned her that problems would soon surface regarding income-tax returns dating back several years. Judy wanted to hear none of it. "You just take care of the goddamned income tax. Do it, and I don't want to hear about it. I'll do my shows, and don't interfere. Don't bother me, or else I'll be so upset I'll blow the whole thing."

The evening ended badly, with Sid tearing up the check and storming out of the house, only to be stopped for several minutes by a petulant Judy, who refused, at first, to open the gates to let him exit the premises.

With Sid out of the picture, Judy turned elsewhere for romance. And so, not long after Debbie Reynolds's reception for

Billy Graham, Judy and Glenn Ford became an item—the second time around, as they had dated briefly some twenty years before.

During the taping hiatus, Norman Jewison had the opportunity to view the handful of Garland programs that had been produced before he entered the picture. "I didn't think the first were as bad as Aubrey said they were," admits Jewison. "I think perhaps they weren't getting the best out of Judy, and that they were working the show more around her, instead of demanding something of her and helping her."

"Garland called me at home," chuckles George Schlatter, "and said, 'Wait until you hear this—Norman loved the shows!' "

New staff writer Bernie Rothman felt even more positively about the previous regime's efforts after screening the videotapes at CBS. "Of the five shows, three were excellent, one was good, and one was so-so. I might have been green, but I knew about averages—I'd settle for that anytime. I went back to the [Garland] offices and said, 'They're fantastic!' and Norman said, 'That's exactly what CBS *doesn't* want us to do!' Aubrey had tested the shows and found out what any one of us could have told him in advance: Judy is a very special lady, and one who is enormously gifted. But she's a very rich dessert. I think the network panicked. What they said was, 'Schlatter and those people are writing it wrong,' which was not true at all. George and his group did very fine Judy Garland shows. But [CBS] wanted Judy to be Dinah Shore. That also made it difficult because I think she sensed that, and sensed that it wasn't going to be a big hit."

To open his batch of Garland episodes, Jewison established a quick, upbeat Garland solo, with Tormé fashioning special lyrics to introduce the guests that week as enormous photo blowups of the stars (printed as negatives) were carted out by the dancers. Just as the guest walked out from behind the blowup, a negative image appeared for a moment; the photo then turned to a positive image while Judy and guest were seen in reversed tones. The first attempt was a Garland production number of "Life Is Just a Bowl of Cherries" with brief appearances by Steve Lawrence and June Allyson. (Only the first four of the eight Jewison-produced hours maintained this opening format, however.)

The overall look of the entire hour was substantially modified as well, reflecting not only the work of Gary Smith and his assistant Gene McAvoy but also newcomer Robert Kelly. Smith's backstage theatrical motif was banished forever. The sets became less abstract, a bit more scaled down but no less sophisticated. And in the desire to form continuity from week to week, much of the nonmusical scripted dialogue was to take place in front of a pair of white latticed shutters that pulled apart at the center to reveal a full set, most likely for a musical number. The goal of conforming *The Judy Garland Show* to all other variety programs of the day had been achieved. But to the credit of the gifted talents involved, it still managed, more often than not, to rise above the average.

Robert Kelly was "terribly flattered" that Gary Smith asked him to leave a staff position at NBC to join the Garland series. "It took me a couple of shows to get my legs under me," he confesses, "because I was a little afraid at first. I liked working with Norman enormously. He was a very nice, very talented man, and he held the show together with a firm but kind hand. And Judy responded to him, too."

Kelly quickly became attuned to the tremendously fast-paced work required for the weekly episodes. "There was no time to do a lot of sketches, have them accepted, signed, and then have them built, decorated, and lit, ready and onstage as they were about to shoot the program. I'd take a little piece of paper during production meetings, and scribble things on the back of an envelope or something. And that's what we'd go from."

He defines the difference between the Schlatter episodes and the Jewison-produced hours: "The sets had up to then been sort of monolithic and hard-edged." In creating richer, more eye-filling sets, Kelly remembers no budgetary restrictions. "But I was never a big money-spender on shows. I don't like big, heavy, cumbersome, unmovable sets. My training early on was in the theater, and it just transferred itself to television."

Beginning with this episode, Mel Tormé's continuing "Be My Guest" special material was introduced, which would be tailored to fit each week's guest. While the six subsequent episodes utilizing "Be My Guest" slotted it at the near-beginning of the hour as a device for Judy to introduce the guests and chat with them for a few moments, here it would appear well into the show. In "Be My Guest," Steve musically reminded Judy of her once-rotund figure, causing her to mock-grimace for effect.

Jewison and the writers opted to diminish Garland's image

June Allyson, Steve Lawrence, and Judy (sans pants) rehearsing the "MGM" medley
COURTESY KIM LUNDGREEN

as "The Legend." With Jewison acknowledging, "Judy had, per-haps, the greatest sense of humor of any actress I have ever worked with," he and his stable of writers attempted to build upon that by debunking Garland's legendary status in hopes of making her more accessible and identifiable to the mass viewing audience. Jerry Van Dyke's character, to bolster this new ap-proach, discarded his "bumbling host" persona in favor of being a glib, know-it-all "expert" in television who would teach "new kid on the block" Garland the TV ropes.

And while Judy and Jerry bantered at a faster clip, the Sul-tan-Worth-Rothman-Nichols team served Garland and company no better than had the Bradford-Waldman brothers trio. The opening Judy-Jerry dialogue for this episode had Jerry encourage Judy to talk to the television audience so that viewers would "get to know her" on a more personal level. Taking his advice, Judy turned to the camera, and admitted that she looked "terri-ble" without makeup, had to "watch her weight," and was "very emotional." As Judy exited to sing "Happiness Is a Thing Called Joe," Jerry cracked, "I don't know how she got this far."

Arne Sultan told the *Saturday Evening Post* that in efforts to "humanize" Garland, the scripts developed a "subtle system of de-glamorizing her by pointing up her problems. We're just being honest." Concluded *Post* writer Richard Warren Lewis, "Instead of guests idolizing her, they say things on the air to denigrate her. The remarks are more painful than funny."

TV Guide's Dwight Whitney attended a late-afternoon rehearsal session for the Allyson-Lawrence show, which was marked by an "on" Judy chatting with old pal "Junie." Beginning to sing, she stopped to laugh, "But this is such a silly song!" Judy, wrote Whitney, was not as high-spirited when she departed from the group for a one-on-one talk with the reporter. She told him that she was "surprised but not disappointed" when Schlatter was fired, surprised because she "didn't know anything was wrong."

He recounts that she said to him—"tonelessly and without much conviction"—that the series was "fun," adding, "You see, I've always played characters and have never been allowed to show my real self before." Perhaps she was echoing Hunt Stromberg: "On the first couple of shows, she was on a pedestal. Now, in a lighthearted way, we are debunking this glamor. She's one of the gang."

No wonder people on the show saw a noticeable change in Judy when they resumed work after the lengthy five-week hiatus. "By stopping the momentum built up in the first five shows, they took a big gamble," said one observer at the time. "But after that break, Judy seemed to sort of fall apart and has never come out of it. She never recovered from the shock of being told the show wasn't good."

Not helping matters was June Allyson's insecurity about performing after the recent death of her husband, actor-producer Dick Powell. As Robert Kelly says of his first Garland episode, "If I was nervous, you should have seen June Allyson. Poor thing, I felt so sorry for her. She was absolutely physically trembling. She hadn't been on a stage in years."

As June revealed to show business reporter Bob Thomas at the time, "It was Judy who made me go back to work." Except for one appearance on a filmed television drama, she had been professionally inactive since Powell's death that January. Not long after, Judy spotted June in a restaurant. "She came over to my table and started to bawl me out. She told me, 'You look terrible! You don't even look like a movie star. Your eyes are all red. Have you been spending all your time crying in the back room?' I had to admit that I had. 'All right,' she said, 'I need you, and you're going to help me out.' " In curlers during rehearsals, June joked that the MGM executives used to say to her, " 'Don't start thinking you're great, because Judy is the big star around here.' The reason we're both so short is that they kept beating us down!"

Newly signed choreographer Ernie Flatt remembers Garland's terror—which apparently brought on a severe case of laryngitis—at facing a collection of top-ranked CBS executives gathered to observe the refurbished Garland show under the direction of Aubrey's right-hand man, Hunt Stromberg, Jr. "All the CBS bigwigs were upstairs, waiting to be told when to come down. And Judy was in her dressing room and wouldn't come out. Norman was trying to get in to talk to her and to get her out. She wouldn't budge. At one point, he came over to me and said, 'Ernie, can you think of anything that we can do to get in there, to tell her that she's got to come out?' At that moment, a guy came with some flowers and asked where he could find Miss Garland. He pointed to her trailer door, and I looked at Norman, and we followed him. When he knocked on the door, it opened a crack, and he said, 'These flowers are for Miss Garland.' When the door opened to take the flowers, we went in. Inside was a makeup room, and he said to the dresser, 'Where is she?' We went into the room, and she was sitting very close to the door and the hairdresser was working on her hair. We stuck our heads in and said hi. She said, 'I'm so nervous. I don't know what I'm doing, I don't know my lyrics,' I don't know this and I don't know that. She was just a basket case. Norman said, in a nice way, 'Well, Judy, that's why you need to come to rehearsals more.' She started calling him every filthy name you could think of. My head was under his in the doorway, and I couldn't get my head out. I thought the whole thing was funny. I said to her, 'Nevertheless, we have to get out of here and do the show,' and she saw the humor, and instantly her whole attitude changed. We stepped out, and in about fifteen minutes the door opened, and Judy came out holding Norman's elbow."

CBS executive Ethel Winant remembers that, unbeknownst to Judy or June, the network was not too keen about the onetime

MGM star appearing with Garland. "Who in their right mind would have put June Allyson on that show? Yes, she might have been the number-one box-office star for ten years, but she wasn't when we used her. Although she sang in movies, it's different from getting her up onstage where you can't support her. She also was a drunk."

According to virtually everyone present at the tapings, Judy, but particularly June, felt the need to fortify herself with a bit of Blue Nun; each perhaps for her own reasons, but the results were just the same. The Garland-Allyson show reflected the too-relaxed atmosphere of the taping—but with occasional, unexpectedly delightful results. Their what-the-hell, off-the-cuff dish-fest is marvelously spontaneous and "inside":

JUNE: You really have to tell them about how they pitted us against each other . . .

JUDY: Yeah, it was terrible. We're talking about Metro.

(BOTH JUMPING IN AT THE SAME TIME, GIVING A LOOK TO THE CAMERA AS IF TO FILL IN THE AUDIENCE, SAYING SIMULTANEOUSLY:)

JUDY & JUNE: That's *Metro-Goldwyn-Mayer!*

JUDY: We were both sort of raised there.

JUNE: . . . We were very young.

JUDY: *Then.* Forget it *now!* She was coming out from New York, she'd just done *Best Foot Forward.* And she was coming out to take my place, you know, when I really failed . . . and I hadn't even failed yet . . . the *first* time!

(JUNE AND AUDIENCE BREAK UP)

JUDY: . . . One thing I really have to talk to you about is *Royal Wedding.* . . . I finally got a vacation from Metro. I had just done about one hundred and eighty-two pictures, and they said, "You can have three weeks off!" So I went to Carmel to play a little golf, and I'd just finished *Easter Parade* with Fred Astaire. You went into *Royal Wedding* with Fred Astaire. They called me and said, "*Get back* here, she's *pregnant* and you've got to take her *place!*" So I went back and learned all these songs and dances, and then, who was it . . . ? I was thrown out and . . .

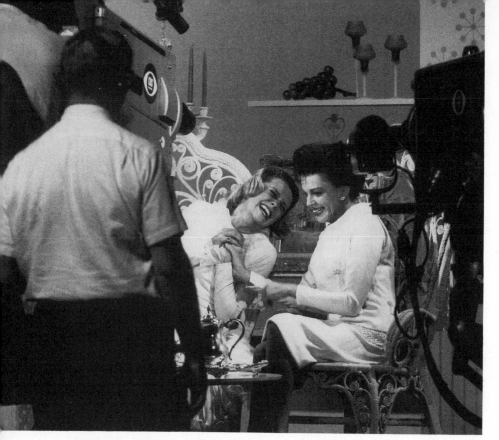

"Jane Powell!"
COURTESY RICHARD CONNOLLY

(JUDY AND JUNE LOOK AT EACH OTHER AND DROP THEIR WRISTS
IN CONFIRMATION, AS IF TO DISH THEIR REPLACEMENT:)

JUDY & JUNE: *Jane Powell!*

(At the same time a second "Tea" segment, with George Jessel, was also taped. At first, it was to be inserted into the Mickey Rooney Schlatter-produced episode to replace the "stuffed bear" comedy sketch, but in the end the Jessel spot was seen in show twelve.)

While the basic structure of show six was solid, and the pacing good, whatever merits the production had overall were largely erased by Judy's loose, slightly off-center performance and June's often sloppy, off-key, and apparently inebriated condition. At various times, she turns her back on the camera during a sketch, stumbles over lyrics, says, "Yes sir—I mean, ma'am!" to Judy, and so botches the novelty tune "Cleopatterer" that when she starts to break up, Garland glares at her, props her up, and continues the number. Their MGM medley was so disconnected, in fact, that pieces of the dress-rehearsal and final-version footage had to be intercut to achieve the semblance of a whole performance.

The same would hold true for Judy's "Trunk" segment, the ad-libbed dialogue from the dress rehearsal cutting into "San Francisco" from the later take.

The unaired version of Judy's "Trunk" anecdote for show six centered around Louis B. Mayer, the head of MGM ("who didn't make any *bones* about it!"), and how he always wanted to "create things," even though he was saddled with handling "the chairman or the stockholders from New York." Judy related how on one occasion, Mayer took a group of board members visiting from the East Coast to the set of the Jeanette MacDonald–Nelson Eddy musical *Naughty Marietta*. Judy joked that Jeanette was supposed to be bidding Nelson a tearful good-bye in one scene, but failed to register the proper emotion of great sadness because "she didn't feel bad about it at all, because they had been on the picture for nine *months!*" Seizing the opportunity to "create artistry," Mayer pushed the director of the picture aside and said to Jeanette, "Wait a minute, *honey!*" Mayer, according to Judy, "whipped" Jeanette's wig off, placed it on his own head, and "walked up the stairs and sang 'Ah, Sweet Mystery of Life' . . . with *steel* tears rolling down his face!" Garland quipped that she was subjected to Mayer telling her the same story "every week . . . I had to listen to this for sixteen years. . . . I never stopped him . . . I let him go the whole way and say, 'Gosh, that's *great*, Mr. Mayer!'"

As newcomer Kelly quickly observed, "Judy was a wonderful talker and storyteller," and was surprised to discover that the "Trunk" dialogue "was not written, it was just outlined. Writers would talk to her and she'd say, 'Well, I'd like to tell a story about the time MGM put me in a loony bin in Gardenia and I made a belt—and that belt ended up costing MGM about twenty-five thousand dollars!' She knew how to build a story and how to give it punch."

Relatively more controlled than Allyson, Judy was hampered primarily by rather severe throat trouble (in contrast to her superlative vocal condition for all five Schlatter shows), causing her to ad-lib during the "Tea" segment to June, "You told me you had laryngitis for three days at rehearsal and I finally got it," adding graciously, if erroneously, "Now you sound like a bell."

Bob Wynn states, "Judy was no problem at all. Judy did one of those looks to June on camera [during 'Cleopatterer'], and when Judy Garland is shaking her head in disgust," he laughs, "you know you're fucking gone! We never would have gotten through that show if it wasn't for Judy. June was really in her cups."

There was also a notorious cake-throwing incident following the taping. To surprise Mel Tormé on his thirty-eighth birthday, a huge, multitiered cake was wheeled on stage. "It was Mel's birthday, but it was June who wound up in the cake," recalls Wynn. "She fell into the damned cake and just started throwing pieces of the cake around. That was a tough show."

The unfortunate incident did not escape mention in the press. Judy did not help matters much when she insisted (and with a straight face), "I never in my life have had too much to drink—when I work or when I don't work." She also tried to defend her guest star with, "I really don't drink that much and neither does June." She added that the cake-throwing incident was "just silliness."

Indelible to new writer Bernie Rothman was a small but most significant incident. "After our opening show, a large cardboard box arrived the next day. A single red rose, which must have been six feet long, was inside. And the card from Judy said, 'I love you and I'm eternally grateful to you.' Judy was a very charming lady and went out of her way to be nice to us. She was the wittiest, funniest woman I have ever met in my life."

Rothman and his fellow writers fervently hoped that the next week's show would be as wonderful and charming as its star. With Schlatter's Rooney show suddenly bumped as the series opener in the wake of his dismissal, CBS had now decided that the upcoming hour (with guest Donald O'Connor) was to be the all-important, make-or-break premiere program to air on September 29—only two weeks away.

12

CBS Television City, reported *Variety* in mid-September, "[is] jumping as no other building in Hollywood as dozens of guest stars roam the corridors and even fill up the choice seats in the audience to watch Garland and Kaye perform. To get a ticket for a Garland or a Kaye dress rehearsal requires 'knowing some-body.' Suddenly, it's become Hollywood's most fashionable pastime."

On September 17, *Variety* announced that George Maharis had signed to appear with Garland on a September 27 taping, mak-ing no mention of the fact that ex-producer Schlatter had signed the ex-*Route 66* heartthrob on July 9. Other guests (erroneously) announced to appear with Garland during the Jewison regime included Trini Lopez, Bob Newhart, sultry songstress Julie Lon-don, Pepsi-Cola "Come Alive" singer Joanie Sommers, Juliet Prowse, and Mitzi Gaynor. In mid-September, Donald O'Con-nor was announced as the guest on the "next" Garland show to be taped, and, as with George Maharis, no mention was made of the fact that he had been signed months earlier by George Schlatter. The same held true for Gene Kelly, expected to guest in late September or early October.

Liza had been away from Judy for several months. Very much missing her daughter, Judy hit upon the ploy of offering her daughter's "beau," Tracy Everitt, a job as a dancer on the series.

Tracy, who was in the chorus of the Broadway production of *How to Succeed in Business Without Really Trying* found the invitation irresistible. Judy's instincts were as sharply honed as always, and Liza promptly quit *Best Foot Forward* and followed Tracy to Los Angeles. And soon after Liza joined her mother in Los Angeles, it was announced that Judy's three children were set to guest with their mother on a special "Christmas Show" edition to be taped in December; producer Gary Smith hoped to sign Mickey Rooney and his family to join them.

Dancer Bea Busch recalls an incident that displayed Garland's perfectionism while at the same time irritating many of the dancers who were used to the precision clockwork of most other television productions. "One time, we were doing a number, and she got so frustrated because it was a step that she couldn't get. Judy was trying to be cool and to stay together, but she just left. She wanted to work on it by herself. It was very hard for her to learn something with us, because she wanted to appear perfect, as if she already knew it, like she was a dancer. And that was very frustrating, because nobody could do that. We were dancers, and we couldn't do it, either. Then the choreographer would be gone for two hours with her, and the assistant would come in and we'd continue to rehearse it until we were perfect. Then Judy would come back later, and she'd fit into it."

Bea was also more sympathetic than some of the other dancers in having to wait for Garland: "Judy Garland was a real perfectionist. She wouldn't come out and sing unless she felt it was going to be just perfect. She forced herself to do so many rehearsals. And if she wasn't around CBS, she was rehearsing at home for hours."

Rehearsals for show seven ended on Thursday, September 19. (O'Connor had briefly visited Studio 43 the week before to shoot promotional photos with Garland.) Under the new Jewison schedule of having the dress rehearsal and final version taped on the same day, the first performance was set from 5:30 to 7:00 P.M., and then after one hour for dinner, notes, and technical preparations, the final version was scheduled from 9:00 to 10:30 P.M.

The script steadfastly maintained the new approach of toppling Garland from her superstar perch and was only minimally better than the material on the previous show:

JERRY: When CBS asked me if I wanted to do the Garland
         show, I said, "Are you kidding! (BEAT) She'll never
         show up!" . . .

Later, Judy mentioned songs she would like to sing on future
episodes:

JUDY: I'd like to sing "Over the Rainbow" sometime.
JERRY: (BLANKLY) What's that one? . . . I don't think I know
         that one.
JUDY: It's from *The Wizard of Oz*! . . .
JERRY: Oh, I saw it last Christmas on TV. That is a great
         song. And that little girl named Dorothy. She did
         it just great . . .
JUDY: Oh, Jerry, you're putting me on. You know that
         little girl was me.
JERRY: (INCREDULOUS) That little girl . . . ? Will you tell
         me something? What have you done to yourself
         since Christmas, sweetie? . . . Let me ask you
         something. What's a nice little old lady like you
         doing on TV?

Van Dyke was hardly pleased with this different, but no better, material. In short order, the comic decided to voice his objections. "I didn't discuss it with Judy," says Jerry. "Judy treated me like a king. She always was wonderful to me the whole time. I was under contract to CBS, and Hunt Stromberg was my man up there. He had said to me, 'If you have any trouble or you have any questions, come to me, my door is always open.' I'm a kid from the Midwest, what did I know? So I went to him. Well, you don't do that. I went over the producer's head, not knowing that you don't do that. The bad material, the 'little old lady' lines stayed in, so I knew I lost the battle." Things became quite frosty between Van Dyke and Jewison. "From day one, Norman Jewison wouldn't give me the time of day."

The opening number was devised as a means to incorporate the now-discarded special-material arrangement of "Sunny Side Up" from the Rooney show. Before "Sunny Side," however, Garland was to spoof her own image by singing "Call Me Irresponsible," with Mel Tormé taking a page from Judy's performance in May at the CBS affiliates meeting. Before Garland jumped into Mel's reworked lyrics, the dancers would give her a big buildup leading into her appearance, only to discover that Judy was late and had missed her cue. A harried stage manager (played by new assistant choreographer Carl Jablonski) would run out looking for Garland. The dancers would quickly reassemble and launch into a frenetic reprise of the song. Judy, all smiles, would then appear from behind Tracy Everitt and go directly into "Call Me Irresponsible."

The idea was a clever one but did risk reinforcing doubts about Garland's ability to sustain a series. Bill Hobin, though, disliked Jewison's approach to open the series for a different reason: "Norman changed the opening to 'Call Me Irresponsible' rather than the overture. It wasn't so much that I loved that overture, I just thought it was a bad choice to come on with a negative idea. The opening should have been upbeat; instead, it had Judy come on with an apology of sorts."

Although Garland's throat troubles were not as pronounced as the week before during the Allyson-Lawrence tapings, her voice was not totally up to par for show seven, either. Judy's (temporarily) diminished vocal condition would lead many viewing the premiere episode to lock into the notion that Garland's voice was fading, an assumption far from true.

Judy looked wonderful on the show, but her laryngitis, of course, worked against her. Her solo, "Fly Me to the Moon," was not really successful due to Judy's vocal problems, but she was seen to great effect in a lavish Bob Kelly set of arched branches (that raised at the beginning of the song and lowered at the close) covered with layers of plumes. "I did that set in all sorts of pale colors," recalls Kelly, "and the look was very soft, very feminine, and very pretty. Judy said, 'This is what I've always wanted!' " Kelly shares credit with lighting director Leard Davis. "He made Judy look good, and he made me look good. And Judy had an innate sense of lighting. She was always exactly where she ought to be. Some people can feel their light, and other people have no idea what you're talking about."

In addition to Garland's throat trouble, the "Tea" segment was a complete misfire. Donald monopolized the spot in telling tales about drinking with old vaudeville cronies, and for the first time the spot seemed to go nowhere. (During the O'Connor taping, Henry Fonda—an old friend of Judy's, who as recently as the year before was reported to be romancing her—also taped a "Tea for Two" segment, which would never be aired.)

The never-aired "Tea for Two" with Henry Fonda
CBS INC.

The running gag on this episode had Jerry, and later O'Connor, lip-synch to Garland's Carnegie Hall performance of "The Man That Got Away" before Judy came on-camera, in a huff because the two had stolen her bit. ("If anybody sings this song," Judy was to tell them, "it's going to be this nice *little old lady!*") After the initial setup of the routine, O'Connor had a solo spot, a production number with the Ernie Flatt dancers (and, particularly, Tracy Everitt) centered around "Sing, You Sinners"—recycled by Mel Tormé from the aborted Nat "King" Cole–Jack Carter episode; the number was mounted with Donald posing as a traveling medicine man.

Then, in a medley built loosely around "Be My Guest," Judy and Donald sang several trademark songs of other performers, including "Indian Love Call" (Jeanette MacDonald–Nelson Eddy), "If You Knew Susie" (Eddie Cantor), and "Mammy" (Al Jolson). It was one of the bright spots of the hour.

Judy's only solo number (with the exception of the "Trunk"

spot) was "Fly Me to the Moon," followed by Judy-Jerry banter. Jerry then performed his *Lone Ranger* bit (which he had taped for, but cut from, the Minnelli show in order to give him a showcase on this premiere episode). A bit of Judy-Jerry-Don "Man That Got Away" lip-synching chatter was next, leading into a production number of "The World Is Your Balloon," with all three in clown makeup and costume. (Because of the elaborate setup, makeup, and wardrobe required for the number, it was pre-taped on Friday afternoon and screened by the studio audiences in video playback.)

A Garland-O'Connor "In Those Good Old Days of Vaudeville" medley was pleasant and charming (including a soft-shoe routine), but it was rather sloppily performed on O'Connor's part. The medley originally included "In Those Good Old Days of Vaudeville" (Don), "Buddy, Can You Spare a Dime" (for Judy, but dropped), "Nagasaki" (Don), "Yacka Hula Hickey Dula" (Judy and Don), "You Can Always Find a Little Sunshine at the Y.M.C.A." (Don), "Hot House Rose" (for Judy, but also cut), "At the Moving Picture Ball"(Judy and Don), and "The Old Soft Shoe" crooned, and danced to, by Judy and Donald. Giving it an aura of being unrehearsed, rather than "spontaneous"—a stagehand's head can even be spotted under a camera, Donald stumbles over the lyrics to "Yacka Hula," and says, "How about this hard-tucker?" instead of "How about this heart-tugger?" Lost for a moment, he then breaks into "In Those Good Old Days of Vaudeville" before saying, "That's even the wrong song!"

The "Trunk" closer had Judy reprise a story from her 1962 Jack Paar appearance detailing the misfortune of an elderly stagehand who unwittingly got caught in a curtain during a 1961 Garland concert, with the gentleman "unfurled after the performance." The incident, which she remembered occurring in Chicago, served as Judy's cue to sing "Chicago" and then "Maybe I'll Come Back."

Judy's stagehand-caught-in-the-curtain story, as she related it in the "Trunk" closing, is somewhat flat—so hilarious, by comparison, in her telling of it on the Paar show earlier—perhaps due to a fairly unresponsive audience. Her "Chicago" is "acrobatic," as one critic deemed it, but her laryngitis prevents it from being an all-stops-pulled, rafter-ringing performance. Not helping the "Call Me Irresponsible" aura at the show's open, Judy

"The World Is Your Balloon": Donald O'Connor, Judy, and Jerry Van Dyke
JOHN FRICKE COLLECTION

goes blank as the violins vamp to begin the number. She scratches her chin and says, "I can't remember 'Chicago'!" before jumping in with "I got the surprise, the surprise of my life," then shaking her head ruefully declaring, "Oh, boy!"

If CBS wanted *The Judy Garland Show* to be a middle-of-the-road, standard-mold variety series, Jewison delivered exactly that. It wasn't a bad show, but it was far from outstanding. Garland's series had been scaled down to weekly proportions, but much of the excitement and larger-than-life theatricality had—if the O'Connor episode was any indication—evaporated as well.

Fate continued to be unkind to Garland. Keyed up and nervous about the premiere of her series the following Sunday, September 29, Judy would not be paired with a musical great to stimulate and interest her for show eight. Instead, she would be surrounded by nonsinging star George Maharis and a country-bumpkin barefooted-hillbilly act known as The Dillards; Jack

Carter, a favorite comedian of Garland's, was also on the bill. The signing of unlikely but seemingly "commercial" guests for Garland was defended by Hunt Stromberg, who had insisted upon such bookings. "I don't like to use the word 'commercial,' " the CBS executive demurred. "It's an attempt to make the show more popular."

Pummeled with bad scripts, hit with laryngitis for the season-premiere broadcast, saddled with second-rate guests ordered by CBS for the next show while bracing herself for the barrage of reviews to hit the newsstands within a week, Judy Garland might well have wondered—now more than at any other time—what indeed was this "nice little old lady" doing on television?

Show number eight stands as the weakest and least inspired of any episode in the series. The script helped little, forcing Judy to play comedy off of a silent down-home novelty act, the nonmusical Maharis, and an increasingly strident Van Dyke character created by the new team of writers. If Judy chose to absent herself from Studio 43 for the week, it is certainly understandable. Ironically, Garland is in fine voice (her laryngitis of the past couple of shows having evaporated) and looks lovely, the effect largely overwhelmed by such mediocrity.

To open the hour, Judy trotted out the Irving Berlin warhorse "Alexander's Ragtime Band." "Be My Guest" followed, the routine serving as a device for Garland to introduce her guests and exchange a few moments of banter. (And to Garland's credit, she would breathe life into the rather flat material, performing it a bit differently—emphasizing random notes and words of the lyric—for the five times she sang it.)

For this taping, Judy had two very important CBS figures in the audience: James Aubrey and Hunt Stromberg, Jr., perhaps leading to Judy's quip at the opening of "Be My Guest" that "one of the most exciting things about doing a television show is just (BEAT) showing *up!*"

And later, when Jerry talks to Judy about The Dillards:

> JERRY: Well, what do you think of the act I brought you?
> JUDY: (INCREDULOUS) Act?

JERRY: Didn't I tell you to stick with me, kid? . . . That
        I'd make you a TV star? Do you know what they
        are?
JUDY: (BEAT) No. Do you?
JERRY: They're hillbillies! That's what people want to see.
        Hillbillies. And they're right here!

Almost erasing the memory of this strained attempt at comedy was Garland's subsequent performance of the bittersweet
ballad, "I Wish You Love," sung with exquisite beauty and control. Her three-minute performance is the highlight of the entire
program and is the first time since the Schlatter programs that
Judy is again in top form; it is a shame that it is buried in this
otherwise completely forgettable hour.

Jack Carter's monologue (framed by a bit of special comedy-
musical material with the comedian and the dancers) is amusing,
with Jack referring to Garland's slender and glamorous meta-
morphosis:

JACK: This isn't the original, you know. This is the twelfth
        Judy Garland, you know that. You think that's her?
        Oh, no. Replica! . . . She went over the rainbow
        years ago! There's a little farm in Pasadena that grows
        Judy Garlands! . . . (LOOKS OFFSTAGE TO JUDY
        LAUGHING) She looks beautiful, doesn't she?

(The comedian's jokes on Garland's astounding weight loss
and physical transformation reflected his first sight of her, in
1960. "I was in Paris, and was shopping at some store, and there
was a little old lady sitting there in black. A little woman. It was
Judy, but she looked like a little old church biddy." A bit taken
aback by her appearance—and having not met her before—Carter
left without introducing himself.)

In a stylized Central Park setting, Maharis then offered a
studied but effective reading of the plaintive "Good-Bye," with
Judy and George dueting for "Side by Side."

The script, recalls Maharis, "said Judy and I were going to
sing a particular number and I said, 'I really don't know it,' and
they said, 'Oh, you'll have plenty of time.' So it got down to the
day before rehearsal, and they said Judy wasn't 'available.' I told
them I was going to speak with Judy, and they said, 'Oh, no

you *can't* speak to Judy!' I said, 'Wait a minute, fuck this!' So I went to her trailer and spoke to her, and she was as nice as could be. And when I met her, I found a person who was completely in touch with herself. She was as friendly as she was open. I told her I had a little problem with the show, the song that we were supposed to sing together. I said, 'I really don't know it.' She said, 'Fine, what do you want to do instead?' And I said, 'I really don't know, I'm basically not a singer.' She said there was a list of songs we could do, and asked me which one I liked. I said, 'Side By Side,' and she said, 'Fine, we'll do that.' I walked out, saying to myself, 'What was the problem about not speaking to her?' I didn't understand it. I don't know what they were all so frightened about. There seemed to be such a protective web around her, like she was some invalid child. And when I met her, I thought, Christ, she's stronger than all of them. I don't know whether they did that because they didn't want anybody near her or because they didn't want to give her any information on what the hell they were doing."

Maharis also remembers a curious moment during rehearsals: "Somebody who was one of her people, and I can't remember who it was, said, 'Do something to make her *insecure*.' I said, 'What?,' and he said, 'Oh, *yes*, it makes her perform better.' "

Dancer Sharon Shore's memories mirror those of Maharis: "It was very tough waiting for her, but once she got into the studio, she was terrific. She was very professional. Her entourage would come in, and she would follow, seemingly very casual, but very insecure and almost nervous. She was a lovely lady, although we [the dancers] never got to know her personally, really. We saw the truly professional side of the lady, who would come in and learn her lines or learn her dance steps, but she was always hustled in and hustled out. I wondered sometimes if they kept her away from everybody. And I would have loved to say, 'Hi, Judy,' just to let her know that we were on her side. They kept her away from everybody. Nobody had a chance."

Garland's uncanny ability to grasp material instantly overrode her absence at rehearsal, says Maharis. "I found her totally professional and delightful. She was just marvelous." Jack Carter concurs: "You had such a feeling of her wanting to be nice and to be helpful, and to go along with everything. She just wanted to give you her show. She was one of the very few performers who could still project when she had to underplay and did it wonderfully."

Gary Smith, who was himself critical of Garland's absence from more than a few rehearsals—and not just on this particular episode—admits, "We didn't have her much of the time to work with her. She'd learn something pretty quick. It was tough for the choreographers, but she'd learn. She was very fast. That was her saving grace. When she wanted to learn, she could learn in two minutes." Ernie Flatt was nevertheless frustrated at the often unorthodox rehearsal schedules week to week: "When she did show up, it was always late. There was only enough time to get done what had to be done, because everything was an emergency. One time I remember vividly coming around the corner of a set, and I ran right into Judy. She was in a bright canary-yellow dress that Ray had done for her. My first reaction was saying, 'You look wonderful in that color.' She put her finger on my nose and kept tapping it, and said, 'I don't know you very well, but I know you well enough to know that you wouldn't say that unless you meant it!' and turned and walked off. That's about as personal as we got."

Assistant choreographer Carl Jablonski took a more sympathetic view, explaining "Often Judy did not show up. But the lady was so bright, you showed her once, or twice, and she had it. And if there *was* something difficult that she couldn't get, or couldn't do, and she was being difficult, Ernie Flatt would say, 'Oh, Judy, now I remember you did that in *The Wizard of Oz!*' and he would trick her into it, so she had no way out. She was incredible. Her brain was so fast."

Although Maharis is himself visibly mesmerized by Garland and, as a result, a bit ill at ease, their duet of "Side By Side" is rather charming; ironically, while Judy was getting heat from CBS for touching her guests, here it was George who frequently hugged, kissed, embraced, or reached for physical contact with her throughout the program.

The "Tea for Two" spot oddly paired Judy with baseball coach Leo Durocher (the only guest to appear on the Garland series "through the courtesy of *Sports Illustrated*"!), a transparent move to grab yet another faction of the television audience—on the order of Hunt Stromberg, Jr.—as in her teaming with The Dillards. While she is, as always, charming and gracious (admitting

"Side by Side" with
George Maharis

absolutely no knowledge of baseball, referring to Durocher's ball
club as the Brooklyn Dodgers, even though the team had relocated to Los Angeles some years before), and enthusiastically
sang "Take Me Out to the Ball Game" with him, it was another
"Tea" misfire. Garland wanted "Tea" with such notables as Noël
Coward, Bing Crosby, and Gene Kelly, but CBS cast her with
the likes of Leo Durocher.

After a mercifully brief Dillards rendering of "Buckin' Mule,"
Judy took a stab at country music. On a rural front-porch setting, the entire company appeared for a medley including "Y'All
Come" (Judy and The Dillards), "Crawfishin' " (Jack and Jerry),
"Somebody Touched Me" (in a wonderful, thoughtful performance of the spiritual by Judy), "Way Back Home" (George),
"Nobody's Business" (Jack, his exaggerated foot-stomping to the
beat causing Judy to break up in delightful laughter), "Way in
the Middle of the Air" (all), and "Y'All Go" by Judy (a counterpoint to the opening song of the medley), bringing the homespun segment to an end.

Garland ended the hour with a brief but amusing story about
"breathing the feathers in her feather boa" during "If Love Were
All," citing it as happening during one of her concerts, when
actually it occurred on the Schlatter Tony Bennett show. Her only
song in the segment was "Swanee." Begun with vigor, Garland

ran out of steam toward the end of the song, and failed to conquer the last two notes.

In a pointed but seemingly good-natured reference, she cut the script's planned nonsensical "Jimmy Durante has a nose like mine" during "Maybe I'll Come Back" to "Hunt Stromberg, Jr., is a cousin of mine." Looking squarely at him while she sang it (evoking a hearty laugh from the unseen CBS executive), Garland—at least to inside observers—made it quite clear that he was responsible for pairing her with The Dillards.

Maharis had met Garland one time before, only briefly. "Even if you had met her eight times before, it was like the first time for her. You know—'what is this new person that I'm seeing?' She was really very childlike, very wondrous, and, like Picasso, was able to keep that throughout her life." He also observed, "She gave me the impression that the show was moving too quickly from the standpoint of how she liked to work, but she dove into it, and she just did it. I always got the impression that she never looked back."

Garland, Maharis, Aubrey, and Stromberg socialized following the show and, on the surface at least, it all was quite convivial. "We went out after the taping, " recalls George, "to some nightclub. When you're out with Judy Garland, people who are supposed to be so sophisticated fall all over her. It was amazing. But Judy was one of those special people who left you with a sense of being bigger than yourself. When you understand what Judy Garland is, and what she does, you also understand that nobody can touch her. Because there is nothing like her around, and there never will be."

As Liza Minnelli explains, "It basically comes down to one thing. And it's so simple. She was fun to be with. That's why people fell all over themselves. She was more fun than you could possibly imagine."

More than her personality, CBS president James Aubrey appreciated Garland's following Stromberg's edict to create an "approachable" Judy. Soon after he observed Garland struggling against second-class guest stars and a third-rate script, Aubrey expressed only satisfaction: "When I see some undisciplined talent elsewhere, I am delighted not at the effort Kaye and Miss Garland put into their shows, but at the way they *listen* to our advice."

Gary Smith recalls the pressure on the show staff from the

network: "They were in their *Beverly Hillbillies* period, so they thought country and The Dillards and that sort of thing would be real folksy. You already had the big-city, sophisticated appeal with Judy; what we really needed, they said, was to get the South and the heartlands."

"When you're a Garland," Maharis offers, "you're a honey pot, and you draw bees. When you're that powerful in terms of your talent, you draw as much negative as you do positive, and it's hard to survive when you're not born with that killer instinct. Suddenly, now she was big money, and they were trying to make her into what they thought she should be. What they should have *done* was let her alone."

Mercifully, Judy was able to throw off the memories of this ill-conceived CBS show blueprint. She had far more important thoughts on her mind. Not only was her show premiering in less than forty-eight hours, she was preparing herself for show nine and the most formidable young singing talent she had yet to face on the series: Barbra Streisand.

13

The day before the premiere of *The Judy Garland Show*, producer Gary Smith told Arlene Garber of the *Los Angeles Citizen-News*, "Judy is going to come on as a more natural human being. She's going to show her imperfect side. That's the part of her that is always responsible for her putting her foot into it, no matter what the situation is." He added that he would be attempting to woo such offbeat guests as Sandy Koufax, Casey Stengal, and even General Eisenhower to have "Tea for Two" with Garland. "We're just going on blind faith now that what we are doing is right for Judy," Gary candidly admitted. "We won't know until these first thirteen have been aired what's really working for us, for her."

CBS, according to rumors circulating the same weekend, apparently had doubts about the series working at all. On September 29—the premiere day—the *Chicago Tribune* ominously reported, "Judy Garland's first taped TV hour tees off tonight, even as CBS asked Eddie Fisher (as well as Bob Goulet) to stand by to sub on short notice in later ones if the weekly pace gets to Judy."

Norman Jewison commented to the *Los Angeles Times*, "You might say Judy destroyed the legend herself when she signed for a weekly TV show." (Columnist Hal Humphrey disagreed, commenting on the first episode aired, "It wasn't Judy who had destroyed a legend but the writers.")

With CBS electing to not screen the O'Connor show in advance of the broadcast, most of the reviews hit the stands the following Monday, and some the day after. *The Judy Garland Show* has been dogged unfairly through the years with the inaccurate notion that the series was a critical flop of mammoth proportions. On the contrary, the reviews were overwhelmingly on the positive side, often glowing effusively with praise.

The few negative notices invariably criticized the show's approach, Van Dyke's character, and the writing in general, saving whatever praise they could muster for Garland herself.

A sampling of the reviews:

Variety: "If Judy Garland as CBS's newest acquisition is of a mind to work every week with the same dedication and zeal that characterized her premiere this week, Bill Paley and his associates should be in clover. . . . For while the premiere could hardly be called the perfect show (being long on nostalgia and short on bounce and zip), La Garland is in a position to whittle down or perhaps even surpass the Nielsen numbers that have been acquiring to *Bonanza*. . . . Miss Garland, youthful and sprightly, was in fine fettle."

San Francisco Chronicle: "It was tasteful, elegant and exciting. If producer Norman Jewison and the star herself can maintain this standard of freshness for the entire season, the whole series, plus Miss Garland, will get over that rainbow with little effort. Style and taste were evident in every detail of the production. Miss Garland herself looked trim and fit and far better than I can remember."

New York Herald Tribune: "When Judy Garland was front and center last night, singing her heart out, all was right in the world of entertainment. And all was right with *The Judy Garland Show*, which started the young veteran off on still another triumph in show business . . . never looking better, Miss Garland worked a wizard's spell in her big variety numbers [and was] sparkling and magnetic. . . . For dark and vivacious beauty, for grand voice and style . . . and for expert showmanship and simple human appeal, there's no one to compare with Miss Garland. . . . Mr. O'Connor may be trying to challenge Dean Martin's public image as the town drunk of Hollywood. . . . Mr. Van Dyke got off the wincer of the evening: 'What's a nice little old lady like you doing on television?' . . . Miss Garland is fine, just fine. The rest of the show, however, needs help."

The New York Times: "What should never happen to Judy Garland did last evening . . . the busybodies got so in the way that the singer never had a chance to sing out as only she can. To call the hour a grievous disappointment would be to miss the point. It was an absolute mystery. . . . Judy never looked more vivacious and sounded in fine voice. It was the network that rattled. . . . In only one number ("Fly Me to the Moon") was there the Judy who has filled theatres the world around. For the other 55 minutes, she was a prisoner of her own production. . . . Those telephones on the 20th floor of the CBS home encampment should buzz this morning with but one directive to Hollywood. Free Judy!"

Los Angeles Citizen-News: "She brought show business excitement back to the one-a-week on the home screen."

Los Angeles Herald-Examiner: "For the plain truth of it, Judy can do no wrong. When she is nervous, the audience doesn't fidget; the crowd 'feels' for her and goes right along with the tension. We tuned in prepared to be belligerent but she captured us within five minutes."

New York Journal-American: "[It] was a delight [and] had that fine, sprightly look of a hit about it from the moment it started."

Albany Times-Union: "It was a great show. One of the good lines came in a little skit when Judy persuaded Jerry that she had played Dorothy in *The Wizard of Oz.* 'What's a nice little old lady like you doing on television?' No little old lady this, but a beautiful woman with a pack of talent. . . . If the show can keep it up for 39 weeks, it will be one of the big winners this year."

Toronto Globe and Mail: "It does not seem possible that Judy will be able to keep up this standard, but no one can doubt her determination."

Dorothy Kilgallen: "Judy Garland's premiere show was a triumph. It was a thrill to see her looking so young, slim, lively and full of zip again."

San Francisco Herald-Examiner: "At the age of 41 years, three months and 19 days, Judy was giving television its tastiest song and dance tonic of the season. The show was a jumping joy to watch . . . she is off and running with what surely should be the smash variety hour of the season . . . She was Miss Show Business adding the Miss Television crown to her laurels. . . . The talents of yore were everywhere evident, but the chassis was new and the model was modern."

"It was a thrill to see her looking so young, slim, lively and full of zip again."—DOROTHY KILGALLEN
CBS INC.

Herald-Examiner television critic Dwight Newton received a letter not long after his review appeared "from a slightly prejudiced corner":

> I am sure you know how very much your October 1 column means to me and everyone else on the program. . . . There isn't an entertainer around who wouldn't thrive on this kind of praise and do everything short of moving heaven and earth to continue doing the best show they can offer.
>
> JUDY GARLAND

Perhaps Judy's most prized review was one contained in a telegram from a beloved, and most distinguished, friend:

> Congratulations on a wonderful show last night. Know it will be a big hit in the coming season.
>
> JOHN F. KENNEDY

Garland's premiere episode was as much of a ratings triumph as it was a critical success. The overnight Nielsen numbers gave Garland a 35.9 rating and a 44.0 share (reflecting the great scope of her urbane, sophisticated audience), compared to *Bonanza*'s 24.7/30.3; *Arrest and Trial* on ABC was at distant third place with a 17.8 rating and 21.8 share. Nielsen's overnight twenty-six-city Trendex report again gave Garland the lead with an average 23.1 rating, compared to *Bonanza*'s 18.4 and *Arrest and Trial*'s 14.2.

Rehearsals were beginning to get under way for show nine with Barbra Streisand (along with the Smothers Brothers) when the reviews poured in.

Garland's renewed enthusiasm for her series was as much sparked by the glowing reviews (and heaps of praise as well for her own performance and youthful appearance) as it was by her keen anticipation at the thought of working with Barbra Streisand. Judy, in fact, had taken Norman Jewison, Liza, her fleet of writers, and David Begelman, among others, to see Streisand's closing night at the famed Cocoanut Grove nightclub in mid-September after taping the Allyson-Lawrence program.

Barbra's Grove opening in August was a star-studded affair

that led Hedda Hopper to write, "Barbra uses her extraordinary voice range beautifully; bats out a high note with full power without straining a muscle. As relaxed as a cat on a hearth rug, she makes old songs sound new." And *The Hollywood Reporter* praised, "Miss Streisand completely captured the jam-packed, celebrity-studded audience at Wednesday's opening, an event, which, veteran Grove-goers said, surpassed any other premiere there in recent history."

Streisand's closing was no less stellar. That night, Barbra introduced Judy as "the world's greatest singer and the world's greatest actress," and invited her onstage to sing. Judy demurred, saying softly, "Tonight belongs to you, Barbra."

"Judy was so generous with talent," remembers Johnny Bradford. "We were all there to see Barbra. Judy was just blown away by her. The night Judy first heard Barbra at the Grove, she said, 'I'm never going to open my mouth again!' She was so stunned by Streisand's pipes." Adds writer Bernie Rothman, "Judy brought us all down to see Barbra and thought she was just incredible."

And when Garland and Streisand met after the show and Judy lavished praise on her, Bradford recalls Barbra's open adoration. "She was thrilled. Are you kidding? Garland was her icon. What an honor."

It was backstage that Judy invited Barbra to guest on her series. According to David Begelman, "Judy said, 'She's *got* to do my show before she leaves town,' and we revised the schedule of whoever the guest was that week, and pushed back a week or so, and Barbra did the show. And it was history."

That July, months of rumors were finally substantiated when the official announcement came that Streisand would play Fanny Brice in the musical *Funny Girl*, to open in early 1964. (Ironically, Garland had been envisioned to play Fanny at the outset but declined, and the role was later discussed for Mary Martin, Anne Bancroft, and Carol Burnett.)

Barbra officially launched her professional career in 1960, when she entered a talent contest at The Lion, a Manhattan gay bar and restaurant. Not surprisingly, she won the contest and fifty dollars, a one-week singing engagement, with meals included— shrewdly adopting an eye-popping thrift-shop wardrobe and such offbeat material as "Who's Afraid of the Big, Bad Wolf?" and

"Come to the Supermarket in Old Peking." Streisand was a bona-fide original from the start.

Barbra then went on to play extremely successful engagements in such top-rate nightclubs as the Bon Soir in Greenwich Village. She launched her television career with multiple P.M. *East* and *Tonight Show* appearances. She scored heavily in the Broadway David Merrick musical *I Can Get It for You Wholesale.* When the play closed in December of 1962, Streisand appeared on television shows headlined by Garry Moore, Dinah Shore, Bob Hope, and Ed Sullivan. She was also booked in at Harrah's in Lake Tahoe, the Riviera in Las Vegas (opening for Liberace), San Francisco's hungri i, and was scheduled for an October 5 Hollywood Bowl concert with Sammy Davis, Jr.

CMA, not unexpectedly, keenly wanted to add Barbra Streisand to its client roster. As early as August 28, one week after her Grove opening, *The Hollywood Reporter* leaked, "LaScala looked like a smoke-filled room Monday night: Barbra Streisand was being courted by the Creative Management menage (Freddie Fields, Polly Bergen, Phil Silvers and a Gaggle of Bright Young Men)."

Liza Minnelli remembers Garland vigorously insisting at the Grove that Begelman at once sign Streisand as a CMA client. Perhaps toying with Judy, in hopes of learning the extent of her enthusiasm for Barbra, Begelman gave the impression that he was not completely sold on Streisand. "David said, 'They want me to sign this girl and I don't know,' " Liza recalls Begelman remarking to Judy, who then added, "I think she looks like a kid from Brooklyn!" David, however, insisted Garland see Barbra perform live, telling her, "You've got to see her because she's the newest thing."

Nevertheless, recalls Liza, "Barbra came out onstage, and David said, 'I'll stick with Robert Goulet!' Barbra sang about eight bars, and Mama leaned over to David and said, 'You're out of your goddamned mind! You are so crazy not to sign this girl. You have no taste whatsoever, but I've always known that!' And then Mama said, 'I want her on my show!' "

Liza notes, too, that Judy was not pleased by some of show business's Old Guard stubborn refusal to take Streisand's talents entirely seriously, preferring instead to dismiss her as a semi-comical, offbeat, "kooky" character. (Streisand once remarked that her "kookiness" was "a big, defensive, rebellious thing. But, at the same time, it was *theatrically right* for me. I *knew* it.")

In May of 1963, for example, *Hollywood Reporter* columnist Hank Grant wrote, "Until we actually saw Barbra Streisand perform on Sunday night's Dinah Shore show, we thought her hot 'Happy Days Are Here Again' single was a satire on schmaltzy torch singers, but this doll isn't kidding! Never such song-chewing have we witnessed. . . . Irony of it is, the gal has a fine pair of pipes, but probably wouldn't make a dime if she sang straight."

"Mama was annoyed that some people were still reacting to Barbra the way they were," notes Liza. "Supposedly the people who really knew talent and how to handle talent. She said, 'Nobody knows anything. If I get her to the public on my show, then the public will know.'"

The taping date for the Garland-Streisand hour was to be Friday, October 4. The evening would be critical for both Judy and Barbra. Not only would Aubrey (along with Dann and Stromberg) again be in the audience, CBS founder and chairman William Paley also would attend, visiting Hollywood from his New York base for preliminary meetings about the 1964–65 season. The evening was extremely important to the future of Garland's series, and was also of tantamount importance in the continuing battle between CBS and NBC for Miss Streisand's services. In August, both Aubrey and NBC talent chief Dave Tebet made special trips to Las Vegas to scout Barbra's act. Both networks began bidding for Barbra, with NBC immediately offering her a two-special contract. (Under CMA management, Streisand signed a $5 million contract with CBS in 1964, for which she was to have headlined one special a year for the next ten years.)

In January of 1969 (only six months before her death), Judy revealed that it was she, and not Mel Tormé, who came up with the idea to pair "Happy Days Are Here Again" and "Get Happy" for the duet between herself and Streisand. During an impromptu appearance at the National Film Theatre in London, Judy said of Mel Tormé, "The Velvet *Smog* was supposed to arrange all of the songs for whatever guests came on, and he was *constantly* fighting with his wife." She then told the audience that Tormé was absent as a result of his domestic squabble, and because she was (as she put it, tongue-in-cheek) "rehearsing for a dance routine with Peter Gennaro, *was* it? . . . Busby Berkeley or *someone* . . . I wasn't aware that Barbra hadn't gotten any music written for her to sing with me."

Garland continued, "I was driving home by myself [thinking], I can't find Mel Tormé and I can't read music. But she was famous right then for that one record, 'Happy Days Are Here Again' and I once did a version of Harold Arlen's 'Get Happy' at a slow tempo. I don't know how to read music, in the first place . . . or play the piano. (I'm really hopeless, but I've been getting *away* with it.) So I went home, and there was a great big piano, and I was sitting in the living room, trying to figure out and I [started to sing] 'Forget Your Troubles' . . . And it all worked out very well.' "

To her great credit, Judy—even at her lowest career, financial, and physical ebb just before her death—remained an unwavering champion of Barbra Streisand's talents. At the National Film Theatre question-and-answer session, when one member of the audience remarked that Streisand's talents were, to many, held comparable to Garland's, derisive cries erupted from the audience. Judy immediately countered the negative reaction by insisting, "She's marvelous, she's marvelous. You just can't deny the fact that she's a star.

"She is a *star*, she makes a *sound*, she has a *look*. No one will be able to really deny the fact that Barbra Streisand is a great talent." Judy pointedly continued, "There doesn't have to be a comparison. She has her way of singing, I have my way. There's enough room for all of us. . . . She's splendid. And very nice."

(In 1965, Judy visited CBS and happened to visit an editing room where a Streisand special was being screened. When several members in her party attempted to brush off Barbra's talents in contrast to Judy's, Garland immediately silenced them, saying, "No, no, no—she's absolutely wonderful." In a similar vein, when Judy appeared on *The Tonight Show* in December of 1968, when Johnny Carson asked Judy to name her favorite singers, Judy immediately responded, "Barbra Streisand," and then, of course, "Liza Minnelli.")

Lorna Luft, although only eleven years old at the time, recalls Judy's delight at working with Barbra: "Mama was so excited about Barbra, because she was so talented, and so unique. She liked the fact that there was someone young, new, and different—but not different, in a way. I remember her sitting at the piano in the Rockingham house, and she was going over the medley of 'Happy Days' and 'Get Happy.' I remember vividly her talking about how excited she was about Barbra. Someone once said that they didn't get along. That's nonsense. She was charming, she was nice, and my mother was a big fan of hers. She thought Barbra was great."

The meeting at CBS between the two singers was no less affectionate than it had been at Streisand's closing night at the Grove. "It was instant warmth," wrote Tormé in his book, "and I knew Garland would be on her toes all week to keep pace with this extraordinary girl."

The taping was not without its share of less-than-sunny incidents, however. Jerry Van Dyke had become increasingly unhappy with his new, strident character. The number of reviews trouncing his second-banana role, his terrible material—some of them discounting him as a performer of any talent—only made matters worse. At first somewhat able to brush off Jewison's cold treatment of him, Jerry had increasingly come to the conclusion that "my days were numbered" after his mentor, Hunt Stromberg, had failed to come to his rescue and, in fact, had turned on him as well.

His marriage was beginning to crumble as a result, and many observers took note of Jerry's drinking. "It got tougher and tougher for him," says Bill Hobin. "I know he felt awkward. He started drinking hard. I remember one morning I walked into his dressing room and found him drinking about eight in the morning."

"I was always on the perimeter," Van Dyke laments. "You just don't do the 'little old lady' lines to Judy. People loved her, and you can't do that to her. I was not a part of writing material for myself. I would have liked to have been part of it. I remember going to Mel and asking him to write some better stuff for me, a special-material song or something."

Another problem was mounting friction between Jewison and Bill Hobin. Before Jewison came in, Hobin had entertained the thought that he might have been made Schlatter's successor; he had, after all, been hired for that same job prior to George's hiring. Jewison represented the second time Hobin had been passed by to produce the series. Norman lobbied to retain Bill, explaining, "I didn't feel he was at fault for the content of the show, and so I did what I could to support him." Still, he adds, tellingly, "I should have directed, but I didn't want to let Bill go." Perhaps sensing this, the two maintained a cool, distant working relationship. "I never had a big rapport with Norman," Bill admits. "George and I did all the editing together. I don't think Norman ever stepped into the editing."

The standoff came to a pitch not long after the new regime got underway, Hobin reveals. "I had a bad time with Norman because he tried to direct, and I told him, 'Fine, but don't do it on my time.' I finally called the Directors' Guild, and this lady came over and saw him in action a couple of times. She told him [to cease] and he apologized and admitted I was right." Bill Hobin and Mel Tormé's once-cordial relationship had also begun to deteriorate. ("I love Mel professionally. He's a wonderful talent. I just didn't get along with him.")

Jewison also experienced a bit of tension when Ethel Merman agreed to guest on the Garland-Streisand "Tea for Two" segment but expected to sing a full song, which would undermine her surprise appearance. A compromise was reached; Ethel would sing a few bars of "You're Just in Love" as a spotlight hit her sitting in the audience. She then would rise and join Garland and Streisand onstage.

The incident was not a serious one, and the Garland-Merman friendship remained solid. As Merman wrote in her 1978 autobiography, "Judy was a pal of mine. I often visited in her home when I was in Hollywood. . . . Anyone who knew her only through the headlines must have thought her personal life was hell. 'Poor soul,' people would say. Poor soul nothing. Judy had a wonderful sense of humor. There might have been quite a lot of melodrama in her life, but what saved her was that she always saw the funny side of her troubles. There was a wide streak of the clown in her. . . . Judy was a very thoughtful girl. Over the years, I seldom made an appearance that I didn't receive a congratulatory telegram from her on opening night—when she didn't show up in person."

With the matter over Merman's wanting to sing a song during the "Tea" spot now resolved to Garland's satisfaction, Jewison relates, "There was a big problem with Barbra and her manager because I had to cut part of Barbra's act because of time. Barbra and I are friends now, but I remember there were some pretty tough scenes about that. Mort Lindsey was incredible. He worked it out. How, I don't know. He was writing some very difficult stuff, very wonderful material."

Although Streisand had made quite a splash in show business, her success was still so recent that many on the show were largely unfamiliar with her. Some of the dancers and even the singers had no idea who she was; the same was true for Jerry Van Dyke. His first encounter with Streisand early in the week was memorable. "I'll never forget this. I said, 'I'm a big fan of yours.' I just said it because everybody was saying it. And she said, 'Yeah, you, too, huh?' She wasn't nice to me. She didn't impress me. Except her singing with Judy."

"One of the greatest thrills in my life in show business, and I've danced for thirty years, was seeing Barbra Streisand in the rehearsal hall," recalls Bea Busch. "Jack Elliott was at the piano. It was early in the day, and Judy was there. Judy knew that this was someone special. You knew just by the way she entered the room. She pulled everything together, and I had not seen her so done-up and chic and reserved. And Barbra came in, and her hair was wild. She was like this wild thing off of the streets of New York. I didn't know who she was. I said to the others, 'Who is *that*?' She had sandals on, and a hippie dress. I thought, This is the *guest*? And, my God, the two of them sat at the piano in the bare rehearsal hall, and you could have heard a pin drop. When they started to sing together, I got goose bumps everywhere. Barbra sang 'Bewitched,' and I couldn't believe this came out of the apparition that had walked in. And then Judy sang like I've never heard her sing, like her telling Barbra, I've still got it. Judy was really on her toes. That competition was a stimulus for her. It was for all of us."

"Judy had a very good relationship with Barbra," says Jack Elliott. "She could sing. And Judy knew that, and respected that." Adds dancer Bonnie Evans, "We were all in rehearsal, and in walks this very unattractive, dirty, scruffy, barefoot girl with stringy hair. We were surprised that she would get a spot on the Garland show. None of us had heard of her. But when Barbra started to sing, it was an electrifying moment, and instantly, everybody realized we were listening to a star."

"Barbra was never intimidated," Evans suggests. "She wasn't afraid to sing with Judy or to appear with Judy. Most people *were* intimidated by Judy, and in such awe of her."

Choreographer Ernie Flatt, however, believes otherwise: "There was great respect on both sides, but I think the greatness of Barbra's talent made Judy extremely nervous. Even then, you could see Barbra's talent, even though she was wearing the freaky clothes and all of that, what I call her 'Goodwill' period. She'd show up at rehearsal with her hair pulled up with a rubber band, and everybody was worried she'd go on the show like that!"

Adds Flatt's assistant, Carl Jablonski, "Judy was kind to all of her guests—I always felt that she was a cheerleader—but she did everything she could to help and guide Barbra. All I saw was encouragement. The only time I can remember her being pissed off was when we were in rehearsal. And in walked Judy's secretary with all these checks for her to sign. And Judy wanted to continue rehearsal, but all these people were on her—sign the checks, do this, do that. And eventually, she just exploded. That's the only time I ever saw her get angry. She was a pussycat, but when things like that happened, she was a tiger."

Barbra's appearance and full vocabulary of expletives quickly became the talk of Studio 43. "She kind of shocked me," says propman Earl Carlson. "Her mouth was really wild. I remember Barbra wanted tea. There was coffee on the set, but she insisted on tea, so we had to go out and get a teapot, go down to the commissary and make her tea. And, she didn't want tea in the *bag*, it had to be *brewed* tea!"

The teaming of Garland and Streisand became the hottest ticket in town. As Tom Cooper remembers, "There were about five hundred people waiting for a chance to get into that show." Getting a ticket for the Garland series—and this show in particular—became near impossible. "The saying was at that time it was easier to get into Fort Knox than it was to get into a Garland taping," states longtime fan Rick Sommers.

The October 4 taping was to have begun with Judy shooting a new opening for the Mickey Rooney show, with "Sunny Side Up" having since been used for the O'Connor program; at the last moment, it was decided that the number would be taped at a later date. Thus, the taping began immediately with "Comes Once in a Lifetime" and displayed a confident, energetic Garland in fine voice.

Next was Streisand and the Smothers Brothers joining Judy for "Be My Guest." The segment gave Judy and Barbra the chance to good-humoredly address the notion that Streisand's formida-

"Can I replace you?"
COURTESY RICHARD CONNOLLY

ble talents were second only to those of Garland. To the tune of "Be My Guest" the young singer turned to Judy and revealed, "I've been a fan of yours since I was two!" Barbra then good-naturedly asked Judy the musical question, "Can I replace you?," to which Garland did a humorous "take" and replied, "Be my guest!"

Garland and Van Dyke were then forced to engage in a weak comedy sketch that led into her solo "The Days of Wine and Roses," later changed to "Just in Time." (This episode's running gag was centered on the Garland series being over budget, Jerry supposedly having sold Judy's car and rented out the den of her home to strangers in order to recoup cash.)

Garland's performance of "Just in Time" is extraordinary. Softly caressing the lyrics to Lindsey's sole piano accompaniment at first, she leans forward and sings directly to the camera and then leans back against Mort's shoulder and continues to sing. As the arrangement switches into high gear for a spirited second chorus, Judy stands and moves stage center to finish the number in grand style, turning to acknowledge Lindsey while blowing him a kiss. (This masterful arrangement of "Just in Time"—featuring multiple-key and tempo changes—was unlike that of any other singer's and was one of Judy's favorites. "That arrangement was the result of Judy, Kay Thompson, and myself spending about eight hours working it out in a lounge at the Plaza Hotel in New York," notes Mort Lindsey.)

The Smothers Brothers comedy-music spot featured "I Talk
to the Trees" and "Dance, Boatman, Dance." While they were
undeniably amusing, Judy reportedly cracked, "I like 'em—I don't
understand them, but I like 'em!" Still, the young men were dazzled by working with the likes of Garland at this early point in
their career. As Dick Smothers jokingly remarked in 1981, "We
were so in awe that we felt we didn't belong in the same building!"

Barbra's solos were next. In a single spotlight and with most
effective simplicity, Judy introduced her by saying, "And now,
I'm very proud and happy to present one of my newest and
nicest friends."

Streisand, also bathed in a single spotlight on her face against
a black background, sang "Bewitched, Bothered and Bewildered" flawlessly and stunningly. She then launched into what
Tormé called her "bombshell" arrangement of "Down with Love,"
one that, he described, "started down here, built to here, and
ended way up there at the top of the excitement range." ("Down
with Love" was recorded by Streisand for her second Columbia
album released that August and "Bewitched, Bothered and Bewildered" was included on *The Third Album*. A Roddy McDowall
photograph of the Garland show performance of "Bewitched"
was utilized for the front cover of the LP, which was released in
late 1963.)

The applause greeting Streisand at the end of "Down with
Love" was loud, sustained, and enthusiastic, led by Garland
herself. Applauding energetically as Barbra left the raised platform where she sang to join Judy, Garland exclaimed, "You're
thrilling—so absolutely *thrilling!*," causing Barbra to giggle after
the two embraced.

"We've got all your albums at home, you know. And you're
so good that I (BEAT) hate you. I really *hate* you, you're so good!,"
Judy said to Barbra.

Barbra laughed, then replied, "Oh, Judy, that's so sweet of
you, thank you. . . . You're so great that (BEAT) I've been hating
you for *years*! In fact, it's my ambition to be great enough to be
hated by as many singers as you."

"Oh, that's a nice thing for you to say," Judy told her, her
reaction to the line causing the audience—and Barbra—to dissolve into laughter. "I love it! Say more, say more!"

"I love you, I love you, too," Barbra assured her. Without

missing a beat, Barbra took on a Brooklyn accent, and added, "But don't stop hating me! I need the confidence!"

"No, no, no," Judy countered. "And if you ever get a little, you know, a feeling of lack of security, call me on the phone and sing a couple of notes to me, and I'll give you *hatred* like you've never gotten before! You're too good. See, I love you, pussycat!"

"I, uh, think that makes me—*happy*," said Barbra, pointedly referring to the duet they were about to perform. "Let's try it," added Judy.

Garland's inspiration to pair "Get Happy" and "Happy Days Are Here Again" was brilliant, and the blending of the two legendary voices was thrilling, particularly when the two opened full throttle during the middle of the medley ("there'll be no more from now on . . . from now on!"). Garland, characteristically, is most generous to Barbra, and subdues her performance a bit to allow Streisand to shine all the more. Their warmth and affection is genuine; they sing arm in arm together, and Judy is clearly no less in awe of Barbra's talents than Streisand is completely mesmerized by Garland's.

Mort Lindsey, however, feels differently: "Judy gave a lot more to Barbra than Barbra gave back to her, I feel, but perhaps it was because Barbra was so young. Barbra is very self-confident, but she is there with Judy—two legends. I noticed Judy giving so much, and Barbra was looking at the camera and not reacting. Judy was always generous that way. It was her show, she wanted it to happen, but she could sense that this girl wasn't giving back."

The "Tea for Two" segment followed, the script indicating that the ad-libbed spot featured "Barbra and Judy chatting. Voice from audience singing 'You're Just in Love.' It's Merman. She joins them for talk re belting out a solo. They discuss new Fanny Brice musical which will star Barbra." After chatting, the three would create even more show-business history by joining voices for the first and only time in a rafter-ringing rendition of Irving Berlin's "There's No Business Like Show Business." Following a bit of banter between Judy and Barbra, Merman was heard singing the opening bars of "You're Just in Love" from the audience before joining the two onstage. Hobin captured the spontaneous feeling of it perfectly by shooting Judy and Ethel embracing in backlit shots looking out into the audience.

After Judy complimented Ethel ("You look marvelous!"),
Merman explained to Garland that she was in an adjacent studio
taping a Red Skelton program. When Judy asked if she was belting there, Ethel shot back, "*I* was belting? I heard *you* two belting. I heard the noise, and that's why I came in! I just came in
to say hello, that's all."

> ETHEL: (TO JUDY) How about this Barbra? Isn't this great?
>   The new belter! . . .
>   (TO BARBRA) What's the next thing after this, the
>   next big thing?
> BARBRA: It's called *Funny Girl*—

As Barbra softly attempts to add that the play is "based on
the life of Fanny Brice and Nicky Arnstein," Merman's booming
voice, declaring, "Wonderful, wonderful," nearly drowns her out.
"Do you have a good composer?" Merman asks. When Streis-
and replies it is Jule Styne, Merman cries out—seizing the chance
to mention one of her own great stage successes—"Jule Styne—
He wrote *Gypsy*! Oh, my goodness! You're in good hands, girl,
you're really in good hands." When Merman also overrode
Streisand's earlier attempt to mention producer David Merrick,
Judy jumped in, sensing Barbra's discomfort, and asked her,
"Who's the producer, darling?" giving her the chance to give
credit to Merrick and coproducer Ray Stark. "The *producer* of
Gypsy!" Ethel exclaimed, getting the last word after all. Following further conversation among the three, Merman suddenly
stopped her train of thought and took in Judy's new, streamlined figure:

> ETHEL: You look–look at you!
> JUDY: (TRAILS OFF AND SLAPS HERSELF ON THE HIP) Fi-
>   nally lost all that . . . Oh, yeah . . .
> ETHEL: (SINCERELY) Oh, you look *wonderful*, Judy!
> JUDY: Listen, you can't get off here without . . . do you
>   want some tea?
> ETHEL: No, I'd rather have the *silver*!
> JUDY: You can't get away without belting one song.
> BARBRA: You've got to. We both did!
> ETHEL: Well, I was belting over there . . . I'm not going
>   to belt unless you two belt with me!

The "off-the-cuff" choice of "There's No Business Like Show
Business" began with Ethel booming the first few bars, subse-

CBS TELEVISION NETWORK

A Division of Columbia Broadcasting System, Inc.

TELEVISION CITY · HOLLYWOOD, CALIFORNIA · OLIVE 1-2345

Dear Judy,

I'll call you as I had to leave — had a date made & couldn't very well get out of it

You look great & it was a "gas" being with you & Barbara

much love Ethel

A previous commitment following her concurrent taping of a Red Skelton program "across the hall" forced Ethel Merman to beg off socializing with Judy following her "Tea for Two" appearance. The Merm's affectionate note to Judy following the program, however, reveals her genuine amazement at Judy's new figure and "the new belter" Streisand, even if she misspelled Barbra's first name. The once-in-a-lifetime teaming of Garland, Merman, and Streisand together, as Ethel aptly described it, was indeed "a gas"—so much so that Ethel quickly agreed to guest on a subsequent Garland hour to be taped in December.

JOSEPH L. GRAMM COLLECTION

quently joined by Judy and Barbra—for the first and only time in her career Streisand almost unheard against the likes of Garland and Merman. (Judy turned it over to the Merm at one point, exclaiming, "*Sing* it, Ethel—*yeah,* baby!") When Barbra seemed totally lost near the end of the song, Judy noticed this and took Barbra's arm to bring attention to Streisand to pull her into the number. The performance stopped the show, one of the great moments in television and one of the great moments in show-business history.

The trio packed such a wallop that *Variety* was led to quip, "The CBSoundmen, incidentally, are threatening to sue Judy, Ethel and Barbra for bustin' their eardrums."

For the second Garland-Streisand medley, Mel Tormé fashioned a tuneful collection of songs familiar to both Judy and Barbra. The "Hooray for Love" medley opened with that Arlen song, followed by "After You've Gone" (Judy), "By Myself" (Barbra),

"'S Wonderful" (Judy), a duet of "How About You?," "Lover, Come Back to Me" (Barbra), "You and the Night and the Music" (Judy), and the two wrapping it up with "It All Depends on You."

Judy and Barbra delightfully worked their way through the song bag, Streisand unabashedly hanging on to every note of Judy's (especially "After You've Gone"); Judy clapped and warmly responded to Barbra's solo moments in return. Barbra mocked erotic remembrance while acting "Lover, Come Back to Me." She sang, "I remember every little thing you used to do . . ." and giggled delightedly before semimoaning, "I'm *so lone*-ly . . ." which broke up Judy. For her part, Barbra delighted in Judy's ad-libbing, "I like a Gershwin . . . and *Arlen* . . . tune . . ." (nodding in agreement) in "How About You?," both holding Harold Arlen as their favorite composer. And Judy's belting of the last few notes of "You and the Night and the Music" caused Barbra to exclaim, "Ohhh!" in admiration.

Judy's on-the-money performance in the "Trunk" spot of "You Made Me Love You," "For Me and My Gal," and "The Trolley Song" was exemplary. Holding an obviously shaken Yorkshire terrier puppy, Judy comforted him and sang "You Made Me Love You" sweetly and gently to calm the dog instead of attacking the song in full-throated vigor. Giving the pup to Joey in the front row, she asked the audience, as was her custom, to join her for "Gal" and then drove into "The Trolley Song" with gusto, hitting the final "to the end of the line!" perfectly.

The Garland-Streisand hour was so spectacular that, after attending the taping, CBS president Aubrey ordered that the Maharis-Carter episode that was set to air that Sunday night be bumped to a future date, and that the Streisand hour be aired instead. Editors, in a marathon session, finally assembled the final broadcast version of the show by 5:00 A.M. on Sunday, only a matter of hours before it was to beam coast-to-coast.

The last-minute switch from Maharis to Streisand was so newsworthy that it even warranted notice in *The New York Times*, and some newspapers, in an unusual move, reviewed *The Judy Garland Show* for the second time in two weeks. *The Hollywood Reporter*'s Hank Grant used the opportunity to make the dig, "If anyone again (this time The Smothers Brothers) refers to Judy as a 'little old lady,' I'll personally horsewhip him!")

"Hooray for Love"
COURTESY RICHARD CONNOLLY

While the show's publicists, not without reason, complained that the sudden flip-flop of the two shows gave them little time to publicize the event, CBS somehow managed to whip up an advertisement overnight that ran in Sunday's *New York Times*: "Judging from her enthusiastic reception last week," stated the copy, "Judy exceeded all expectations. Tonight her guests are Barbra Streisand and The Smothers Brothers."

Variety raved: "It's little wonder that a last minute switch was made. . . . All concerned seemed awed by the result of the session with Barbra Streisand. . . . The combination of the Misses Garland and Streisand with Ethel Merman in a brief bit, was a combine of major talents and styles which resulted in superb entertainment. Judy and Barbra have diverse singing manners. Miss Garland is sentimental, open and frequently joyous. Miss Streisand is sophisticated, sometimes ironic and frequently devious. Yet there was an extremely harmonic play and a sympatico feeling between them. When sitting on a pair of stools and bantering tunes back and forth, it was a true delight. It proved a vocal highlight of the season even though the current annum is only two weeks old."

The program was no less a triumph for Streisand. While she had already committed to guest on subsequent television programs—including one special with Bing Crosby—Barbra successfully asked to be released from those obligations. As Streisand's manager, Marty Erlichman, concluded, "Once she did *The Judy Garland Show*, I told her, 'There's no more reason to be a guest artist on these cockamamy television shows. You just couldn't top that.' " (And, after her Garland appearance, Streisand's weekly salary for concert appearances reportedly jumped from $2,500 to $8,000.)

The pairing put both Garland and Streisand in a unique situation. In 1964, Judy was nominated for an Emmy Award for her continuing performance on the series, while Barbra (in an unusual combining of categories that year) was nominated in the same category and thus pitted against Judy for her single appearance on *The Judy Garland Show*.

Barbra was said to be "apologetic" when she learned that she and Judy were in Emmy Award competition. "I should have been in a different category," declared Barbra at the time. "It was silly to put me up against the people who had a weekly show like

Judy, Danny Kaye, Perry Como, and Andy Williams." She added, "I'd hate to do a weekly show. How can you get good material every week?" (Kaye was the winner.)

The Hollywood Reporter on May 4 of that year revealed: "Barbra Streisand is eager to split a fall special right down the middle with Judy Garland, so grateful is she that her very first Emmy nomination was pegged on her guesting in a Garland show." (Judy spent most of that year abroad and, in her absence, along with a dramatic decline in her health, caused this projected second teaming of the two giants never to materialize.)

Through the years, Barbra has unwaveringly spoken of Judy with great fondness and respect. When asked by Geraldo Rivera during a 1984 *20/20* interview whether Judy was "jealous," Barbra replied, "No, I don't think so. [She was] generous, very generous. My heart went out to her. She was holding on to me—tight. She was scared, too. Sometimes, you get more scared as you get older, maybe."

In 1986, in her One Voice fund-raising concert at her home in Malibu, Barbra—for the first time—sang "Over the Rainbow." In introducing the number, she made her feelings toward Judy quite clear:

"Recently, I've done some research for an album that I'm planning to do, some songs from movies. And I came across what is one of the finest songs I think [was] ever written. But I thought I couldn't sing it, because it's so identified with one of the greatest singers who ever lived. But the lyrics felt so right, so relevant tonight, [so] what the hell, I decided to sing it anyway. But I would like to dedicate it to the wonderful woman who first sang it—this woman who I had the privilege of working with, who touched me so deeply. Who knows . . . she may even be listening . . . "

Barbra also never forgot a helpful warning that Judy gave her. Sensing Streisand's extraordinary future ahead of her—and perhaps willing her as successor to her crown as the greatest singer in show business—Judy took her aside. Her advice was simple but profound.

Looking the twenty-one-year-old Barbra straight in the eye, Judy told her, "Don't let them do to you what they did to me."

14

For show ten, the producers conspired to team Judy Garland with two performers who shared with her memories of MGM and the golden age of Hollywood: Jane Powell (Garland's replacement in *Royal Wedding*) and Ray Bolger, the Scarecrow in *The Wizard of Oz*. And the very day the writers turned in their script, once again *The Judy Garland Show* was unexpectedly plunged into turmoil.

Without giving him any warning, CBS fired Jerry Van Dyke and the Powell-Bolger episode would be his last appearance on the series. "We didn't know what to do with him," admitted an unnamed CBS executive at the time, echoing the words of George Schlatter five months before. Some reports indicated that Van Dyke was "asked to be let go," but he admits that he was fired.

Van Dyke got the news one night after leaving the studio. "I remember going home, coming in the door, and my wife saying, 'You're off the show.' I don't even remember if I called anybody or talked to anybody after that. I was devastated." He also admits that the turmoil resulted in a bout with alcohol. "It was really a traumatic experience," he offers. "I had never drunk in my life. But I started drinking."

Judy also was devastated when she was told that CBS had dropped him from the series. "I'm going to pretend like it's just not happening," she told him. "I don't even want to talk about it. If I don't talk about it, I won't think about it."

During a 1965 newspaper interview, Jerry Van Dyke stated, "Judy Garland treated me great. At first all went well. I was the bumbler, the likeable, loveable goof . . . Then they get a new producer and new hotshot writers and . . . these know-it-all guys said, 'Look, sweetie, the concept is all wrong. The way we read the smoke signals Judy herself is the bumbler—not you.' They said, 'From now on, Van Dyke, your characterization changes. You tell Judy what to do.' I'm not kidding. One week I'm the shy yokel. The next week they . . . made me into a heavy. When I started with Judy, I figured, wow, this'll make me a big star. After what happened, I'm lucky to be working!"

Without missing a beat, CBS already had another candidate in mind: Jack Carter. Word had actually leaked out about the network's interest in the comedian *before* Jerry was officially given his notice of termination. CBS then announced that Jack Carter was being eyed as Garland's "steady comic foil" for a minimum of ten appearances. In the end, Carter was a guest on show thirteen with Peggy Lee. While he remembers that he was quite eager to team with Garland on a regular basis, Carter could not extricate himself from other already-set TV guest shots and club dates; he also was under contract to Desilu for his own situation comedy to begin pilot filming soon after CBS approached him for Garland.

With Garland still reeling from Van Dyke's dismissal and yet another go-round of changes made beyond her control, Bill Hobin's departure was announced only days later. The result was even more bad press for *The Judy Garland Show*.

Judy had trusted and respected Hobin and hoped that he would change his mind and remain. But Hobin's desire to flee the Garland operation had intensified due to his strained relationships with Jewison, Tormé, and even Freddie Fields ("He walked onstage during a taping, and I had to cut. I chewed him out, and I don't think he liked me after that"). Clinching his decision was an incident surely known to Garland that occurred at the George Maharis taping. "That's when I got into a fight with Norman, as a matter of fact. I couldn't understand booking [Maharis] . . . he was hot then, but he couldn't perform. [Norman] was out there [onstage] trying to direct George, spinning a bench around, trying to find some business for him to do. I think he realized he'd booked a dud. And I didn't think Maharis had any business on a musical show."

"Bill was very upset by it all," says Bob Wynn. "He is a very nice man, and I don't think he could stand the amount of rat-fucking that was going on—the truly political rat-fucking between Fields, Begelman, Aubrey, Stromberg, and Iannucci. Bill was badly shaken."

Hobin remains adamant that Garland was not to blame in his departing the show. "As far as Judy was concerned, I love her," he said at the time. Hobin now adds, "Judy was always most cooperative. The only problem was when she'd drink a little, but even then, she was on the stage and she was always there. Once that audience was there, she was always up. We ran pretty well on time every week."

The Judy Garland Show had by now been irrevocably branded as a chaotic, desperate, doomed failure—after barely three weeks on the air. As *Variety* put it, "Old rumors are being hashed over regarding the Judy Garland show and its prospects of longevity now that Jerry Van Dyke has been dropped and director Bill Hobin departs after four more shows. The CBS high command, western section, insists that the show 'isn't breaking up' and 'everybody is happy with it so far.'"

Reports of Hobin and Van Dyke's exits also pointed out that executive producer Jewison was about to leave. Also, although it was not yet announced, Garland was aware that her senior writers Arne Sultan and Marvin Worth had struck a lucrative deal with CBS and would depart after show thirteen to move on to their own projects.

Seeds of discontent were springing up everywhere around Judy. Her show was sinking, and she had become filled with dread that she was sinking along with it. And her archrival competitor *The Danny Kaye Show* was left untouched by network interference.

Kaye's director, Bob Scheerer, revealed the extent of Kaye's freedom with CBS not long after Van Dyke made headlines following his dismissal: "Danny realized the importance of having regulars on his show, but figured it was worth the gamble to build his family on the air instead of following customary procedures and signing individuals to seasonal pacts . . . only an actual trial on the air would tell. Our auditions were most comprehensive—some 500 performers—but not one selected was signed beyond just a single show. And this plan has worked out extremely well. . . . As a result, we recently signed pacts with

Harvey Korman and Jamie Farr, strictly on what they put forth on their initial performances. Comedian Howard Morris was so impressive on his one-shot that he was inked for several repeats. Others set for returns include Art Carney and Nancy Walker, so you see even guest stars have made single appearances before the pact, so to speak. This radical procedure . . . isn't really as much of a gamble as risking multiple contracts with players who later prove, through no fault of their own, not to fit the show. Danny may well have more regulars at the end of the season than other series have at the start of their shows!"

Garland's situation was the fault of Fields and Begelman, according to CBS executive Ethel Winant. "She had bad luck and bad management. They didn't give her a Perry Lafferty [Kaye's producer]. Her people didn't know what they were doing. The difference was that Kaye had a very skilled, unemotional, professional producer who looked at what he had and tried to create a show that would work. And the show became a hit. It wasn't an accident. Judy seemed so insecure, she seemed to listen to everybody."

Orval Paine ruefully agrees with Winant, recalling how easily Judy was maneuvered as she desperately sought to follow the advice of the army of so-called experts who passed in and out of the Garland operation. "She wondered why people couldn't come to her and talk to her as a real person and not somebody they were going to benefit from. Judy was a very outgoing, very loving person. She liked everybody until they would do something against her. She was a very trusting person. There are a lot of phonies out there in show business, but she wasn't one of them."

Judy, who had an innate, extraordinarily sensitive ability to sense such layers of discontent festering around her, became sharply aware of growing factions of discontent and "camps" forming, one group pitted against another. She became alternately upset, angry, and frustrated, no longer buffered by her unbridled enthusiasm and goodwill. As star of the show, and as president of Kingsrow Enterprises, Judy began to be more vocal about her objections; she also rebelled by increasing tardiness and absence from rehearsals. She was increasingly coming to the conclusion that she had, in effect, been sold a bill of goods, and vastly inferior goods at that.

A phenomenally quick study, Garland seldom showed the

lack of formal rehearsal in the final product; she still delighted in working with her guests and rarely skipped rehearsals when the performer playing opposite her needed her there. "She was a big girl, and she showed up," says Bob Wynn. "And she performed well. Yes, she missed some rehearsals. But she always had respect for her fellow performers. She would get it together with them, somehow. There was never any major kind of problem."

Wynn signals Schlatter's firing as the turning point. "It lost her attention, that really was the key. Because she had to be constantly reassured and constantly stimulated." Stromberg's presence did not help matters. "Hunt was so heavy-handed, and Judy just didn't understand that. You had to get down to basics for her. Or make her laugh. Then she would do very well."

During this new cyclone of panic and change, Judy renewed her late-night calls to staff members. Gary Smith and Norman Jewison made it clear to her that they were not to be included in her nocturnal pleas for telephone conversation or visits to the Rockingham house until the early hours of the morning. Smith deems his refusal to be part of "the Dawn Patrol" as the beginning of his relationship with Garland turning sour. "I didn't play the social game, that was one of the problems. I didn't know all those old MGM stories. I couldn't sit up until five in the morning schmoozing. I was a twenty-seven-year-old kid. All I knew about was TV. I said, 'I'll do my job, but I cannot be at the house to two or three in the morning.' And Judy would call, and I'd say, 'No, I can't come over.' "

Gary offers that Garland's unhappiness with the series became more and more directed at him. "I had to say, 'Judy, rehearsal with the orchestra is tomorrow at two. You didn't make it last week, we wasted three hours, the orchestra was just sitting there.' She'd say, 'Let CBS pay for it.' I said, 'Judy, CBS is not going to pay for it. It's your responsibility. It's our responsibility—why should they pay for it?' 'Well,' she would say, 'because they got me into this mess.' She got really negative. I think she felt terribly hurt."

Bob Wynn, however, suggests that tensions between Garland and Smith largely resulted from Gary's being supportive of the CBS position regarding the show. "Garland didn't have the family that CBS wanted. Gary, on the other hand, tried to create the family for CBS, which didn't work, either. Gary wasn't her type. George Schlatter was a Judy Garland person. George could do fart jokes. Gary couldn't. Judy would get out there and raise all sorts of hell. But it was all manageable, and George handled it quite well. The first five shows had a momentum. Where we got off the track was when we had to stop and deal with 'the family.' Judy just wanted to get out there and sing." Gary Smith, to Judy Garland, came more and more to represent CBS and all of the poor decisions and choices they had put upon her.

Although from the start Jewison was always considered a temporary employee, his firm resolve to distance himself from Garland on a personal level still left her with one less source of comfort or support. "She'd call me up at three in the morning. I was one that rarely went over. I was very close to her, but I was trying desperately to keep it on a very professional level. I felt there had to be one relationship that she could count on that was professional."

Self-described "kid writer" Bernie Rothman vividly remembers a warning from Jewison when Judy invited him, along with several others, to the Rockingham house for an evening of card-playing and conversation: "Judy was pretty social and loved to play poker. I was in Hollywood [from Canada] and didn't know anybody there. Once, Judy called and invited me over to play poker. Norman said, 'Bernie, be very smart. Have a nice professional relationship with this lady and don't get involved.' " Rothman remained swayed by Jewison's advice. "Professionally, we were close. We had a great professional relationship. Norman made sure I didn't make the mistake of trying to be Judy's friend."

However well-intentioned Jewison's advice to the young, relatively inexperienced Rothman, the pervasive view held by her colleagues that befriending Garland was a "mistake" could hardly have been of comfort to her, particularly when she remembered convivial nights with Schlatter, the Waldmans, and Johnny Bradford—whether at the Rockingham house, on the town in Hollywood, or during a weekend jaunt to Las Vegas. (Schlatter and Bradford remained friends with Garland after their firings; George and his wife, Jolene, were invited to Judy's Christmas party at her home, and Bradford, among many other evenings of socializing, was asked by Judy to attend Streisand's Grove closing night.) At this point, she could only have felt abandoned by nearly everyone.

Mort Lindsey astutely offers, "Judy liked Norman. But Norman was a different kind than George. She called George at two in the morning, and he'd say, 'Okay, Okay, what do you want to do, Judy?' She'd call Norman, and he'd say, 'Listen, I'm sleeping. I'll see you in the morning.' But you had to do that. If you did your job, Judy respected you. Judy was very bright. Her IQ must have been one-fifty, one-sixty. You couldn't fool her. But you could bore her easily when she went through your bag of tricks. And with these people, she did just that. But if you did your job, you didn't bore her."

That Judy chose to absent herself from most rehearsals for the Powell-Bolger show is thus hardly surprising. (Garland's lack of preparedness is perhaps more obvious in this hour than on any other episode.) Bill Hobin's memories of Jane Powell as being "a total professional and a real doll" are sentiments voiced by everyone present near Studio 43 that week.

Ray Bolger was quite another matter.

Hobin enjoyed an old friendship with the rubber-faced, gangly dancer, and the two got along well, but the director acknowledges that Bolger had a reputation within television circles as being "difficult." Mel Tormé was taken aback when Bolger rejected his idea of having Ray, in a routine, refuse to perform his trademark song, "Once in Love with Amy," instead singing a medley of any number of "girl" songs—*except* "Amy." Ray only agreed to do the material after it was altered to his satisfaction.

Then, Ernie Flatt announced he was quitting the show. He had been increasingly frustrated not only by Garland's tardiness but by the chaos permeating the entire endeavor. "I had nothing but respect for the lady, but she was just impossible to work with, because she never showed up for work. They'd say, Miss Garland's going to be in at ten, so we'd rehearse and plan schedules around that, and then they'd call and say she's not coming in until two, and then four, and it just went on and on like that. She took uppers to be able to get to work, and then she'd be so alive that she couldn't sleep at night, so she took downers to go to sleep. The normal working hours of motion pictures or television were daylight hours, and she was on a nighttime schedule. She just couldn't bring herself to come to rehearsal. She was scared to death because she'd have to face the audiences and never felt she knew what she was doing. As brilliant as she was— she possibly was the wittiest, the brightest talent that ever was— under those conditions, it just didn't work. Wherever she went, she was followed by her hairstylist with an ice bucket with a bottle of Liebfraumilch in it, and she herself with a glass of wine. Not only was she taking pills, but she was taking alcohol along with it. At that time, nobody understood it. It was really sad to see that great talent involved in such a mess." (Garland favored the light white wine, highly diluted in a large glass of ice cubes, both to reduce the nervous effect of the amphetamines she needed to control her weight and to counteract the throat-drying effect that such medication brought about.)

Mort Lindsey takes another view. "Judy always had personal problems—the kids, the show, her personal life—her habits weren't that regular. That was her nature. But we didn't have to be *up* or as *bright* as she was. She showed up when she was supposed to show up."

While many of the dancers were critical of Garland's tardiness, none of them recall Garland under the influence of alcohol or temper tantrums. "Judy was there," says Sharon Shore. "Judy never did not show up. But she was always late. I do not remember any day that Judy, at some point, didn't show up when she was supposed to. She would occasionally say, 'Oh, could we do this?' or 'Could I wear my hat here?,' and they would always let her. But there was never a big confrontation. And she asked for very little. She was a very professional lady and would never cause a confrontation in front of everybody. And although the wine was always there, and she was drinking it, it was never apparent that she was incapacitated or could not cope with what she had to do." Adds the dancer pointedly, "Judy never slurred her words. She was directed, and she did what she was told and she did it well."

Jane Powell was an unfortunate target during the week of rehearsals for a rather startling predilection of Ray Bolger, who brought a whole new meaning to the phrase "guest appearance." Laced with a bit of uneasy laughter, Jane reveals, "Ray liked to take his clothes off—he loved to expose himself!

"I think that was just the exhibitionist in him. He didn't do it all the way," Jane hastens to add, "but he loved to tease! At the time, I was terribly prudish. I'm not as prudish as I *used* to be, but I just found him to be kind of a dirty old man. I don't mean that to sound so terrible. I mean it endearingly." When asked if she was aware of Ray's unusual habit during her MGM days, Jane chuckles, "Well, I think he must have always been that way—that just doesn't come on *overnight!*"

Despite the rampant tensions swirling around *The Judy Garland Show* at precisely the time of Powell's appearance, Jane remembers the experience as a happy one: "Judy was well at that time, and she was pampered. She wasn't temperamental. She was on time. I felt the men behind the scenes had more input than Judy, because they were so talented. I think that Judy probably went along with almost anything they had to say because they were protective of her and also very good at what they did."

Jane's lavish production number of "Dear Friend" was one of the most opulent and successfully realized of the entire series, a concept she credits to Jewison and Smith. "That was such a gorgeous song, and that all came from Gary and Norman."

The week of rehearsals was brisk and efficient. "We didn't have that many meetings. We got the script, and they talked to me on the phone about it. I went in and worked with the arranger and the choreographer. I really had very little input as far as doing anything, because I always did what I was told. Maybe Judy did, too. She had her numbers, but she worked with her own people."

While the Powell-Bolger show had moments of charm and freshness—with Garland enjoying tremendous rapport not only with *Oz* cohort Bolger but with "Janie" to an equal degree—the final product has a thrown-together, piecemeal quality, ranging from nearly excellent to only fair. The nearly excellent was Judy, the musical material, and her guests; the mediocre was the pedestrian comedy material.

Lindsey created a spectacular arrangement (and Tormé some fine special material) of "A Lot of Livin' to Do" for Garland. Again utilizing the revolving light board, Judy took the stage, wearing a rather simple white dress, and lip-synched the number. The effect of the performance, however, was marred by Garland's forgetting the lyrics three times during the song, having to lower her head rather noticeably when the words left her.

Jane Powell and Ray Bolger join Judy for "Be My Guest."

(Wearing the elegant slacks outfit she wore for the unaired Henry Fonda "Tea" segment shot during the Donald O'Connor show, Judy also taped another lip-synched number, "I Feel a Song Comin' On," set to be the new beginning for the revamped Rooney program finally scheduled to be aired two weeks later.)

"Be My Guest" was next, and was offhand and enjoyable. Judy introduced Jane in song ("We've got Jane Powell, she's sweet and witty. She sings each ditty so pure and pretty . . .") and then Ray ("Here's Ray Bolger, and like I told ya, I'm such of a fan of this lovely man, especially when he sings those great old songs . . ."). Upon his entrance, Judy warmly embraced Jerry Van Dyke (sighing, "Oh, darling!") for more than a few seconds and affectionately kissed and hugged him—knowing that this was their last time working together.

Jerry displayed his own, genuine sense of humor during his audience warm-up for the Powell-Bolger hour. Holding up a stack of reviews panning him for the premiere episode, he cracked, "Reviews don't mean anything. Oh, by the way, this is my last show with Miss Garland!"

Experiencing a bit of a rough throat for this show, Judy is touching and quite wonderful in her solo of "That's All," even though she is vocally not in peak condition. Then, in a bar setting, Judy began to croon "One for My Baby," which served as a comic sketch for a boisterous birthday party (a huge cake, placed on the bartop as homage to Garland's agent, reading HAPPY BIRTHDAY, FREDDIE). Garland's soulful rendering of the Harold Arlen "saloon" song is broken when the party goes into full swing, with a drunken Van Dyke (the birthday boy) staggering in, causing the guests to be thrown out into the street by the indignant bartender. (Before singing the final "long, long road" words of the song, Garland does a take, looking behind her to see if it's safe to finish the number without further interruption.) While the sketch is humorous, a serious reading of the song would have been preferable, because Judy never recorded or performed the song on radio or television before or after.

Bolger's song-and-dance routine is tedious going, with the performer shamelessly mugging, pratfalling, and working very, very hard to be charming and achieving quite the opposite effect. (Even Judy, who adored Ray, was said to have once cracked, "Every movie, same goddamned dance!")

Jane Powell, a most accomplished performer and excellent dancer, offers an astute assessment of Bolger's performing style: "I think he thought he was funnier than he was. He was an interesting dancer, or dancing cartoonist. But his jokes, his timing, always seemed to be off. It's not so much what he did, or what he didn't do, it's *when* he did what he did. At the time, it seemed that he was trying so hard to be 'now' that he just pushed too much."

After Jane's "Dear Friend" solo spot, she joined Judy (who forgot the special material and threw it to Jane to sing alone) and Jerry for a somewhat amusing "Leading Man" sketch, based on the notion that Van Dyke had to sub for MGM male leads of Hollywood's golden age, due, so the gag went, to the show's "limited budget." ("He's it?" Jane asks Judy when Van Dyke makes his appearance. "He's *them*!" corrects Garland.) Intercutting Garland into Maurice Chevalier's "I Remember It Well" (from

Judy and Jerry mimic Jane Powell and Vic Damone reaching for a glass-shattering note.

Vincente Minnelli's *Gigi*), Jerry impersonated the famous Frenchman to her obvious delight. Jane then took a turn at a Kathryn Grayson impression, amusingly dropping to her knees to sing a duet to Jerry's Howard Keel, who towered above Grayson singing "Make Believe" from the MGM version of *Show Boat*. Judy then had a chance to do a good-natured send-up of Jane in *Deep in My Heart*, with Jerry lip-synching the Vic Damone part to "Will You Remember," both Garland and Van Dyke mugging hysterically as they mimicked Damone and Powell's overwrought reach for their shattering high notes. (Jane and Jerry were to impersonate Garland and Astaire warbling "Snooky Ookums" from *Easter Parade*, but the idea was dropped before the taping.)

Ray and Judy had a brief but beguiling spot together, with Ray tapping to Judy's singing of "On the Sunny Side of the Street." Judy threw off most of the high notes at the opening of the song (giving the impression that she was attempting to sing it in the same key as she did on her 1942 Decca recording!), but opened up full steam for the final chorus. Ray, obviously surprising Judy, picked her up near the end of the number. Delighted, she nevertheless struggled to put her high heels back on the stage floor in short order, playfully spinning Ray around in her chair after they finished.

Their "Tea for Two" segment was warm and wonderfully nostalgic, including, in part:

JUDY: Do you remember a song in *The Wizard Of Oz* called "The Jitterbug"?

RAY: Oh, golly. Where the monkeys came down? Oh, sure. Hey, that was a great song.

JUDY: They cut it out!

RAY: I know they did. And we had a very cute number.

JUDY: They cut out "Over the Rainbow" once. . . . Yeah. In Pomona. Yeah, they did!

RAY: They didn't know what they were doing.

JUDY: They thought it would take up too much time with "this little fat girl" singing!

RAY: Listen, of all the things in the world that leaves me with the fondest memories, it's *you* in that picture.

Upon Judy's prompting, Ray sang a marvelous rendition of his "If I Only Had a Brain" that caused a sentimental Judy to warmly put her head on his shoulder as he sang. Then the conversation turned to the Cowardly Lion, Bert Lahr, and his fights with MGM over his *Wizard of Oz* contract:

RAY: He fought with the studio. They wanted to give him a five-week guarantee. And he insisted on a six. And it was five, he said six, they said *five*, he said *six*. They settled for six—

(JUDY BEGINS TO BREAK UP AND JUMPS IN TO FINISH THE SENTENCE WITH HIM)

RAY: And the picture ran *seven months*!

With Judy asking him, "Shall we go down the Yellow Brick Road?" (Garland comically in search of a comfortable key for them to meet in the middle), the two ended the spot with an energetic performance of "We're Off to See the Wizard." At the finish, she exclaimed, "Well, we *made* it, darling!" The song-and-dance production number of "The Jitterbug" was next, with Bolger playing it in a polka-dotted cape and hat in pursuit of Judy and Jane. This latter-day interpretation of the cut *Oz* tune is great fun, if not really memorable.

The "Trunk" closer was fine, Judy singing a song new to her, the haunting ballad "When Your Lover Has Gone" to the strains of a single guitar in the background. (She wore a simple white turtleneck and matching slacks, which had become her standard "Trunk" costume of this period, possibly because several of the broadcast versions were dress-rehearsal takes.) Changing moods instantly, she then launched into her brief but sensational version of "Some People," running the length of the stage, whipping the microphone cord like a lion tamer. In homage to the crane cameraman whom director Hobin had close in on Judy for the whole of "Maybe I'll Come Back"—much to her surprised amusement—she ad-libbed, pointing, "This cameraman is a cousin of mine!," mugging, winking, and darting about through the number.

Reflecting on the experience of working with Garland, Jane says, "Judy was wonderful. She really was unique. There was nobody like her, there never has been, and there never will be. Judy really was spectacular." And after viewing a tape of the program in 1989, the first time she had seen the show in twenty-five years, Jane remarked, "Sometimes you don't appreciate someone until you haven't seen them perform in a long time, and then you say, Yes, that's what it all means. *She's* what it means."

Show number eleven (with guests Steve Allen, Mel Tormé, and Jayne Meadows) would begin rehearsals immediately. Norman Jewison could not have known that what was to be his most successful entry in *The Judy Garland Show* was due largely to the man whom he had replaced—George Schlatter.

Judy had not given up on the idea of having Schlatter return as her executive producer, even though his initial talks in early September with Mike Dann resulted in nothing conclusive. With Norman Jewison set to depart after only three more episodes, Judy had become even more vocal in her demands to reinstate Schlatter.

One strong indication that CBS was taking Garland's suggestion seriously came when the network slotted a Schlatter show (Lena Horne) to be the third episode aired, instead of broadcasting one of the Jewison-produced hours already in the can. After the show aired the Sunday following the Bolger taping, Judy had every reason to hope that chances to snare Schlatter were quite good, if trade-paper reaction was any indication. As Hank Grant raved in his "On the Air" column in *The Hollywood Reporter*, "Sunday's Judy Garland show was indisputably her best. No strained informality this as Judy tandemed provocative chatter with her guests Lena Horne and Terry-Thomas. And her vocal duets with Lena highlighted the show as much as Lena's splendid solos and Judy's single belting of 'The Man That Got Away,' which CBS should be mournfully singing as an apology to their axed producer George Schlatter!" In the same issue, Mike Connolly in his "Rambling Reporter" column praised, "Just for the record, Judy Garland's giving us our TV kicks of the season, as per Sunday's 'Foggy Day in London Town.' "

Syndicated television writer George Laine offered, "The show created the kind of electricity for which Judy is famous. . . . So impressed was CBS after the Horne program aired that the network ran back to the library and grabbed another Schlatter effort, this one featuring Mickey Rooney, for next week." (With the George Jessel "Tea" segment now out of the Rooney show, slotted instead in an upcoming Jewison hour, Mickey and Judy decided to tape a new music-comedy sketch in its place; as a result, the Rooney hour would not air until December.)

Laine added, "Sources close to Miss Garland report that Judy called Schlatter and [Johnny] Bradford after the program had aired and said it was the best job she'd seen done on her for television. Judy also reportedly told the two men that she was going to demand their return—immediately." Obtaining the services of either Schlatter or Bradford was questionable, however, as they both had other commitments.

Judy, after quite a dry spell, was the recipient of even more good news. After the Horne show beamed Sunday night, CBS told her that her series was picked up for another thirteen programs. And two days after *The Hollywood Reporter* noted that Garland was "prodding producer George Schlatter for a return engagement," CBS decided to renew Garland for not only thirteen episodes, but for nineteen more programs—news of this breaking the day the Steve Allen-Mel Tormé-Jayne Meadows hour was taped.

No wonder that for this show Judy was as sparkling, rested, rehearsed, and confident as she had been during the Schlatter regime. She was also bolstered by a first-rate script (no doubt polished and improved by Allen's comedy genius), Mel Tormé's

superb musical choices, Mort Lindsey's incomparable arrangements, and Judy's great rapport with Steve Allen and wife, Jayne
Meadows, who were both close friends of hers during this period.

The idea for Steve to be a full-fledged guest on the show
(thereby cutting his "Tea" spot with Judy during the Tony Bennett hour) came only hours after his initial appearance was taped.
Tony Bennett invited Steve and Jayne to a party after the taping.
As Jayne recalls, "We went back with him to the studio, and
there was Judy. We went back into her trailer, and there was a
piano in it, and suddenly I thought of *Sophie* (an ill-fated April
1963 Broadway musical based on the life of "Red Hot Mama"
Sophie Tucker, which closed after only five performances). And
Mel was there, and Steve and Mel were friends since going to
high school together in Chicago."

Mel remarked to Judy that Steve had written innumerable
songs, and Jayne piped in. "I spoke up and said, 'You know,
Judy, my God, you've got the voice for the songs Steve did for
Sophie.' " Judy asked to hear some of the songs from that score,
and Steve sat at the piano and played the defiant "I'll Show Them
All." "And while he was playing it, Judy jumped up and went
over and stood by the piano and said, 'Why, that's the story of
my life! I want to sing that song on my show and dedicate it
Louis B. Mayer!' "

Later, "Steve got a call from Freddie Fields, who was also
Steve's agent, that Judy wanted to do several songs from the
score on her show." Allen was unabashedly excited when Judy
told him she wanted to sing his songs. "I was so thrilled when
I heard about the possibility of her not only doing a number
from the show, but actually talking about the show," Steve recalls. "Speaking as a songwriter, it was a great honor that she
was in love with it."

The Allens and Garland—and particularly Judy and Jayne—
immediately developed a fast friendship. "We got a call that Judy
wanted us to come to her tapings, and the first time Freddie,
Steve, Judy, and I all went to some Italian restaurant for supper,
and the next thing we knew, we were with her almost every
single night. Every Sunday night, we went to her house for dinner. It would be Mickey Rooney, Freddie and Polly [Bergen],
and strangely enough, Sid, and the children. It would be, maybe,
twelve of us." (After the series went on the air, Judy began a
weekly practice of having close friends to the Rockingham house

for Sunday night informal dinner parties. In addition to coworkers and her children, often Roddy McDowall, Roger Edens, and a few other close friends would attend as well. Once Roger and Roddy made an especially grand appearance, Roger walking in carrying Roddy over the threshold! Judy, remembers Jayne, was "particularly thrilled" with the Allen-Tormé-Meadows episode.)

"Judy took a shine to us," says Jayne, "I guess because we thought she was the greatest, and all I did was laugh with her. I adored her. We loved going over there. And she would sing, and Mickey would sing, they were so adorable together, and Roger would play the piano."

Jayne became Judy's confidant, and one of the very few people she had told about her affair with Begelman. As Jayne reveals, "She took me one night into the bedroom, shut the door, and made a phone call. It was to David. She said, 'You know, I'm madly in love with David.' "

Jayne also remembers an incident that occurred after her show with Judy was taped, when Judy was preparing to leave for New York for meetings with CBS. "One Sunday, she was packing, and she said to me, 'Well, of course, I'm in love with him, but he'll never marry me. He's not in love with me. You know, Jayne, he's not fooling me.' " Meadows astutely observes, "Many actresses, especially the ones who were child stars like Judy, so many of these people are manipulated by agents and very easily because their egos are so fragile, because they did not have a normal childhood because they were onstage all the time. And they're in a world of imagination and lack of reality. Consequently, everything is a romance. Judy had many romances with very attractive men with power. . . . She had a crush on David, but he was nothing like the men that she was usually attracted to. She was attracted to very handsome men. She was crazy about David probably because he resurrected her career. Which is the role that Vincente served for some time. And Sid, too. She wasn't sure what she wanted, whether she wanted that father figure or the romantic guys that mistreated her."

Glenn Ford, Jayne insists, "was never there. It was David. That's all she talked about to me. She was mad for him."

The shooting script for show eleven was turned in on October 16, two days before taping. Jack Elliott fondly recalls an incident occurring at that week's rehearsals: "What kind of a mind Judy had! My son was about three or four weeks late being born.

The girls in the vocal group, Ginny Mancini and the others, were really sweet and gave me a shower. Finally, we had the kid. I hadn't spoken to Judy directly, really, in a very long time. We were rehearsing 'Here's that Rainy Day,' and she said, 'Did your wife ever have the baby?' I told her yes. She said, 'When?,' and I told her, 'A couple of weeks ago.' She asked what his name was, and then asked if he had a middle name. I told her it was David. She said, 'Mmmmm, David.' And then, to the tune of 'Fascinating Rhythm,' she walked by and sang. 'Alan David Elliott, you've got me on the go . . .' It was that fucking razor-sharp sense of humor of hers." (Ginny Mancini—wife of composer Henry Mancini, who also was part of Tormé's 1940s vocal group The Mel-Tones—also got a glimpse at eleven-year-old Lorna Luft's already-developed sharp wit. The two crossed paths in the backstage ladies' room the following week. Attempting to make conversation, Ginny asked Lorna, in a manner perhaps a bit too cloying, childlike, and condescending, if she got "a lot of goodies on Halloween." Swinging the powder-room door open and beating a hasty retreat, Lorna shot back, "Oh, just a lot of shit!")

Art director Robert Kelly decided to frame Garland's "Here's that Rainy Day" as a beautifully choreographed production number. Garland would wear the trench coat from the never-aired version of Schlatter's "Stormy Weather" spot at the "Trunk," while several dancers were to frame the haunting, melancholy ballad wearing trench coats and carrying umbrellas. The number was so beautifully executed, and Garland's rendering of the song so perfect, that it stands as perhaps the most successfully realized set piece of the entire series.

But, says Bob Kelly, "Here's that Rainy Day" presented considerable challenges: "We took everybody, all of the singers, all the dancers, and put them in raincoats, and I lacquered about twenty-five umbrellas, so that when the revolving turntable turned, the umbrellas flashed and made them appear wet. It was a gorgeous number, and there again, Leard Davis just lit it beautifully. It was a very rich creative time. Ideas set you on fire. After we had done a few shows together, after all the false starts and stops of those first couple of shows, we all kind of developed a language that meant something to us. It saved a lot of time and promoted a great deal of creativity."

The dress rehearsal of "Here's That Rainy Day"
CBS INC.

Kelly credits Tormé with creating the white motorcycles-on-platform (Mel was an inveterate cycle enthusiast) look for his solo number, "Comin' Home, Baby" and then the duet of "The Party's Over" with Garland, each of them on a white motorcycle. "I loved that," says Bob, "We welded about six or eight motorcycles together. We made a big pyramid out of motorcycles, and then we put high-fashion models on them. It was Mel's idea, completely out of left field, but a really good idea for the number. He knew somebody who was a motorcycle dealer and said, 'I can get you all the motorcycles you want!' Which he did—and they didn't care whether we bolted them or welded them or what we did! So we made a marvelous number out of that."

"From the standpoint of total production," Kelly states, "I think the Garland series was some of the best television that was ever done. Not necessarily as a body of work, but as moments in that body of work. An awful lot of love went into that show. I think the show was ahead of its time."

Although she wasn't at first scheduled to be on the show herself, Jayne was there at Judy's insistence. "I was on the set every day. And the week that Steve was on the show, some important magazine [*Saturday Evening Post*, for a lengthy story to be titled "The TV Troubles of Judy Garland"] had spies around, and they were running around asking everybody about her drinking. I wished they'd come and asked me. I never, ever saw her drunk; however, I never saw her without a glass in her hand. What was in the glass, I don't know. I never asked.

"She would sing, she'd sit on a stool, she'd work with the band. She was a woman on top of everything, who was brilliant in every area, never late," stresses Jayne. "I *never* saw any tantrums, temperament, anything. She was just fabulous. Judy was in the most terrific spirits, like a performer who was in the biggest hit on Broadway. I have never seen such energy. She was in all of the rehearsals and knew every song, and I never saw anything but professionalism and happiness. And I never, ever saw a sign of drunkenness."

Steve, Jayne, and Judy socialized often. Out at dinner, Jayne recalls fondly, "We would all sit at the table and *listen*. Now, *I'm* a big talker, but she did all the talking. And *we* did all the laughing and the listening because it was so fascinating—her stories about vaudeville, MGM. I had been under contract to MGM, too, so I appreciated them. She would tell all kinds of stories, it got to be God knows what time, she'd sleep about four hours, but she'd be the first person at the studio every morning. And then Steve and I would drag in at nine in the morning. She had been there for I don't know how long, ahead of everyone. And we had gone home so tired, and we hadn't even *talked!* We sat there laughing so much that *we* were absolutely exhausted."

Jayne, however, remembers that Mel Tormé that week was far from animated. "Mel, who had been such a good friend of ours, was not Mel at all. He seemed very heavyhearted, very depressed. He was the real downer personality on that show."

Meadows recalls a most unusual conversation with Judy that week: "One day, she took me in her dressing room. She said, 'Jayne, I want you to carry my phone number with you all the time. I want you to have my phone number everywhere you go, always. You are my new best friend.' And then she said, 'If you ever, ever have any fear of suicide, I want you to call me immediately.' Now, I'm the last person in the world who would ever think of suicide. I told this story to someone who was very close to Judy and me, I can't remember who it was, but this person said, 'Jayne, that's a call for help. She wanted you to have her phone number with you always because she felt you were so well-adjusted.' Very often psychiatrists will say that a person will say something like that about you, when they are actually talking about themselves."

Steve says of his wife's relationship with Judy, "Jayne was sort of motherly to Judy, and she responded to that." Adds Jayne, "Judy knew that I loved her, and she respected me and admired me as I did her. She felt I was someone she could turn to."

Jayne should not have been surprised, then, when Judy made the sudden decision to have her be the "Tea" celebrity guest. "The night before the taping, I was shampooing my hair, and it was soaking wet and the phone rang, someone saying, 'Judy wants you to come in tomorrow and do "Tea for Two"!' They said, 'You'll just talk.' I said, 'About what?' and they said, 'Judy wants you to tell one of your hilarious stories.' I said, 'I don't know what stories she's talking about.' So they got Norman on the phone, and he said, 'Judy said you told her a story about Steve's show.' I said, 'I haven't got the vaguest idea of what Judy is talking about.' I used to sit and listen to *her* stories. Finally, I said, 'Get Judy on the phone.' She said, 'Come on down!' I said, 'Judy, what story do you want me to tell?' and she told me back the story. She said it was hilarious, and she wanted to do 'Tea' with me."

Her hair still in disrepair, Jayne wore a wig for the taping. After running through the segment during the dress rehearsal (done without an audience since Jewison's reign), Meadows remembers, "Norman said to me, 'I've never seen anybody as relaxed as you in my life—you've relaxed Judy, she's having so much fun doing it with you.' "

Judy, indeed, is enormously comfortable and self-composed for the entire show, but her chat with Jayne during "Tea for Two" is particularly splendid and a highlight of the hour. With great aplomb, Jayne related how she agreed to appear on one of husband Steve's television programs, with the promise that they would do something "glamorous with her." But when Jayne arrived on the set, the producer "started to read the rundown of what they were going to do. And he said, 'The opening shot finds Steve and Jayne in a *manhole* in the middle of Vine Street.'

Jayne Meadows and Judy in the gown that got away
CBS INC.

Now, ordinarily, I'd speak up and say, 'Look, fellows, I'm not the manhole *type!*' " Jayne good-naturedly agreed to go along with the gag. Descending "way, way down," Jayne hung on to ancient steel rungs running down the manhole like a ladder, but two of them were so rusty that they broke, leaving her "hanging, like a *gorilla*, inside this thing!" Then, laughed Jayne, Steve's entrance was so successful, and his laughs so prolonged, that he "forgot" about his wife waiting in the manhole to make her own entrance, "and there's *gas* in manholes—and I was getting . . . well, I was getting *gassed!*"

"Television shows *are* kind of peculiar," Judy agreed, relating how, during the week of rehearsals for the taping of the first show in the series, she came to the studio already made up and wearing a dress, but on the day of taping decided to come to CBS dressed casually in slacks, a sweater, and without makeup. "They stopped me at the gate," deadpanned Judy. "They wouldn't let me in. They'd forgotten to leave a *pass* for me. And that was a bit *demoralizing*," she quipped. She added that, when she finally was allowed into CBS Television City, her production staff "was so *busy*, nobody recognized me. It's so *hasty*, television!" Judy bemusedly noted, "I couldn't just holler "Over the Rainbow" and *identify* myself!" After laughing delightedly at this, Jayne quipped that show business was indeed a "kooky business."

Also "kooky" was the dress Judy was to have worn for the "Tea" spot, as well as "The Party's Over" duet with Tormé and the subsequent songwriter's sketch. Ray Aghayan designed a beautiful soft chiffon gown for the second half of the show, but it self-destructed during the dress rehearsal. Ray laughs, "It literally fell apart. We could have fixed it, but there was no reason when we could just put Judy in something else." For the final version, Garland wore a glittering white gown seen in "Fly Me to the Moon" and the "Tea" segment in the Donald O'Connor program.

The rest of the show was no less fine than the Meadows "Tea" spot. Judy made a grand entrance among snow-covered trees in a winter sleigh. Dazzling in a fur-lined coat with matching hood, Garland ripped through a (prerecorded) sparkling arrangement of Steve Allen's "This Could Be the Start of Something Big"—her finger-snapping, alas, not in time with that heard on the prerecording!

"Be My Guest" here was the strongest of them all, with Judy self-mockingly rendering her "school song" (assuring Mel and Steve, "Yeah, I went to school!"):

> We're from old Metro
> in Culver City,
> that great, big, busy town!
> We had to learn our lines and our arithmetic;
> With all that overworking,
> no wonder we are sick!
> Mickey Rooney, Judy Garland,
> Lana Turner, "Deena" Durbin
> and Freddie Bartholomew—
> that's why we're speaking so loud of it,
> because we're so proud of it—
> old Metro, we're true to you!

Steve Allen's solo segment (with him racing through some of his renowned characters, including sportscaster Big Bill Allen and the Question Man) is first-rate, as is the *Sophie* medley, comprised of the tender "I Love You Today," the lilting "When I'm in Love," and the powerful "I'll Show Them All," which Garland turned into a stunning tour de force.

Judy introduced "I'll Show Them All" by eloquently noting, "Next there is a song that everybody will understand, because all of us have been too criticized, and told to get out of the business, whatever business it may be. And we're made to feel not very pretty, and not very worthwhile, and not very brave."

Judy—perhaps silently "dedicating the song to Louis B. Mayer" as she had said that night in her dressing room when first hearing the number—bit into Allen's powerfully affecting lyrics:

> I'll show them all.
> I'll show them every one.
> I'll do my damndest now
> and make a vow to everyone.
> They'll give me praise,
> some of these days.
> They're really gonna see
> this "Red Hot Mama" blaze
> I'll show them all
> I'll let 'em watch my dust.
> I'm on my way,
> and there'll be hell to pay—
> the top or bust!
> Some day I'll win.
> Some day, they'll crawl.
> Believe me, when I say—
> I'll show them all!

Moving from her chair to stage center for the final moments of the song, Judy is so electrifying, and the final note so soaring, that composer Allen, in the background, leads the applause and looks at her with rapt admiration, beaming, praising, "Marvelous, you were just marvelous!"

Mel's solo spot was engaging, with him delivering the instantly forgettable "Comin' Home" with the right amount of tongue-in-cheek good humor; his subsequent duet with Garland of "The Party's Over" was warmly sung, the two voices again blending beautifully as they had during the Count Basie show. The songwriter sketch is as well done musically as it is in the comedy-material department (again, the mark of Steve Allen's influence). When miserable songwriters "Rise & Shine" (Allen and Tormé) ask Garland if she saw one of their Broadway musicals, she deadpanned, "No, I had tickets for the *second* night." Tormé fashioned what he dubbed a "round-robin" collection of over a dozen tunes sung by the three, in harmony and in counterpoint, including "Tip Toe Through the Tulips," "Mean to Me," "Ain't Misbehavin,' " and "My Heart Stood Still," all sung to delightful effect.

The "Trunk" spot is one of the very best of them all, Judy (in a straw hat, maneuvering it no less rakishly and spectacularly than she did her fedora in "Get Happy") romping through "Island in the West Indies."

She introduced "Through the Years" poetically, by saying, "Well, we have a whole new year ahead of us. And wouldn't it be wonderful if we could all be a little more gentle with each other, and a little more loving, have a little more empathy. And maybe next year at this time, we'd like each other a little bit more." Judy sang "Through the Years" beautifully, rich with meaning and emotion. Then, reflecting her good humor, after thanking her guests as she was about to begin "Maybe I'll Come Back," she asked the audience to tune in next week, when, she quipped, "Old, *undependable* Judy will be back!"

This program was a smashing success, with not one weak moment in it, standing as the finest entry in the series of the standard variety-program mold, equal to Schlatter's best efforts (the Rooney and Minnelli episodes), although his differed in concept and were admittedly larger in scale; the Allen-Tormé show ranks among Garland's finest hours on television.

Judy had scarcely time to reflect on the week's triumph. She had to leave immediately for CBS headquarters in New York, where she was to meet with James Aubrey and a battery of other network officials to determine the future course of *The Judy Garland Show*. All the series needed to complete the next nineteen programs was its third executive producer, a second director, a fourth choreographer, and a third team of new writers.

"Judy is a legend in her own time. She is a combination of Sammy Davis, Jr., Aimee Semple McPherson, and Greta Garbo."

—Norman Jewison, 1963

15

Singer Vic Damone and actress-dancer Zina Bethune (of the then-popular CBS medical-drama series *The Nurses*) were booked as Garland's guests for show twelve. While the writers worked on the script, Garland flew to New York to confront Jim Aubrey and present a list of demands. Judy quickly discovered that the network president had some definite opinions of his own to share with her. Although the talks between the two were to remain private, details quickly leaked out.

The ratings story for the show had not been good, with Garland's series hovering near sixtieth place, according to an A. C. Nielsen Company report issued at the end of October. Garland could take some solace in the fact that Danny Kaye fared little better. As a result, *Variety* tipped that Judy "is said to have expressed dissatisfaction with the format since Schlatter left and the poor ratings [and is] nervous over departure soon of rest of the crew."

The Hollywood Reporter revealed, "The way we hear it, the minute Judy Garland set foot in Gotham over the weekend she put the screws on CBS prez Jim Aubrey to get George Schlatter back as producer of her series. Aubrey, who took the responsibility of firing Schlatter in the first place, is thinking about it. The second thing Judy did was to personally latch Noël Coward for a guesting to be taped in January. The third thing she did was ask Aubrey if he'd made up his mind yet [about Schlatter].

He's still thinking about it." (Judy did leave the CBS boardroom while in Manhattan; she dined with Noël Coward and asked him to guest on the show. Regrettably, that once-in-a-lifetime pairing of two old friends never materialized.)

Schlatter, understandably and as a matter of pride, pointedly told CBS that he would consider returning to the Garland show if they would not only match, but better, the princely sum of $12,500 the network paid weekly to Norman Jewison. The network resisted, halting negotiations. But money was still not the only mitigating factor to Schlatter. The other was his irrevocable stand against Aubrey over how Garland should be presented on television; he held to his "weekly series of specials" concept as much as before and, as he remembers, Aubrey stubbornly held to the folksy, standard variety-show mold. With the show largely a critical success but a ratings dud, one would think Aubrey might have reconsidered his position at this point. He did not.

"There were a lot of talks about my coming back," George now reveals. "But what it really was, was that Judy was upset, and CBS, mostly, was saying, 'Okay, we'll try to get him to come back' as a kind of pacifier to her. And I told them since they were paying Norman Jewison twelve thousand five hundred dollars, they would have to pay me fifteen thousand dollars a week, which is not a lot now, but it was a hell of a lot of money back then. The pressure to get me back was coming from Judy. . . . [She] talked to me about it, and I explained that CBS and I had a basic disagreement on what the show was. She was a legend, and it's very difficult when you have a star and try to remold that star. It's not only difficult, it's unnecessary, and usually unsuccessful. Gleason was Gleason. Danny Kaye was Danny Kaye. They didn't make them somebody else. They were trying to make Judy somebody else. And she was fantastic just as she was. That was the biggest problem I had with CBS.

"There were an awful lot of egos running around then," Schlatter adds. "You had Jim Aubrey with his ego, you had Hunt Stromberg with his monkey. You can't really have a serious discussion with a program executive who has a pet monkey. You don't know," he quips, "whether to talk to him or the *monkey*." When Schlatter ran into Stromberg at Judy's Christmas party, George remembers Hunt whining, "I'm so confused about the show. And I'm having trouble with my monkey." Without missing a beat, George cracked, "Why don't you just *fire* it?"

Although Schlatter did not return to her series, he did remain very close to Judy until her death. After he was initially fired, George recalls, "I went over to her house, because what I wanted at that point was just for her to make it. That's why I did not cause any kind of problem. I didn't even talk to the press, because I was bewildered, too, and I didn't want to do anything that would hurt her. She was a good friend. And as far I was concerned, the woman worked for me. She did everything I asked her to do. I couldn't have expected any more out of a performer."

Jim Aubrey, on the other hand, expected more from Garland.

He made it clear that she was to stop "touching" her guests on the air, a complaint he made to Schlatter and then to Jewison. Now, with no producer to act as buffer, Aubrey confronted Judy directly. Although his charge was ridiculous, Judy was forced to take a defensive stand. She told *Newsweek,* "I touch. I've always touched people. All the time I touched. It's a habit. It isn't nervousness. It's pure affection. I'm a woman who wants to reach out and take forty million people in her arms, but I've been told that I must watch myself. I've also been told that I shouldn't kiss my leading ladies on the cheek, that it offends some viewers. I've been a hit for years," she pointedly added, "and I always kissed and touched." Judy, however, said she would bow to network demands. "I'm the original take orders girl. CBS knows more about television than I do. All they want for me is a smash."

Schlatter did not find Garland's need for physical contact disturbing or, for that matter, a problem that did not have a solution. As the producer reflected in 1989, "She was a toucher. It was a simple thing, actually. Judy just felt better if there was some physical contact. We solved this problem by having the guest star just reach over and put their hand on Judy's, which immediately relaxed her and freed her up."

Judy, not long after being admonished by the network, took a typically humorous view: "They told me I was a *toucher,*" Judy giggled when relating the story to *TV Guide's* Vernon Scott in 1964. "They sent me back to New York and called me on the carpet for kissing my guests and touching them with my hands. The room was full of executives. Maybe even some from NBC. They said, 'Don't touch the guest stars!' I explained that I've always been demonstrative. Some of the guests were nervous, and I'd give them a pat of reassurance or hold their hands. But the executives showed me letters from viewers accusing me of being either drunk or nervous or both. They even wrote that there were supposed to be some sexual implications. So I said, 'OK, I'll be absolutely sterile. I won't touch a soul.' But, on the very next show, Zina Bethune kept touching *me*. So did Vic Damone. They were nervous, I guess. And so was I, for fear I'd touch them back!"

At the same time, Judy made it clear that she sided with Schlatter's, and not CBS's vision of showcasing the star. "The network wanted me to be sort of the girl next door. But they couldn't find the right house, or the right door." She flatly added, "I've never been the girl next door."

Judy, in typically candid fashion, admitted to *Newsweek* during her New York stay, "You know, I used to watch *Bonanza* all the time, and if my show doesn't get better, I'll go back to watching *Bonanza*. What do I think *The Judy Garland Show* should be? Well, like my own life, really. Full of interesting personalities." She added, "You just can't barge into people's living rooms and say, 'I'm a big star.' I like them to get to know me. And I'm not that experienced with so much taping. You get the feeling that if you miss one word, you get shot. Maybe that's why I wanted so much to do the weekly series. For years, everybody's been saying I couldn't stand the pressure every week. Now it's kind of like sticking my tongue out and saying, 'See, I'm doing it.' And I'm hoping someday to be very rich from this."

At the same time, Mike Dann jumped in to offer his plans for the future of Garland's series. Although the team of Marc Breaux and Dee Dee Wood would join the show as a stopgap—due to Ernie Flatt's sudden departure—and to complete the first thirteen-week cycle, Peter Gennaro (now in Los Angeles for the filming of *The Unsinkable Molly Brown* with Debbie Reynolds) signed as the new choreographer; alternating with him would be Carol Haney, perhaps most remembered for her sizzling "Steam Heat" number in the hit Broadway musical *The Pajama Game*.

Dann continued to put the nail in the CBS coffin by remarking, "We told her what we think, and she's listening. She's far too insecure about TV to exercise her own judgment. She knows we know what's good for her." The CBS head of programming, not long after, made it clear that CBS was still quite intent on making Judy Garland "homespun," if not quite giving up the idea of having her surrounded by a "television family" of one sort or another. Dann exclaimed, "There will be no regulars . . . but we will use such guest stars as Don Knotts, Andy Griffith, Jackie Cooper, and Danny Thomas." (The CBS executive also noted Danny Kaye would make an appearance on Garland's show.) Dann admitted, "Judy is a fine comedienne . . . but we found it difficult to get comedy material suited to her"; Danny Kaye, however, found it easy, simply by hiring the best writers available.

The primary perpetrator of this chaos, Hunt Stromberg, Jr., could not resist joining in the CBS chorus. In the middle of this new round of revamping *The Judy Garland Show* from top to bottom, as a third production team had to be assembled after only eleven completed shows and as the ratings projected doom, Stromberg somehow mustered the nerve to declare, rather idiotically, "Not in any way, shape, or form is this show in trouble."

In an attempt to generate some publicity, Garland consented to be interviewed by several television newspaper editors across the country—after curiously being told to avoid the press during the entire preproduction period and the premiere week.

Judy admitted to *Chicago American* reporter Bill Irvin, "I think the show has a pretty look, don't you? I'm very new to TV. I didn't know we weren't a hit. I understand they change writers regularly," adding, "It's a bit disconcerting at times." And while Dann wanted to put the likes of Don Knotts and Andy Griffith on Garland's show, the star had other ideas, revealing she was hoping to woo Bing Crosby for a January appearance. "Maybe I'll be on his show in return, if he asks me. Maybe he won't want me, but I want him on my show."

Judy added further that Liza ("I expect her to be supporting me soon," she laughed) was in the running to headline Judy's time slot as a summer-replacement series. "I would love it if she would," said Judy.

Norman Jewison attempted to deflect Garland's low ratings with "I don't believe in ratings—ratings are a false yardstick. They're for the birds." Unfortunately, they were also for networks and sponsors. The cutthroat ratings contest was best illustrated by a *Variety* article titled "It's '30 Share' or Drop Dead: Madison Avenue Loads Up on Aspirin" as the first ratings report of the new season was issued. It offered: "Joining the ranks of shows failing to hit a 30 share (the percentage of viewers tuned into a particular program) are such items as Judy Garland and Danny Kaye. . . . While Miss Garland was hardly expected to top NBC's high-rated *Bonanza,* nonetheless her 28 share in contrast to *Bonanza's* 38 has all the earmarks of a shocker. And whereas Kaye was expected to take his Wednesday 10 to 11 time period, his 29 share was outclassed by NBC's 36 for *Eleventh Hour."* the paper summed up that "the biggest surprise of the 30-market count was the failure of either . . . Garland . . . or Kaye . . . to hit a 30-share stride."

Illustrating the television climate of the times, a bland, insipid new ABC situation comedy series starring former child star Patty Duke had already become a major hit, winning a whopping 48 share; *The Beverly Hillbillies* and *Bonanza,* respectively, remained the number-one and number-two programs on television.

The Hollywood Reporter's Hank Grant took an unusually harsh jab at the accuracy of Nielsen ratings on October 16, stating, "Though the ratings systems took a few governmental slaps last year as being anywhere from inconclusive projections to outright farces, it's still the only game in town and the tastes of a miniscule fraction of one percent will continue to determine the fare presented to some 56,000,000 homes."

Then, rumors began circulating that, due to her poor ratings performance, Garland might switch to doing a show every other week.

Judy later found humor in her sad ratings story: "I'd really like to know who this guy Nielsen really is—and what's his *first* name? Is it *Ned* Nielsen? I don't think there is such a person! I think there's just some guy who didn't make good with a network once and then just named himself *Nielsen* and became very important somehow!"

CBS obviously had turned a deaf ear to Garland's dim view of how they were "packaging" her for mass-media consumption, the singer candidly remarking only a couple of weeks after her round of CBS meetings, "I would like to see the shows become a little simpler. I don't think I'd like to look at my show every week. It's just enervating. I think it should be a bit easier for people to watch. We're in trouble unless we all calm down a bit."

While Judy's show might not have been a ratings smash, it

nevertheless was one of the most watched, and discussed, programs in show-business circles. Because she was in New York,
Judy unfortunately missed the annual Thalians charity ball in
Hollywood the last weekend of October; one of the chairmen
was her beau Glenn Ford. Although she was not present, Garland was the highlight of the show. Her two good friends Debbie Reynolds and Carolyn Jones, noted *The Hollywood Reporter*,
did a "wickedly funny takeoff on Judy Garland and guest star
'Barbra Strident' in which they kept congratulating themselves
until ringsider Jerry Van Dyke jumped to his feet and hollered,
'I want out, out, OUT!' and walked out."

Aubrey and the other CBS executives gathered in Hollywood
the weekend that Garland's twelfth episode was shot. To some
CBS insiders, as well as most of those on Judy's production staff,
it was at this point that Aubrey dismissed both Garland and her
series as having any future on his network; to many, he now
became openly hostile toward her, having fully come to the conclusion that Garland was nothing more than an expendable multimillion-dollar mistake.

Norman Jewison remembers having more than a few stormy
confrontations with Aubrey during this time. "I said to him, 'Don't
you realize the talent you have here, for God's sake? You're the
one that was impudent enough to believe that you could put her
on the air every week! You're the guy who forced all this on
everybody. Why don't you now back off, why don't you just
support it, why don't you give us a decent time slot? Give us all
the support you can and sit back and let us do all the work.' I
even suggested at one point that we do one show a month. I
kept pounding that home. Nobody would listen. They seemed
to be out for the dollar at that point, too."

Jewison sadly adds, "There was a renewed energy and enthusiasm when I came in. Then it started to slip again. It was a
matter of demanding too much from someone. You can only demand so much from certain people, and when they have a gift
as special as Judy had, it should be preserved and protected and
be utilized sparingly. Not flogged. I felt she was being exploited
in a way by everybody."

Gary Smith reveals, "When Aubrey realized that she was
fucking up his Sunday nights, he wrote her off. I think he made
that decision after the third show aired."

Hunt Stromberg, Jr., by all reports, followed Aubrey's lead. "When you get minds like Stromberg and Aubrey working together, it's pretty frightening," says Bob Wynn. "Hunt was one big son of a bitch. He threatened to run me out of the business, and he was very devious. Aubrey was an authoritarian dictator." Upon Aubrey dismissing the Garland show as a hopeless failure (despite public and critical protests to the contrary), Stromberg did the same and, after creating irreparable damage, vanished.

Bob Wynn says much the same of Fields and Begelman: "They were nonexistent. In all of the turmoil, in all of the fights, they were never there. In all of the meetings we had, if CBS showed up, they might come in. David showed up for the first one or two shows."

Despite the turmoil regarding the future course of *The Judy Garland Show*, its star still had the immediate present to contend with, flying back to Los Angeles to immediately begin rehearsals for show twelve.

Garland's enthusiasm to do well on this program came not only from the presence of the CBS executives but also from her long-standing friendship with Vic Damone and a strong kinship with young Zina Bethune who was a friend of daughter Liza.

"I fell madly in love with Judy instantly, as did many people," Zina remembers with great fondness. "When I was asked to do the show, I was excited and really wanted to do it. I had begged my producers for a week off to get in better shape, but they wouldn't give me the time off. Because of that, I was under a bit of strain, because I didn't feel I was in the top condition that I needed to be."

Judy, however, instantly befriended the young performer. "We struck up a friendship very quickly. I voiced to her my concern about not being in shape. And Judy being Judy, the minute she hears that anybody is concerned about anything, she's there for you. And she was there for me. She attended rehearsals. She called me every day when we were rehearsing, saying, 'How's it going, what do you need?' She was quite extraordinary. Judy certainly was not needed for some of the things that she showed up for. From my perspective, she went out of her way to be there."

The two socialized during the week of rehearsals, "having dinner, just becoming friends. She was very lovely, very warm, and very much a real human being to me. And very aware, extraordinarily astute. If anybody knew what they were doing artistically, she did."

Judy also hinted at her problems with the network during their conversations, Zina recalls: "She genuinely felt, from what she told me, that the network had some difficulty in thinking that she was going to be successful in this area. Judy joked that because the show had lasted even as long as it had, 'Well, I guess somebody likes us somewhere!' If anybody had an extraordinary sense of humor about her own failings, it was Miss Garland. I never laughed so much in my life [as] the night that I met her. And most of what she was zapping and zinging was herself. Most of the time, it was a joke." But, Zina pointedly notes, "she was no fool. Absolutely not."

Zina expressed her unhappiness as well to choreographers Wood and Breaux, whom she felt had saddled her with a second-rate dance routine for the show. "I really didn't feel they wanted me to do anything interesting or different, and I was not happy with them as a result. I thought my capabilities were better than what they thought I could do. I had been in the New York City Ballet, and I could have done more than the simplistic routine they had for me." (The "Crazy Rhythm" choreography crafted by Breaux and Wood was pleasant, if only adequate, placing Bethune and several boy dancers in a stylized rehearsal hall, and giving Zina little more to do than go through a few kicks, turns, and leaps.)

Recalling Judy's good-natured joking that both Bethune and Damone's touching her throughout the show (which was indeed true) sabotaged her own efforts to keep her hands off the guests, Zina laughs: "What made it worse was that we both are touchers. I heard later that CBS wanted her to stop touching everybody. But we genuinely liked each other, so it was an expression of the warm camaraderie that we shared."

Garland and Damone shared a long-standing appreciation for each other's talents (and, reportedly, a brief romance—which Vic denies—in early 1963 before she reconciled with Sid Luft). But as the talented singer reveals, his friendship with Judy had actually begun just as she was exiting Metro, and he was about to sign with the motion-picture studio: "When I had my first screen test at MGM, I can't remember the name of the director, but he was asking me questions and had me turn this way and that way, and I was uptight, because here I was at Metro, and they were giving me a screen test. And, God, I wanted to be with those people. All of a sudden, I heard this voice behind the director, this pretty little woman's voice, and I recognized it. She said, 'You're not doing this right! If you're going to give him a screen test, these are the questions you should ask!' And it was Judy. She pushed him out of his little chair that he was sitting in, and said, 'Now, let's start this.' And she was the one who did my screen test. She was the one who sat there and asked me the questions, and we laughed. And she was so cute. So that was my first introduction to Judy Garland." (Judy was his good-luck charm, with Damone soon after signed by the studio.)

They did not work together professionally, though, until 1963, when Judy asked him to appear on her show; Vic, who head-lined a series in the 1950s, had also enjoyed a recent success on an NBC summer-replacement series called *The Lively Ones* the previous two seasons.

Jewison deferred to Damone's judgment and asked him to select his material for his guest appearance with Garland. He also, remembers Bill Hobin, played producer in a rather unique way. "Norman bought him a seventy-five-dollar haircut," the director laughs. "I remember being with him out in the CBS parking lot. Vic was driving a Cobra sports car, and his hair was going everywhere, and Norman offered his own barber, saying, 'Let me send in Jay to give you a haircut and I'll pay for it!' "

Hobin held Damone's talents in high esteem. "Vic is a great performer and a fine, fine singer." Garland, of course, was eager to sing with Damone, Gary Smith remembering, "Judy adored Vic. She thought he was the greatest." And, notes the producer, unlike other previous Jewison hours, Judy was indeed present for rehearsals. "She came in, and she came in on time, because she wanted to work with Vic very much."

Damone, curiously, remembers having little contact with Mel Tormé. "I didn't work with Mel at all, really. I would say, 'How about doing *Porgy and Bess* with Judy, or *West Side Story* [which they would do on the series for his second guest appearance],' and they'd say, 'Great, she'd love it.' And then they'd come up with the medley and send it to me. I'd listen to it, I would go and work on it with Judy over at her home. She was wonderful. And she was so *humble*. I couldn't believe that with all the talent that she had, she would be scared to death. I would have to keep saying to her, 'My God, that was beautiful!' And it was. And, she'd say, 'Really?' "

Garland and Damone were both under contract to Capitol Records, and the label planned to release not only albums of Judy's solos from the series but an LP of the Garland-Damone duets as well. (Capitol, in the end, released only one series LP; *Just for Openers* featured eleven Garland solos.) Because of Capitol's plans, the bulk of the musical material for this show was prerecorded to obtain superior audio quality, including Judy's opening "From This Moment On," Damone's "Let's Take an Old-Fashioned Walk," as well as their medley together, a glorious collection of songs from George Gershwin's *Porgy and Bess*.

Prerecording the numbers was scheduled for October 31, the day before the actual taping. Following the usual procedure, Garland and her guest would run through the music with Lindsey and his orchestra and other production staff members in the orchestra cube off to the side of the main stage. "We would prerecord some things," recalls Damone, "and we would sit there and listen to what we just had recorded the night before, and one time she just looked at me, and said, 'You know, we're good—we're really good.' She would be surprised at her own talent, the notes that would come out of her. And they were pure gems, pure, beautiful gems that God had given her, this wonderful talent. She was so thorough. When we'd be working together, or rehearsing, she'd want to know exactly where it was going musically—and then she'd want to know why. Why that note, why couldn't we do this one? She was very thorough.

"Working with her was a great thrill for me," Vic says lovingly. "She had all that raw talent and something that was very unique. Judy lived everything, and she lived every word of her music and what she sang."

Damone was baffled by her reputation for tardiness and temperament. "She might have been ten or fifteen minutes late, but she was getting ready. So what? I didn't care. Just to work with her was a thrill for me." The singer candidly offers that, because of performing with Judy, he thought little about his own solo turn, saying, "What was important to me was really not my solo numbers, it was the medley with Judy that I cared about. That was really why I did the shows. Just so I could sing with her." (Judy's great respect for Vic Damone is evidenced by the fact that he was the only performer—other than Mel Tormé, who

The *Porgy and Bess* medley with Vic Damone

was contractually promised multiple guest spots on the show as part of his Kingsrow employment deal—to be invited for three appearances within her twenty-six programs.)

Vic also clearly recalls a good relationship between Garland and Jewison: "When we were finally shooting the show, Norman Jewison comes to mind. He was so patient, wonderful, and was strength to Judy. She would look to him when we recorded the medley and see if she had his approval."

The *Porgy and Bess* medley was magnificently realized and brilliantly performed by Garland and Damone; Judy, particularly, is at her zenith. The staging was simple, the direction unobtrusive, and both were in flawless voice.

However, Tormé's mannered, superficial arrangement of Cole Porter's "From This Moment On" did not serve Garland well, seemingly designed more with his style and voice in mind than with hers. (And while Garland looks great in the Damone duet, this is the first show in which she looks noticeably drawn and tired and older than her years, obviously a result of her harrowing last several days with CBS and no rest before plunging into rehearsals for this program.) Her next solo, "Moon River" (sung live) redeemed Tormé. In a wonderful, slow-tempoed, haunting arrangement of the poignant song, Judy sang exquisitely to the strain of a harmonica against an Americana setting of a grandfather clock, a rocking chair, and a stovepipe furnace.

Damone's solo of "Let's Take an Old-Fashioned Walk" was nicely performed, Vic even engaging in some dance steps with a collection of blue-jeaned girl dancers. The number was imaginatively set on a construction site, with Sharon Shore operating a forklift, lowering Vic down to sing. The inventive staging of Damone peering through a huge pipe while singing, framed by sweeping camera angles and breezy choreography, again illustrated how richly creative was the Garland series at its best; *Porgy and Bess* further underscored the program's sophistication and artistic excellence.

Following Bethune's dance routine, Garland joined her for their duet. (In the earlier "Be My Guest," Mel Tormé had Judy sing, "We've got lovely Zina, our ballerina!") Sitting side by side on stools, the two romped through an easygoing and warm "Getting to Know You."

Judy, Vic, and Zina later attempted an "All-Purpose Holiday" medley of songs that included, "Yankee Doodle Boy," "Happy Birthday to You," and "Seasons Greetings." While the performers are fun to watch, attempting valiantly to make a go of the second-rate routine, it nevertheless misfires. (The best moment was, of course, ad-libbed by Garland. When a hyperactive chorus rushed on stage to recite an endless parade of Irish names saluting Saint Patrick's Day, Judy quipped, "There aren't that many Irish people!")

Judy's "Trunk" segment ranged from fair to excellent. Stricken with a bit of a dry throat, she listlessly walked through "Smile." Aware that her throat was slightly rough, she conserved it, avoiding most of the high notes and, as a result, most of the effectiveness of the song. In a sudden switch, she then launched full throttle into the warhorse "Rock-a-Bye Your Baby (With a Dixie Melody)." (Originally, she was to have sung "What'll I Do?" and "Puttin' On the Ritz" before "Rock-a-Bye Your Baby.") Deciding midstream to go with it, Judy attacked the number with vigor (the tempo slightly faster than usual) and made this one of her very best performances of the oft-repeated tune she originally sang in tribute to Jolson and then made her own.

The "Tea for Two" segment with George Jessel (taped during show six with June Allyson) was inserted into this program. The result is not only historically important—Judy appearing with the man who changed her name from Gumm to Garland some thirty years before—but completely beguiling:

JESSEL: Many years ago, I met you. You were a tiny girl in Chicago. Do you remember?

JUDY: . . . Yes, I *do* remember. You were so nice to me.

JESSEL: We were playing at the Oriental Theatre in Chicago. . . . We were doing six shows a day. . . . I remember, you were a baby doing an act: the Gumm Sisters.

JUDY: Terrible name!

JESSEL: Yes, it was a bad name. I was sort of the big . . .

JUDY: You were the *star*.

JESSEL: And they got rid of a lot of the acts, not that they weren't good. [They said] we don't need them, you know, Georgie, you talk so much, people want to see you, which they did *then*.

JUDY: (INTERJECTING) They still *do*, darling.

JESSEL: (DISMISSING IT) One woman in Pittsburgh! (LAUGHTER) . . . I introduced you, you came out alone, a little baby girl. I said to the audience, [Here is] Frances Ethel Gumm. . . . And it sounded like some funny little kid with pigtails, and the audience used to giggle. I told your mother, "Gee, I don't like that name for this lovely, warm little thing" . . . and she said, "Mr. Jessel, well, she's just starting, call her anything you like!"

(JUDY LAUGHS ABUNDANTLY AT THIS)

JESSEL: There was a great actress called Judith Anderson, and she was opening in a Broadway show that night. . . . I [sent] a very flowery telegram: "Dear Judith, may tonight add another rose to the garland of successes that adorn your great great. . ." something, and I walked on. And I said, now, ladies and gentlemen, here is a little girl destined to go very far in the show business, Judith Garland. And I said, "That's you, honey!," and you went out.

JUDY: (WARMS AT THE MEMORY) That's right!

George Jessel with Judy for "Tea"

Judy offered George tea. "This is delicious!" he enthused while sipping some, adding, "With *beer*, I'd like this!" Jessel continued his story of naming Garland at the Oriental Theatre: "Then, I said, 'And now little Miss Garland will sing, and I lifted you on the piano. First I sat you on my knee [beat, eyeing her newly gorgeous face and figure], which I would like to do *again*, now!'" to which Garland gamely replied, "Okay!" This led into Judy's singing "My Bill."

While it was planned that she was to sing the full measure of the Helen Morgan torch song, Judy sang only a few bars, preferring to let Jessel shine in a rendition of his chestnut, the unabashedly old-fashioned but still touching "My Mother's Eyes." Garland, obviously delighted in Jessel's capturing a bit of the old glory, turned her attention completely to him, instigating the audience to applaud when he began the number and then leading the applause at the finish.

Show number twelve was a solid and good show, elevated to moments of greatness during the Garland-Damone medley of *Porgy and Bess*. The final show in the first thirteen-week cycle would begin production immediately, and the company of friends Peggy Lee and Jack Carter as her guests would surely give Garland comfort. It was, nevertheless, to be a sad affair, with Norman Jewison, Bill Hobin, and her latest collection of writers bidding farewell.

Peggy Lee and Jack Carter reported to CBS Television City the first week of November for rehearsals; the tape date for show thirteen of *The Judy Garland Show* was Friday, November 8. The script, for once, remained virtually intact from its initial draft through the final rundown. In tribute to Miss Lee's songwriting talents, Judy opened with one of her hits, "It's a Good Day," and followed with "Never Will I Marry." (Both numbers were prerecorded, and, perhaps recalling the large amount of music she lip-synched rather than performed live on the last episode as well, Judy quipped, "I think I've been singing 'Japanese Sandman' when I was supposed to sing 'It's a Good Day'!")

After the second Garland solo, she was joined by comedian Carter in a fashion similar to earlier opening-show patter with Jerry Van Dyke, suggesting that Carter was still being considered as a series regular. And while the strained Judy-Jerry talk more often than not brought the proceedings to a dead halt, Garland and Carter were a perfect pair. Jack's stridency was tempered by his obvious admiration and warmth for Judy, and his strength—in contrast to Jerry Van Dyke's—made the material that much stronger.

They struck such a good balance that it is a shame that he was not involved in the show from the beginning, or from this program on:

JUDY: Let's welcome back my old friend, Jack Carter!

(APPLAUSE)

JACK: An old friend? I'm an old buddy to you now! Thank you. Well, an old friend would like to say, Judy, you sure look beautiful tonight. . . . I've been meaning to tell you that I may be doing a show with your lovely daughter Liza very soon.

JUDY: I know, I think that's wonderful.

> JACK: Of course, she's a very talented girl, and she's very normal. Especially for a kid that's around show business. But you wouldn't understand about that, Judy, because you were never a kid!

(JUDY DOES A TAKE AS THE AUDIENCE LAUGHS.)

> JUDY: What do you mean? . . . Didn't you see *The Wizard of Oz*?
>
> JACK: Big deal—so you were a kid for one picture!

After more of this—really a setup to Jack's production number and comedy monologue—Carter more than adequately engaged in a song-and-dance routine built around "Kids" from *Bye Bye Birdie*. (When a guitar began to play ahead of its cue, Carter quipped, "No, wait for me, sweetheart!")

He then launched into a very funny routine about the foibles of "the youth of 1963": "My own mother, a little old lady of sixty-five, is affected [by the youth craze sweeping the country], she's wild today! She's in love. I wouldn't mind if it were a dignified man, someone who could be a companion—but *Fabian*? She's got his pictures all over, buys his records. I called my father, I said, 'It's terrible, what are you going to do, Dad?' I said, 'Teach her a lesson. Hang Ann-Margret pictures all over the bedroom.' He said, 'What—and take down my *Brenda Lees*?' "

Peggy's solo (with Judy introducing her off-camera) displays "the Magnificent Peg" at her peak in a stunning tour-de-force performance of the haunting ballad of lost innocence, "When the World Was Young." (Garland was also to have sung the number during the run of the series but, in the end, never did.) With Peggy in a tight black gown with a plunging neckline and posed against a completely black background, the total effect was mesmerizing.

Peggy and Judy got along very well together; they were old but not extremely close friends. Mel and Peg were friends of long-standing, and the musical portions of the show were particularly harmonious.

"We had a lovely time and really enjoyed singing together," remembers Peggy. "Mel suggested some of the songs for the 'I Like Men' medley, but they're all songs that are known or identified with me." She adds, "I wish Judy and I could have done

The "I Like Men" medley with Peggy Lee
CBS INC.

more shows together. We had a wonderful time, and just told each other a lot of jokes. What I enjoyed most about Judy, I think, was her sense of humor." Although the show marked the departure of the director and writers, Miss Lee recalls no problems on the set, "nothing extraordinary—I only remember the enjoyment of working with Judy and the laughs we had. People always think there was sadness all the time with Judy. But she was really very, very funny, and anyone that knew her would say the same thing."

In a chapter devoted to Garland in her book *Some Are Born Great*, veteran newswoman Adela Rogers St. Johns described an evening at Peggy Lee's home, watching the Garland program with her, and quoted Peggy as telling her, "One thing she has that no one else ever has had—remember how they begin to applaud and shout *before* they can see her? The mere announcement of her name, the news of her approach, fires them with enthusiasm, and she gets a welcome as no one else in our profession ever has. They'll do the same on television."

After Lee's solo, Judy and Peggy joined for a throwaway, fun medley of numbers, including another Lee composition, "I Love Bein' Here with You." The song also included bits of "Under the Bamboo Tree," "It's a Good Day," and "Witch Doctor."

Judy and Jack then had great fun—and delighted the audience in equal measure—in a "Broadway" medley, giving each of the two talented mimics the chance to run through impressions. Those included: a brassy Ethel Merman ("They Say It's Wonderful"), a drawling Ray Middleton doing "My Defenses Are Down," both from *Annie Get Your Gun*; Judy donning a perfectly ridiculous wig and tattered robe to the tune of "I'm Gonna Wash that Man Right out of My Hair" from *South Pacific*; Carter doing a perfect Rex Harrison biting through "I've Grown Accustomed to Her Face" and "A Hymn to Him" from *My Fair Lady*; Judy donning a scruffy newsboy sweater and cap (rather like in "Lose that Long Face" from *A Star Is Born*) and finding a note out of nowhere to growl through "Wouldn't It Be Loverly?" in an outrageous Cockney accent; and, finally, in a salute to Carter's own Broadway show, *Mr. Wonderful*, the title song from the score as well as a tuneful, snappy "Too Close for Comfort." Both stars shone brilliantly, particularly when given such top-rate material and had great chemistry together.

The harmony between Judy and Jack scarcely reflected the backstage happenings this week. Dormant personality clashes were coming to the surface; barely disguised in-fighting was brought out into the open. As writer Rothman reveals, "Gary hired me because I could write good musical material. Mel was in charge of the special musical material, but he would take my ideas, a lot of the time, and rewrite them. I also felt strongly that the things he wrote for Judy were better tailored for himself than for Judy. Too often, it sounded like the Mel-Tones."

Rothman continues, "At the end of Norman's tenure, Gary called me in and said, 'Norman's going, but we'd like you to consider staying.' It had been so horrendous working with Mel, Sultan, and Worth from an emotional point of view that there was no way that I could hang around. I called Norman to say good-bye and he said, 'I think they'd like you to stay.' I said, 'If this is big-time Hollywood show business, you can keep it.' It

The "Broadway" sketch with Jack Carter
CBS INC.

was too tough. It was too scary. And there were too many major egos on the line. Mel was very tough to take. He had an ego as big as a fucking house. We all indulged him. Norman is an enormous talent; Tormé didn't give a fuck about anybody. He didn't give a fuck about Judy, either. He wanted to look good with Judy, but he didn't care about her. I don't mean that we were all rushing to protect her in any spiritual way. I think we were all aware that we were dealing with a very substantially talented person, a legend of sorts, and that whatever we could do to protect, help, and support her, we were there to do. Mel, on the other hand, was a scene-stealer. He took credit from everybody."

Bernie Rothman does not spare his fellow writing team from sharp criticism as well: "Would you have hired them for Judy? I don't think so."

CBS interference only made matters worse, stresses the writer. "Hunt was a pretty rough guy. One of the things that made it such a difficult show was the regime at CBS, which was very tough. Stromberg was Aubrey's hatchet man. When those guys walked in, you saw that. We were made painfully aware that writing 'good Judy' was not what CBS wanted. They cited Dinah

Shore. They wanted Americana, and that's wrong. Make no mistake about it—Judy Garland was a funny lady. I don't know anybody who delivers much funnier than she did. What they gave her was television stuff, and that's not what Judy was. She was fine with it, and we did the best we could. If a star is going to carry a series, they've got to go with their best show. The second best—or in this case—fifth best, isn't good enough."

Norman Jewison adds bitterly, "Things did start to deteriorate. All I was doing was shaking my head, wondering why everybody was headed down this very self-destructive road. And then it started to take up speed. If anybody was conductor of the train, it was Aubrey. He could have made changes which he didn't. He could have saved it." Judy "was very worried," says Norman. "I tried to explain that everything was going to be okay. That she had Gary, that she had support. She was concerned, but she was also concerned about other things, her finances, and she was concerned about her children."

Judy, he remembers, tried to keep a brave face in spite of it all. "She had, perhaps, the greatest sense of humor of any actress that I have ever worked with. We had some great times. When everything was falling down around her, she'd make some absurd reference, some joke, and we'd just take off laughing." He says with more than a trace of emotion, "Of all the people I've ever worked with, Judy Garland inspired me the most. She gave me constant inspiration." Unable to top the experience of the 1962 "comeback" special and the subsequent Garland series, Norman Jewison left the medium altogether, never to return. "That was the last television I ever did," Jewison remarked in 1989.

Bill Hobin, because of their strained relations, did not go to a farewell party for Norman Jewison; instead, he attended a party in his honor given by several of the technical crew on the show. "They were my guys. They did it for me. I felt more obligated to them than I did to Norman Jewison." His parting with Judy was brief but emotional; silence said more than anything else. "That was the last time I saw her. We just said good-bye and that it was fun working together. I wished her luck. We never discussed the show."

In spite of the backstage melodrama and the ever-changing show personnel, Bernie Rothman says of Judy, "I thought she was great. She cheered everyone on. She was a real team player.

She was the star, she knew who she was, but she liked to get the team together."

Sweet and nice was the Judy-Peggy medley saluting "various kinds of males." Based on Peggy's tune, "I Like Men," done more for comic, rather than musical, effect, with the two donning voluminous and very, very long feather boas at the end.

Although it was taped the previous week, Carl Reiner's "Tea for Two" segment (the last one in the series) was aired in this episode. "Judy was so humorous and charming. There was no rehearsal, we just went and *did* it!," exclaims Carl. "I couldn't believe I was on with Judy Garland—and I was an established performer. I adored her. That wonderful lower lip and those black eyes and the way she moved, her left-handed movements. I told her, 'I don't mean I adore you, I really love you! I wanted to date you, but I would be too ashamed to ask!' We were exactly the same age. When I first met her, we were both thirty-seven, and she said, 'What a shitty age, because it's past thirty-five and it's not near forty,' adding, 'Thirty-*eight* is all right, but thirty-seven is just awful!' "

He had another experience, although a poignant one, involving Judy many years later: "My wife, Estelle, was singing at a club in Hollywood, and we met Liza in front of a theater one night, and she mentioned that she wanted to hear [Estelle] sing." Carl offered to be Liza's escort. "I was thrilled. I picked her up at her father's house, just before he died, and I rang the bell. It was very dark, and I didn't know how to get into the house. I was very ill at ease. Vincente's wife, Lee, opened the door and told me that Liza was upstairs with her father. I wanted to say hello to Vincente. He wasn't well. I didn't know him; I had only met him once, I think. I said hello to him and there was Liza, with tears running down her cheeks. She said, 'Excuse me while I repair my face. I haven't sat with my father and watched *Meet Me in St. Louis* with him in years.' They watched the whole picture together, and they were both crying. I never forgot that day."

The highlight of the Garland-Reiner spot:

> CARL: I remember you singing "Balboa" in a movie called *Pigskin Parade*!
>
> (JUDY IS ASTOUNDED THAT HE REMEMBERS THIS)

JUDY: (LAUGHING) *"Balboa"*!
CARL: Was it *Pigskin Parade?*
JUDY: *Yes!*
CARL: And everybody loved you, and you made a success
       then. And you can get to be *eighty,* and they'll still
       think of you as Dorothy and they'll go (EXAGGERAT-
       EDLY PINCHES HER CHEEKS), "Oh, *Bubbeleh!"*

The "Trunk" segment of show thirteen was pure Garland. Offering a poignant "How About Me?," Judy then shifted gears and signed off with an energetic, fully charged "When You're Smiling." Augmented with special lyrics by Roger Edens, the song was one of Garland's standard concert openers. This time, though, Judy altered Edens's special verse of "If your husband bluntly tells you you're too stout . . . don't you pout," and ad-libbed on-camera, "If your banker proudly tells you that you're broke—hah! That's a joke!"

It might have been a harmless change of pace (Judy's new figure hardly made the "stout" reference as pertinent as before), but it could also have been a signal that her eyes were being increasingly opened to the state of her financial future, so dependent upon the future of *The Judy Garland Show*—suddenly no longer as certain as it seemed.

Only a few weeks before, *The Hollywood Reporter* announced that four foreign countries had purchased the series, "although only two of the shows have been seen so far in this country." The item stated that England, France, Australia, and Japan "have purchased the Garland program sight unseen. Deal was finalized by Creative Management Associates, which represents the Garland series exclusively in all areas."

The truth of the matter is that *The Judy Garland Show* was never sold, nor would it be seen in any foreign countries until later, when it was no longer under the representation of CMA. (Syndication proved equally unprofitable for Garland, an initial sporadic attempt in 1966 largely a fizzle.)

Whether it was a ruse to promote interest in the sale within the industry by a false story planted in the trade paper, or even assuming that sales were pending but ultimately fell through, Garland never received any monies from foreign sales.

According to Sal Iannucci, who negotiated with CMA for

Garland's services, the promises made by her managers that international sales were a significant source of income were highly exaggerated: "Since the show was shot on tape, there was no after-market value for those shows. Plus, there were a lot of technical union and musician's union problems with clearing rights for international broadcast. There was no residual value to those shows."

Freddie Fields boasted at the time that "the best part of Judy's deal" was that "Judy owns the tapes, and they're worth at least three to four million. She can release them over and over again. She can sell the syndication rights, the foreign rights, anything she wants. For once in her hectic life, this little dynamo is going to be financially secure. And it's about time." He added, "Judy is forty-one. She's done everything there is to do in show business, from vaudeville to one-night stands. She's earned fortunes for other people, but she's been victimized over and over again. Before we made this deal with CBS, she was practically broke. But television is going to give her what it's given others much less talented than she—security. These shows are going to bring in money so that she doesn't have to sing her guts out in concerts night after night to support her kids."

For her part, Judy said simply, "It's nice to think that these shows will make me rich." She expressed those sentiments to Norman Jewison more than a few times: "Judy was always saying that she was going to make millions on the series. She was very excited by the deal." In May of 1964, one month after the series had ended, Garland, by this time, held a radically different view of her financial state: "I've made a lot of money for a lot of other people, but I don't know who wound up with most of it. We didn't—not my family."

As far as Judy Garland making millions goes, Iannucci deems that impossible under the terms of her CBS contract. "You could not make millions on a variety show. Ed Sullivan was on the air, I think, maybe with forty-four shows out of fifty-two weeks, and he was making two million dollars a year. No way could anybody walk away with that kind of money."

"If your banker proudly tells you that you're broke," indeed. And contrary to what Garland sang that night, it certainly was no joke.

16

Although the Garland series had a three-week break before beginning its second thirteen-week cycle, there was little time to waste in choosing a new executive producer, director, and writing team with pre-production set to begin on November 18.

CBS presented Judy Garland with a list of "approved" director candidates, including Dwight Hemion, Bill Colleran, Dean Whitmore, or Charles Dubin, all talented and respected craftsmen. Judy chose Bill Colleran (a CMA client since 1961) as executive producer—and not merely producer—reversing CBS's promise to Gary Smith that he would be Jewison's successor upon his departure. Having twice been denied the title of executive producer, through no fault of his own, Smith was involved in an adversarial relationship with Colleran from the start.

Before his departure, Jewison had suggested two fellow Canadians, the writing team of Frank Peppiatt and John Aylesworth, to raise the quality of Garland's scripts. Having worked with them on her 1962 "comeback" special, Judy liked the two, a pair of unpretentious, extroverted, and talented men. (The three shared a favorite story of working with Kay Thompson. "Judy flew her in from Rome," says John. "In New York, Jewison, Judy, Frank and I met with Kay. We had a wonderful meeting. At the end of the day, Norman said, 'Let's all get together tomorrow.' Kay said, 'I can't—I'm busy tonight. I have to fly back to Rome because I think I left my apartment unlocked.' It wasn't a joke. She flew back to Rome. And when she came back, she said, 'I was right. I *did* leave it unlocked!' ")

Aylesworth offers a humorous, and rather telling, insight into David Begelman when the CMA executive first courted the writers to join Garland's series: "We went to Begelman's office, which was enormous. He kept saying, 'Peppiatt and Aylesworth—I've admired you fellows for *years*, you are the *greatest*, we *must* have you for Judy!' " David then dismissed the writers' contractual obligation to ABC for country-western singer Jimmy Dean's New York–based variety series—produced by onetime Garland producer candidate Bob Banner. "Don't *worry* about Banner, I'll take care of that!," Begelman promised them, adding, "Judy is a legend. She *needs* you!"

"He gave us such a wonderful tribute. For an hour he kept wooing us, saying how he had always followed our careers," laughs Aylesworth. "After all of this, we said, 'Wow, yes, sir—we'll do whatever you say!' He said, 'Let me call Bob Banner as long as you fellows agree with me. You'll *never* regret it! I want you guys to know that you are doing me a *personal* favor. If you guys ever need *anything* from me, don't hesitate to call!' We left dizzy with praise. A few days later, Frank and I were going to the theater with our wives. We went to Sardi's. We were taken to a banquette directly beside David Begelman and his wife. We saw him and said, 'Hello, David!' And he didn't know who the *hell* we were! Totally mystified, he said, 'Oh, uh, hello,' and turned away. When we realized he hadn't a clue as to who we were, we spent the whole evening asking him questions, 'Isn't that *right*, David?' It was then we realized that show business was such bullshit."

Begelman's offer to CMA client Colleran was couched rather differently; Bill remembers David telling him, "She's a mess, she's impossible to work with, she's crazy. It's a hell of a thing to ask you to do, but I think it would be good for your career and you'd be good for the show, with new, fresh ideas." Begelman (as he had promised Peppiatt and Aylesworth) assured Colleran, "if there were any problems at all to call him or Freddie and they'd come right down." Colleran adds, "That's the *last* I heard from them."

A more recent brush with the past came with the return of

Johnny Bradford. Embroiled in a dispute with CBS and Kingsrow (namely, Fields and Begelman) over the terms of his contract since his termination in the Schlatter purge, Bradford was rehired and returned as associate producer. He received dual billing and was also credited as the third writer following Peppiatt and Aylesworth.

Peter Gennaro, an even more distant echo of Judy's embryonic television career (the 1956 G.E. special), had been hired as choreographer but had to bow out after only a handful of programs. "While I was on the Coast, I stayed four extra weeks, just to do the shows with her," recalls Peter. "She was so quick to learn things, it was a pleasure to work with her." (His assistant, Wally Seibert, took over upon his departure; contrary to Mike Dann's announcement at the end of October, Carol Haney never joined the Garland series.)

Bill Colleran and Judy struck up an immediate friendship as well as forging an excellent working relationship. Unlike Norman Jewison, Bill was not deterred in expressing his lifelong admiration of her talents; at this stage of her television career, she responded warmly and gratefully to his genuine interest and concern. And they shared a similar sense of humor and a sophisticated appreciation for music. The fact was likely not lost on Judy that Bill Colleran was perhaps an amalgam of the best qualities of George Schlatter and Norman Jewison.

Judy and Bill's bond was formed when he related to her a story of how, as a young farm boy, he braved a 1938 Minnesota winter to see Garland as she traveled across country by train, stopping in nearby LaCrosse, Wisconsin: "She was the dream of my life. I adored her since I was twelve years old. When I read in the *LaCrosse Tribune* that she was going to be coming through town at five in the morning, I couldn't believe what I had read. On that day, I got up before dawn and rode my bicycle to the railroad station and sat there until the train came in. It stopped, and I was at the back of the train, and held on. Judy saw me, came out, and reached over and took my hand. I rode home on my bicycle with one hand all the way, with my other hand over my heart, because that glorious creature had touched my hand." When Bill told her the tale during their first lunch at Chasen's, "Judy cried and cried. She told everybody that story. Another time we were there, she called Jack Carter over to our table, told him the story, and started crying *again!*"

Bill Colleran reveals his obvious admiration for Judy at the postperformance party honoring the taping of his first Garland hour.
COURTESY BILL COLLERAN

Colleran notes, "We had a very good relationship from the beginning because she liked me at once. For some reason, she thought I was terribly funny. She just loved to laugh with me and was nice to me from the start. We knew we'd get along when she knew I could make her laugh. She was very sweet at that first meeting. And it just got better and better. She wouldn't leave my side." (Bill was Judy's escort at a party following the taping of his first Garland episode; among those present were Judy's CMA agent, Alan Ladd, Jr., and publicist, Guy Mc-Elwaine.)

Colleran held a dim view of the previous Garland regimes, favoring the recent Jewison programs no more than those of Schlatter's. "They put me in a screening room and I looked at all the shows," says Bill. "When I came out, I was so depressed, seeing that staggering talent go to waste. I came out saying, 'CBS, what have you done? You're going to wreck a career, trying to destroy her legend.' She was not the girl next door. Judy Garland was one of the most beautiful creatures that God ever created. I knew it had to be completely redone, to just let her sing and that is *it!*" All those awful comedians on those earlier shows. It was so embarrassing. They didn't belong on the same stage with her."

Colleran immediately recognized the serious sound deficiencies of Studio 43 that had only been modified, not cured. He brought in Bing Crosby's top audio man, Murdo MacKenzie.

"Christ, it sounded like she was singing under a bale of cotton or something. It was really the worst sound I had ever heard. And on her numbers, it was particularly bad sound. So I brought Murdo in, and from then on, the sound was just dandy." The producer not long after replaced the standard CBS microphone Judy used in the "Trunk" spots with a custom-made, state-of-the-art Shure microphone costing in excess of three thousand dollars. (His improvements were remarkable; the Colleran-produced episodes are comparable in audio quality to studio recording sessions.)

With Colleran locked in as executive producer, he then successfully championed his friend Dean Whitmore for director. Bill, a soft-spoken, gentle, and articulate man, was a contrast to the businesslike style of Norman Jewison; Whitmore, thought Colleran, had a low-key, sensitive approach to his work that might well be a calming influence on the highly strung, intense Garland. ("He knew my work so well, and I wanted someone like that. He was a master at the kind of camera work, the kind of lighting that I wanted for Judy," explains Colleran, who adds that he also delegated the directing in order to devote as much time as possible to Garland.)

His reasoning proved correct. George Sunga notes, "Dean did things soft and easy," and lighting director Leard Davis adds, "Whitmore and Hobin had extremely different styles. Two different types of people, really. Bill was more of a man's director. He did Skelton forever. He would approach things kind of hard-handed, although not with Judy. Dean was rather a quiet, sweet man. But they were both easy to get along with and very understanding."

Colleran, of course, was aware of the chaos that enveloped the Garland series, but nothing prepared him for Jim Aubrey. "The first day at CBS," recounts Bill, "Aubrey sat down at the big conference table and said, 'What are you going to do with that fucking cunt?' I thought, Oh, my God, what is this, what's happening to me? All I could manage to say was, 'Well, I'll try to make the show better, Mr. Aubrey.' He just loathed her." Gary Smith recalls another such meeting, where Aubrey snarled, "I won't have that cunt ruining my Sunday nights!"

Aubrey moved quickly to make his wish a reality. Being bound by Fields and Begelman's unique contract giving Garland, and not CBS, the power to continue for a second thirteen-week cycle—even if the network did not wish to do so—only fueled Aubrey's hostility. (Garland refused to give up the fight for television success for artistic as well as financial, reasons.) Ignoring Norman Jewison's earlier pleas to move the show away from *Bonanza*, Aubrey kept the series mired in the same deadly time slot. Additionally, the network still, according to Colleran, would not relent and let him break Judy out of the standard variety-program mold and shift the emphasis to music.

As early as November 15, *Variety* reported that *The Judy Garland Show* had become television history; the trade paper further indicated that CBS planned to move Danny Kaye to Garland's spot the following season. Echoing the exact philosophy when slotting Garland on Sunday, a network spokesman stated "Naturally, we don't expect Kaye to beat *Bonanza*." While CBS felt that Kaye's ratings, which had improved somewhat since its premiere (while Garland's continued to drop) would give it leverage against the NBC western, Kaye apparently balked at the move, remaining in his original midweek position for its entire four-season run.

With CBS already renewing Kaye for the coming season and contemplating his time period, Garland being dropped was tacitly, but clearly, a fait accompli.

While the trade paper deemed Judy's series as "the most conspicuous and, next to Jerry Lewis, the mostly costly failure of the season," apparently unimportant to Aubrey was the fact that "surprisingly, she is garnering *substantially higher* Nielsens than did *Real McCoys* and *G.E. True* in the same hour a year ago." Aubrey, it seemed, preferred to focus on the fact that CBS claimed nine of the top ten-rated programs, with only NBC's *Bonanza* (in second place) preventing the network from making a clean sweep.

With the luster of Judy's series now dimming within the industry, the steady flow of announced guests turned into a trickle; during this time, operatic tenor Sergio Franchi and dancer Juliet Prowse were inaccurately said to be signed for a February joint appearance. Albert Finney, who was riding the crest of his motion picture hit *Tom Jones*, was another guest-star candidate for Garland. That inexplicable booking was announced hastily after a trade paper item stated that Garland and Finney (then appearing on Broadway) were a romantic item after the two met in

New York during the production break. His "guest appearance"—announced only one day after the same column broke the "romance" news—was likely created as a means to squelch rumors of an affair.

That same week, it was announced that Gerold Frank had signed to ghostwrite Sid Luft's autobiography. It was to be titled *I'll Laugh Saturday*, based on a "private joke" between Luft and his estranged wife. Nothing came of this, although more than a decade later Frank went on to write a Garland biography with the cooperation of her family, including Sid Luft.

The night of Friday, November 22, Bobby Darin was due to fly in from Las Vegas. He and his fellow guest star, comedian Bob Newhart, would begin rehearsals for *The Judy Garland Show* on Monday. The taping of show fourteen was scheduled for the following Thursday.

The Friday Darin was to arrive in Hollywood, President John F. Kennedy was assassinated in Dallas. Television production was halted, television and radio commercials were dropped, and all regular programming was canceled for the next three days as the networks devoted their entire schedules to provide unprecedented round-the-clock coverage.

The shattering impact of Kennedy's death upon Judy Garland cannot be overstated. She had actively campaigned for him as he sought the presidency; the Lufts were guests at the White House and the Kennedy compound in Hyannis Port the summer of 1961. Judy had been a guest at many Kennedy political galas. More recently, she was invited to the White House in late November of 1962 along with Danny Kaye and Carol Burnett. The following month, *A Child Is Waiting* premiered at a Washington charity function. After the screening, the president lavishly praised Judy for her outstanding performance as a social worker in the uncompromising, grimly realistic John Cassavetes film dealing with the plight of mentally retarded children and their families.

Since its beginning, JFK had championed Judy's series. He not only sent her a congratulatory telegram when the premiere episode aired, but declared not long after that it had become the Kennedy family's favorite program. When the series faltered in the ratings, the president gallantly consoled Judy by publicly stating that "fine art was never for the masses."

The day of JFK's assassination remains indelible to Orval: "I

Judy, President Kennedy, Carol Burnett, and Danny Kaye at the White House, November 28, 1962

was on my way to her house when the announcement was made. Ray Aghayan and Bob Mackie arrived just ahead of me. They had come for a final fitting on a gown she was supposed to wear on one of the shows. She wouldn't even let them open the box it was in or show it to her. Judy wanted absolutely nothing to do with that dress, never wanted to see it again. She was terribly upset." Judy then immediately rushed to console her friend Pat Lawford (sister of the president and wife of her old friend Peter Lawford). Although Lorna's eleventh birthday was the day before, Judy had planned a birthday party that Friday night so that she and her friends would not have to worry about school the next day. "Oh, God, it was so awful," Lorna remembers. "Although I was little, I knew he was Mama's friend, and I remembered spending time with him, riding with him on his golf cart that summer we had gone to Hyannis Port. We were all in shock. Mama just couldn't believe it. Mama was at Pat Lawford's house at the beach a lot of the time after it happened, but she couldn't go to the funeral because she was doing the television show."

Completely spent, Judy canceled a Capitol Records recording session that week that had been scheduled for her to complete an aborted 1962 album titled *Judy Takes Broadway*. Also scuttled was the scheduled broadcast that Sunday of Garland's Ray Bolger-Jane Powell episode. (The firing of Jerry Van Dyke perhaps jinxed that particular show, which in February was preempted yet a second time, not airing until March of 1964.)

Garland and a grief-stricken world watched the tragedy on television, unfolding day after day. Judy, comforted by the presence of her three children, kept to herself at home. Most remaining show staff members, knowing of Judy's friendship with Jack Kennedy, feared that Garland, already shaken by the apparent failure of her series, would be unable to function in the wake of JFK's assassination.

Her CBS team—a collection of seasoned, often jaded professionals—had been unabashedly amazed during the preceding weeks when Judy would casually pick up the phone, call the White House, and instantly get the president on the line. They were even more astounded when the public-address system announced on more than a few occasions that the president was on the phone for Miss Garland if she might be available. Their warm, chatty, informal conversations were so frequent that Judy once quipped, "I can get the president on the phone easier than I can get my *managers!*"

"I was with her more than once when Judy would call and immediately get Jack Kennedy on the phone, and very easily," says Orval Paine, who stresses that the president was of enormous comfort to her as the series was in disrepair. "And after seeing one of the shows, or for no reason in particular, she'd get a call from him. I'd answer the phone, he'd made the call directly, and asked for her. Naturally, after that, she'd be on an all-time high, that he would be such a friend and call her. Many times Judy would call him because of the fact that she couldn't get ahold of Freddie or David or certain people on the show. Calling him would lift her spirits."

Liza remembers similar telephone conversations between her mother and Jack Kennedy at the Rockingham house. "Mama used to call him once a week, on Sundays. And always at the end of the conversation, he'd say, Sing something. She'd say, 'What do you mean?' And he said, 'Just sing eight bars of something.' He knew *bar* numbers. Mama used to sing a bit of 'Over the Rainbow' or 'When You're Smiling.' One day, I was walking to the living room, and there's my mother on the phone singing 'The Battle Hymn of the Republic'! I thought, What is she *doing*? After Mama hung up, she told me that she was talking to President Kennedy, and he wanted her to sing that. It was only the two of them. None of the conversations were taped. It was real friendship."

Gary Smith believes that JFK's death had lasting consequences on Garland. "There's no question that the turning point for her was the assassination. She couldn't sleep. We'd work with the others, and Judy would show up in the afternoon. We'd call her to come in at ten, she'd come in at one or two. She'd sit in the trailer." (Gary later hit upon a way of having Judy show up on time: "She'd come in two or three hours late every time, so we started the practice of calling her two or three hours *early*, and it worked for a while, until one day she showed up on time and blew the whole thing.")

"We had a conversation one day that I will never forget as long as I live," continues the producer. "Judy began talking about the White House and mentioned that she knew the president very well and went to visit him there. He lifted up the rug in the Oval Office to show her the holes from Ike's golf shoes. Judy thought that was hysterically funny. Then she decided to call the White House. She was depressed. *Bonanza* was beating her out. She calls and says, 'I want to speak to the president.' Sure enough, a minute or two later, I heard, 'Hello, Mr. president!' He did a lot of talking. We learned later that what he had said was that the Kennedy family had changed their eating time on Sunday nights to be finished with dinner so they could watch Judy. It was the first time in quite a while that she'd heard someone say the show was terrific. And then she sang, 'Over the Rainbow,' the whole song, to him. He was assassinated four weeks later, and it devastated her."

Judy wanted the Darin and Newhart program scrapped. Instead, she decided to do a one-woman concert of patriotic songs. More than a homage to the president, it represented Judy's fervent desire to do something for her country, to offer an affirmation of America's strength, hope for the future, and the need to press on, despite the tragedy.

"Judy never worked harder in her life," recalls Gary Smith. "She had an extraordinary program planned. She did research. She was absolutely focused, and she did it all by herself, too. It was all her."

Garland's plan was rejected by Jim Aubrey. Smith was summoned into the network president's office and told, "When we go back on the air, we don't want any tributes on any shows." Gary was ordered to inform Judy of Aubrey's decision; not wanting to give her the news by phone, Gary drove to the Rockingham house. "Her first reaction was anger, saying, 'Fuck CBS! They're *not* going to tell me I can't do this. I *knew* him. He was my *friend*. I'm telling you, I'm *doing* it!' "

Judy was incensed at the decision, and the relationship between her and Aubrey now became openly hostile. With the show already bound for the CBS graveyard, she had little reason to put on a facade. The fate of her series was, for the moment, of no importance; Aubrey's refusal to allow her in her own way to offer hope to a nation stunned with grief was unconscionable.

With CBS rejecting her concert idea, there was talk that the taping with Bobby Darin and Bob Newhart might be canceled. But Garland had to perform; she had been told by the network that she would not be paid for any expenses incurred as a result of shutting down production, whatever the reason. The show would go on, although the tape date was moved to Saturday, November 30. To force her to perform against her will was to invite trouble, but Judy was the picture of professionalism throughout the week.

Spotted by a group of fans the afternoon of the taping at Television City, Judy managed a smiling face although she felt far from cheerful. As she walked downstairs toward Studio 43, wearing orange Capri slacks and a bulky beige pullover sweater, without makeup and clips in her still-askew hair, she paused for

Judy and "The Mighty Mites"

effect and cracked, "Do I look *glamorous* enough for television?" She told the group she would see them after the taping, and that she had to prerecord vocal tracks for the show's opening, a medley of football songs with a Venice, California, football team called "The Mighty Mites." One of the fans asked if he could attend the session. Pausing for a moment, Judy stopped in her tracks and said, "All right, come on!"

The run-through began badly. The stage speaker was not functioning, and Judy was unable to hear the music from the band in the enclosed cube off the stage; several takes of "Buckle Down, Winsocki" and "You Gotta Be a Football Hero" were recorded. After Judy ripped through "Winsocki" perfectly and began "Football Hero," she made a gaffe. Instead of singing "a pretty coquette," she realized she had said "*croquette*" and stopped the music. "Croquette!" she laughed, "Oh, Lord! Croquette!" Mel Tormé, standing on the sidelines, did not catch the mistake, and Judy kept insisting to him, "I said *croquette*!" After everyone had a good laugh, Judy joked, "Mother is cracking up!"

When Bud Lindquist, the audio man up in the control booth, was being called by someone onstage, Judy attempted to help out, shouting, "Buddy!," and when that didn't work, she started to *sing* "My Buddy." Through all of this, Judy was having trouble with the zipper on her slacks and kept having to hoist them up, only adding to the humor surrounding the afternoon session. Then, after an attempt at the lightening-fast "Jamboree Jones"—which was too fast for Judy to sing without sounding as if she were mumbling the already-nonsensical lyrics—another try was made at a slower tempo, with Garland singing *"Jennifer Jones,"* instead of "Jamboree Jones," causing everyone to break up once again. A third take was successful, and a one-hour break before the dress rehearsal was announced. The loyal group of fans was given choice seats for the performance.

They were astounded when, following the appearance of "The Mighty Mites" in football uniforms, Judy came out of her alternate dressing room offstage, gamely sporting a complete football outfit herself, including shoulder pads, helmet, and spiked shoes. One of the fans, Elly Oleson, remarked, "She was hilariously adorable. She wasn't any taller than some of the boys, and I kept losing her with them." Elly added, "It was kind of funny to see what looked like a little kid running around with a *cigarette* in her hand—you sort of felt like you should go up and take it away and scold her for breaking training!"

Several takes were attempted, with someone in the control booth barking, "Cut!" in the middle of one attempt. Judy stopped, looked around, and asked, "What happened?" Between takes, Judy was having as much trouble with her football pants as she had earlier with her Capri slacks. Shutterbug Roddy McDowall ruined one take when he accidentally got in front of one of the low-placed cameras. Peering out from beneath her helmet, Judy looked at Roddy and said, "Awwww, baaa-by!"

The routine had one of the boys ask Judy, "You said you gotta be a football hero to get along with the beautiful girls?" After Judy replied, "That's right," he asked, "Well, where are the girls?" Judy answered, "Oh, I see what you mean. I'll be right back." She then went off-camera and in one minute reappeared, dressed in a stunning Aghayan creation. The boys whistled and shrieked. "Time! Hold it! Whoa!," Judy declared, and then told them she wanted them to all grow up to be "big football heroes," mentioning the upcoming Rose Bowl game on New Year's Day. Changing again to white slacks and top, she sang "Jamboree Jones."

Ironically, after all the effort, the routine was scrapped, never to be seen. On December 18, Judy taped a miniconcert segment as its replacement featuring "Hello, Bluebird," "If Love Were All," and "Zing! Went the Strings of My Heart." (That opening would also be repeated for the March 1964 broadcast of the Powell-Bolger broadcast version. The miniconcert segment replaced "That's All" and "One for My Baby," which in turn had been removed from that program and spliced into show five to make up for the Steve Allen "Tea" segment, which was cut because of his appearance on show eleven. And because of the elimination of Jerry Van Dyke from the series, all five Schlatter shows were reedited to cut or greatly minimize Jerry's participation. The Rooney show was substantially altered, cutting the original opening and bear sketch. Judy was so displeased with this jarring lack of continuity that she commented to *TV Guide*, "They'd edit the tapes without my knowledge. So a song with a guest star would pop up in a completely different show. My hair-do and wardrobe would mysteriously change from scene to scene.")

Despite her good-spirited demeanor, the harrowing events of the last several days had taken their toll. Although Judy tackled the material with as much vigor as she could muster, she was unable to conceal her fatigue, quite evident on this program; not surprisingly, her voice is a bit ragged due to her lack of sleep.

Judy found Bob Newhart amusing (he was subsequently announced as a guest on two more episodes, although neither appearance transpired) and was fond of Bobby Darin. "She liked them both very much," notes Colleran, "and [they] worked very easily together." (Mickey Rooney reported to Studio 43 that same Friday to tape an insert for show one. Peppiatt and Aylesworth concocted a clever, affectionate send-up of the Garland-Rooney MGM films of yesteryear—Judy even calling Mickey both "Timmy" *and* "Tommy" throughout; the so-called "premiere episode" finally aired on December 8, the lengthy overture now more mystifying than exciting.)

Other elements of the hour included Newhart's solid comedy monologue; "Take Five" performed by the Peter Gennaro dancers; and Darin's solo spot, two tiresome folk songs, sung in a belabored, self-conscious manner. (Judy was perhaps bored with the numbers as well. She was heard singing in her dressing room during the dress-rehearsal taping as he sang them!) Garland sang the current hit "More" (the theme from *Mondo Cane*), although she had been dead-set against singing the relentlessly banal tune. "She hated that song, but she sang the hell out of it, anyway," remembers Colleran.

Garland and Darin performed an ambitious "Train" medley featuring such "travelin' " songs as "Sentimental Journey," "On the Atchison, Topeka and the Santa Fe," "Bye, Bye Blackbird," "Toot, Toot, Tootsie," "Lonesome Road," and "I've Been Working on the Railroad." The latter tune inspired the set design to frame the medley, an old-fashioned railroad car with seating only for Judy and Bobby. Darin, already on board, was greeted by Judy. "Do you mind if I join you?" she asked. "All the other seats are taken—*away*." (She then noted that she was taking the train to Oz. "I don't usually take a train though," she assured Bobby. "I usually go by house!") While hardly a musical milestone, the medley was well put-together, the performances fine, and the pairing of Darin and Garland successful.

For the first, and only, time in the series, a comedy sketch was as much a highlight of a Garland program as the music, indicating the new writers might indeed have found success in giving Garland decent comedy material. The sketch had Garland (wearing frumpy bedtime clothes and her Ben Franklin glasses) and Newhart (equally prepared for bedtime) playing an average American couple—watching Garland and Newhart on television.

Garland's "Trunk" spot featured the sensual "Do It Again" (its frankness about two lovers never to see each other again after their one-night stand rather provocative for television of the day) and "Get Me to the Church on Time." Before singing, Judy opened the segment with a story, later cut completely due to the show's running length after the football opening was replaced by the lengthier "miniconcert" insert. Never heard was Judy's delightful account of her legendary 1961 Hollywood Bowl concert that continued despite a downpour. She introduced "Do It Again" by noting that she had sung it at Carnegie Hall as well. Of the *Carnegie Hall* album, she said: "That was the first time I ever sold a million copies, and I've been recording since they had *cylinder* records! . . . We did those concerts all over the country . . . and one of them was at the Hollywood Bowl . . . It's outside, you see, and it was a rotten night, a terrible night. I had particularly asked them to build a runway over this great big pool of water, you know, the audience separated from the artist by this vast ocean. So they built a runway without any *bulbs* on it, just to confuse me! It started to rain at the beginning of the overture and I thought, Well, what the heck. I had to come out with a hand mike, and there was about 108 feet of cord in back of me. As they finished the overture, and I started to come out onstage, the stage manager stopped me and said, 'Don't let *any* of that cord get in the water or you'll be *electrocuted!*' So I went on, and did the *dodgiest* performance you've ever seen! . . . The first violinist was married to the harpist [and] he was so worried about her harp that she put her raincoat over her *and* the harp, and that made the whole show look terrible! And then the first violinist walked off with his wife and, oh, it was just a mess! Anyway, I'm glad we played Carnegie Hall and made the album."

Garland's rendering of "Do It Again" was exquisite, its hypnotic effect enhanced by Dean Whitmore's sweeping, but unobtrusive and graceful, framing of the number, utilizing only one camera for the entire five-minute performance. (At the dress rehearsal, Glenn Ford made an appearance onstage during the number, causing Judy instantly to brighten, and ad-lib at the end of the song, "but until then, I will sing it for Glenn!") "Get Me to the Church on Time," approached by Judy as a brassy throwaway tune, was made all the more exciting by multiple camera work and quick cutting; the broadcast version of the song was, in fact, imperceptibly pieced together from the two tapings of the song.

Before signing off with "Maybe I'll Come Back," Judy wished all "a happy and peaceful 1964" (with the hour scheduled to air the last Sunday of 1963) and, referring to either her third professional staff or the football fracas that afternoon, quipped, "I'll be back next week—if I can get through these many changes!"

"Oh, yes, my children watch the show," Judy told reporter Lloyd Shearer in late 1963. "They come to the studios on Friday when I tape it, and I must tell you this. The other week, they were sitting down front and they fell *asleep* while I was doing the show! My daughter, Liza—yes, she's out here, in fact, she's so busy I have to make an appointment to see her—I've done one show with her, and I'm doing the Christmas show with my other children, too."

When asked what she did when not working, Judy said, "I stay at home with my children. I play a little golf. I wait around for Tuesday and work to begin." She added, "I like TV better than any of the other jobs I've had in the past. It's hard work, but we've got it down to a pretty good routine now. I work four days a week and have Saturday, Sunday, and Monday off. It's inspiring, and not too much hard work."

Shearer, noting Garland's ratings troubles, offered, "It is ironic at this point, when she is healthier and happier than she's been for years, that Madison Avenue and the advertising fraternity should interpret Judy and her show in the light of disappointment. . . . Judy Garland has never failed in any avenue of show business. If her weekly TV series ends in statistical failure [it is] because it has been incorrectly targeted by network masterminds"; the reporter noted that Schlatter and Jewison still held that Garland had a substantial chance for success if Aubrey would relent and move the show to 10:00 to 11:00 P.M., Monday nights.

Under that plan, with the benefit of a strong comedy block lead-in of *The Lucy Show*, *The Danny Thomas Show*, and *The Andy Griffith Show*, Garland's variety program would be a refreshing change of pace. Furthermore, its competition would be far from formidable. Aubrey, however, would not consider the suggestion and let the show continue to sink in the ratings quicksand that *Bonanza* created.

"It seemed that he wanted to sabotage the show," confirms Bill Colleran. "After he put it on the air, it was as if he thought later, I shouldn't have done that—so I'll *kill* it."

Garland's television tribulations were lessened by the presence of her three children on the next hour taped, a special Christmas program. Her appearance reflected her good spirits, and she looked glamorous in a red velvet fur-trimmed hostess gown. Other guests on the show were Mel Tormé, Liza's "beau," Tracy Everitt, and Jack Jones. Garland was particularly delighted to have Jack on her Christmas program; she greatly admired the singer, whose father, singer Allan Jones, had appeared with a very young Judy in one of her earliest MGM films, *Everybody Sing*.

The production was a homey, informal affair, even replicating Judy's Rockingham living room as the sole set. The program was taped on December 6. Songs included Judy's "Have Your-

"Judy's living room set" for the Christmas show
JOHN GRAHAM COLLECTION

self a Merry Little Christmas" (the show's opener, Garland sing-
ing the song to Lorna and Joe) and "Little Drops of Rain" (from
Gay Purr-ee); Judy and Mel singing "The Christmas Song"; Lorna
belting "Santa Claus Is Coming to Town," and, from *Oliver!*:
"Consider Yourself" (Judy, Liza, Lorna, and Joe), and "Where
Is Love?" (Joe).

A highlight was Liza's solo of "Alice Blue Gown," offering a
first-rate Roger Edens arrangement of the old tune, which he
had written many years before for a very young Judy to sing on
the radio. "It was an old, old arrangement, and Mama said, 'You'll
sing this great, sing this!' And she sang it for me and I loved it,
because it was so funny."

At the time, Roger Edens was still under contract to Metro
and thus prohibited from writing for Judy's CBS series. When
Hedda Hopper asked Judy whether Roger might write her some

special material, she replied, "Oh, no. He's writing for Liza now." But these plans never came about. "Mama wanted him to do something, but it just slipped by, and I got busy. And I kept going back to New York, because I was doing theater."

Also part of the bill was a Minnelli-Everitt song-and-dance routine of "Steam Heat," featuring Tracy's choreography; and Jack's solos of "Lollipops and Roses" and "Wouldn't It Be Loverly?" Judy, Jack, and Liza performed a medley including "Sleigh Ride," "It Happened in Sun Valley," "Winter Wonderland," "Jingle Bells," and a Peter Gennaro routine of several dancers outfitted in oversized Santa Claus suits unexpectedly bursting in the door (twice), to offer a frenetic, quasi-Charleston turn.

Traditional carols performed included "What Child Is This?" (Judy); "Hark! The Herald Angels Sing" (Jack and Mel); "It Came Upon a Midnight Clear" (Liza and Tracy); "Silent Night" (Lorna and Joey); and a finale by all of "Deck the Halls." After the dancing Santa Claus—and Judy—did some spirited high kicks, they vanished. ("Merry Christmas," ad-libbed Judy, "*whoever* you are!") Then she and the children sat on a sofa, and with "Mama" in the middle, Judy crooned "Over the Rainbow" with her arms tenderly around Joe and Lorna to close the hour.

There were a few mistakes, a few flubbed lyrics, a few unexpected happenings—Tracy conking his head on a swinging lamp as he was putting a punch bowl down on a table, for example—but they only added to the delightful, informal quality of the hour.

The Christmas episode became Judy's favorite of them all; the program was no less memorable to her three children and was such a success that a similar Easter edition was planned. (Judy later took an audio tape of the Christmas show with her everywhere, along with a treasured photograph autographed to her by JFK.)

"The Christmas show was the best," remembers Lorna. "First of all, to get a week off from *school* was the best thing in the world! That was really sensational. Plus the fact that that was when I decided that I really did want to be in this business. I got a week off from school, and I got to really know what it was like to shoot a television show—to watch Liza rehearse, to see Joe learning his numbers, learning to sing with everyone else, to be able to sing on Jack Jones's *knee* was a great experience! My mom made it fun for everybody, and it was just great."

Lorna's solo of "Santa Claus Is Coming to Town" revealed a powerful and outstanding voice, rather surprisingly emanating from a lovely eleven-year-old girl in a simple green velvet dress; Judy, not long after, said that she was "very, very proud" of Liza's career, and immediately jumped in to add, "I've got an eleven-year old daughter who's got the best voice of all, and she isn't even out of the gate yet!" and, laughing, "She has more talent than all of us put together."

Lorna acutely recalls a moment when she stumbled during her solo, chuckling, "Something caught in my throat, and I was so embarrassed," but she recovered instantly, Jack almost having to hold her down, so enthusiastic was her performance. She recalls, though, being "really self-conscious, and I was at that funny age then, too. But I remember, when I looked over at Liza, or Mama, I'd feel a lot better, because they were sitting there with so much encouragement, not disapproval or anything like that, and that was so wonderful. We were treated like guest stars, and we all had such a wonderful time. Mama was so happy, and we all had such a great time doing that show."

"She loved it when her family was around," says Liza. "She was so family-oriented, and we were all so very, very close."

Joe recalls his mother coaching the children at home, as well as at CBS: "She showed me how to do most of it at home, and then we went once or twice into the studio to make sure we had it right. My mother really loved Christmas. It was her favorite time of the year, and she wanted us to be with her. We went to rehearsals a lot. I knew most of the numbers before, it was just to make sure that I had it all memorized. The first time I did 'Where Is Love?' was in one of those neighborhood plays. My mom really liked it, so she wanted me to do it on the show. I said no at first, because I was very nervous. And I was nervous doing the show, especially at the beginning. But after I sang the song, I had fun doing the rest of it." (This particular program offers evidence that Judy Garland was an incomparable mother. She and her children unhesitatingly hug, embrace, kiss, and encourage one another, and their mutual joy at being together alone makes this show memorable; a single shot of Judy's glowing, proud face in the background as Joey in profile sang "Where Is Love?" is unforgettable.)

Although Garland's children were clearly the product of exceptional parents and a resultant extraordinary upbringing, Lorna states, "We weren't show-business children. Unlike Liza, Joe and I were not around a lot of sets. We were in school. It was pretty normal, although that's probably not what a lot of people think. When we went to the tapings each week, to us it was like going to see a Broadway show every Friday."

"Steam Heat," as performed by Liza and Tracy, had already become a favorite routine of Judy's, and one that she would call upon them to perform at more than one party on Rockingham Drive. "Tracy choreographed the whole thing and taught it to me," says Liza. "I started to learn it, then we worked on it for a long time, and then he kept *changing* it, but finally we had it down! I'd seen him do the whole number by himself, and I said, 'Let's do that on the show,' because Mama had said, 'I want you to dance with Tracy on the show because you two dance so well together.' " Liza laughs, "I think she was getting a dig in at me about how much time I was spending with Tracy, because every time we'd go on a date, I'd say to her, 'Oh, we have to *rehearse!*' But she was so wise."

Mel Tormé suggests that Judy was absent for most of the week, to which Liza counters, "She was always there. She was there at every rehearsal. But she was trained like that. She was trained that you get up and you go to work and you come home.

RAINBOW'S END   **289**

Mama liked very much the routine of going to work in the morn-
ings and coming home for dinner, except on the taping days. It
gave us a sense of order."

Further discounting Tormé's recollection was a report filed by
the television editor at the *Cincinnati Enquirer*, who observed rehearsals and tapings for show fifteen and wrote, "The afternoon
was an organized chaos of deciding on camera angles, costumes
that didn't quite fit, lip synchronization with pre-recorded songs.
. . . Was Miss Garland the temperamental star I'd read about in
newspapers, lo these many years? Not that afternoon, that's for
sure." Instead, Judy "was a model of patience and good humor
during all the turmoil. 'Sorry, sorry, that was me,' she'd say when
she made a mistake. Or she'd interrupt good-naturedly above
the din, 'May I suggest something, boys—I can't hear the directions.' Judy sat placidly while lengthy camera adjustments were
made and was quick to join in the laughter during such horse-
play as guest Jack Jones's surprise whirling of a pretty female
dancer outfitted as Kris Kringle while he exclaimed, 'I never believed in Santa Claus before, but, now—wow!' "

James Devane further observed, "The [Garland] family group
was as happy as the show. There's no doubt Judy's a doting
mother. She was Liza's best possible audience as she watched
her uninhibited daughter perform, and her eyes followed Liza
fondly as she strolled hand-in-hand with Tracy, or huddled with
him in far corners where they seemed to have an endless number of things to tell each other during breaks. 'It looks serious,'
laughed Judy. . . . For somewhat shy Joey, Judy had happy
knucklings of the head and extravagant praise to make him feel
better about perching on a piano to sing the wistful 'Where Is
Love?' from 'Oliver!' 'Marvelous, darling, marvelous,' she'd tell
him." Lorna's powerhouse "Santa Claus" number won praise
from Judy and stunned the crew, noted the reporter, with the
buzz among them being, "The kid's really *good!*"

When Devane had a moment with Judy, he asked about why
her voice varied from show to show. "It takes me awhile to warm
up, to feel an audience is with me, even after all these years,"
she answered.

Tormé's book recounts a harrowing evening the week of the
Christmas-episode taping. Tormé details being summoned to
Rockingham Drive late one night, where he encountered a wildly

out-of-control, inebriated Judy. The episode was triggered, he wrote, when Garland told him that she had just learned of the death of her oldest sister, Sue, from cancer. However, Sue Cathcart did not die until May of 1964, one month after the series ceased production; in addition, Sue's death was not due to cancer, but an overdose of sleeping pills, following the dissolution of her marriage to Judy's onetime musical conductor Jack Cathcart, who left her for a younger woman. Furthermore, Judy received word of Sue's passing not on Rockingham Drive, but in a Hong Kong hospital. Glenn Ford has denied that the incident occurred, and Bill Colleran recalls that the week was a happy one.

According to many observers, Garland and Tormé's relationship was on a downward spiral. Mel had balked on more than one occasion about coaching Judy off-camera and, when the second thirteen-week cycle of shows came up, Tormé used the opportunity to negotiate a hefty raise in salary. Garland was also aware that Bill Hobin, Bernie Rothman, Norman Jewison, and even Orval Paine, her hairdresser, were among those who had strained relationships with Mel, the situation further exacerbated by the fact that Tormé and Gary Smith (with whom Garland had become less and less enchanted) were close friends, and, in her mind, "in the same camp."

This particular program had itself triggered friction between Judy and Mel after he strongly objected to appearing on the Christmas episode, feeling second in status to primary guest-star Jack Jones; the lower-than-usual fee offered him mirrored his lesser stature on the show. For his part, Jack admits, "Mel and I are friends now, but it was quite tense then. Mel felt very competitive with me. There was a lot of that going on." Tormé agreed to be part of the show only after Judy personally prevailed upon him to reconsider.

Unlike their other two previous appearances together, the on-camera relationship between Garland and Tormé on the Christmas program suggests that all was not well between them. Although she had inadvertently called Mel "Mort" (referring, obviously, to her musical anchor Lindsey) on the Steve Allen episode, and he, in turn, later in the hour quipped, "Just call me 'Mort'!," at the open and the close of the Christmas show Garland referred to him again as "Mort," exhibiting some sort of mental block against him. As he sat at the piano waiting to begin "The Christmas Song," she stumbled a bit in introducing him; then, a few moments later, she erred slightly on a couple of words of the song to no ill effect. Instead of letting it go, however, Mel pointedly said, "Close!" in noting her mistake. Although she laughed it off, Judy, instead of singing "reindeer" in the bridge of the song, deliberately sang *"rainbows"*—making the lyric non-sensical, but shrewdly calling up her own trademark song while the attention was to have been on him instead. A brief but withering look to him underscored her point. And, though completely willing not to dominate the camera on their past appearances, this time Judy, effortlessly and almost subliminally, stole virtually every scene they shared. Her incomparable bag of tricks gave her the uncanny ability to steal even the two-shot, in which all Garland had to do was stand at the piano as Mel sang. Judy pulled no stunts, did no business, but pulled the rug out from under him just the same.

The "Over the Rainbow" finale was wonderful, richly sung as a lullaby to Lorna and Joey, cuddled next to her, wearing bedtime clothes. Joey, in fact, seemed to forget for a moment that they were on television, speaking matter-of-factly to "Mama" during the musical bridge and as she began the final chorus, causing her to smile and kiss him lovingly. "Joey was so little," laughs Lorna, "that whenever Mama sang or did anything, he would feel that we were at home, and could say, 'Excuse me, could you stop that so we can talk to you?' " Although older, Lorna felt much the same way. "It was always special when she sang 'Over the Rainbow,' and when Joe and I were sitting there, we couldn't get close enough to her. We forgot that we were on a television show." (Lorna and Joe did, however, pick up their AFTRA cards after guesting with their mother!)

The Christmas show was singled out for praise. The *New York Journal-American* deemed it "warm and subtly stylish [with] flavor and point of view. It reflected good taste in tunes and trailed a nice sense of respect for the sentimentality of the holiday season. Judy's three children . . . added more warmth than any blanket, including electric . . . these were simple elements, but television finds its most difficult times trying to elicit such warm, attractive, simple moods. It was a fine show, unpretentious, shrewdly effected in every department. It was a show which caused quite a few TV fans to [feel] that indeed, it would be unfortunate if *The Judy Garland Show* fell by the Nielsen wayside."

Glenn Ford was a source of comfort to Judy; more often than not he was present for the tapings (often accompanied by his mother)—Garland would rush to him in the audience and hug him between takes.

Judy convinced Glenn to buy a grand piano for his home "because the room needed it"; so fond of the flattering effects provided by soft amber lighting, Judy surprised Glenn one evening by showing up on his doorstep with a bag of *one hundred* amber bulbs that she proceeded to install in every light socket in the house. Judy gave him a photograph of her inscribed, "Glenn, dear one, now I can look upward and see the beauty of the sun and moon, and the love you give to me. You have my heart and I adore you."

Judy greatly enjoyed her Sunday night parties centered around the broadcast, which, of course, included Glenn when he was not working on a film. The evenings were invariably sparkling and upbeat, no matter what the ratings situation of the moment. "Mama would always be very happy then," recalls Lorna, who notes that Judy made a point to appear positive. "It seemed that it was a happy time for her. I loved that house, because it was a big house, and I always liked a house with a lot of noise. It made me feel good when there was a party going on, and somebody was playing the piano, and all of that." The conviviality of the evenings notwithstanding, Judy strictly maintained that the younger children had to go directly to bed the moment the show was over.

"My mother loved watching the show, especially watching it around other people," recalls Lorna. "Everybody who came over knew what was going on, knew what happened at rehearsals, so the atmosphere was always great. One thing I do remember—my mother never really criticized herself when she was watching herself in front of us. She liked her work. She was very proud of her work. I learned from her, if you're going to do something, do it the best you can, do it the right way, and then enjoy watching it. Every time I was around CBS, which was quite a lot, she was having a good time."

With the seventeen-year-old Liza, Judy would "giggle at things

and she'd always point out the mistakes, or she'd say, 'I could have sung that better,' but she'd say that quietly to me." Still, notes Liza, "she'd watch the shows with pride."

Judy's enormous reserves of strength, sheer will to continue, and the determination to make the series a personal triumph even if it was not a ratings success cannot be undervalued, insists Liza; indeed, Garland continued long after her detractors predicted her television demise and, furthermore, gave some of her best performances.

"Mama never seemed terribly depressed," remembers Liza. "I said to her, 'Isn't it slightly distracting that they keep changing things?' And she said, 'Look, television is always musical chairs. You go with it.' My whole life, my mother was truly hilarious. And people would go, 'Oh, really?' They just want it to be such a tragedy, and it wasn't. The series kind of shows that."

Liza continues, "I'd ask her, 'Why do people keep talking about you like you're this little bird who's *dying*, or something?' and she'd say, 'I don't know, let them talk. It doesn't matter as long as *we* know the truth.' People would just hate to hear that she could sing 'Over the Rainbow,' and as people were standing up and falling down and screaming and crying, I'd rush up to the middle of the stage [in the blackout] every night thinking, Oh, my God, she's a wreck, and she'd look at me and say, 'You want Chinese food tonight?' People don't want to hear that, but that, in fact, is the truth. She understood that her vulnerability in performance was something that we all recognize in ourselves. She knew how to portray somebody in flux, somebody in pain, very well. She understood it deeply enough to be able to portray it.

"*She* created the legend. She did it, and she knew *exactly* what she was doing. And it instilled a great need in people," continues Liza. "She'd say, 'Don't correct *anything*, let the legend build, it's going to build anyway—and if you fight it, you're going to drive yourself nuts!' She understood that. That's hard for some people to understand, too. It takes enormous courage and discipline and patience to understand that about her."

Indeed, the very next week, Garland would openly defy Jim Aubrey, stand up to CBS, and show tremendous determination and strength. As a result, Judy would create a moment of television history.

17

For show sixteen, Garland was once again vexed by taping a show on Friday, the thirteenth (this time of December), an ominous date that launched the Jewison regime three months earlier to the day. On the plus side, Judy had as guests her old friend, Ethel Merman, as well as comedian Shelley Berman (originally to have been Jack Carter, who was unavailable due to a scheduling conflict); Peter Gennaro would also contribute some bright moments to the production.

However, rumors that the series was about to face the Aubrey guillotine within a matter of days were now rampant. The most recent A. C. Nielsen Company tally set Judy's show at a crushing sixty-sixth place among approximately eighty regularly scheduled programs. Even worse for Judy was knowing that Aubrey had already renewed *The Danny Kaye Show* for the 1964–65 season (one of the earliest renewals announced by the network for the next year), although Judy's 14.0 rating was not much worse than Danny's 17.0 and his time slot had little competition.

The writers turned in the final draft of the Merman-Berman program on Wednesday, December 11. The "Trunk" spot became the focus of the hour among the writers and producers. Judy insisted on singing "The Battle Hymn of the Republic" in tribute to President Kennedy. If Judy had lost the battle to do a one-hour concert program of patriotic songs, she was determined, more than ever, to have her way now. To ensure that CBS would not interfere, Judy conspired to have "Battle Hymn" purposely deleted from the initial rundown until the very last minute. Says Bill Colleran, "It was a secret that she was going to do it. Judy didn't want anybody to know."

CBS, remembers Colleran, indeed objected strongly to Judy singing "The Battle Hymn of the Republic" when word finally leaked out. "Hunt Stromberg said absolutely not," says Bill. The CBS executive, recalls Colleran, attempted to justify the edict by telling him—with no trace of emotion whatsoever—"The country will have forgotten Kennedy by then." (January 12, 1964, the scheduled air date of the show, was barely six weeks after JFK's assassination.) Garland would not relent. With Colleran backing her, "Battle Hymn" was set to close the "Trunk" spot.

The memories of JFK's death and reports of Aubrey likely to cancel the series any day made Judy fearless in defying the network—more weary, angry, and resentful every passing day. Garland's bitterness was reflected in her absence from Television City for rehearsals, and she did most of her preparation for the show at home. This practice would be the rule for the remaining days of the series. CBS had become to Judy the dreaded factory that MGM was to her years before; it now became unbearable for her to be there. Says writer Peppiatt, "We sat with her at the house and rehearsed. The studio was, to her, like going to see the principal at school. At the house, she was wonderful."

By this time, Mort Lindsey's wife, singer Judy Johnson (formerly of *Your Show of Shows*) had been hired as Garland's stand-in. "My wife used to do preliminary rehearsals," says Mort. "Judy would watch in the booth and see where she was supposed to move. Sometimes my wife actually worked with the guests for a day or so until Judy came in. It would save Judy's energy." Orval adds, "Judy wanted to rehearse at home because it was a more relaxed atmosphere; it would make it easier not only for her to get away from the pressure, but for everyone else, too." Colleran adds, "Judy followed Judy Lindsey's mark on the stage. She only needed one rehearsal. Once you told her where to go, she never forgot it. She knew where the cameras were, where the lights were; she knew every time, just one time through."

"My feelings of Judy are of great affection and admiration," says Shelley Berman, "but I felt that she was desperately ill and desperately out of control with what was happening with her life, that she was in trouble. Every day, Ethel would come in and just sit and wait to rehearse. She'd wait, go to lunch, and wait, and then go home. Judy was not able to rehearse. I never saw Ethel nervous or upset. And when Judy got there, it was gangbusters. They didn't really rehearse until the day of the show, but what they did together was incredible." (By all accounts, Ethel remained unruffled, and their relationship was no less cordial and warm than before.) Adds Berman, "I think she saw the show as her salvation. She wasn't a kid anymore. There were no more *Star Is Born*s, and I think she realized that. Seeing the show in jeopardy must have been awful for her."

It was indeed a wrenching week for her; according to John Aylesworth, Garland's managers offered little comfort or guidance: "Fields and Begelman were never there. They just left her high and dry. When it wasn't working for the network, they walked away from her." (Judy jokingly referred to them as "Leopold and Loeb.") Orval states, "When she could get ahold of them, or they would show up, Judy would always pick up, and she felt better if they were around. Out of the twenty-six weeks of shows, I doubt if more than half a dozen times either one or both of them were at the studio. Judy realized that they could not be there every show because they managed other people. But she couldn't get them on the phone to talk. It had its effect."

Facing the cameras—and all that "Battle Hymn of the Republic" represented to her—was clearly an ordeal. "In the makeup chair, and then with Orval, Judy was a wreck," Bill sadly recounts. "She had one of the greatest laughs I have ever heard in my whole life. And then I'd be laughing so hard, I'd start crying, and that would start her laughing all over again. The things she would say. Funny as hell about people, about things, and very quick. A mind like a trap. Nobody could keep up with her. When she was sober, and she was clean, her mind was unbelievable."

This time, the solution to dissolve Judy's tension with laughter was only a temporary one. Despite the attempts to lessen the tension with humor, Garland, recounts Colleran, "stayed in her dressing room. I'd go back now and then to see how she was, and if she was better, I'd stay. She was inclined to get angry easily. But she never got angry with me, ever. All of her trouble was fear. That fear was there all the time." And, recalls writer Aylesworth, "once she got on the stage, it went smoothly."

The Garland-Berman comedy sketch, another inspired Peppiatt and Aylesworth routine, was taped but never aired. ("She was a little the worse for drink that night, and it was never used," states Aylesworth.) For his part, Shelley notes, "We tried it twice. She flubbed a few lines, but the audience loved the sketch. We had a ball, but they cut it. I was told that she had been drinking, but I think it was an overreaction. She didn't slur her words, she didn't stagger, she didn't do anything wrong. I think there was an overreaction to her few flubs." (For this program, Judy appears a bit puffy, and, not surprisingly, tired; her voice remained strong and powerful.)

Berman's recollection is accurate; while Judy stumbled a bit at the beginning, she quickly got in sync with the material, and the two pull the sketch off quite well. The routine was to directly follow Judy's solo of "Shenandoah":

JUDY:	My name is Lorelei Gumm, and I'm from *Personality News Magazine,* and we'd like a story on you.
SHELLEY:	You seem like a nice lady, so go ahead. What would you like to know about me?
JUDY:	(SWEETLY) Well, how long have you been a member of the Communist party?
SHELLEY:	I have never been a member—
JUDY:	Oh, still *denying* it, eh? . . . Now when did your wife get out of burlesque?
SHELLEY:	She was never in burlesque!
JUDY:	Couldn't *make* it, eh? . . . Now, I understand you're on *The Judy Garland Show* this week . . . How are you and Miss Garland getting along?
SHELLEY:	We're getting along fine. We're the best of friends. . . .
JUDY:	I understand she hit you with her trunk!
SHELLEY:	Of course not. (BEAT) She missed by a mile!
JUDY:	Was she *really* born in a trunk?
SHELLEY:	Well, I don't know. I know she *lives* in it! . . .

While "Battle Hymn of the Republic" tended to overshadow the rest of the hour, the show, overall, was quite solid. The only negative aspect of this installment was an obvious move to cut

**Judy as muckraking reporter Lorelei Gumm with hapless interview subject
Shelley Berman**
COURTESY RICHARD CONNOLLY

production costs, with a minimalistic (or, more accurately, nearly
threadbare) look, contrary to the usually visually rich approach
of the series as a whole.

The opening "Let's Do It" routine had no scenery whatsoever, with Garland sporting the jacket she wore on the O'Connor episode, with everyone else wearing a copy; Merman's
backdrop for her solo segment was only a few painted panels;
the comedy sketch was done on two stools against a flat backdrop; Gennaro's dance number used only a few flag banners (he
sported a hat worn during Garland's dance routine on the Count
Basie show, and was decked out in the very same outfit *Judy*
herself would wear two shows later!); his dancers wore more
recycled costumes from past episodes; and last, the Garland-
Merman medley was framed sparsely with several thin strips of
lights. The only production values to speak of on the entire hour
were Berman's office set for his comedy sketch, and a rustic motif (a wooden fence, a barrel, and other pieces of Americana) for
"Shenandoah."

Ethel's "Gee, But It's Good to Be Here" and "I Get a Kick
Out of You" were full-bodied vintage Merman, and Berman's

sketch as a harried office worker was quite amusing. Gennaro's "I Love a Parade" dance routine was well performed, while Garland's pensive solo of "Shenandoah" is one of the more successful—and overlooked—set pieces of the series. Using only one camera throughout, with Garland shot in profile against the rustic backdrop, the camera slowly moved in and then, as the number neared its close, pulled back. The simplicity was enormously effective.

"Makin' Whoopee" displayed an energetic, playful Garland who threw up her heels and engaged in high kicks with Gennaro. Wearing similarly tattered white tuxedos (complete with starched, curled tails, the sort of costume that Judy loved), the two played patty-cake and pantomimed, all to delightful effect. Berman then joined the two, pleading with Judy and Peter to show him how to be "cute people" like them. Taking him in hand (after ripping his once-perfect tux), Judy, with Peter and Shelley, high-kicked to "Makin' Whoopee," with the comic breaking Judy up at the end when he took off his high top hat and crushed it under his foot. It was the most sparkling, and perhaps the best, dance routine in the entire run of the series. (Colleran remembers that Peter, who wore hearing aids in both ears, adopted the gesture of throwing his arms out after doing a turn. "He did that," Bill laughs, "to catch his hearing aids as they flew out of his ears.")

From the first song ("Friendship") to the last ("It's De-lovely") in their duet, Judy and Ethel were magnificent together. Although the medley was little more than one song strung immediately after another, seeing the "last of the big belters" (as Ethel referred to herself and Judy immediately before jumping into the routine) head-to-head in song remains an incomparable experience. Making the meeting of the two powerhouse singers all the more delightful is the chance to observe the disparate styles of Garland and Merman at work. Ethel unerringly played directly to the camera (if not the parking lot outside CBS Television City), only occasionally glancing at Judy or reacting to her. Merman, or so it seemed, chose not to alter her delivery, whether she was on Broadway or in the comparative broom closet that was Studio 43.

Judy appeared most amused at Ethel's single-minded, full-throttled blaring; indeed, Garland's performance is comprised mostly of her "takes," playing off of Merman's straight-on, dead-

"The Last of the Big Belters"
CBS INC.

ahead delivery. And even though "You're Just in Love" is in Garland's key, and not Merman's (it was, after all, *Judy's* show!), Ethel stole the song anyway—pushing Judy against her bosom when singing the line "Put your head on my shoulder . . ." causing Garland to look up at Merman towering above her in bemusement. Judy faltered for only a moment during the routine, but laughed so uproariously at getting tongue-tied that it only added to the fun. She seemed stimulated by Merman's presence, and Ethel, in turn, responded to Judy with genuine warmth. Where one might have expected competition, there was only mutual respect and generosity on both sides.

The rundown for the "Trunk" closing had "Puttin' On the Ritz," followed by "A Pretty Girl Milking Her Cow"; by showtime, the order was reversed. Both numbers were also well-performed and energetically sung but were, in essence, throwaway, undemanding numbers building up to "The Battle Hymn of the Republic."

Colleran had reinstated the policy of having a live audience

attend the taped dress rehearsal. The second version was the
one chosen by CBS to air; during the first, Judy mentioned JFK,
on the second she said only, "You know, one of the greatest
songs that was ever written is very seldom done on television,
and I would like to sing that song for you tonight."

It mattered not at all that "Battle Hymn" was not technically
perfect—Judy faltered over a few words, her microphone shorted
out during the middle of the song, requiring the engineers to
graft the audio from the dress-rehearsal performance onto the
second take. Garland's performance is one of the most indelible
and greatest of her entire career and stands as one of television's
most shining moments—the electrifying arrangement building and
building and capped with a final, soaring note. (Liza and series
dancer Harvey Evans sat transfixed together in the front row for
both tapings.)

Never before, or since, has the anthem been sung so movingly or been given a delivery so rich in emotion. Perhaps grasp-
ing this, CBS relented, and James Aubrey, to his credit, allowed
it to air, even if it was done in tribute, albeit tacitly, to President
John Fitzgerald Kennedy when "no tributes" were to air on Aubrey's network after the assassination.

Bill Colleran vividly recalls both performances of "Battle
Hymn":

"The first time Judy sang it was at dress rehearsal. The first
one, I think was even better, if that is possible, than the one that
aired. That's when, right before she sang it, she looked straight
into the camera and said, 'This is for you, Jack.' It was a powerful moment in my life. I will not forget that for as long as I
live. Never. There wasn't a dry eye in the house. People on their
knees crying. It was devastating. I was sobbing out loud. I've
never been so moved in my life by anything, anybody, or any
drama. Nothing compared to what that did to me the first time
she sang it. She gave every bit of her soul to that number. Everything that was Judy Garland was there and on the line at that
moment, everything she had to give. The final taping was an
hour later. She felt so deeply, she knew what she had. She got
a standing ovation. The audience was crying, they were so moved.
When she came backstage, she was crying and I was crying. She
was pleased at doing it for Jack. She knew what she had done.
But she was very easy, very quiet. Everyone just quietly went

home. I was handling her very carefully that night. She was very, very fragile. She had given so much. I can still see that little four-foot-eleven-inch gal standing there, her head going higher and higher, tears streaming down her face, as she sang her heart out. It's moments like this that make you forget your problems."

For episode seventeen, Vic Damone was invited back for a second guest appearance. Comedian Louis Nye (a regular on Steve Allen's television programs) and singer-dancer Chita Rivera also were to guest on the show. To fill in the hole left by the departed "Tea for Two" segment, CBS provided Garland Ken Murray and his "Hollywood Home Movies." Murray would show clips from his collection of informal films, and Judy would comment. For spontaneity, she decided not to see the footage in advance but to wait until the segment was taped. Murray was a CBS favorite who was for a time considered to host his own series; when that failed to materialize, he was contracted for several Garland appearances.

The final script was completed on December 17, three days before the tape date. The schedule had Garland tape the new opening for the Darin show on December 19, and later that night prerecord a *West Side Story* medley with Damone, as Capitol Records planned to release this performance (along with the earlier *Porgy* duet) on an album in April; it never materialized. December 20 was reserved for the dress rehearsal and, later that evening, the final taping.

Garland's frustration toward the series at this point was enormous, and she often expressed her anger by tardiness or even threatening not to do the show. "I'd say, 'Fine, you don't want to show up today,' " recalls Bob Wynn. " 'Instead of making twenty-five-thousand dollars this week, you'll make twelve-thousand dollars. It'll cost us twelve-thousand dollars to buy the day.' She'd say, 'Maybe I'd better take an aspirin and show up.' She understood very clearly the idea of getting her salary cut in half was not a good one."

Indicative of her dark mood, a distraught Judy made a late-night call to Bill Colleran. "She called me and said she was going to go to *Paris*," remembers Bill. "I said, 'Can I go along?' That stopped her in her tracks, and she said, 'What about the *show*?' I said, 'What show?,' and she said, 'Oh, *shit!*,' and we both laughed, and that ended that." Admits Colleran, "It was very bad by this time. Judy didn't know what she wanted to do with the show. Everybody was a nervous wreck, afraid for their jobs, afraid of what Judy would or wouldn't do. They'd tiptoe around her. I think it was absolutely doomed by the time I walked in. Judy was not happy with the show; she was bored with it. Coming to work, she wasn't excited anymore. But she needed the money. David and Freddie knew that, too. That's why they knew they had her."

Vic Damone was again a powerful stimulus and source of comfort to Judy. "She was like a little bird that you wanted to hold in your arms and protect, but became a giant when she started singing. We had one rehearsal at the house, rehearsed it with the orchestra at CBS and then taped it on the stage the night before the show. We prerecorded it to make sure it was absolutely *perfect* vocally." (The medley, the highlight of the hour, was no less brilliantly performed than the earlier *Porgy and Bess* performance on show twelve. Garland and Damone are vocally at their zenith, their collaborations ranking among Judy's greatest musical achievements. And it was fortuitous that she prerecorded *West Side Story* on Thursday night, being in better voice for the medley than she was for the actual taping.)

The visual treat of seeing Garland and Damone work their magic on "Maria," "Something's Coming," "Somewhere," and "Tonight" was marred, however, by a glaring mistake on Judy's part, that, astoundingly, was not retaped before airing. In the middle of "Something's Coming," she forgot the lyrics and, as her prerecorded vocal continued, she threw up her hands and stopped singing. After several seconds, she returned to the lyrics, and the segment continued to the end of the medley. Although she was once noted to have remarked, "Keep the mistakes in—at least it's honest," this went far beyond the boundaries of wanting to achieve a spontaneous effect in performance. The memory of this obviously rankled Judy, who, months later, felt the need to explain the gaffe to *TV Guide* with, "Vic Damone and I never did rehearse our 'West Side Story' songs. We prerecorded them and went right on the air," adding, "A couple of times I learned the music as I sang it on the show, reading the words from idiot cards. I don't know how to read music. Never have. But we got by. How? Black Irish luck, I guess." Garland's great pleasure at working with Damone is reflected in her ap-

"I Believe in You" with Chita Rivera and Louis Nye
CBS INC.

pearance on the show, Judy again looking rested and well—despite the fact that she and Glenn Ford had apparently separated by this time, reportedly because he was away shooting a film.

"They Can't Take That Away from Me" was a bright opener, a beaming Garland appearing first with a bevy of females; not happy with this development, Judy snapped her fingers and, thanks to stop-action photography, the girls were replaced by a collection of boy dancers outfitted in top hat and tails. The production number was first attempted with Garland using a hand microphone; the version that aired had her sing without a mike but to the prerecorded track from the earlier performance. "I Believe in You" is engagingly performed by Garland and Rivera, Louis Nye's forlorn self-doubting character visibly amusing Judy. Louis's comedy routine, one of his best-known monologues about a hapless group of army inductees ("You're now going to be marched over to a theater to see some army hygiene films—and after that, *breakfast!*") is very funny, and, unlike many solo spots of many other comedians on the Garland show, holds up well with the passing of time.

Damone's "You're Nobody Till Somebody Loves You" elevates the pop tune into something memorable, made all the more entertaining by his singing to Garland off-camera, smiling and pointing to her the whole time. Rivera's "I Got Plenty o' Nuttin' " showcases her song-and-dance abilities well, and Chita is noticeably moved at the enthusiastic reaction from the audience at its finish.

The Ken Murray spot was not only the first, but best, of his four appearances on the show. (In 1982, Murray spoke fondly of Judy, remarking, "I'd be there at nine in the morning, and it seemed that she wouldn't show up until nine at night. But when she got there, you had to love her. She was the best, and you forgave her anything. And the waiting was always worth it.") Flashes of Mickey Rooney, June Allyson, Van Johnson, and others flew by, and Judy's quips kept up with the pace. A youthful Ralph Bellamy, beaming in close-up, caused her to gibe, "He looks like Lillian Gish!" When a shot of a 1930s Judy appeared at a tennis tournament, Garland cracked, "Quite plump. Now I know what Louis Mayer had in mind!"; and when Mayer himself appeared for a moment, Judy cringed; "Oh, my *dear!*" Finally, there was projected a 1933 shot of Joan Crawford from *Dancing Lady*, the star glamorously bedecked in a lavish evening gown. Murray commented, "I just saw a wonderful [new] picture she did called *Strait-Jacket.*'" Without missing a beat, Judy shot back, 'She hasn't got it on *here!*"

Garland at the "Trunk" was in good, but not great, form. After speaking briefly of Fred Astaire and Irving Berlin, she began the beautiful ballad "Better Luck Next Time," starting in the wrong key (unusual for her, and likely due to lack of rehearsal), but slipping into the correct lower one after singing the title phrase; still, her simple, understated performance was quite wonderful. A last-minute replacement for "That's Entertainment," a driving, energetic "Almost Like Being in Love"/"This Can't Be Love" was terrifically entertaining. (This "Trunk" segment marked the last time Judy sang "Maybe I'll Come Back.")

Although a private Christmas party was held at Matteo's later in the evening, a large-scale celebration for the staff and some audience regulars was given on the soundstage directly after the taping. While she was charming and friendly and chatted with anyone who approached her, observers recall that Judy (escorted by Beverly Hills real estate tycoon Mike Silverman) was uncharacteristically subdued, and kept to herself, drinking next to nothing all evening. Most noted an aura of melancholy about her; some attributed it to lingering sadness about Kennedy's passing, others to the end of Judy's romance with Glenn Ford.

"Almost Like Being in Love"/"This Can't Be Love"
CBS INC.

She was also aware that, at that very moment, James Aubrey and his colleagues were determining the programming schedule for the 1964–65 season. She expected to hear news of her cancelation in a matter of days.

The first week of 1964 brought no news, good or bad, from CBS. Despite the network's silence, the fate of the show, according to virtually every TV columnist, was certain. Reflecting the majority view, Jack O'Brien in the *New York Journal-American* lamented, "The saddest news of this early moment of the New Year is that *The Judy Garland Show* won't be renewed when it finishes its first CBS season. It's a shame. For it's a good show, sometimes a very good one, occasionally a warm and rare gem in TV's tacky crown."

A "Save Judy" campaign was launched in New York by a Garland fan named Stephen Matthews. News of his efforts quickly spread, and letters from all over the country began to pour in to CBS. Jack O'Brien reported, "The keep-Judy Garland-on-TV feeling is high, by our mail." Columnist Earl Wilson did his part to help, printing Matthews's address, urging viewers to mail him their letters of protest to forward to CBS.

It is worth noting that in the 1963–64 season, thirteen of the top-rated fifteen shows were comedy programs; musical-variety programs (compared to comedy-variety programs such as Kaye's) were on the decline in popularity. Still, Garland's ratings were consistently above those of other shows in her genre, including *The Bell Telephone Hour, Sing Along with Mitch,* and *The Garry Moore Show.*

Perhaps in response to the campaign, rumors circulated that, even if her weekly series was dropped, CBS was "opening negotiations" for Judy to headline a minimum of six specials for the upcoming TV season. Addressing such speculation, Hank Grant of *The Hollywood Reporter* stated, "It's my guess if Judy Garland elected to return next fall on a strictly specials basis, she'd never want to do another weekly series again. It's tragically sad but true that even a revered performer is wide open for critical and even viewer abuse when launched on a weekly series, yet is treated with praise and respect when TV visits are made on a special basis."

Garland and Colleran hatched plans of their own to "save Judy." *The Hollywood Reporter* announced, "Give Judy Garland credit for leaving no stone unturned in her battle to bolster her sagging ratings. Judy just gave exec producer Bill Colleran the OK to go after the biggest name guests money can buy. Highest on Colleran's latching-list is Cary Grant, a real scoop if you can get him, 'cause Cary's turned down all TV offers to date." Judy also was interested in a dual booking of Sid Caesar and Nanette Fabray, which would have marked their first reunion since their old *Show of Shows* days, and still hoped to snare Noël Coward as a guest.

Gary Smith, on the other hand, was interested in having a steady flow of comedians on the show, a different one to appear each week opposite Garland. Smith left for New York to book such comics as Buddy Hackett for a two-shot deal, Jackie Mason (to appear on show twenty-one with Mel Tormé and Diahann Carroll), and a return for the Smothers Brothers. The pronounced difference in approach between Colleran and Smith only added to the difficulties between the two. And, with Garland favoring Colleran's accent on music, Judy's relationship with Gary rapidly deteriorated as well.

With Garland's worries about the series at an all-time high, the timing could not have been worse for Gary Smith to schedule the taping of two episodes back-to-back in the same week. Show eighteen (with Martha Raye, Peter Lawford, and Rich Little) would go before the cameras on Tuesday, January 14, with another program (with guests Louis Jourdan and the singing group The Kirby Stone Four) to be taped on Friday, January 17.

Meanwhile, Judy attempted to fill the void left by Glenn Ford. While dating Mike Silverman for a time, she met a relatively unknown actor by the name of Mark Herron (who had recently returned to the States after appearing in Fellini's *8½*) at a party hosted by Ray Aghayan. He was attentive, theatrical, and shared with Judy a similar sense of humor and an appreciation for the outrageous. (Once, Mark escorted Judy to a costume party at Ray Aghayan's. Walking in the door, she saw her art director, Bob Kelly, dressed exactly like Judy Garland. Judy looked him up and down, turned to Mark and said, "You know, there's only one thing that bothers me—he has better *legs* than I do!")

Judy invited Herron to several of her tapings, but their relationship at this point was far from serious. According to Bob Wynn, Judy began a brief romance with Hollywood attorney Greg

Bautzer (noted for his highly publicized, stormy love affairs with such glamour girls as Lana Turner and Joan Crawford). Wynn states that, while the romance with Garland was not long in duration, Bautzer (now deceased) deliberately cultivated the opportunity for long-term personal and professional gain. CMA might have the lock on managing Garland, but Bautzer felt he might profit handsomely by taking on her tangled legal affairs and get a sizable monthly retainer fee. According to Wynn, Judy was dazzled by the charming attorney and left a trustworthy law firm solely upon his recommendation.

Says Wynn, "Judy went to a cocktail party one night and met Greg Bautzer, who stuck it to the law firm that had straightened out her life and took the entire account away from them. He took an astronomical fee per show away from her. They had a meeting up in Bautzer's office, they had everybody there. Judy and Bautzer made their entrance, and he sat her at the head of the table, put his arm around her, and said, 'What do you want, Judy?' She said, 'I want an independent income that I don't have to work for.' Eddie Traubner said, 'Well, Mr. Bautzer, I think I should tell you that there are no resources or assets that an independent income could be drawn from.' Bautzer said, 'Sit down and shut up, that's not important.' I couldn't believe this man. He stayed with her until the show was over, and that was that. He took the money and ran." (By 1965, Bautzer's law firm still represented Garland, who by then was on the verge of bankruptcy; she nevertheless was billed by Bautzer for a monthly retainer fee of more than thirty-seven-hundred dollars.)

Judy, says Wynn, at the same time grew more suspect of her financial dealings with Fields and Begelman and came to believe that funds had been misappropriated: "She was aware of it, all right, but it never got really bad until David severed whatever relationship they had—but not bad enough that she would do anything about it. Towards the end, she screamed, 'I want them investigated—get me the president of the United States!' We were sitting there, at her house, eating breakfast, and Orval calls the White House. The president wasn't available. So we continued to eat, and the phone rang. The paper on her tray somehow unrolled, and on the front page was [Lyndon] Johnson holding a dog by the ears. She said, 'Fuck *this*, look what's he's doing to that *dog*!' Then she went to the attorney general [Robert Kennedy]. But she never got them investigated." (Sid Luft filed a lawsuit against CMA and Garland's managers on January 30. His motion was against Fields and Begelman in the amount of $1.45 million, charging the two with "defrauding" Garland by charging her fees in excess of 10 percent of her earnings, listing that amount at $350,000. He also alleged that "within the last few years Miss Garland has given them an additional $100,000." Luft asked for return of the $450,000 plus $1 million in punitive and exemplary damages.)

Focusing her attention on show eighteen was almost impossible, but Judy's week was made bearable by Colleran's support and the presence of old friends Martha Raye and Peter Lawford. Judy and Peter dated for a time during their MGM days and remained close thereafter. Garland and Raye not only were good friends, they shared David Rose as an ex-husband; the composer divorced Raye and married Judy soon after (in 1941). (Coincidentally, David Rose scored *Bonanza* each week, and had written the western's popular theme song.)

While Garland was obviously tired (looking puffy and carrying a few extra pounds as well), her flagging spirits were buoyed by the outrageous Martha and the urbane Peter; still, the final product had the same slapdash, lackluster quality that the Jane Powell–Ray Bolger show also possessed. Some moments were good, others fair; some segments were taken from earlier runthroughs, some from the final take. (The dress rehearsal of the Garland-Raye medley—a collection of Glenn Miller tunes—aired, with Garland noting the fact during her introduction of the segment.) The "Trunk" spot, with Judy looking much better than she did on the rest of the show, was taped later and inserted into the final broadcast version. In it, she wore a peculiar Aghayan zebra-striped creation and only *one* earring.

Championed by Mel Tormé and fellow Canadians Peppiatt and Aylesworth, impressionist Rich Little made his American television debut with Garland on show eighteen. She alarmed everyone with the news that her first encounter with Rich would be on-camera. Wanting to achieve the same spontaneous effect of the past "Tea" spots, and the fledgling Ken Murray segments, Judy nonetheless stunned everyone with the unorthodox decision.

Judy, laughs Rich, did not want him booked on the show,

Judy and Martha Raye rehearsing the "Glenn Miller" medley
CAPITOL RECORDS

telling Mel, "I don't want an impressionist on my show—they make me *fart!*," deliberately using the "*F*-word" that Tormé particularly disliked. "There was such turmoil going on because they couldn't get her out of her dressing room. Although she never rehearsed with me, it was a big plus for me, because she would be reacting to me for the first time. I can't think of any performer who didn't sort of fake it once they knew what I was going to do. In her case, she didn't know what was coming next, and that really worked to my benefit."

A good deal of socializing among the guests marked the week; Lawford, a noted drinker, drew the taping to a halt on several occasions. Says Little, "Peter Lawford could not remember his lines, going through sixty takes or something. I found him to be very aloof and in his own world. I don't think I spoke two words to him. I never saw a man flub so many lines before in my life. He couldn't put three words together. We didn't finish until two in the morning. Martha was fine. I went on around midnight. I don't know how they ever kept an audience for that show. Judy was very sweet to me, very nice, no temperament at all. She said, 'Let's cut out of here and go to the movies, let's get away from these despicable people!' I was new in the business, I didn't know much, but the drama going on backstage was better than what was going on in front of the cameras. But the show went over big, and she couldn't have been nice enough."

Rich did not escape some of the turmoil. "I was staying at the Farmer's Daughter Motel across the street from Television City. We sent my suit to be pressed, and the guy who brought it back had no idea that the trousers had slipped out on the street. An hour before the show, they unwrapped my suit before makeup, and there were no pants! They told Bill Colleran that I had no pants for the show. He said, 'Stop doing jokes!,' and I said, 'No, really, I have no pants!' I was having an absolute fit. My first big break on TV. I had to try on all these trousers belonging to CBS pages!"

Rich credits the Garland show as being a significant launching pad for his durable career: "It did wonders for me because of Judy's reaction as I did the impressions. She did me a tremendous favor by *not* showing up!" (The segment is quite wonderful, Judy amazed by Rich's uncanny impressions of over a dozen stars, mostly done talking the lyrics to "The Man That Got Away"; his James Mason was so accurate that Garland visibly gasped. At the close of the segment, Judy spontaneously invited him back for another appearance.)

The show opened with a prerecorded production number of Garland singing "76 Trombones" (a strident, pointless tune that really didn't suit her), flanked by the orchestra on raised platforms. The routine was fun but not really memorable; Garland's voice was strong but a bit rough around the edges. Martha's song and dance solo of "Taking a Chance on Love" was done as much for comic as musical effect, the brazen-voiced singer bumping into one of the boy dancers, startling him, saying, 'Oh, sorry, dear!" Peter Lawford walked through a rather flat routine, playing a world-weary bachelor on the prowl for virginal Judy under the watchful eye of his butler, played by Bert Mustin. In an obviously early run-through of the routine, Garland looks quite tired, wearing only minimal makeup, the segment saved by her warm rendering of the beautiful ballad "I'm Old-Fashioned." Ken Murray's spot was merely adequate. Garland, Raye, and Lawford teamed for a comedy-music routine of "Hit Parade 1964," featuring a solemn introduction by Lawford (requiring multiple takes) leading into such currently popular songs as "Be True to Your School," a rock version of "The Boy Next Door," and "Dumbhead" (whereupon Martha actually bit Peter's hand, visibly angering him for a moment, when he put his hand over her mouth to stop her singing). The spot was amusing but forgettable.

The Garland-Raye "Glenn Miller" medley is the highlight of the hour, Martha completely unleashing her comic talents. Mugging, shimmying, sticking her head in Judy's close-up (with Judy delightedly attempting to beat Martha at her own game), Raye is great fun. During "At Last," Martha exaggeratedly mouthed, "I love you!" repeatedly as Judy attempted to continue the ballad with a straight face; finally giving up at the end, she pointed to Martha and changed the lyric to ". . . and *she* is mine at last!," causing Raye to break up. At the close of the routine, Judy turned to Martha and said, 'You're outrageous, you're absolutely outrageous!" (Some recall that the final version did not air because the dress rehearsal could not be topped; others remember that the taping got so late and Martha's humor so "blue" that it was far too risqué for television.)

The one-earring "Trunk" spot showed a Garland appearing rather bored and uninterested; still, in great voice, she crooned "All Alone" to perfection and then closed with a powerful, brilliantly sung "Oh, Lord! I'm on My Way." Garland was to have sung "Maybe I'll Come Back," but instead, underscoring her apathy, abruptly turned and exited the stage—leaving the orchestra to vamp and director Whitmore to shoot perhaps two dozen shots of a bare stage and stationary trunk from every conceivable angle over a three-minute span. "Maybe I'll Come Back," at this point, was hardly a song that Judy felt like singing any longer.

Bob Wynn cannot forget one night of socializing: "We went to a Mexican restaurant. It was Judy, Martha, Peter, Johnny Bradford, and myself. After that, we all went to Judy's house. Remember, I was only twenty-eight at the time. I said, 'Boy, that Mexican food is tough on you!' Martha looked at me and said, 'The trouble with you, young man, is that you don't know how to *fart!*' Judy got into the act. So, Judy Garland and Martha Raye taught me how to fart. I sat there and never laughed so hard in my life. These two women were demonstrating a sneaker, a wet one, the explosion, the shaking one out! Poor Peter was sitting over there with his head down, saying, 'Life is a bowl of shit!' They really had it down to a science—God, they were funny!''

Martha Raye remembers the week with great fondness, saying, "Judy was a dream to work with, just wonderful, and was one of the most *unselfish* performers I've ever worked with. She was there for rehearsals and worked very hard." Raye adds, "We had a ball."

The sets for show eighteen were barely carted off the stage before taping of the next episode was to commence. In addition to rehearsing and taping two complete shows within a single week, Judy knew that James Aubrey, Michael Dann, and Dr. Frank Stanton would all be in Hollywood to take "a final look at next season's potential product," according to *The Hollywood Reporter*. The CBS executives would begin discussions on Thursday, January 16, the day before show nineteen was to be taped.

Then word leaked out that the network was holding off on deciding Garland's fate, perhaps taking into account the tremendous outcry to keep Judy's show on the air; the critics were much in her corner, the "Save Judy" campaign was in full force, and CBS was deluged with mail. The official decision, either way, would come after the CBS executives met in Hollywood.

Show nineteen, however, was hardly the model to gauge the future potential of Garland's series, a flat, lackluster effort that had only a few bright moments. Judy was originally set to open the hour singing "Great Day," one of her favorite songs. Perhaps not wanting to bother learning a new arrangement, she elected instead to do "San Francisco." (Garland here began the practice of repeating numbers that she had sung on previous episodes and, for the most part, bettered her earlier attempts on the series.)

The Kirby Stone Four, an innocuous group of middle-aged male warblers, raced through a nondescript "Baubles, Bangles and Beads" and "You Do Something to Me." Judy joined them for "Whispering," but she had trouble remembering the prerecorded lyrics, and (as she had done with "A Lot of Livin' to Do") dropped her chin to her chest when the words escaped her. Louis Jourdan offered a pleasant but unexciting, "I Want a Girl Just Like the Girl that Married Dear Old Dad" with a bevy of girl dancers. Garland then soloed on "Paris Is a Lonely Town" (a last-minute selection) from *Gay Purr-ee,* revealing a dry throat; she skirted most of the high notes as a result. Then, against the same set (a lavish room overlooking the Eiffel Tower), she sat at a small table and clutched a handkerchief. In the same dramatic fashion as she had framed "Paris," she began to sing "Smoke Gets in Your Eyes." As she sang plaintively and longingly, smoke slowly appeared, followed by a ax breaking down the door and firemen racing in. The inspired routine (an idea of Colleran's and Garland's, with the song being among Judy's least favorites) is brilliant. Judy's incredible comedic sense and timing are in sharp focus, and her performance hilarious. Finally, after the firemen have stripped the room bare (their "carry-outs" including life-size cutouts of the Tin Man and the Scarecrow used as props by CBS in promotion of the yearly telecast of *The Wizard of Oz*), Judy was picked up bodily by a fireman. As she was hauled out of the room, she grabbed the chair she had been sitting on, dragging it with her, singing the final "Smoke gets in your *iiiiiiiieyes* . . . !"

The Ken Murray segment was again adequate, but by now had overstayed its welcome and lost most of its freshness; Judy's quips provided welcome leavening. A medley of children's songs with Judy and Louis was surprisingly quite good, the two warm and relaxed together. Seeing Garland work her way through such songs as "Popeye, the Sailor Man," "Give a Little Whistle," "When You Wish Upon a Star," and "Zip-a-Dee Doo-Dah!" is an unexpected delight, and her solo of "Some Day My Prince Will Come," while not vocally first-rate, is a treasure. The segment closed with a dreamlike waltz danced by Judy and Louis, conjuring up a bit of the old MGM magic.

The "Trunk" closing was to have included "Just You, Just Me," "What'll I Do?," and "Rock-a-Bye Your Baby," a song she had sung on show twelve with Vic Damone. At the last minute, Judy decided to drop "Just You" and "Rock-a-Bye" and instead repeated "Battle Hymn" after "What'll I Do?" (the latter sung tenderly and effectively to the sole accompaniment of Mort Lindsey's piano). Mentioning the response the song had generated, Judy remarked that a search for a similar song led her to con-

"Smoke Gets in Your Eyes"
COURTESY RICHARD CONNOLLY

clude that "Battle Hymn" was irreplaceable. As the orchestra struck the first note, the audience broke into applause; Judy's performance is fine but cannot be compared to her first, and this time she inadvertently went for a higher, barely reachable final note. Judy erred in repeating the song, but the final result is far from embarrassing. Garland won a tremendous ovation and exited triumphantly.

CBS was poised to cancel *The Judy Garland Show* within a matter of days; when it finally happened, the decision was hardly a surprise, but it crushed Judy just the same.

"People said, 'How can you put her through this terrible torture?' states former CBS programming executive Mike Dann, "and also [said], 'You're making her work so hard.' She was the same Judy who was performing all those concerts in far-off places under adverse conditions as compared to the studio and her little trailer. CBS was the most sheltered place she was ever in in her whole life, and the safest for her. She was really the happiest that I'd ever seen her in her whole life. She really loved those days. There was always a huge group of her close friends who were always dropping in on her in the trailer. The studio was like Grand Central Station. Once I got a call first thing Tuesday morning. The show had gone very late and over budget. I was called down to her trailer. Out of the kitchen and into the living room stepped Judy. All dressed up in a prisoner's black-and-white striped outfit. She must have been in makeup for an hour and a half to get ready. She said, 'I know I belong in jail—I'm ready!,' and we roared. That kind of thing happened all the time.

"She treated me like Louis B. Mayer, because she always had to have a father figure," says Dann. "Even after the show went off the air, I'd very often get these calls at three or four in the morning from Judy, wanting to know what happened. She always would say, 'Why did you do it?—*why*?' "

18

CBS notified Judy Garland that her series would be terminated upon completion of her twenty-sixth program, scheduled to air on March 29. In a gallant move, the network allowed Judy to make the announcement, stating that it was she, and not CBS, who chose to end the series. The formality fooled no one, but it did allow her a graceful, dignified exit. The network released the news on January 22, 1964, in the form of a letter from Garland to James T. Aubrey, Jr.:

> Dear Jim:
>
> I've done a great deal of thinking recently about a decision that I have made and I hope that I might be able to say briefly and unemotionally what is terribly important to me in a letter, rather than attempting to do so in a meeting or on the phone.
>
> Firstly, I am most grateful for the support that I've had from CBS these past months, both personally and professionally. I have found my experience on weekly television a most gratifying one and a part of my career that I will always remember as exciting and fulfilling, as well as challenging. Now, however, in spite of all this, I have had to make the decision not to continue after the production of my twenty-sixth program. I have found the

involvement that I must give to production and performing these programs to be incompatible with the time and
attention that I must give to family matters. Frankly, I
find it impossible to give my children the time and attention that they need and also continue the demanding
schedule of a weekly program. Needless to say, since my
children's interests come before anything, I know this decision to be the right one and I would have no difficulty
or hesitation in sending this letter had it not been for the
personal and professional affection that I have for you
and the other executives at CBS and for all the kindness
and consideration that you and they have shown me. . . .
There will be many opportunities for us to work together
in the coming years, and I look forward to them with
great excitement. . . . On a somewhat lighter note—let's
be happy about all the bets we've won from all the wise
guys who said we'd never get our first show on the air.

　　With deep affection, I remain,

Sincerely,
JUDY GARLAND

　　CBS released a response, obstensibly written by Aubrey, no
less carefully worded than was Garland's statement:

Although I can appreciate the compelling reason for Miss
Garland's action, I would like to say how genuinely sorry
all of us at the Network are that she has reached this
decision. Judy's great talent and electrifying personality
have added distinction to this television season, and we
are proud that the CBS Television Network was able to
provide, through this gifted artist, so many hours of
heartwarming delight for the nation's viewers. We look
forward to her return to television—hopefully on the CBS
Network."

　　John Aylesworth and Frank Peppiatt went to see Judy at home
as soon as they learned of the cancellation. "She was in a rotten
mood," recalls John. "She glared at us and said, 'What do you
guys want?' And Frank stood up and said, 'Judy, we've come to

kill you.' And she just dissolved in laughter and said, 'Please, I've already been killed *once* today!' "

The public and press rushed to Judy's defense. *TV Guide* published an unprecedented number of viewer letters lambasting CBS and praising Garland. Expressing the sentiments of many television critics, Harriet Van Horne in the *New York World Telegram and Sun* wrote, "Poor Judy Garland! After triumphing over the bureaucratic idiocy that sought to remake her personality . . . [she] now faces a springtime cancellation. It hardly seems fair. . . . In truth, Miss Garland's ratings weren't awfully low, especially if you count in millions rather than Nielsen points. But the opposition—that ugly, violent, always-vulgar, ever-predictable *Bonanza*—continued to delight the masses. . . . Watching [Judy's] show last night, I was struck by its enormous improvement, and by the good humor, the sly comic gifts of the star . . . how nice it would be if CBS would find another time spot for Judy . . . and brought her back next season."

CBS's most enduring and beloved female star, Lucille Ball, was not afraid to speak out against her own network: "I was furious when one of the biggest stars in America, Judy Garland, was given lines like, 'I'm a little old lady,' and someone started talking about 'the next Judy Garland.' I bet she's glad her series is over. She's the best."

(In 1989, James Aubrey declined to be interviewed for this book. He did offer, rather ironically, praise for *The Judy Garland Show*. Speaking of how the quality and star power of Garland's series could not be equaled by future network programmers, Aubrey stated, "They would watch those shows again today and would only hope that they could be able to duplicate them today in television—but they can't. There's no way that they can.")

Bolstered by this resurgence of public and critical support, Judy and Bill Colleran decided to go completely against network policy. Judy and Bill were determined to adopt an all-music "concert format." The comedians hired by Gary Smith were scrapped; as a substitute of sorts, ten additional musicians were added to Mort Lindsey's orchestra.

"We had bad audio problems from the beginning," Judy said a few weeks later. "Half the time, I couldn't hear the orchestra because it was off to one side. I was told it was a unique television technique. It left the stage free for sets and backgrounds.

I got tired of the *television look*. And I wanted to hear the music. So I yelled, and they finally put the band on stage behind me." Judy further remarked, "I thought we could use movie techniques to get away from pure television quality. But everyone kept telling me, 'This is television, Judy. It's not like movies or concerts. You have to get used to this medium. Just take our word for it; we know what we're doing.' And I took their word for it. I believed they *did* know what they were doing." She ruefully added, "We had nine different formats. We spent four or five weeks drifting around on the air looking for a format. They never consulted me about changes. They didn't want to upset me, they said. I followed orders until I began to listen to my own instincts."

One of Judy's first attempts to exert some control was her decision (made at the start of the Colleran regime) to abandon the use of the revolving turntable. "It had a lot of noisy machinery under it and turned in a full circle so they could build back-to-back sets and swing me around. But I suffered dreadfully from motion sickness. I'd get violently ill. Or the table would come to an abrupt halt, and I'd lose my balance. Once, I stepped off while it was still going and staggered around like I'd jumped off a train or something."

Says Colleran, "When I thought of the concert idea, it was because I just couldn't take what was happening any longer. I thought, I cannot do this show and not contribute something to this woman, because I loved her deeply. I had to help her in some way. She loved the idea, and said, 'Let's go ahead and do it.' I said, 'They'll all hate me.' She said, 'Tell them to call *me*.' "

It was, from the start, an uphill battle, not only with CBS, but with Garland's production staff. Says Colleran, "Judy got pissed off at Gary Smith because he didn't want to do the concerts. He had other people he wanted to put on the show. He thought the show needed it. I said, 'It hasn't worked so far, it's become embarrassing.' The people coming on with her were second-rate, and it was bad for Judy. I told Gary and everybody else not to sign anybody for the show." Colleran then faced CBS. "Aubrey and Stromberg hated the idea; Stromberg said that she couldn't hold a show on her own, and Aubrey said she had lost her talent," says Bill ruefully.

Artistic considerations notwithstanding, the move to the concert format had significant financial advantages for Garland; this allowed her the means to recoup, at least in part, some of the losses she had incurred by going over budget on previous shows. With the realization that she would exit CBS with far less than the "twenty million" promised her, she knew her financial future depended largely on whatever she could save on the last handful of episodes. The show's lavish design, top money paid to guest stars, and delays caused by Judy and a variety of other factors put the show very much over budget. As art director Bob Kelly notes, "By the eighteenth show, we were so much in debt, she couldn't stop. They had to do those concert shows. We were recouping money." (Kingsrow was to have been paid seventy-five thousand dollars for each repeat aired, but none were shown that summer, even though as late as March 18, *Variety* reported that CBS would rerun seven episodes, including three concert programs, and the hours with Barbra Streisand and Martha Raye.)

According to Colleran, Garland confronted Aubrey directly. "I said, 'Judy, I need help,' so she called Aubrey. She said, 'Do what Bill wants or you don't have me. It's that simple.' And that's what did it." Perhaps no longer caring at all and willing to throw in the towel, Aubrey acquiesced to Garland's demands. The victory was sweeter because the concept for the first concert hour was, in fact, based partly upon Judy's "Americana" tribute that CBS had rejected in the wake of JFK's death.

Judy's enthusiasm, excitement, and spirits climbed instantly; it also would give her a much-needed bolster of self-confidence to triumph in a one-woman show, unencumbered by second bananas, second-rate guests, and the standard variety-programming mold of the day. Garland, Colleran, Tormé, and the writers worked together to formulate the program for the all-music hour. The songs comprising the hour went through several revisions, but all versions contained an inspired mixture of spirituals, nostalgic and patriotic numbers, as well as several Garland trademark tunes. The taping date was set for Friday, January 24; a party held in Judy's honor at Matteo's followed.

Thursday, January 23, was set aside for early morning technical discussions, a rehearsal with Jud Conlin and his singers with orchestral run-throughs. Friday included a 2:00 P.M. rehearsal, a 6:00 to 7:30 P.M. dress taping with audience, and a final taping from 9:30 to 11:00 P.M. (Garland's call was not until 2:00 P.M.)

From the moment Garland walked onstage for the final taping it was clear that a revitalized Judy had appeared. She was at the top of her current form and in fine vocal shape. Judy threw up one hand in an expansive gesture as she began "Swing Low, Sweet Chariot." The movement, as it happened, was not made to punctuate a point in the lyric. As Judy once explained, "You stand there in the wings, and sometimes you want to yell because the band sounds so good. Then you walk out and if it's really a great audience, a very strange set of emotions can come over you. You don't know what to do. It's a combination of feeling like Queen Victoria and an absolute ass. Sometimes a great reception—though God knows I've had some great receptions and I ought to be prepared for it by now—can really throw you. It kind of shatters you so that you can lose control of your voice and it takes two or three numbers to get back into your stride. I lift my hand in a big gesture in the middle of my first number, and if I see it's not trembling, then I know I haven't lost my control."

Judy clearly had not lost her control and, from that first moment, was in total command, hitting the final, sustained note with power and confidence. Asking for her "Camelot dressing room" to be moved onstage, Judy changed from her glamorous Aghayan gown to a spectacular jeweled top and white Capri slacks. She threw open the dressing room door and launched into a medley of World War I songs; her performance of such tunes as "Give My Regards to Broadway," "Over There," "Boy of Mine" and "Keep the Home Fires Burning" was stellar.

Judy pranced, skipped, and even swatted Mort on his behind during the musical bridge of "That's Entertainment"; when Bill Colleran had asked her if she wanted Wally Siebert to assist with some choreography for the number, Garland laughed, "Oh, no, don't bother—I'll just do some 'Judy steps'!"

The script then had Judy and director Whitmore engage in a bit of dubious banter, with Judy instead asking Mort Lindsey, "What has four wheels and lies on its back?" The hapless Mort replied he didn't know, and Judy said, "A dead bus!" The joke never made it to the broadcast version, with the segment instead beginning with Judy noting "Make Someone Happy" as a song that she hadn't done before, and then adding that what would follow would "make three very special people in my life very happy . . . you'll see what I mean later."

Sitting next to Mort at the piano, Judy crooned a beautiful, touching "Make Someone Happy," giving it meaning and substance far beyond the ordinary. Then, standing at the piano, she sang "Liza"; while not matching her earlier version on the Schlatter show (which, after all, was a full-blown production number with Liza present), it was wonderfully sung, simply and direct. "Happiness Is a Thing Called Joe," by contrast, was far superior to her version on the Allyson-Lawrence episode. Not only was Judy in much better voice, her performance was extraordinary due to the presence of her son, Joe. Walking to the edge of the stage during the first chorus, Judy sat at the apron. She kissed Joe tenderly, and spoke to him during the musical bridge; and then, with great love, sang the final chorus, looking at him directly as she changed the lyric to ask, "Do you love me good? . . . That's all I need to know . . ." It was theatrical, it was enormously effective, it was an outpouring of love that was genuine and unrehearsed.

Judy then addressed the fact that, until that moment, there had never been a song for her third offspring:

"I have another child, and she's pretty angry. She really is. And her name is Lorna. And *nobody* ever wrote a song about *Lorna*! And we looked everywhere. We found songs like Linda, and Lily and Lola and Lorraine and Lulu and, of course, Cincinnati Lou, and even Lydia the Tattooed Lady. But we couldn't find a Lorna. We just couldn't. . . . We have a lovely theme that was written on our show by Mr. Mort Lindsey, our musical conductor. It's such a pretty melody, and we thought it would be nice to put some words to it. So we thought of asking one of the finest lyricists in the country if he could come and help us out, and I'm pretty thrilled, because his name is Johnny Mercer, and you can't do better than that! . . . I want to thank Johnny for writing such a beautiful lyric and for making *Lorna* a very happy little girl. . . . Let's do your song, now. . . ."

Lorna stood up, and, as both were seen in profile, Judy sang:

> Lorna—
> I can't believe what I see,
> What I see astounds me!
> Mirrors of love
> are your eyes to me.

Judy croons "Lorna" to the song's inspiration.
CBS INC.

> Stars up above
> must delight to see them.
> Lorna—
> you won't believe what I say.
> What I say
> I almost should pray . . .
> pray for the day
> I can shout from the rooftops,
> Lorna loves me too!

As the music played before the final chorus, Lorna reached out to her mother and the two embraced, Judy patting her gently. The moment was pure magic. The number was so magnificently performed that a reprise of "Make Someone Happy" was eliminated from the final broadcast version of the show; "Lorna" could simply not be topped, the emotion stirred by Judy and her children making anything after anticlimactic.

Yet, as Bill Colleran remembers, the creation of "Lorna" was a story in itself. In order to obtain the services of Johnny Mercer, the executive producer had to take a red-eye flight to Detroit, where the composer was embroiled in the out-of-town tryouts for a Bert Lahr show called *Foxy*. Colleran quickly discovered that the supremely talented Mercer was, for this night anyway, rather under the influence: "The song was Judy's idea. She called Johnny Mercer to write the lyric. She came back to me and said, 'Johnny will do it if we go back there and take him a tape of the song.' I made the arrangements and got to Detroit. Johnny greeted me at the door. I had the tape with me. He put the tape on and said, 'Okay, sit there and wait for me—it shouldn't take too long.' About two in the morning, passed out with his head on the typewriter, he looked up for the first time and said, 'Who the fuck are *you*?' I said, 'I produce Judy's show and I'm here for the Lorna theme.' He said, '*Whose* theme?' 'Lorna!' I told him. 'Oh, yeah,' he said. This went on all night, until eight in the morning. He woke up about five or six times, and the same thing happened each time, 'Who the *fuck* are you?' He was one of the greatest lyricists of all time, but this was the comedy of all time. About ten in the morning, he finished the lyric, and I left, totally exhausted. I went out to Judy's house with the tape, showed her the lyric, and she sang it. Judy just adored it."

Continuing show twenty, Garland's "Rock-a-Bye Your Baby" was first-rate and even greater than her performance at the "Trunk" on show twelve. Judy's "Camelot dressing room" was wheeled onstage. Garland changed into her tramp costume and makeup ("This gets worse looking every time!") as she prepared to do her "Couple of Swells" routine. Garnering perhaps her biggest laugh of all twenty-six shows, she announced she'd have to do the routine as a solo; partner Fred Astaire, she quipped, was unavailable: "I think he's busy choreographing *Bonanza!*"

The song-and-dance routine was so good that Fred's absence was hardly noticed. Hampered a bit by using the microphone for most of the number (it was rather incongruous to see a tramp carrying a three-thousand-dollar Shure mike!), Judy growled, danced, and re-created the choreography from *Easter Parade* without missing a beat.

A rousing "America, the Beautiful" ended the hour. After

Judy in her "Camelot
dressing room" changes
into her tramp costume
for "A Couple of Swells."
CBS INC.

Mort helped her scrape the tramp-black paint from her tooth, she threw off her hat with a casual gesture that had it land perfectly on Mort's podium right side up. Garland planted her feet on the stage and began singing the anthem. In the tramp outfit—the effect here is Chaplinesque—she seemed to reaffirm patriotism while facing adversity. The final result, rather than being cloying, calculated, or artificial, exemplifies Judy Garland's genius. Her sincerity transcended theatricality and made a moment indelible. The audience responded with a standing ovation, a gesture quite uncommon for television audiences of the day. Judy, taking tiny steps in her oversized clown shoes, came back for several bows.

Although the program would not be seen by the public until February 9, the trade papers were quick to report Garland's dazzling success. *Variety* noted, "Bill Colleran, Gary Smith and the cast and crew of Judy Garland's show gave her a standing ovation after taping her one-gal show." The bash, noted Army Archerd, did not break up until three in the morning. *The Hollywood Reporter*'s "Rambling Reporter" Mike Connolly noted that Garland, "headed for her last CBS roundup" did such a spectacular show that he concluded, "One can hardly blaze out more gloriously than that."

Bill Colleran was thrilled at Judy's greatly improved de-

"America, the Beautiful"
CBS INC.

meanor. "I used to try to distract her from her troubles by making her laugh. I couldn't hide the pills, I couldn't stop her. Nobody could. I knew the only thing I could do was to make her forget, to make her laugh, [then] I got her back to thinking that she was okay. Once the concerts started, it worked. She was happy. The difference to me was amazing. I couldn't believe it was the same person."

Show twenty-one, to be taped the following Friday evening on January 20, would be the first of several "miniconcert" installments. A Garland solo performance would occupy approximately the first half of the hour, with guest stars Diahann Carroll and Mel Tormé featured in the second. Garland would perform with both singers, and, as always, close with the "Trunk" spot. Discarded by Colleran was another Ken Murray appearance, as well as comedian Jackie Mason.

While the "miniconcert" was enormously effective and properly put the accent on music, the elaborate setup required did not endear Garland or Colleran to the technical crew. Dress rehearsal for the guest segments began at 2:00 P.M. and ended at 3:30 P.M., with their final taping set for 5:30 to 6:30 P.M. Then, from 6:30 to 8:30 P.M., the entire stage had to be reset, bringing Lindsey's forty-piece orchestra onstage, followed by extensive audio and camera checks. As George Sunga says, "It meant a traumatic move to get the guys out of the shell and get them up onstage." After Garland's stand-in, Judy Johnson, did an audio balance with the orchestra, the taping of the concert segment began at 10:00 P.M. The hours were perfect for Garland, but set the crew to grousing; the late taping time guaranteed, however, that Judy would be at her best. (The concert audience was first routed to adjacent Studio 41, where a videotape playback of the "production segments" was shown, before they filed into Studio 43 at 9:45 P.M.)

Judy cared little about any complaints. She was, for the first time in months, enjoying her television career. Garland (who had six distinctly different "looks" during the course of the series) took on an ultraglamorous, sophisticated aura. Her makeup became more pronounced, more theatrical than natural; she chose to remain with her teased "Jackie Kennedy" pompadour hairstyles; and she reveled in wearing sleek, low-backed Aghayan-Mackie gowns the likes of which she had never before worn in her life. The new approach, states Aghayan, "was absolutely very carefully thought out." Garland's new sophisticated evening gowns had another purpose, adds Mackie: "She loved getting dressed up and going out—everything that was made for her on the show, she took home." Garland's newfound glamour was not without a price, however. As production consultant Bob Wynn laughs, "I know the first bill that I questioned was for six hundred dollars. Ray built her a new ass for those tight formfitting gowns, and the invoice read 'new *derriere* for Miss Garland—six hundred dollars'!"

Ray Aghayan and several others note that before the concert shows aired, the lavish Rockingham screening parties had dwindled to but a few people in attendance. (Bill Colleran was absent for some broadcasts of the early episodes, attempting to salvage his marriage to Lee Remick.) "Most people just started turning off their phones," says Ray. "But when she'd call me late at night, I'd drive all the way to Brentwood and sit there. I liked her. We were friends. I used to be entertained for hours at a time. She was absolutely compelled to entertain you. I don't think you could ever be bored around her." But, states Bob Kelly, as Garland trimmed the show budget and staff, her CBS "family" became far less supportive: "Time after time, Bob Mackie, Ray Aghayan, and I went out to Judy's house to watch the show with her. She was absolutely alone. None of the producers showed up, none of the writers, nobody. She'd order in Mexican food or the cook would whip something up, and we would watch the show with Judy. And Ray would arrange it all, put it all together. He'd call me and say, 'Let's go to Judy's Sunday night, because nobody's coming, and we don't want her to be alone.' "

The taping of show twenty-one went on schedule. First done was Carroll's solo spot of "Quiet Nights" and "Goody, Goody," both sung and performed extremely well against a simple black background peppered with lights. Kelly and his staff had a field day creating a stunning train station set for Tormé's solo of "Blues in the Night," using props from "Shenandoah," and the train tracks and signals from the Bennett-Garland "traveling" medley on show five. Garland introduced Tormé with an unfortunately brief bit of his "Stranger in Town," which was beautifully sung; his "Blues in the Night" (which Garland purportedly dubbed "pretentious" after the taping) was, in fact, overwritten and overwrought. Intent on being a ladies' man of sorts, Mel conspired to have a bevy of beautiful dancers circle him (wearing the same costumes and exaggerated wigs from his earlier "Comin' Home, Baby" of show eleven) while he sang, with a trench coat à la Frank Sinatra draped over his shoulder. His fun, but pointless, duet with Judy of "The Trolley Song" was rather odd, Mel even snarling "boo" at Judy on-camera, which noticeably startled her. The routine ended with Judy lip-synching to an obviously prerecorded loop of the final note of the song, while Tormé sang nonsensical counterpoint lyrics about his shopping list while riding on the trolley. Judy and Mel, despite the material and backstage turmoil, were good together, but the final on-camera meeting of Tormé and Garland should have been better.

A Garland-Carroll medley of Harold Arlen and Richard Rodgers songs was quite good, with Judy obviously delighted in being paired with the young Diahann; often overlooked, this medley stands as one of the best in the series.

For the concert segment, Judy strode on the stage and was, from the start, in total command. "Hey, Look Me Over" dis-

Judy and Diahann Carroll

played Garland improvising a bit of the lyric on the spot, but her confident, sure delivery began the hour with great effectiveness. "Smile" was near-perfection, infinitely better than her earlier "Trunk" performance on show twelve, sung richly and poignantly. "I Can't Give You Anything but Love (Baby)" was the first and only time Judy sang her complete arrangement on television, and, in a daring move, the camera remained on her during the entire orchestral interlude midsong. It was a stunning six-minute performance captured by one camera. "After You've Gone" followed, and, done in a tempo a bit faster than usual, was first-rate.

Director Whitmore followed Colleran's very specific directions on how he wanted to frame Judy: "When you have Garland, a real talent, leave her alone. That's why most of my numbers with her were one-camera numbers. Move in and stay there. Let her sell the number. Leave her alone. Just light her beautifully."

Garland began the next segment by striding out of the wings to sing "Alone Together," framed in dramatic lighting. Her performance of the romantic ballad was extraordinary, topped only by her next number, "Come Rain or Come Shine." Colleran held the song (and Nelson Riddle's arrangement) to be his very favorite ever written; although Judy had performed it on a Schlatter hour, he prevailed upon his star to repeat the song. Judy attacked this most difficult routine with vigor and made it one of her greatest performances in a version different but no less remarkable than the one on show three. The earlier rendition built more slowly to its thunderous climax; this attempt is more vital, more energetic, more fiery from the start. At one point, the audience became so caught up in Garland's compelling, powerful performance that it applauded spontaneously when she walked toward it and sang, *"You're* gonna love me, like nobody's loved me . . ."* in affirmation of that sentiment. Her ovation at the end was loud, long, and pronounced, and Judy was visibly moved by the tremendous applause.

The "Trunk" closing segment was actually pieced together from two performances over a three-week time period. "Don't Ever Leave Me" was sung effectively but had to be reshot during the taping of the next show due to an audio problem; "Great Day" was taped twice. The first take was slower and ran out of steam before it finished. The second (which aired) was more driving, with Garland spontaneously singing along with the off-camera chorus even though it was not part of the arrangement. The final broadcast version had "Don't Ever Leave Me" followed by a lengthy cutaway audience shot (always a clue of editing underfoot) and then Garland, in a slightly different hairstyle and in the same gown—but inexplicably without the earrings she had worn only five seconds before—attacking "Great Day" with gusto.

The series went on a two-week hiatus following the taping of the Carroll-Tormé hour. Judy and her younger children escaped to New York, where Liza was appearing in a production of *The Fantasticks* at the Mineola Playhouse in Long Island. The vacation was not without incident, however. The night before the first concert was to air, Judy suffered a mild concussion from a fall in her suite at the Sherry-Netherland Hotel. She spent the night at Mt. Sinai Hospital but was released the next day "feeling great." So enthused was Judy about the first concert show that when Liza phoned her from a friend's apartment, Judy advised her to watch the program. Liza recalls, "I asked her if she was okay, and she said, 'Oh, I'm fine, I'm fine.' She said, 'Watch the show tonight—it's a good one!' "

Judy was so excited about the show that she took Lorna and Joe with her to CBS headquarters in Manhattan, where she watched the broadcast hand in hand with them; photographs of the three arriving at CBS show Judy beaming with pride, hugging Joe and Lorna.

CBS even relented and placed advertisements in newspapers

across the country heralding the first concert show. The public and critical reaction was overwhelmingly positive.

The Hollywood Reporter enthused, "Judy Garland sure showed 'em she could carry any old show anytime, anywhere all by herself in spades on her solo shot, didn't she?" *The Chicago Tribune* stated, "While Judy's weekly series has been cancelled after the last Sunday in March, she did a brilliant one-hour show on her most recent performance, singing everything from 'Happiness Is a Thing Called Joe' to 'America, the Beautiful.' . . . Judy's shining and electric personality was reflected on this one-woman show. She sang a flock of songs with the warmth that only she can impart. . . . She has a lot of style."

Buoyed by this success, Colleran announced that three future Garland shows would be in the same concert-format vein after the first received "such favorable reaction" that Garland and CBS executives "mutually agreed" to follow the same successful format. In addition, the last show would be a black-tie affair to be taped by Capitol Records. (This would be yet one more series disc never to materialize.)

The New York Times was most supportive: "After five months of production trial and error in which the show has been subjected to various and ill-fated formulas, CBS is going to let Miss Garland do what she does best—sing. . . . Miss Garland did her solo performance of the season, singing songs with which she has been identified for years. Seemingly a simple format, the show still contained certain production techniques used to instill excitement for the audience. In the center of a huge stage was this little girl, everybody's Judy, singing her heart out for her public . . . the solo performance probably got better response than any other show Miss Garland has done this season. The next day, many people who had known mostly disappointment in watching the Garland show were commenting about the delightful change. No wonder that CBS is going to put that same little girl back on that great big stage alone three Sunday evenings [in March]. It could be that the Garland show will register its highest rating of the season. . . . Maybe even the Cartwrights will be watching."

The reaction to the "new" Garland on television was so positive that *Variety* announced that ABC was actively negotiating for a series of ten specials to be taped next season around the world. Bill Colleran, who was to be executive producer, created the concept that he would showcase Garland in the greatest concert halls of the world, including Tojo Stadium in Tokyo, the Forum in Rome, the Tivoli in Copenhagen, the Comedie Française in Paris, the Palladium in London, a venue in Russia, and, in the United States, Carnegie Hall and the Palace. The plan triggered international interest, with one British syndication company interested in cofinancing the series of specials with CMA.

"The audience picked up, and people started talking about the show again," remembers Colleran. "People in Hollywood, the industry, started talking about it. The audience began to build." But in the eyes of CBS, it was too late. "The ratings, to them, were not going up fast enough." The personal and professional satisfaction that Judy received after months of turmoil, criticism, and failure was inestimable. Mark Herron even recalls Judy once remarking to him that "the time I spent with Bill Colleran doing the concert shows was the best time of my career."

When the concert programs began to air, Bill would go to Judy's house and watch the shows with her; no one else was invited. "We used to sit on the floor at Rockingham. Some of my favorite memories are holding her and hugging her as we watched the concert shows together. She was so happy and so proud of those last programs. She would just be beaming, and laugh and carry on." (Bill remembers an unexpected moment one evening while they watched the show. "We were sitting on the floor, and I was hugging her as we looked at the television. She was laughing a lot about something, and she suddenly reached around and put her hand on my *dick*! I said, 'Judy, that's not for me. I can't. I'm married.' She stood up, walked across the room, turned around, put her hand on her hip, and said, 'You know, nobody wants to fuck a *legend*!' " And a few minutes later, we were screaming with laughter about it, and it was forgotten as quickly as it happened.")

In all their moments together, Bill holds one memory most dear to him: "I can never forget the times when she would come running offstage after having done a spectacular Garland performance. She'd come offstage to the wings and run into my arms. I'd hold her tight, and she'd look at me with those great big eyes and say, 'Was I okay?' to get my approval. Every time she did that, I damned near died right on the spot."

19

The acclaim lavished upon the concert shows caused Judy's self-confidence, as well as her sense of authority, to blossom. Not coincidentally, her relationships with Gary Smith and Mel Tormé became increasingly acrimonious. Unwilling to continue her clash of wills and battle of egos with either of them, Garland took action.

Smith was the first to go. His relationship with Judy had been fragile for some time, but his lack of support for the all-music format shattered it. Sealing his fate was her desperate quest to conserve cash; the revamped format did not require his services.

Gary Smith had a number of detractors, but some supporters who credited him—more than anyone else—with creating the sophisticated, expensive, high-gloss look of *The Judy Garland Show*. (Norman Jewison was among the most vocal, stating, "I honestly believe the show wouldn't have continued without his efforts.")

Smith's determination to cast Garland opposite such ill-suited guests as Buddy Hackett and Jackie Mason was clearly misguided, but his willingness to follow the CBS blueprint for success reflected not his desire to sabotage the series, but rather to give it a chance for survival. Garland, however, focused much of her resentment upon Smith. The success of the concert shows—which he disdained—only heightened her fury. Bill Colleran recalls, "Judy said, 'Get rid of him—*now!*' I had to call David and Freddie and tell them that she wanted him out. He left right away. When we started the concerts, there was nothing for him to do."

For his part, Smith offers, "Mel and I used to give each other pep talks, because we were the two that really did work our buns off and care about her and not necessarily about all the other nonsense that was going on. Mel was shocked when she finally fired me after twenty-two shows. I was twenty-seven years old. I made some mistakes, but I worked diligently to keep her on track." Smith concedes that he and Garland often were at odds about his choice of guests, noting, "She had never heard of the Smothers Brothers or Jackie Mason. There were some artists that were booked that she didn't know."

Gary recounts his last days on the show: "I was sitting in my office packing up. And I was really sad. I didn't want to leave, I didn't want to be fired. It was my first job as producer. Everybody knew it wasn't justified. Judy used to run around saying, 'Gary's the only one who tells me the truth around here.' And that ran out, too. She fired me because she didn't want to hear the truth anymore.

"The show was in the hands of her entourage," he says of the final days of the series. "She wanted people around who only treated her gently and eased her through this difficult process. She tried to save as much money as she possibly could at the end, and therefore she didn't need me. I think it started when I had to be the one to tell her that she couldn't do the concerts."

The triangle of bad blood among Gary Smith, Judy Garland, and Bill Colleran continued long after Smith's final week as a Kingsrow employee. *The Hollywood Reporter* bannered his termination on page 1 of its February 17 edition, the news somehow suppressed until three weeks after the fact. The paper stated that the firing was confirmed by Colleran, who was quoted as stating that Smith "had not been involved in the past five segments of the series."

The news item turned the private squabble into a bitter public dispute. When Bill advised his public-relations firm of Smith's termination, he mentioned that Gary had not been actively involved in several recent episodes. Although he assumed his remark was off the record, his publicist inadvertently included it in a prepared statement. Colleran's claim infuriated Smith, who promptly took action against him. "Gary brought me up on Directors' Guild charges," Bill reveals, "which was my union. I was a DGA member as well as a producer." Although the DGA did not discipline Colleran, he nevertheless was forced to "recant and say it wasn't true, that he offered a lot on the last several shows. Everybody that I cared about knew the truth anyway," he laughs, "so it didn't matter to me at all."

Smith sued Garland in Manhattan Superior Court in 1965 for twelve thousand dollars, citing breach of contract; Kingsrow countersued for fifty thousand dollars, charging that he "did not supply proper services." Judy summed up their professional differences by telling Justice I. L. Levy, "I didn't agree with his choice of material." Levy threw Smith's case out of court. Despite her victory, Judy cracked afterward, "They should call me 'Sweet Sued' because I'm always being sued," adding ruefully, "I've been in more courtrooms than I've been on the stage."

Mel Tormé was fired three weeks after Smith. Garland could no longer tolerate Tormé's ego, which adversely affected others on the show as well. Also, her determination to save Tormé's three-thousand-dollar weekly salary made him expendable. Rehearsal pianist and dance arranger Jack Elliott states, "It took [Tormé] two years, it seemed, to put a medley together, and it would always be the same old thing. He had a guy on staff being paid six hundred or seven hundred dollars a week just to transcribe for him, waiting for him to make up his mind and decide what songs to use. We were all trying to figure out what the hell Mel was doing. As an arranger, Mel was late all the time, and we couldn't move until Mel did something. He made an enormous amount of money and really did very little work. He laid out a bunch of tired old medleys that were done for a hundred years, and she sang them well and so did the people she worked with, but there was nothing unusual or fresh about those things."

Jack says also that Tormé "had a tendency to buy a lot of things and charge them to the show. He had this one pencil sharpener which must have cost thirty or forty dollars, and he used to brag about it. He kept saying to Peppiatt and Aylesworth, 'Mine's bigger than yours,' so they *stole* it and hid it in a desk somewhere. He came back from lunch, and it was really the Caine Mutiny."

Elliott claims that Tormé, who was on the brink of divorce, spent a good deal of work time in pursuit of a young dancer on the show, "an adorable kid, just came out from New York, she might have been eighteen or nineteen. And Mel landed on her and just made a career out of trying to trap that girl. Mel was never around. He would come in, try to nail the blonde, leave, and come back. He was bailed out week after week by the arrangers."

"Mama ignored it so as not to embarrass him," states Liza Minnelli, "but she was very funny about it. She used to say we'd have to buy him new soles for his shoes, or *crepe* soles."

Elliott stresses, "Judy knew what was going on. She knew *everything*. Judy was very smart, clever, very bright. She knew who did what and who didn't do what." Adds Bill Colleran, "A lot of people didn't know that about her, but she knew it all. She knew what the smallest person was doing, and whether they were doing it well. It was her money. It was coming out of her pocket."

After the two-week hiatus, another semiconcert episode (with guest Jack Jones) was to be shot on February 14. As Judy had done so often before, she escaped to Manhattan. During her stay, she frequented Jilly's, one of her favorite nightspots. It was there she met piano player Bobby Cole, a chance encounter that hastened Mel Tormé's departure from *The Judy Garland Show*.

"Judy was with Peter Lawford," Cole recalls, "and she and I hit it off right away. She was just charming, sitting at the piano bar. She had on a black boa and hat to match. I started kidding her. I made her laugh—she loved that, when you weren't agog. She enjoyed it when I was rough with her, in a joking way." Jack Jones was also in Manhattan and was present for one memorable evening. "There was an impromptu party with Judy, Bobby, Sinatra, and Tony Bennett. We were all hanging out at Jilly's. It was a wonderful moment where everybody was just singing."

When she returned to Los Angeles, Judy brought Bobby Cole with her. He enjoyed being her lover (leaving a wife in New York to pursue Garland), but claims he was completely unaware that Judy viewed him as Tormé's successor. For Judy, simply firing Mel was not enough; she delighted in puncturing his ego even further by replacing him with an obscure piano-bar player. As Liza assesses, "She'd never embarrass anybody—unless they embarrassed her, and then she could hold her own. She really knew how to say, Don't push me like that, don't do that to me, it's not fair."

Early in the week of rehearsals for show twenty-two, the production staff buzzed with gossip that Judy planned to install Cole in some undefined musical capacity. Mel bristled, subsequently advising Colleran that he would no longer be Garland's off-camera musical prompter. Predictably, this annoyed Judy further.

For her duet with Jack Jones, Judy asked Tormé to create a medley of Nelson Eddy–Jeanette MacDonald songs. During a band call, Judy faltered over a passage and asked Mel's assistance. Irritated that the medley had been substantially rewritten (likely by Bobby Cole), Tormé entered into a heated exchange with Garland. Mel stormed out, and Judy commanded Colleran to fire him. Bill phoned Mel in his office and told him to leave the premises.

"Bobby Cole is what did it with Mel," says Colleran. "He thought he was being replaced. His ego was so huge, he couldn't handle it. She got testy about Bobby Cole, and so did he. She only said once, 'Where's Mel?,' and he wasn't around, and she said, 'He's O-U-T.' I do like Mel. But he stopped helping her. No matter what he thought of her, that was not professional. Do your job or get out."

Bobby offers, "Judy started bad-mouthing Mel from the get-go. I listened, but I had nothing to contribute. I still have the greatest respect for Mel. Mel must have thought I was sniffing around for his job, but I wasn't. There were a lot of problems, but the problem wasn't Judy. She was not a malicious, vindictive person.

"Judy got me an apartment," he continues, "but I spent most of my time at Judy's house. She came home one night and said she had just fired Mel. I said, I can't take Mel's job. I told Colleran I couldn't do that. I sure didn't come out here to take Mel's job; he was doing just fine. I don't know whether she did it to justify paying me a thousand dollars a week."

Judy turned to George Schlatter for advice before making her final decision about Cole. "I told her it was okay for her to fuck him," he laughs, "but *not* to put him on her show."

But Judy remained undeterred in her plan and took the vendetta one step further when she booked Cole—and his trio, flown in from New York—for his first network television appearance, knowing that Tormé was rankled at not securing all the guest shots he had been promised. "I wanted to write, that was my big love. I did not want to perform on the show," states Cole. Despite his objections, he signed to appear on show twenty-five. The booking scotched Judy's earlier hope that Mary Martin might agree to guest on her second-to-last episode—reminiscent of Mary's historic television encounter with Ethel Merman years before. The Cole booking also canceled plans for André Previn, who had been announced as the original guest for show twenty-five. (Nor would there be an Easter show with her children or a concert show with guest Sammy Davis, Jr., as Judy had wished.)

According to Jack Jones, "Mel was having lots of problems with her, and although she did believe that I was good, I think he felt that Judy was rubbing me in his nose. But she was so sweet to me. Judy was there when I opened at the Cocoanut Grove the first time. She was the greatest audience, totally unselfish when it came to supporting other performers. There were no problems in our working together."

Although she had tumultuous relationships with Tormé and Smith, Mort Lindsey and Garland had only a single argument over the years. "Judy called me up and said, 'Where's my tape recorder?' I said, 'Jesus Christ, I'm writing the arrangements! That's not my job, it's Gary Smith's.' She said, 'Well, you're the musical director, why don't I have a tape recorder?', and she hung up on me. So I called my agent and said, 'I'm leaving.' I didn't talk to her for two days. Judy came up to me and said, 'I hear you're going to quit. I didn't mean anything by it. I'm sorry. I was upset.' And we hugged and kissed, and of course I didn't quit. That's the only time we had a scrape." As for the others, Lindsey remarks, "That little girl could chew you up and spit you out in two minutes. She was very bright and no fool. You had to do your job."

Mort had assumed the lion's share of the musical chores each week. "I never had a lot of time," says Lindsey. "I used to do at least fifty percent of the writing myself for the whole show. I'd even write for the guest, if there was any. Judy usually made suggestions on her own songs. If it was a number with Judy and somebody else, it was Mel's job to put it together. Sometimes he did it, and sometimes he didn't." Mort also supported the concert format. "Musically, it was better than some of the other shows. We weren't distracted with all that other stuff. Some of the numbers were great, but some she did with guests were klutzy. She could dance, they couldn't, she could sing, they couldn't, she could *act*, they couldn't."

Judy did not, however, offer Cole the position vacated by Tormé until asking Mort if he harbored any objections. "I told her no," Lindsey states. "They were an item at the time. He didn't step on my shoes."

The week of show twenty-two was not completely without humor. Just as she was about to face the cameras, Judy turned to Mort and asked, "What do you think of this gown?" As Mort laughingly recalls, "It was this striped black-and-white zebra thing. I said, 'Jesus, you look like the upholstery at the *El Morocco*!' She said, 'You *son of a bitch*! What do you mean?' I said, 'Listen, you want to ask me about a G-seven cord, fine, but don't ask me about your *dresses*! I'm not here to do that, I'm here to take care of your music.' She respected me for that and didn't ask me again. She told that story around, laughing about it."

Nevertheless, the taping got off to a rocky start. Garland was seized by panic as the taping was to begin and she barricaded herself in her trailer. "There was all this chaos going on," recalls Jack. "All these people were in her dressing room, begging her to go on. Somebody had the great idea of starting the overture. She heard that music and threw everybody across the *room* and ran out and went on."

Whether or not the stunt had any real effect, Garland is arguably at her very best among all seven concert programs. *Sans* overture, Judy immediately took the stage with "Swanee" (an odd but riveting choice for an opening number) and was in total command; her voice had a purity and richness that equaled her best moments on the Schlatter episodes.

Judy was quite touched when the technical crew surprised her during the taping with a Valentine's Day gift of a large box of candy. She passed it around to her crew and thanked everyone profusely. She was no doubt bolstered by this display of affection from her coworkers after her well-known battles with Smith and Tormé.

Show twenty-two featured several numbers sung by Garland on previous episodes—including "Almost Like Being in Love"/

"This Can't Be Love," "Just in Time," "A Foggy Day," "If Love Were All," and "When the Sun Comes Out"—but her performances here, without exception, outshone those earlier versions. The familiarity of the songs was offset by the freshness Garland gave each number. As Mort Lindsey explained, "She sort of sang the songs the same but never really did them the same. She always approached them as if they were new." Her other solos were equally good. "Just You, Just Me" (bumped twice before) was given a brisk, spirited workout, Garland backed by a combo. The "Judy at the Palace" routine remains a priceless link to her famed 1951 and 1956 Palace appearances, neither of which was preserved visually.

Colleran also prevailed upon Garland to sing Arlen and Harbury's haunting "Last Night When We Were Young." (Judy once said of it, "I think lyrically and melodically it is one of the great love songs of all time.") Her beautifully shaded performance was framed perfectly by Whitmore's poetic camera work—shooting her in silhouette for most of the number—and Davis's dramatic lighting which was far removed from the flat "television look" that Judy disdained and more reminiscent of her appearance in a lush MGM motion picture.

The taping was peppered with several unexpected happenings. "Just in Time" was fashioned with a new—and challenging—ending. Judy's delivery was a bit off from the start, and at the end she transposed the words to the new "tag," yelling above the band in frustration, "Stop it!" as they continued to play. The mistake was likely deliberate, a ploy Garland often used to allow herself to repeat the number when she instinctively felt she could do better; invariably, the second take would be letter-perfect. Technical mishaps required both Jack's solo numbers ("Love with the Proper Stranger" and "Wives and Lovers") and Judy's introduction at the top of the segment to be retaped twice. (At one point, the microphone made an annoying noise, and someone in the control booth yelled, "Feedback!" Judy shot back, "*Feedback*? Wherever it is, let's go there!")

Ken Murray's last appearance was shot on January 31. Originally intended as part of the Diahann Carroll–Mel Tormé hour, it was inserted into this show instead.

The Garland-Jones medley of MacDonald-Eddy songs was well-crafted and delivered with tongue-in-cheek good humor. The

The unaired version of the "Jeanette MacDonald–Nelson Eddy" medley with Jack Jones
COURTESY RICHARD CONNOLLY

rundown included Roger Edens's special verse of "San Francisco" (Judy and Jack); "Will You Remember (Sweetheart)?" (Judy and Jack); "Rosalie" (Jack); "I'll See You Again" (Judy and Jack); "Lover, Come Back to Me" (Judy); and a duet of "The Donkey Serenade," the novelty tune associated with Jack's father, Allan Jones. The most delightful moment of the routine was unrehearsed. Judy's "Lover, Come Back to Me" began with proper poignancy and longing. Then, instead of warbling "this aching heart of mine . . ." she sang, "this *eeking* heart of mine . . ." Judy did a double take in Jack's direction, saying, "*Eeeking* heart?— aching heart!" She could sing only two more words before chuckling at her own gaffe. Judy recovered, and built to such a climax that Jack sat upright in his seat, turned to face Judy, and gazed upon her with rapt admiration; she, in turn, reacted with delight during his solo moments.

The "Trunk" closing, originally to have been two numbers,

was ultimately whittled down to "When the Sun Comes Out." Vocally, Judy far outshone her performance on the Rooney show; her earlier attempt, though, is perhaps more interesting with an against-the-grain interpretation. Her first version had more impact in that Garland was unencumbered by the trunk and a hand-held microphone.

Judy Garland gave among her greatest performances at the close of the series—when many expected her to, at worst, self-destruct or, at best, stumble through the final handful of shows—but it is equally true that the concert format was not without its limitations. The contrast of the two performances of "When the Sun Comes Out" illustrates some of the strengths and deficiencies inherent in the all-music approach.

The concert shows were completely devoid of Garland solos mounted as lavish production numbers. Also, Judy sang virtually every number with a hand-held microphone. This perhaps reflected her desire to control the audio problems plaguing the show from the beginning. The mike also served as a device giving her business to do with her hands—such as whipping the cord about or caressing the mike during a tender ballad—but it instilled a sense of sameness that an occasional number done instead with an overhead boom would have eliminated.

Another drawback in the all-music episodes is the bare minimum of dialogue, some of Garland's concert segments devoid of a single spoken word. Judy's live performances were noted as much for her engaging patter as her singing. The concert programs would have been better balanced had Judy ad-libbed or told a story or two. Garland's jumping from song to song without a respite is a bit overpowering.

Episode twenty-three was set to tape on Friday, February 21. The show was to be a one-woman concert of "Music from the Movies." Garland was in excellent form, although she did not quite meet the level of uniform brilliance of the previous program. One contributing factor might have been that Judy was burdened with rehearsing for two programs simultaneously. The latest two-week layoff put production behind schedule, and episode twenty-four (with Vic Damone) was slotted to be shot on February 23, only two days after the "Music from the Movies" concert was taped.

Judy was a bit hesitant at the top of the hour, slightly botching the lyrics to the new (for her) "Once in a Lifetime"; she recovered sufficiently to tackle her old-faithful "I Feel a Song Comin' On" with confidence. "If I Had a Talking Picture of You" was pleasantly forgettable, "Toot, Toot, Tootsie" great fun, Garland playfully growling the words when she became tongue-tied. "Love of My Life" (shot in silhouette) displayed Garland giving first-rate treatment to a second-rate Cole Porter song. She then instantly metamorphosed from sultry siren to innocent schoolgirl for a charming "Boy Next Door"—even though she came in too fast at one point and decided to upgrade "I live at 5135 Kensington Avenue" to "6135 . . . and he lives at 6133," indicating that if Garland did make a lyrical mistake, at least she remained consistent. She erred also during "Steppin' Out with My Baby," transposing the lyric—and thus, losing the rhyme—singing, "Can't be *good*, I feel so *bad*, never felt quite so sunny and I keep on knocking *wood*." Otherwise, the number, along with "Alexander's Ragtime Band" and "You're Nearer," both featured in the same segment, were fine.

"I'm Always Chasing Rainbows" was properly wistful and well-sung, but "I'm Nobody's Baby" was hampered by a peculiar, strident arrangement with which Judy seemed to be at odds from the start—she was, more often than not, a beat behind the music, nearly flattening a few notes here and there, stumbling over "but he only said . . . good . . . good-*bye* . . . and kept on walking down the avenue." Judy tore into "The Man That Got Away" in her traditional, straight-ahead delivery, never again to approach it from the more subtle, unorthodox manner of the Schlatter "Trunk" version on show four. This version, however, was powerfully sung and excitingly presented.

The final "Be a Clown" segment, as it aired, had Judy silently making up for the number in her "Camelot dressing room" as circus music played. Garland's ad-libbing was, unfortunately, cut: "I'm going to make a change of costume . . . I've always done rather spectacularly *glamorous* things in the movies . . . I always played clowns or tramps or old *newsboys*! . . . I feel like I'm in a steam bath—but we can't change in front of the audience!" Judy's first attempt at "Be a Clown" was aborted when she transposed some of the lyrics at the beginning. Getting hopelessly tangled in the words, she continued with the melody, singing, "Well, I don't know what I'm saying!" and good-naturedly boomed, "Let's start it again!" The second take was successful.

Mort Lindsey at the piano for "You're Nearer"
COURTESY RICHARD CONNOLLY

Judy ended the program with a soaring "Once in a Lifetime." She pulled out all the stops—sitting on the edge of the stage, kicking off her oversized clown shoes, pulling the clown hat away in the middle to muss her hair, standing as she reached the crescendo. This moment, perhaps more than any other in the series, came the closest to replicating the magic of a live Garland performance.

The show's highlight, however, was "Dirty Hands, Dirty Face." The song stirred up such emotion in Judy that she insisted upon writing a recitative without assistance from her writers or her producer. Bill Colleran notes, "It was absolutely her. I was there when she did it at the house for the first time. It was all Judy."

"Dirty Hands, Dirty Face" was sublime. Judy's great sincerity transformed an old-fashioned, cloyingly sentimental, and banal chestnut into a profoundly moving experience. Her "What Is a Boy?" recitative has lost none of its impact in the passing years:

"Now, I suppose I could recite a poem about my son, or maybe

Judy kisses Joey while taking bows after her "Once in a Lifetime" finale.

show you a photograph, or tell you about some of his little ways. But that wouldn't be telling you what he means to *me*. I've seen acclaim that's changed into disapproval, and success melt into failure, and the applause of *thousands* of hands *diminish* to the sound of just one shutter hitting one window in a very lonely house in the nighttime. But through all of this, *his* applause, and *his* acclaim, and his love for me haven't changed. My deeds, right or wrong, remain *unquestioned*. And my perspective, and my strength, are soothed by, and kept together by, one freshly washed hand on my face, and the clean, sunny smell of his outrageous pajamas. And the most eloquent phrase in the world— 'Good night, Mama. I love you.' So I love *him*. I love him, because he feels, and knows, that he can fill the space that I feel keeps me away from the world sometimes. I love him because he makes me aware of the fact that I'm truly *alive*, and not just drifting somewhere. I love him. And I need him. But you know something? I love him because he needs me, too."

Immediately after the show aired, New Orleans–based television critic Bob Sublette praised: "It would appear that ever since CBS announced *The Judy Garland Show* was going off the air, the shows have steadily improved. Miss Garland's last two hours were particularly impressive. She is making more and more viewers wish that CBS would reconsider its decision. Perhaps the knowledge that the show is doomed took some of the pressure off Miss Garland. Maybe she is going all out to make CBS regret its early announcement the show would not return . . . [Judy] needed awhile to adjust to the medium on a weekly basis. This she has apparently now done but it is too late."

Show twenty-four was another semiconcert hour, Garland alone for most of the program. Vic Damone's spot included "Who Are You Now?" and "I'm Gonna Miss You." For their duet, Bobby Cole crafted an intricate medley of songs from *Kismet*. He dismisses his first effort for Garland as "overwritten" and "much too complicated for the show," yet the medley stands as one of the most ambitious and difficult Garland attempted on the series.

"Vic came over to Judy's house. I said, 'Hi, Vic, here's your part!' recalls Cole, who adds that Damone was so nonplussed at the difficulty of the material that "he disappeared for three days and got together with his piano player." Judy at first resisted tackling such substantial material. "I had no intention of throwing together a little ditty. She knew that I, unlike her other playmates, would fight with her and tell her to fuck off. We had really wild fights. Lots of walking home in the middle of the night, stuff like that. But she respected musicianship." As he expected, Judy soon warmed to the challenge and rehearsed in earnest.

The *Kismet* medley, which included "Night of My Nights" (Vic), "He's in Love" (Judy and Vic), and "This Is My Beloved" (Judy and Vic), was indeed electrifying, exceedingly well sung by both Garland and Damone. Getting through the routine, however, required three takes. In the middle of the first attempt, Judy hit a wrong note, and yelled over the orchestra, "Hold it, hold it, hold the phone!" She then cracked, "Mother *blew* it!" The second take went well, until Judy faltered on one of the

Judy and Vic Damone rehearse the "Kismet" medley.
CBS INC.

climactic notes, causing her to shriek in frustration. Vic gamely went on—there was only one note left to sing—causing the audience to laugh and then break into applause as Judy reacted. Refusing to merely retape the final moments, Garland insisted upon reshooting the whole medley. The decision was a good one, with both Judy and Vic noticeably improving vocally with each take, as their confidence in the material increased. This was the last medley of *The Judy Garland Show,* and it was a shining finale indeed.

Almost every concert episode displayed Garland warmed up by the middle or end of her first number, but on this program she did not hit her stride until the fourth song. "Lucky Day" was adequate, but "Sweet Danger" and "Do I Love You?" lacked her full concentration. (Judy improvised the lyric several times for "Sweet Danger" and, during the latter number, the microphone fed back for a second, causing Judy to mock-grimace and pull away from it briefly before continuing.) Only a few seconds after finishing a somewhat wobbly "Do I Love You?," she launched into "I Love You," a challenging song (new to her) that completely energized both her voice and performance. Judy tackled the difficult arrangement with authority and built to a stunning climax.

She had sung "When Your Lover Has Gone" at the "Trunk" on the Bolger-Powell hour accompanied only by a guitar, but Bobby Cole wrote an excellent, fully-orchestrated arrangement for this show. (This version included the verse, while the other did not.) The number was staged rather oddly, Garland seated in the forefront of a row of highbacked chairs, which looked to be either spirited from the Television City cafeteria or the Rockingham dining room. Despite the peculiar setting, Garland's performance was outstanding, far better than her earlier attempt. Next was a slightly fumbled "Down with Love," with the mistakes ("bee-yoo-hoo-manity" instead of "boo-hoo-manity" for one) making Garland's offhand delivery all the more enjoyable.

Judy was in complete command by the middle of her set. "Old Devil Moon" and "Never Will I Marry" were excitingly performed and well-sung. It was Judy who brought the Frank Loesser tune (originally sung by Anthony Perkins in the ill-fated musical *Greenwillow*) to Mort Lindsey in 1961. He recalls, "I had never heard of it. Nobody had ever done that song outside of the show, and it was a big challenge. I didn't know what to do with the number, and I wasn't too keen on it, but she got me to like it. I did a loud arrangement, played the second melody against what she was singing, and she loved it. I think I blasted Judy right out of her *seat* when she heard it for the first time."

This "Never Will I Marry" bettered her previous (prerecorded) version on show thirteen, the excitement of Lindsey's driving arrangement heightened by Judy's wielding the microphone cord and strutting about the stage. Her expression of concentration—and a touch of apprehension—visibly dissolving into sheer delight while sustaining the final, difficult note are fascinating to observe.

"Any Place I Hang My Hat Is Home" and "Chicago" were first-rate, the latter far surpassing her performance on show six. At the onset of the concert shows, Garland demanded that her fans be admitted to the tapings and seated in the front rows; this time, after singing "and you will never guess where," she leaned toward the audience and asked, *"Where?"* and the reply

Judy puts a bull's-eye
through the final note of
"Never Will I Marry."
CBS INC.

was a booming "*Chicago!*" She mugged, gestured, assumed the patented Garland stance, and whipped the mike cord around, and shot a clean hole right through the final note.

Damone's solo numbers were more relaxed, but smoothly and ably delivered, Vic charmingly acknowledging Judy off-camera and blowing her a kiss before singing.

At the "Trunk," Judy introduced "Lost in the Stars" by saying, "Some of the most beautiful poetry ever written in America can be found in the lyrics of our popular songs. One of the most outstanding examples can be found in a song called 'Lost in the Stars.' Maxwell Anderson's lyric attempts to explain the universe and its creation to a small child in the simplest of terms, and I think you'll find his words to be as inspired and touching as I always have." (Bill Colleran had taken the Kurt Weill song to Judy only two days earlier!) Judy attempted the song twice; the broadcast version featured the second take of the song cut into her speech from the first version. (She ended her aborted first attempt of "Lost in the Stars" by breaking into a few bars of "He's in Love" from *Kismet!*)

Friday, March 6, was scheduled for taping Garland's next-to-last episode. The hour, essentially a one-woman concert, featured "Mister Robert Cole" and his trio in a ten-minute segment near the close. (Cole's solo numbers were to be "From This Moment On," "I Wonder What Became of Me?" [later cut], and "The Lady's in Love with You.") By popular demand, Judy elected to repeat "Old Man River" at the "Trunk"; that number had been interrupted by a news bulletin throughout the Eastern seaboard and the Midwest when the Rooney hour aired December 8.

The week was a most difficult one for Judy. Although she rehearsed thoroughly (spending hours at the piano with Bobby and Bill Colleran at the home of Orval Paine and his new wife, Marge), she was inundated by legal battles with Sid Luft.

The child-custody battle between Judy and Sid reached its zenith when the estranged couple appeared in Santa Monica Municipal Court the day before Garland was to tape show twenty-five. In order to secure custody of Lorna and Joe, Luft filed an affadavit against Judy in which he charged that she had "attempted suicide on at least twenty occasions."

The *Los Angeles Herald-Examiner* noted that "the court file of charges made by Miss Garland and Luft against each other since the battling began over the children is one of the thickest on record for such squabbling." The two were compelled by the judge to enter a "four month cooling off period" to resolve their differences. Judy (accompanied by Liza for moral support) and Sid met at the Santa Monica courthouse the following month and agreed that she would have the children six days a week; Sid was granted custody on Saturdays and alternate Wednesdays.

Judy, of course, bore the brunt of the bad press. Luft's allegation that Garland had attempted suicide on "no less than twenty occasions" was splashed across newspapers from coast-to-coast. The very day the sordid story hit the papers, Judy had to report to Television City to begin rehearsals. "She was very upset by reports of the suicide attempts," recalls Bob Wynn. "She said, 'I just *can't* go out there, I'm too embarrassed.' I said, 'Judy, you've *got* to go out there, I've got thirty-five musicians waiting for you.' She said, 'I can't do it, I just *can't.*' "

Then her sense of humor—and ability to laugh at herself—

came into play. "Judy thought for a moment," Wynn continues, "and said, 'Well, is there a *nurse* in the building?' I told her yes. She said, 'Get her up here, and tell her to bring *everything* she's got with her!' I went to the nurse's office and brought her down. Judy bandaged herself up and came out to the orchestra on *crutches*, with bloody bandages, and said the reports of her demise had been vastly overrated. 'I'm ready to sing!,' said Garland with great flourish, adding dramatically, 'The show *must* go on!' "

Despite this display of bravado, Judy admitted to Bill Colleran that she was so distraught that she had not slept in the last three days. While her fatigue is evident in her appearance, Garland is in good voice (though slightly husky) throughout the hour.

The show began with Lindsey's overture of "Old Man River," "Love," "By Myself," and "Get Happy." Confident from the moment she walked onstage, Judy launched into "Sail Away," followed by the equally well performed "Comes Once in a Lifetime" (sung devoid of special material, unlike her first version on the Streisand hour), "I Am Loved," and "Life Is Just a Bowl of Cherries."

One of the best moments of the hour was Judy's exquisite and poignant treatment of the ballad "Why Can't I?" ("Everybody has someone . . ."). Next was the torch number "I Gotta Right to Sing the Blues." As the piano struck up the first few notes, Judy went blank for a second and cracked, "I know that this is being taped, but how does this one start?" And then, after a beat, she added, "What's the *song*?" Ready to begin, she stopped and asked her director, "Do you want to start again, Dean, or just leave this in, like it's *live* television?" Whitmore asked her to start from the top, requiring her to be posed against the proscenium arch. "Now, you want me back here?" Judy joked, adding, "I want a cigarette and a blindfold!"

The remainder of Garland's set was taped without interruption, and all of the numbers were well-sung. Judy offered "Joey" to her son in the front row, playfully bit through "Love" (included briefly in her medley with Lena Horne, but delivered with full gusto here), and offered a definitive "Get Happy," in her original, fast-tempoed arrangement far removed from the one featured in her duet with Streisand. (Judy had asked Ray Aghayan to design a glittering, tight fitting, Marlene Dietrich–type gown

Judy in concert on show twenty-five

that would " 'out-Marlene' Marlene." His efforts were almost too successful. The outfit was indeed dazzling, but Judy could barely move in it—most evident when she vainly attempted to lift her dress and kick up her heels during "Get Happy." Bemused, she had no recourse but to jump up and down as an alternative.)

"As Long as He Needs Me" did not vocally match her earlier attempt on the Minnelli hour (she was a bit out of breath after the athletic "Get Happy"), but Garland instilled in it even more power and immediacy by performing seated on the edge of the stage—causing the audience to give her a standing ovation. (This time, though, she bowed to network demands and sang, "but still, I've got my pride" instead of "the *hell*, I've got my pride.")

Judy introduced her guest as "a fine singer, an excellent musician, and very talented composer and lyricist," and emphasized that he "is one of the most *attractive* performers I've ever seen." She added, "On last week's show, he wrote an *exciting* medley from *Kismet* for Vic Damone and myself, but probably the most *outrageous* thing is that he's never been on a network-television program before, so I think it's high time he be seen by you, and I know that you'll love it. It's my great pleasure to present Mr. Robert Cole." Appropriately framed in a nightclub setting, Bobby and his trio offered smoky, jazz-infused versions of "From This Moment On" and "The Lady's in Love with You." Garland joined them for "Poor Butterfly," the number as notable for her singing as it is for the interplay throughout between Judy and Bobby. "Old Man River" at the "Trunk" was the climax of the hour but remains a distant second to her incomparable performance on the Rooney show; it was nevertheless powerfully sung and a strong ending to an excellent program.

Although there was to be only one more episode, enthusiasm for the series remained in full force. In his syndicated "Hollywood Is My Beat" column, Sidney Skolsky wrote, "I can hear the Madison Avenue Executive Cell Block. They're saying, 'Well, alright, so Judy can do a one-woman show; maybe she can do it twice, three times, but that's it. No singer can make it alone for 13 weeks, maybe 26 weeks.' Judy did three or four of the shows and she could have done six more, twelve more, twenty-six more, thirty-nine more."

To her production staff and her network, the question was not if Garland could triumph in "thirty-nine" concert programs, but if she could endure the taping of her series swan song. The hope was to end on a glorious note of triumph, yet everyone had a sense that disaster was ahead.

20

Ominously, the final episode of *The Judy Garland Show* was scheduled to be taped on Friday, March 13. The event was guaranteed to be a melancholy, emotional one under the best of circumstances. Garland, however, was under enormous strain—fighting for custody of her children and facing lawsuits from disgruntled former staff members. On top of this, it was the end of her dream of financial security.

At the same time, Garland was determined to end her series on a note of triumph. The taping, she decided, would be a black-tie affair. Judy hired Matteo's to cater an after-show party for the staff. Capitol Records planned to release an album of the last program. Garland, Cole, and Colleran compiled such an ambitious, abundant collection of songs, it could have filled not one but two programs—perhaps allowing Capitol to release two albums, or to select the best moments for one. (In the end, the LP was never released.)

The original rundown began with a lengthy overture, Garland then opening with "After You've Gone." The second segment featured "The Nearness of You," "Love Walked In," "Time After Time," and "That Old Feeling" (all new to her repertoire), concluding with "Carolina in the Morning."

Next came a recap of opening special-material tunes from some of Garland's greatest stage triumphs. (It would be Garland's only visual recording of these songs.) Included were "Bonjour, Paris" (1960 Paris engagements); "It's So Lovely to Be Back Again in London" (the Dominion Theatre, 1957); "Call the Papers"/"On the Town" from the original 1951 Palace show; a "Take Me Back to Manhattan" medley (Palace Theatre, 1956); and "Here I Am" from her 1951 London Palladium appearance.

"The Last Dance" was next; then Garland would offer a one-woman version of "Born in a Trunk" sung in its entirety. "Suppertime" and "Almost Like Being in Love"/"This Can't Be Love" followed. A pair of Billy Barnes songs ("Something Cool" and [Have I Stayed] Too Long at the Fair?") was the second-to-last segment. To wrap up the show, Garland would dress as a clown and pantomime another Barnes composition, "Where Is the Clown?," as a chorus sang off-camera.

Still in the clown outfit, Garland's series finale would be "Here's To Us" (from the Broadway musical *Little Me*), with the star venturing into the audience to pour glasses of champagne.

"For a guy who was on the show for such a short time, I certainly caused more goddamned trouble," ruefully admits Bobby Cole. "I inadvertently picked three Billy Barnes numbers. I wanted to get her away from the usual stuff and do something different. I picked out a song called 'Something Cool.' I also loved 'I Stayed Too Long at the Fair' and 'Where Is the Clown?' She said she wanted to do it. She wanted to let me know that she was still enthusiastic about the show."

Judy not only admired Barnes's songs but his bitingly satirical revues as well, which by this time were a staple at the Coronet Theatre in Los Angeles. It was not uncommon for Judy to attend a single Barnes revue numerous times, invariably joining the cast afterward for an impromptu songfest lasting until the early hours of the morning.

("Judy had a mind like a vise, once she learned something," offers Barnes. "After one of the shows, she taught Ken Berry the 'When the Midnight Choo-Choo Leaves for Alabam' routine from *Easter Parade*. She did *all* the choreography, she remembered *everything*—her steps, *Fred's* steps. All of our mouths were hanging open. We couldn't believe it. Ken asked her, 'How do you *remember* that?' She said, '*That*? Oh, it's nothing!' "

Although Billy Barnes and Judy "had become friends" by this time, he was unaware that Cole was actively courting Garland to perform several of his songs for the last show. One night, Barnes gave her sheet music of several of his songs and, as Bobby later told him, Judy "went home and put them on the piano." A few evenings later, Bobby conspired for Judy to "accidentally" hear the tunes. "He was diddling on the piano while she was getting ready to go out, and she said, 'What song is that? It's a great song.' He played the rest of "Something Cool" and the others, and she said, 'My goodness, I think I'll do the whole bunch.' "

Soon after, Barnes was contacted by Peppiatt and Aylesworth. "They said, 'Judy's going to do some of your songs on the show. She wants to say something about you, and we were wondering if you could come over to Television City.' I thought I was going to die, I was so excited. I went down there, they read the copy, and I was so pleased."

Barnes was at first unhappy with the concept of having Garland pantomime "Where Is the Clown?" as a male chorus sang it off-camera. "I always thought pantomime always bordered on the pretentious. I like words and music. But then I thought, Wait a minute, it was an honor just to have her associated with it." For Garland, its tempo would be slowed, and the number would take on pathos, the clown clutching a flower in a single spotlight. Barnes did not object. "It was very pretty; they did it very slowly, and she just loved it."

Judy, recalls John Aylesworth, "was really up for the last show," determined to view the occasion as a triumphant ending rather than as the footnote to a dismal failure. "She said, 'I'm going out on *time*, have everybody in *black tie*, and have one *hell* of a party.' " Judy invited many of her close friends, including Tony Bennett, Peter Lawford, and Jayne Meadows.

On March 10, Mel Tormé filed a $22,500 breach of contract suit against Garland and Kingsrow Enterprises. Tormé claimed that his May 2, 1963, contract called for four guest appearances at $4,500 each, but he had only been paid for one program; he asked $13,500 for the three other appearances. Tormé demanded an additional $9,000, asking his $3,000 weekly salary for the three programs following his termination which he stated he was contractually owed by Kingsrow.

Tormé filed the lawsuit three days before Garland was to tape her series finale. Judy was already walking an emotional tightrope—with a conspicuously absent Fields and Begelman providing no visible means of support. Suddenly, her enthusiasm plummeted as her fragile optimism crumbled.

Judy was required to attend an 8:00 P.M. orchestra rehearsal the evening of Thursday, March 12. The warning signs that the taping the following night was headed for trouble were clearly evident when it came time for Garland to learn the choreography for "Where Is the Clown?"

Cole continues, "In order to get the idea to jell, we had to record the band the night before because we had to clear the stage. And we needed depth to choreograph this number. When we got together to discuss it, the choreographer was *nowhere* to be found. And all Judy wanted to do was drink. She tried to wing it, but she couldn't get it. She was afraid of attempting the number, she was afraid of facing the end of the series, afraid of everything."

This was only a hint of what was to come. By the time Garland arrived at CBS Television City the next afternoon for show twenty-six, she was completely distraught.

"Judy had gone through the songs the day before, and I was worried about her then," Bill Colleran recalls, "but when she came in on Friday, the minute I saw her, I said to Dean, 'We're in *big* trouble today. Don't push her, be very, *very* gentle with her.' " He sadly adds, "She was already falling apart."

Midafternoon Friday, a nucleus of Garland fans gathered outside Television City, hoping to get into the 9:30 P.M. taping. After an hour or so of waiting, the group was pleasantly surprised when told by CBS that Judy wanted the fans to attend the dress rehearsal, even though originally it was to have been a closed session. They formed a line outside Studio 43 and waited to be admitted. After three hours, a CBS representative ventured out to announce, "So sorry, Miss Garland is *not* ready to start the dress rehearsal yet. We also just discovered it will definitely *not* be an *open* dress rehearsal."

Garland surprised Billy Barnes with a 4:30 P.M. phone call requesting him to come immediately to CBS. Judy was unsure of "Where Is the Clown?" and wanted his suggestions, as well as additional moral support. When he arrived at Television City, "Judy dragged me into her dressing room to show me how she was going to mime the number. She was so cute, because she had her distinct way of how she was going to do it." In that initial, impromptu run-through, he somewhat warmed to the mime approach. "She did sort of a soft-shoe, which I thought was beautiful."

But Judy's morale had completely disintegrated. Overwhelmed by a combination of dread, fear, despair, and mounting panic, she was unable to face an audience—however supportive—and refused to tape the number with any outsiders present. A taped run-through was attempted. To Barnes, the routine, as it was staged, was meandering and unfocused. The songwriter cites the absence of a choreographer to pull the routine together into a sharply defined, fully realized whole. "They had taken the time and the money, but without a choreographer, it just wasn't that effective and somehow seemed oddly out of character for her."

Two complete takes of "Where Is the Clown?" were attempted, the first shortly after eight o'clock. Judy's frustration and irritability mounted as the routine seemed to fall apart. She did a second complete take and had to reshoot the ending when it was determined that the last several bars were unsatisfactory. Judy left the stage; the fate of "Where Is the Clown?" remained uncertain. At the same time, Garland's guests waited outside the doors of Studio 43.

At approximately 8:30 P.M., the invited audience was ushered in. The doors closed about thirty minutes later. Rumors circulated as the scheduled 9:30 P.M. start time passed without explanation or any sign of Judy. Backstage, Colleran and Garland decided to first shoot the "Here's To Us" finale while she was still attired in the clown outfit.

Mort Lindsey struck up "Over the Rainbow" as Judy appeared. She was greeted with a thunderous ovation, and launched immediately into "Here's To Us." Though she changed a word here and there, no other song could have more perfectly expressed her strength, determination, and devotion to those she loved and to those who loved her in return:

> Here's to us, my darling, my dear.
> Here's to us tonight.
> Not for what might happen next year,
> 'cause it might not be nearly as bright.

But here's to us, for better or worse
and for thanks to a merciful sky—
skies of blue, and muddlin' through,
and for me and you as we are!
And here's to us for nothing at all,
if there's nothing at all we can praise—
just that we're together at last
for the rest of our beautiful days!

"Yes!" Judy heartily shouted above the band in affirmation to the audience. She then left the stage to pour glasses of champagne for the audience, saying, "For *you* and for you!" The orchestra continued to play "Here's To Us," and after several minutes, Judy returned to the stage to finish the song—mustering every resource at her command to remain in control. She sang the second verse, and not a reprise of the first, as planned:

Here's to us, for all that we have
and the road that we've traveled so far—
skies of blue, and muddlin' through,
and for me and for you as we are . . . !

Judy then improvised this declaration of courage and love to the audience:

And here's to *you*
for letting me do
what I'll *do to the end* of my *days!*
Apropos of nothing at all
but for feeling like throwing bouquets . . .

She paused for an instant, her voice now shaking with emotion as she sang the final words and held the last, soaring note:

And here's to us
forever and *always!*

After being presented with a bouquet of roses, she went over to Mort, kissed him, and gave him a rose, kissed Bobby Cole, and went back out into the audience and poured more glasses

"Here's to Us"
CBS INC.

of champagne—the audience cheering and applauding throughout. (The closing credits, so it was planned, would roll as Garland took her final bows while the orchestra vamped "Here's To Us.")

Judy burst into tears and fled the stage. There was no announcement when, or if, the show would continue. Members of the audience who elected to wait were invited into another studio to watch clips of past episodes to pass the time.

Judy barricaded herself in the trailer. There, she discovered an orchid plant sent by Hunt Stromberg, Jr. Billy Barnes vividly recalls the card Stromberg attached to the orchid plant: "You were just great. Thanks a lot. You're through. Hunt Stromberg, Jr." Billy sadly recalls, "Judy was reeling from this cruelty. She said it was the worst day of her life."

Bill Colleran, Bobby Cole, Mark Herron (who accompanied

her to CBS), Mort Lindsey, and the few others genuinely close to her did everything possible to calm and comfort her. Judy was alternately livid and inconsolable and attempted to fortify herself with pills and liquor. Colleran had experienced his share of a despondent Garland over the months, "But for that final show, she went down to rock bottom."

Judy's despair quickly turned to rage after she summoned Bob Wynn and Shep Fields (Freddie's brother) to her trailer. Judy had been frantically—and unsuccessfully—attempting to locate both David Begelman and Freddie Fields. "Everyone had deserted the show," recounts Bob Wynn. "Freddie Fields, David Begelman, and the entire CMA organization were in New York for Barbra Streisand's opening of *Funny Girl* on Broadway. It was Shep Fields and myself, alone with her in the dressing room. She was angry, she was crying, she was upset, she was remorseful—every possible emotion. Judy attacked Shep, who said, 'Judy, it was a personal emergency or they would have been here.' Later, he said, 'Do you think she understood?' I said, 'She will, until I tell her that the "personal emergency" was *Barbra Streisand's opening*, that's why your entire goddamned office is there and not here.' He didn't want to hear that."

When Wynn revealed the truth behind the "personal emergency" keeping Fields and Begelman away, Judy was enraged. Ironically, it had been the revenue from Garland and her series that gave CMA the leverage to add Streisand to its client list. And Freddie Fields and David Begelman were, at that very moment, courting their new client. One can imagine the devastating impact this brutal truth had on Judy as she sat alone in her dressing room.

Meanwhile, a number of fans remained in hopes that Garland would continue the show. At 12:30 A.M., a harried Bill Colleran appeared and announced, "Due to problems too detailed, technical, and unionized to go into, Miss Garland cannot do her show with an audience." A groan erupted, and everyone was ushered out. While most of the group disbanded, about fifty people remained in hopes that Judy would again change her mind and allow the audience in.

The specter of Garland's onetime optimism for a happy and punctual ending came in the form of a Matteo's catering truck, which appeared, on schedule, at 12:30 A.M. The hired hands put out the lavish spread ordered by Judy on adjoining Stage 33. John Aylesworth recalls Colleran "running around saying, 'Keep that bar next door closed—if the musicians get in there, we're *dead!*' "

It was not until she spoke with Bill that Judy agreed to continue with the show. "She turned to me and said, 'Bill, what's next?' I said, 'We're going around the world, do concerts for TV in Greece, Rome, Paris, big concert shows.' She loved the idea, but said, 'I've got to rest.' I said, 'Of course you need a rest. Afterwards.' I was doing it to bring her up again so we could get the show finished. But I meant it. Money was my last card. I said, 'Judy, they won't pay you, and you need the money.' I wanted her to do enough only so she'd get the check from CBS. I knew she needed it badly."

Bolstered by her talk with Bill, Judy agreed to continue. She also asked for the faithful fans still waiting to be admitted back into the studio. Many of the group had gone to Kelbo's Restaurant across the street, where two CBS pages appeared at one point and ordered twelve bottles of quinine water. "We have problems," was all that was offered by way of explanation. Longtime Garland fan Rick Sommers left Kelbo's and went back to CBS. He recalls, "Judy came out of her dressing room wearing a gorgeous four-thousand-dollar floor-length gold lamé gown. I said, 'Judy, what is this I hear about you not taping the show in front of an audience?' She said, 'Come on with me.' There were enough fans around to fill one side of the runway. Later, the audience had to get up and go sit on the other side, so they could shoot from the right side."

The fans enjoyed the curious sight of the cast party occurring while the taping was under way. Production staff members were going from one studio to the other, availing themselves of the food and drink in the adjacent studio during breaks in the taping.

A perfect first take of Lindsey's overture and "After You've Gone" was deemed unusable for technical reasons, and the opening had to be reshot. For the first attempt, Judy was bolstered by the enthusiastic reception given her by the group of hard-core fans. The second take (which aired) did not share that advantage.

Judy, not surprisingly, was not in peak vocal condition although she was in reasonably good voice; it should be noted also that she does not appear under the influence of pills or liquor on the program. During the taping, Garland was never less than professional, remaining in good humor in front of the audience—and unerringly assumed the blame for mishaps, whether actually her fault or due to a technical problem. (Interestingly, Judy was in such anguish she could not face the television cameras, and, for the entire taping, played instead to the studio audience.)

The next segment began with "The Nearness of You"; Judy completed the number in one take. "Time After Time" followed. She began strongly, but thought the musical bridge was longer than it was and jumped in past her cue. Judy finished the number gamely, and instantly after hitting the last note, she cracked, "I blew the *whole* thing! I did. I forgot to come in. I'm sorry." The audience applauded her efforts, and her second take was fine.

The taping was an off-again, on-again affair, Judy discarding many songs from the rundown and substituting others. Several of the numbers seen on the final-broadcast tape were actually assembled from fragments of various takes; Judy could only get through one or two songs before rushing offstage. "She couldn't do more than ten minutes at a time," Colleran notes, "before falling apart. She wouldn't be able to remember what she was doing. Most of the audience stayed all night. I was back and forth from the dressing room to the stage, trying to help her. She'd either be in her bedroom in the trailer with her door closed, or she'd be trying to get out of there and attempt to perform, and I'd lead her down the stairs, she'd do something, and then go back to bed and lie down. I told Orval, 'Call me when she gets up again, then we'll go back and try it all again.' She was physically and mentally exhausted."

"Love Walked In" was ultimately dropped and, after several attempts, "That Old Feeling" and "Carolina in the Morning" were satisfactorily done in a single take. Attempting a complete performance of the lengthy, involved, special-material opening-numbers routine—as well as "Born in a Trunk"—seemed out of the question. (Still, it is remarkable that Garland retained and successfully performed so much new material in the course of the taping.)

The dependable, familiar "When You're Smiling" was a last-minute substitution, but it, too, required several takes. Judy faltered when she came to the spoken special-material bridge, her quick wit pulling her out of the fire. Her mugging during, "And for heaven sakes, retain a calm demeanor, when a cop walks up and hands you a subpoena," caused the audience to laugh, which in turn prompted Judy to break up. She gamely continued, "If the groom should take a powder, while you're marching down the aisle . . ." and paused, totally lost in the lyrics. She bemusedly scratched her head, ad-libbing, "Don't be upset . . . it'll be better yet . . . and, remember . . . aw, *heck* . . . all the while . . ." (The broadcast version of the show cut at this point to another take concluding the number.) Several tries at "Almost Like Being in Love"/"This Can't Be Love" followed, the take selected for the final show performed at a slightly slower tempo than usual.

For the next segment, the audience dutifully moved to the other side so that Garland could be photographed sitting on the edge of the runway for the old Ethel Waters tune "Suppertime." (The camera work skillfully avoided audience shots throughout the finished product; the audio track was sufficiently "sweetened" to add applause and laughter.) Judy was not completely confident with the song, and her delivery was slightly off-center. She attempted to work her way through it until the very end, when she suddenly stopped and remarked, "I'm sorry, I have to start again. I do, I must," joking, "I ran out of gas!" (Her next attempt was successful and was included in the final program.)

At one point, Judy took a sip from a glass at her side, and spilled some of the contents onto her gown. This caused another lengthy delay while the dress was removed, cleaned, and pressed. Between takes, Judy spotted Tony Bennett in the audience. She put her hand on her hip, looked directly at him, and cracked, "Tony, if you had any *class*, you'd come up and give me a hand!"

After some delay, Judy chose "The Last Dance" as her next number. The song featured a huge globe that hung suspended over the stage. When it revolved, it gave a "startling, glittering effect," according to one observer, who noted that Judy asked that it be made to stop turning. "Would you stop that thing? It makes me dizzy!" she said, adding, "It'd even make a *legend* dizzy, I think!" And when Mort was tuning up the orchestra, Judy yelled to him, "Let's have a few pear-shaped tones for *Mother!*" Judy's first try went well, until her voice broke during "They're hoping we'll go . . ." She stopped and said flatly, "All right, *hold* the phone! There was a *frog* in 'go'!" before clearing her throat. A second take was interrupted by the director; the third take was included in the program.

Garland once again left the stage. It was now after 4:00 A.M. The stagehands brought out a lounge table with an umbrella for "Something Cool." By 5:15 A.M., they announced that it would be "at least another hour before it would be taped," says Rick Sommers. Astoundingly, most of the fans remained in their seats, and the crew in the control booth waited. Bob Wynn says, "We knew she'd go out onstage, because she couldn't afford to lose the money."

Finally, Judy appeared and fumbled the introduction to Billy Barnes, ending with, "Shall we do this *whole* thing over again? . . . I really 'fumphed'!"

The second, and final, version:

"There's a wonderfully talented young man who's done several exciting revues, and his name is Billy Barnes. He's such a fine talent and has a captivating mind. Billy has written so many famous and fabulous songs, it's kind of difficult to choose a favorite. But there's one called 'Something Cool,' and I think that, maybe, it's just a little more marvelous than the others. And I'd like to sing that for you now, if that's okay. . . ."

Although the segment was originally to have begun with "(Have I Stayed) Too Long at the Fair?" Judy elected instead to sing "Something Cool." As Mort struck up his lush, haunting arrangement, she crossed to the lounge table and chair, sat, and began singing. She performed it well (slightly improvising a bit of the lyric to no ill effect), but got annoyed at herself when she faltered halfway into the number. She stopped and impatiently remarked, "Oh, *heck!*" She stood up suddenly, turned on her heels, and stormed off the stage. Bill Colleran took his cue and announced to the beleaguered audience that Judy was unable to continue. The endurance contest had finally come to an end. It was 5:54 A.M.

Barnes followed her as she walked offstage. She was crying at this point, shaking her head from side to side, exclaiming,

"It's too much, I'm just too tired. I can't go on." Barnes was, of course, disappointed, but it was harrowingly clear to him that she was too exhausted to continue. Sobbing, Judy said, "I can't be treated like this!" as she closed the door to her trailer. Inside, Bill Colleran tried to console Garland. "Judy was broken-hearted," he remembers. "I had the distinct feeling that, deep down, she was thinking this was the end of her life. She knew it was her last chance, her last act. She was in her death throes. It was horrible to see. She died there at CBS that last concert. It frightened her." He added, "It frightened me, too."

Several days later, Garland and Colleran viewed the unedited videotapes of the marathon session; much of the footage was unusable, but it was obvious that a good deal of the material needed to be retaped.

Then, on March 18, Judy was rushed to Cedars of Lebanon Hospital. Her physician, Dr. Lee Siegel, stated that Garland was in "good condition, but possibly suffering an attack of appendicitis."

Garland recovered sufficiently to escape to San Francisco with Bobby Cole several days later; he recalls that she was in a reflective, relaxed mood during their stay. They had a telling conversation about Judy's state of mind at the time: "Judy said to me, 'You know what I'd like to do? I wish I could open my own club, and host and greet people. And maybe sometime during the night, get up and sing a song.' Judy probably would have been very good at that. I can't really say that she liked the idea of working at this time. But she could have handled that. In the situation she was in, the pressures were enormous. But she did the best she could."

Although Judy had agreed to retape material for the last show, her hospital stay fueled rumors that the final program would be comprised of clips from previous episodes. In spite of her exhaustion and suspected appendicitis attack, Garland adamantly refused to end the series in such a manner. She told Colleran to arrange an evening taping on Thursday, March 26, only three days before the final episode was to air. Judy and Bill elected to shoot "Born in a Trunk" as the second-to-last segment. ("Where Is the Clown?," at this point, was still part of the rundown, slotted to air before "Born in a Trunk.") "Here's To Us" was dropped from the revised rundown, necessitating that Garland, the same night, shoot a new "Trunk" closing. (The number was still un-decided the day of the taping.)

Erroneous reports circulated in the trades that Garland would retape the entire program that night, but the papers did accu-rately note that the performance was not open to the public, Judy, so grateful for the support the hard-core group of fans had given her that tortuous night two weeks before, sent out word they would be allowed into the taping.

Despite her good intentions, and although the evening was shorter in duration, it was no less agonizing than the March 13 attempt. At 5:20 P.M., Judy walked through the doors of CBS Television City, although she was not expected until her 6:00 P.M. call. A run-through with the orchestra was scheduled from 8:00 to 9:00 P.M., with the actual taping to begin at 9:30 P.M. and wrap one hour later. Garland was outfitted in the same gown she had worn for the March 13 marathon session. Ken Young, attending the March 26 taping, noted "Judy looked very chic, but also very pallid. Later on, I heard that Judy was still feeling ill when she arrived at the studio and that she was still sick. I believe she was trying her heart out for us so we could have a memorable last TV show."

When the group was admitted into Studio 43, Garland's stand-in, Judy Johnson Lindsey, was running through "Born in a Trunk" for lighting and camera setups; until then, most of the fans had no idea Garland was going to attempt a complete version of the fifteen-minute routine. When Lindsey finished, Mort started playing "The Stripper," and Garland, remembers Young, came "bouncing out, keeping time with the beat of the song. She ban-tered with the audience and joked about her television trou-bles." Despite her energetic entrance and attempts at "being a clown" to amuse the audience, "Judy just couldn't remember some dialogue to 'Born in a Trunk' and couldn't get a sense of timing," recalled Ken Young. (She made odd gaffes throughout, such as singing, "And *Mama* shouted . . ." instead of "Papa"; saying "the tricks of *my* trade" instead of "tricks of *the* trade"; and then changing "but the hardest one of all" inexplicably into "the *strongest* one of all. . . .")

Young stated, "I got the distinct impression that Judy was enduring physical pain—she kept touching her stomach and side as if it hurt her—and that [her] fast ad-libs and joking were a cover-up for the pain she was having." Judy had remained standing at the "Trunk" during the lengthy delays caused by the stops and starts and finally asked a stagehand to bring out a chair. "Anything!" she joked, "any old chair. A *box*, I don't care!"

When she made her first flub, she exclaimed, "Oh, darn it!" but added, "Keep it in!" and the audience applauded in support. At one point, when she missed a line, she cracked, "No wonder I forgot it. Jack Warner must've cut that line from the movie!" A telling moment occurred during one taping delay. Judy turned to the audience and stated, "Now, let's be *honest* and *serious*. This series has really been *disastrous*, hasn't it?" The small group heartily replied with an emphatic *"No!"* Warmed by this show of support, Judy modified her past remark by noting it was the fans who were "good" but reiterated that she knew the series "had been a disaster." (Many of Garland's comments that night "were very funny," noted Ken Young. However, and many others agreed, they "kind of tore me up inside.")

Though she was determined at the outset to get through the routine, her concentration was visibly broken where her voice broke over a note, prompting her to talk, and stumble, over the lyric: ". . . and I can't forget the endless nights . . ." She never fully recovered from that point. Later, she instructed Mort, "Take it back to 'I learned very quickly the tricks of the trade . . .'," and quipped to the audience, "I never *did*, you know!" When another take was attempted, her temper flared for a moment, causing her to snap impatiently to herself, "Oh, come *on*, for Christ's sake!" Judy recovered in a second and cracked, "Sorry out there in Nielsen Land!" She turned to the audience and sincerely said, "I *am* sorry. Please forgive me." Garland became so upset with herself at one point that she addressed herself in third person, admonishing, "Oh, come on, Judy, now, Judy, stop that!" She then cracked, "Stop that, Judy Lindsey! It's not really *me* up here, it's my split personality. I *am* a Gemini."

Later, as the stage manager appeared with his clapperboard, Judy quipped, "What *are* you doing?" She grabbed the clapperboard eraser, positioned it as if placing a head on a guillotine, and cracked, "Put your *puff* in *there*!" The audience roared and the band sounded a drumroll. Judy promptly removed the pad from the clapperboard and erased the writing off the board, giving the hapless stage manager no recourse but to announce "Take four!" As he exited laughing, Garland countered, "Take *one!*," adding "*Maybe!*" Judy joked her way through "You Took Advantage of Me" and, after comically improvising, "You had your chance, you took advantage of my '*anse,*' " the taping came to an abrupt end.

According to observer Dick Connolly, Judy attempted to continue until she heard a disgruntled lighting man complaining above. She looked up, and the electrician groused, "Come on, Judy, hurry up. It's hot up here." At the end of her rope, Garland shot back, "Well, it's hotter down *here!*" Not letting the exchange end there, the grip shouted, "Jesus Christ, we're broiling up here." At her breaking point, Judy fumed, "I don't care if you *fry!*" and marched off the stage.

The Judy Garland Show ended that moment as she stormed into her trailer for the very last time. Suddenly, it was all over— the hopes, the dreams, the optimistic view toward the future. Judy chose to face the end of her weekly series in solitude. Bob Wynn, nearly heartbroken, appeared: "She stood there alone. It was all over for her. Judy didn't ask me to, but I walked out with her, put her in her car, and sent her home. She insisted on taking tons of stuff with her. Sheets, pillowcases, all kinds of crap from her trailer. It was very sad."

With "Born in a Trunk" unusable, Colleran and the CBS engineers worked fervishly to assemble the bits and pieces from the March 13 taping into a complete performance. Out of the footage came more than thirty minutes of acceptable material. To fill out the hour, however, Colleran inserted "By Myself" from show twenty-five, which had been deleted from the final version due to time restraints. He had no choice but to use part of Garland's concert segment, as well as the "Trunk" closing, from show twenty-two with Jack Jones.

After much handiwork, Colleran finalized the rundown for show twenty-six: Lindsey's overture was followed by Garland's "After You've Gone," "The Nearness of You," "Time After Time," "That Old Feeling," "Carolina in the Morning," "When You're Smiling" and "Almost Like Being in Love"/"This Can't Be Love." The "By Myself" insert from show twenty-five was next, followed by "The Last Dance" and "Suppertime." Show twenty-two footage of "Just in Time," "A Foggy Day," "If Love Were All," and "Just You, Just Me" comprised the next segment. Lifted from show twenty-two, "When the Sun Comes Out" was Garland's swan song at the "Trunk." With just Judy's trunk in a pool of light on an otherwise empty stage, the final credits rolled; the "Over the Rainbow" instrumental theme and applause were lifted from a previous episode.

Garland and her series were championed until the very end. The *San Francisco Chronicle*'s Terrence O'Flaherty ensured that it would end on a complete note of triumph:

> The final Judy Garland show has come crackling over the air. It was the most crisp and stylish musical series of the season. In fact, I cannot recall any in television's history where the production was so polished or where the star burned with any brighter intensity.
>
> For Garland fans—as well as viewers who seek showmanship and sophistication—the demise is a disaster.
>
> Tomorrow night her vacancy is filled by two half-hour game shows described by the CBS press department as "frivolous and fun-type" programs. I hope those who so bitterly attacked Miss Garland will be happy with the new shows as well as the critics who called her series a flop, and particularly James Aubrey of CBS who gave her a false facade and mercilessly pitted her against *Bonanza*, the greatest audience attraction on television. . . .
>
> Despite saying in her letter of resignation that she was quitting "to be able to give more attention to her children," Miss Garland was actually dropped. But she walked out of CBS a bigger star than when she came in. She mastered the uneasy relationship between star and camera. She tackled new kinds of songs with moods and emotions difficult to sustain and managed to bring them off successfully. . . . In my estimation, the creative elements backstage were superior at all times. The lighting was top quality, the dancers excellent. The art direction made the whole show sparkle.

He concluded:

> Backstage stories were as lively as a Punch and Judy show. I have little sympathy with the producer's woes.

All those associated with the program were well aware
that they were working with a highly charged superstar
whose ups and downs are as well chronicled as the decline and fall of the Roman Empire. They were well paid
for any inconvenience they may have suffered. It is a miracle the program didn't reflect the backstage confusion . . .

The show wasn't a flop; it just happened to be up
against the stiffest competition on TV. It is far easier to
fly over the rainbow than to beat a good horse opera. The
fact that Judy Garland attempted it provided some of the
high spots of the season.

Offers Bill Colleran, "Yes, it was difficult. It was an ordeal
like I've never known before or since. But it was all worthwhile
because of her. The happy moments far outnumbered the bad,
and there were long, long stretches of good times without any
problems. And usually the problems weren't caused by Judy.
When it was miserable, it was because Judy felt miserable about
how the series was going, what it meant to her life and career.

"But I remember the wonderful times. I don't think Judy had
much simple love—or at least as much as she needed to support
her, to hold her together. And she tried to grab that from everybody. She was so filled with doubts about herself that she covered them up with the pills and drinking, everything.

"It was worth it all," he affirms, "because she was so goddamned *good*. She was so absolutely brilliant. When she felt right,
there was no one else like her in the history of the world. Nobody could touch her.

"And somewhere inside, Judy *had* to know that she had what
nobody else ever had," concludes Bill Colleran. "She just had to
know that."

EPILOGUE

The Judy Garland Show ended its network run on March 29, 1964. Its star returned to the stage and immediately triumphed in Sydney, Australia—two months to the day after enduring the March 13 marathon taping for the final episode in the series. *Variety* stated, "Miss Garland won the greatest audience ovation in the history of Australian show-biz. She had the audience in the palm of her hand from the moment she stepped on the rostrum."

The two instantly forgettable game shows that replaced Garland quickly faded from view; faring no better were the pair of situation comedies that CBS placed opposite *Bonanza* in the 1964–65 season. *The Joey Bishop Show* moved from NBC to CBS after three years to battle NBC's western, only to be so trounced by *Bonanza* that it was moved mid-season to Tuesday nights; it nevertheless was canceled at the end of the season. The other half-hour occupying Garland's old time slot, *My Living Doll* (with Robert Cummings in a role originally designed for Jerry Van Dyke), was a single-season casualty and quietly vanished without a trace.

Judy Garland's health and, not coincidentally, her career, sharply declined in the five years following the demise of her series, exacerbated by an increasingly harrowing financial state. (The Rockingham house, for example, went into foreclosure in

1967.) "I loved the idea of not working," Judy quipped that same year, "but then I found out I couldn't afford it."

Hospital stays, illnesses, a sometimes elusive voice, a marriage to Mark Herron in November 1965 (dissolving only six months later), and then a fifth and final attempt at matrimony with discotheque manager Mickey Deans three months before her death were among the incidents that marked Judy's increasingly difficult final years.

The widely publicized disasters that occurred in the twilight of Garland's life often, still, overshadow her triumphs. Among the latter: a surprise appearance at *Night of 100 Stars* in July 1964; two sold-out concerts with Liza that November at the London Palladium; a 1965 Forest Hills, New York, concert; a four-week, record-breaking Palace Theatre appearance (with Lorna and Joe) in the summer of 1967; and many successful concerts from 1965–68. Her last United States concert came before an audience of twenty thousand at the John F. Kennedy Stadium in Philadelphia in July 1968. Backed by Count Basie and his band, Garland was in fine voice and spirits and was a great success.

From 1965 to 1969, Garland was a frequent television guest and the quality of her work reflected her highly variable physical and vocal condition—ranging from near-excellent to poor. Yet, even the handful of her outstanding performances did not equal the quality of her work on the series. Judy appeared on variety programs headlined by Andy Williams, Sammy Davis, Jr., and Perry Como. She was also seen on *On Broadway Tonight, The Ed Sullivan Show,* twice (as hostess) on ABC's *Hollywood Palace* series, and on ABC's telecast of the 1965 Academy Awards, singing a medley of Cole Porter songs arranged by Roger Edens.

In her last years, Judy also became a frequent talk-show guest and appeared on programs hosted by Jack Paar, Johnny Carson, Mike Douglas, Gypsy Rose Lee, Merv Griffin, and Dick Cavett. (In December 1968, Garland joked about her up-and-down career when she remarked to Cavett, "I can't go to the *powder room* in a restaurant without making a *comeback* when I come out!")

But as Randall Henderson astutely observed in his 1983 *Emmy* magazine critique of Garland's television career, "Often these appearances found her with no voice to speak of; yet the essentials of her phrasing, of communication with her audience, and the sense that she meant every word still came across. But the

years of physical, emotional, and psychological turmoil showed—
the great inner mainspring that had sustained her was failing.
. . . Viewers might still find Judy looking reasonably well, in
fairly good voice, or in high spirits, but it was harder and harder
to find all three at the same time."

Her 1967 comeback at the Palace Theatre was so phenomenal
that it was reported that Garland was in the running for another
weekly series, but nothing materialized. That same year, it was
also rumored that Judy and Liza had attempted to purchase the
television rights for an adaptation of *Gypsy* with Garland as "Mama
Rose," Liza as Gypsy Rose Lee, and Lorna and Joe also in the
cast. Warner Bros., however, had recently sold the television rights
to the film version of *Gypsy* and would not grant permission for
a concurrent small-screen adaptation.

After making the rounds of the Carson, Cavett, and Griffin
talk shows at the close of 1968, Garland began a five-week cab-
aret engagement at the Talk of the Town in London. In January
1969, she replaced at the last minute an ailing Lena Horne on
the British *Sunday Night at the Palladium* live television series.
Looking wonderful, full of joy and excitement—and in reasonably good voice—Judy captivated the audience. It was to be her
final television appearance.

Garland's last "live" performances came during a Scandina-
vian concert tour (with Johnny Ray) in March 1969. A documentary of the tour revealed an obviously frail Judy but one filled
with humor and optimism; and although she would be dead in
only three months, her voice had somehow maintained strength,
control, and range.

Throughout her controversial last years—and even on the final tour—Judy continued to be rhapsodized by audiences and
critics alike, her magic almost always fully on tap and her performances incomparable. While she admittedly was without voice
on occasion, it is equally true that Judy Garland was *never* without talent.

Upon her passing, Vincent Canby in *The New York Times* remarked of her live performances of the final couple of years, "It
didn't really make much difference when finally [her] resources
were comparatively meager. She used them with such skill and
with such humorous (sometimes mocking) self-awareness that
she could conquer anything and anybody." Of her 1967 Palace

triumph, Canby noted, "There was displayed the kind of magic that has very little to do with the fun of being fooled. The voice was gone [but] the performance was full of energy, transformed and shaped by her intelligence into a momentary triumph of style."

Judy died in her London home of an accidental overdose of sleeping pills on June 22, 1969. Her passing made front-page headlines around the world. More than twenty thousand people came to pay her their last respects at Campbell's Funeral Home on Madison Avenue in New York; Judy's *A Star Is Born* co-star James Mason delivered the eulogy at her funeral where "The Battle Hymn of the Republic" was sung and "Here's to Us" was played.

The Judy Garland Show proved to be the last sustained, concentrated endeavor of her career. As Christopher Finch noted in *Rainbow*, it is the only preserved body of work we have of Garland as a mature artist unencumbered by a motion-picture characterization or plot. And perhaps most important, the series captured Garland's last moments near her zenith, in fine voice and in complete control of her resources.

Initial attempts to syndicate the series in 1966 were truncated by legal problems; it was not until the 1970 publication of Mel Tormé's *The Other Side of the Rainbow* that Garland's series once again became the focus of attention, controversy, and debate. Norman Jewison offers: "I was upset by the book. I felt the book came out too soon, and I felt it was exploitative in nature. It certainly didn't do justice to Judy and to the other people who were part of that scene, because Tormé was looking at it from his own ego and his own perspective." Succinctly adds George Schlatter, "As an historian, Mel Tormé is a great singer."

Glenn Ford vilified Tormé's account of Garland and their relationship and called it "despicable—Mel obviously didn't have the nerve to write those things when she was alive. I was going with her at the time, and I know that the things he wrote were just not true."

Liza Minnelli and Lorna Luft have remained vocal in their objections to Tormé's account. "When somebody who was as famous and revered as she was dies, it's interesting to see who is the first one to take advantage," Liza notes. "I felt that it was vaguely self-promoting. And it's a pity, because I know my mother believed in his talent, and I'm sure would have agreed with me that he didn't need to use anybody else. He tried to make himself so special that he just came off as typical." She laughs, "Mama used to call him 'Mel *Torment*.' "

Adds Lorna, "He never wrote a book while he was on the television show. He never wrote a book while she was with us. He waited, and [then in a later 1988 autobiography] got the date of when she passed away wrong. I just find it repulsive."

The mid-1970s experienced a great burst of interest in Judy Garland and her film and television work. Jack Haley, Jr.'s 1974 compilation of great moments from MGM musicals, *That's Entertainment!*—with Garland prominently featured—was such a hit that it inspired two sequels. A plethora of Garland biographies emerged. Among them were Gerold Frank's *Judy* and, the most noteworthy, Christopher Finch's *Rainbow*.

After lengthy legal battles, Sid Luft was awarded full ownership of the Garland series and specials in 1979. An entrepreneur named Barnett Glassman purported to own the rights to the programs and sold six episodes of the series for broadcast over seven Metromedia-owned television stations. Luft states that he "put Metromedia on notice not to air the programs," due to questions of ownership which, according to Luft, "they ignored because they thought I had nothing to do with the shows." Unaware of the alleged deception, "Metromedia went along with Glassman." (Glassman, states Luft, was unable to copyright the Garland programs in his name, which are now fully held by Sid Luft and his production company.)

Sid Luft has released various Garland shows (complete programs and compilations) to the home-video, cable, and syndicated television markets domestically and internationally over the years. His efforts to both preserve the programs and make them available to the general public have served to heighten interest in Garland's television work with each passing year. *Video Review* deemed a 1983 Luft video compilation "85 minutes of a certain kind of euphoria, the chanteuse at her best. . . . Her incomparable voice, her sincerity and her personal sense of music's drama all come through. This is Judy in her prime." *The New York Times*'s Stephen Holden praised another Luft home video release that "reveals an impressively high level of professionalism from one who was supposedly teetering on the abyss."

Further fueling appreciation and fascination with Garland are the home-video releases of all but a few of her feature films— from 1938's *Love Finds Andy Hardy* to *A Star Is Born* to *I Could Go On Singing*. The 1989 fiftieth-anniversary release of *The Wizard of Oz* remained in the top five on *Billboard*'s best-selling-videocassette chart—and sold more than three million units—in its seven-month issue. A concurrently released book, subtitled *The Official 50th Anniversary Pictorial History*, has met with equal success; John Fricke's definitive study of the film (and all things Oz) entered into its third printing after only three months in release.

Capitol Records, which had Garland under contract from 1955 to 1965, released only one album culled from the series, *Just for Openers*. In 1989, several tracks from that 1964 issue were included in *Judy Garland Live!* (The album, however, primarily featured the *Judy Takes Broadway* live 1962 session, which had never before been released; the five cuts selected from *Just for Openers* were considered "bonus tracks" for that compact disc/cassette.) *Judy Garland Live!*, and the concurrently released reissues of three 1950s Garland albums in the compact-disc format, have all been best sellers; the 1962 Broadway album, in particular, has been a great success and has doubled Capitol Records' initial sales projection.

In 1990, Sid Luft announced plans to release various audio compilations from Judy's series and earlier specials, but it remains uncertain whether or not they will be a co-venture with Capitol Records. That same year, Luft produced a spectacular color-enhanced version of the 1962 "comeback" special with Frank Sinatra and Dean Martin. The program has received glowing notices following broadcasts on the BBC and Danish television and a videocassette release of *Once in a Lifetime: Judy, Frank and Dean in Concert* has met with equally positive reviews in the United States and abroad.

"Eventually, Judy's series and specials will be shown again on television and made available in home video domestically and internationally," Sid Luft stated in 1990. "Not all of them, but most of them. Some of the material will be packaged in two-hour 'Best of Judy Garland' collections. Some of the material might possibly be color-enhanced as well."

Episodes of the series have been screened at universities and colleges throughout the country. A 1986 Museum of Broadcasting seminar on Garland (produced by the author), held at the Los Angeles County Museum of Art, was a sellout success. The "Music from the Movies" concert episode and the Silvers-Goulet special were screened, with Mort Lindsey, Bill Colleran, and Sid Luft appearing in person. The audience so enthusiastically applauded after each number that Sid remarked backstage in the din of such cheers, "She still does it to them, doesn't she?," which caused a beaming Mort to nod his head and reply, "She does it every time."

An interesting phenomenon had occurred by this time. An entire new generation had discovered Judy Garland through the television series and not from her earlier MGM films. Those classic movies, always appreciated, had also always been available; the television programs were a veritable new gold mine of Garland. As a result, a formidable number of new admirers increasingly had come to view the series as their indelible frame of reference for the singer; ironically, many of them had come to embrace the latter-day Judy although they were too young to have seen her in concert. (And the so-called television failure that was *The Judy Garland Show* continues to entertain and enthrall, while the long-running small-screen series headlined by Danny Kaye, Dinah Shore, and Garry Moore hold scant, if any, latter-day interest or fascination; none of these programs has even found its way into the home-video market.)

This swelling respect and interest in *The Judy Garland Show* reached new heights in 1985 upon the broadcast of PBS's documentary *Judy Garland: The Concert Years*. While reviews of the actual *Great Performances* production were, largely positive, Judy's actual performances were universally acclaimed. One critic commented, "Garland is as good—if not better—than we remember her, with a delicious sense of humor." Another reviewer, Philip Purser, noted, "She never gave anything less than 105 percent of herself. . . . The program enlarged a myth."

Terrence O'Flaherty of the *San Francisco Chronicle* called upon his 1964 review of Judy's last episode to proclaim: "I cannot remember any series in television history where the production was as polished or the star burned with brighter intensity."

The Gannett newspaper syndicate summed up Judy's incomparable, still-potent magic by concluding, "This special shows that Garland was one of the greatest singers ever to take the stage."

Liza Minnelli offers a fundamental clue to explain why *The Judy Garland Show* has not only endured in the passing of time but has won such great critical and popular acclaim: "People will *always* be affected by her delivery and by her art. The shows were very sophisticated but they were also very simple. There is something wonderful in *every* show. And it had a pace that was a bit different than any other show. My mother, her whole life, was truly *hilarious*. I think they showed a side of her humor that was the closest somebody who didn't know her would ever get to knowing her.

"She could put herself down *better* and with more *wit*—I mean *really* witty, not just funny—than anybody else. And she was a brilliant raconteur, the charm and imagery that she used. Mama could make you see things, smell things, visualize things. She could put you right where she wanted to when she told you a story—and take you with her. The television shows were closer than anything else to what she really was. Mama wasn't playing a role—she was playing herself. She was *being* herself. And you could see her go in and out of characters when she'd sing," affirms Liza.

"The series makes me miss her so much. And yet there's that other feeling, which is grand, of, my God, I'm lucky that I have something like this of my mother. It makes me so homesick," Liza concludes, "and yet I'm so glad that it's there."

APPENDIX

THE JUDY GARLAND SHOW—
EPISODE RUNDOWNS

THE JUDY GARLAND SHOW #1   Taped: 6/24/63

Guests: Mickey Rooney, Jerry Van Dyke   Aired: 12/8/63

Overture: "Rock-a-Bye Your Baby (With a Dixie Melody)"/"By Myself"/
"I Can't Give You Anything but Love (Baby)"/"You Made Me Love
You"/reprise: "Rock-a-Bye"/"Swanee"—Mort Lindsey and Orchestra
* "Keep Your Sunny Side Up"—Judy
** **"I Feel a Song Comin' On"**—Judy
"All I Need Is the Girl"—Mickey (brief dialogue with Judy follows)
* "I Believe in You"—Judy and Jerry
**Medley: "When I'm Not Near the Girl I Love"/"Girls"/"Thank Heaven
for Little Girls"**—Mickey (with girl dancers and youngsters)
"When the Sun Comes Out"—Judy
* "Unseen Audience" sketch/"Exactly Like You"—Judy, Mickey, and
Jerry/"Stuffed Bear" comedy sketch
"You're So Right for Me"—Dancers, then Judy and Mickey sing and
dance, then look at old MGM stills while reminiscing. Mickey pan-
tomimes golf-tournament sketch with Judy as commentator. Reprise:
"You're So Right for Me"
*** **"MGM" Mickey-Judy sketch/medley:**
(a tongue-in-cheek spoof of the let's-put-on-a-show musicals)
"Where or When"—Judy and Mickey/"How About You?"—Judy and
Mickey/"But Not for Me"—Judy sings; Mickey plays drums/"Fasci-
nating Rhythm"—Judy and Mickey/"God's Country"—Judy and
Mickey/"Could You Use Me?"—Mickey/"Our Love Affair" and re-
prise: "How About You?"—Judy and Mickey
"Born in a Trunk": **"Too Late Now"**
"Island in the West Indies" ****

**** "Two Ladies in the Shade of the Banana Tree"
"Who Cares?"
"Old Man River"
"Maybe I'll Come Back"—Judy
(joined after song by Mickey, Jerry, Dancers, and Dancing Youngster)

*deleted
**insert taped 10/11/63
***insert taped 11/29/63
****dropped from final rundown; "West Indies" was performed on show #11.

THE JUDY GARLAND SHOW #2   Taped: 7/7/63

Guests: Count Basie, Mel Tormé, Judy Henske,   Aired: 11/10/63
Jerry Van Dyke

Medley: "I Hear Music"/"The Sweetest Sounds"/"Strike Up the Band"—Judy and Count Basie and His Band
"Fascinating Rhythm"—Mel
"Memories of You"—Judy (Basie accompanies her on the organ)
"Shiny Stockings"—Dancers
"God Bless the Child"—Judy Henske
"Peter, Paul and Irving" comedy sketch—Henske, Mel, and Jerry
    "Walk Right In"/"Low-Down Alligator"/"Lemon Trees"/reprise: "Walk Right In"
"Count Basie" medley—Judy, Mel, Count Basie and His Band:
    "One O'Clock Jump"—Basie and Band/"I Can't Stop Loving You"—Basie and Band/"I've Got My Love to Keep Me Warm"—Judy/"Don't Dream of Anybody but Me"—Mel/"April in Paris"—All
"One-Note Samba"—Jerry, Count Basie and His Band
"Soul Bossa Nova"—Judy and Dancers (no vocal)
"Born in a Trunk": **"A Cottage for Sale"**
    "Hey, Look Me Over"
    *"As Long as He Needs Me"
    "Maybe I'll Come Back"
*dropped from the final rundown
(A Garland solo of "Witchcraft" was possibly taped but deleted from the final broadcast version.)
(Garland and Van Dyke also taped a "Share with a Child" commercial, a General Mills charitable endeavor to provide Christmas gifts to underprivileged children; it aired during this program.)

THE JUDY GARLAND SHOW #3   Taped: 7/16/63

Guests: Liza Minnelli, Soupy Sales,   Aired: 11/17/63
The Brothers Castro, Jerry Van Dyke

"**Liza**"—Judy (tag of number includes a few bars of "My Heart Stood Still"; Liza appears at conclusion of song)
"**Come Rain or Come Shine**"—Judy
"**Together (Wherever We Go)**"—Judy and Liza
"**Put On a Happy Face**"—Liza and Boy Dancers (Judy does brief comment off-camera)
"**I'm Calm**"—Jerry and Soupy (Judy appears at tag)
Garland-Minnelli medley:
    "We Could Make Such Beautiful Music Together"/"The Best Is Yet to Come"/"Bye, Bye Baby" (brief dance interlude with both)/"Bob White (Whatcha Gonna Swing Tonight)"
"**You Are for Loving**"—Liza
"**Judy's Number-One Fan**" comedy sketch—Judy and Soupy
*Jerry/Liza talk into Jerry's lip-synching of *Lone Ranger* radio-program comedy routine
"**Malaguena**"—The Brothers Castro
"**You Make Me Feel So Young**"—The Brothers Castro and Girl Dancers
"Born in a Trunk": "**As Long as He Needs Me**"—Judy
    "**Let Me Entertain You**"—Liza (tag with Judy; in tramp costumes)
    "**Two Lost Souls**"—Judy and Liza (in tramp costumes)
    "**Maybe I'll Come Back**"—Judy and Liza (in tramp costumes)

*deleted

THE JUDY GARLAND SHOW #4   Taped: 7/23/63

Guests: Lena Horne, Terry-Thomas, Jerry Van Dyke   Aired: 10/13/63

"**Day In, Day Out**"—Judy and Lena
Terry-Thomas comedy monologue
"**I Want to Be Happy**"—Lena
"**Where Is Love?**"—Lena
"**He Loves Me**"—Lena
"**Tea for Two**": Terry-Thomas/"**A Foggy Day (in London Town)**"—Judy
*"**Brush Up Your Shakespeare**"—Terry-Thomas and Jerry
"**Judy Sings Lena Sings Judy**" medley—Judy and Lena:
    "Honeysuckle Rose"—Judy/"Meet Me in St. Louis"—Lena/" 'Deed I

Do"—Judy/"Zing! Went the Strings of My Heart"—Lena/"It's All Right With Me"—Judy/"The Trolley Song"—Judy and Lena/"Love"—Judy and Lena

"Mad Dogs and Englishmen"—Judy, Lena, Terry-Thomas, and Dancers

"Born in a Trunk": **"Losing the Academy Award" story/"The Man That Got Away"**

"Maybe I'll Come Back"

*deleted

THE JUDY GARLAND SHOW #5 Taped: 7/30/63

Guests: Tony Bennett, Dick Shawn, Jerry Van Dyke Aired: 12/15/63

*"Yes, Indeed!"—Judy, Tony, Dick, and Dancers

"Honestly Sincere"—Dick and Jerry (talk with Judy prior to number was deleted)

"True Blue Lou"—Tony

"Keep Smiling at Trouble"—Tony

Garland-Bennett medley:

"Night Train"—Boy Dancers/"Lullaby of Broadway"—Tony/"Carolina in the Morning"—Judy/"Kansas City"—Tony/"When the Midnight Choo-Choo Leaves for Alabam' "—Judy/"Big D"—Judy and Tony **/"I Left My Heart in San Francisco"—Tony (reprised with Judy)

***"Tea for Two": Steve Allen

****"That's All"**—Judy

****"One for My Baby"** (comedy version)—Judy, Jerry, Dancers, and Chorus

"My Buddy"—Judy and Dick

*****Dick Shawn comedy routine (with Judy and Terry)

"Born in a Trunk": **the Greek Theatre "moth story"/"Stormy Weather"******

"Maybe I'll Come Back"

*"If Love Were All" was originally taped as the opening number, but deleted; dropped as opening numbers were "Sail Away" and "Comes Once in a Lifetime."
**dropped by show time
***Roddy McDowall was the announced "Tea" celebrity guest; when he dropped out, Schlatter surprised Garland on-camera with Steve Allen. This segment was deleted due to Allen's later guest appearance.
****taped 10/11/63 for show #10 but inserted in this program instead
*****Shawn was to have sung "When the World Was Young" and also performed a

different comedy routine than aired, with Judy appearing throughout—even being the foil of his knife-throwing act.
******replaced "Alone Together," which was dropped from the final rundown.

THE JUDY GARLAND SHOW #5-A
(Scripted/Not Taped)   Script completed: 8/2/63

Guests: Nat "King" Cole, Jack Carter,   Scheduled tape date: 8/7/63
   Jerry Van Dyke, Gene Kelly

"Sing, You Sinners"—Judy (joined by Nat, Jack, and Dancers)
Jack Carter comedy monologue
"In the Still of the Night"—Judy
Medley: "Hi Lilli, Hi-Lo"—/"There's a Lull in My Life"/"The Song Is Ended"/reprise: "Hi Lilli, Hi-Lo"—Nat
"Tea for Two": Gene Kelly
Garland-Cole medley:
   "Straighten Up"—Nat/"Sweet Lorraine"—Nat/"It's Only a Paper Moon"—Judy (alone, then joined by Nat)/"The Christmas Song"—Nat/"Nature Boy"—Judy and Nat/"Mona Lisa"—Nat/"Too Young"—Judy and Nat/"Put 'Em in a Box"—Judy and Nat/"Orange-Colored Sky"—Judy and Nat
"The Company Way"—Jack and Jerry
"Born in a Trunk": "How About Me?"
   Reprise: "Sing, You Sinners" (joined by Nat and Jack)

THE JUDY GARLAND SHOW #6   Taped: 9/13/63

Guests: Steve Lawrence, June Allyson,   Aired: 10/27/63
   Jerry Van Dyke

"Life Is Just a Bowl of Cherries"—Judy and Boy Dancers (Jerry, June, and Steve appear)
"Happiness Is a Thing Called Joe"—Judy
*"I've Got You Under My Skin"—Steve
"Time After Time"—Steve
"Be My Guest"—Judy and Steve
"The Doodlin' Song"—June and Dancers
"Tea for Two"/"The Doodlin' Song"—Judy and June
"Tea for Two": June Allyson/**"Just Imagine"**—Judy and June
"I'm in the Mood for Love" (comedy version)—Judy, June, and Steve

"MGM" medley—Judy, June, Steve:
  "Buckle Down, Winsocki"—Dancers/"(I'm in Love with You) Honey"—
  June/"Cleopatterer"—Judy and June/"Thou Swell"—Steve/"Look for
  the Silver Lining"—Judy/"Till the Clouds Roll By"—Steve/tag: "Till
  the Clouds Roll By" and "Look for the Silver Lining"—All
"Born in a Trunk": **"Naughty Marietta" story/"San Francisco"**
  "Maybe I'll Come Back"

*"Just in Time" was the original choice but was dropped by show time.
("Tea for Two" with George Jessel was taped during this show for insertion into show
#1 but ultimately placed in show # 12.)

THE JUDY GARLAND SHOW #7   Taped: 9/20/63

Guests: Donald O'Connor, Jerry Van Dyke   Aired: 9/29/63

"Call Me Irresponsible"—Judy and Chorus
"Keep Your Sunny Side Up"—Judy, joined by Donald and Jerry
  (revised arrangement from show #1)
"Sing, You Sinners"—Donald, Dancers, Chorus
"Be My Guest"—Judy and Donald
  "Songs We're Famous For" medley:
  "Inka Dinka Doo"—Donald/"If You Knew Susie"—Judy/"My
  Mammy"—Judy and Donald/"Indian Love Call"—Judy and Donald/
  "Rose Marie"—Donald/"Will You Remember (Sweetheart)?"—Judy/
  "Stout-Hearted Men"—Donald/"Italian Street Song"—Judy/reprise:
  "Indian Love Call"—Donald/"Be My Guest"—Judy and Donald
"Fly Me to the Moon"—Judy
"The World Is Your Balloon"—Judy, Donald, Jerry, Dancers, and
  Chorus
*"Tea for Two": Donald O'Connor/"H-A-R-R-I-G-A-N"—Donald
"Vaudeville" medley—Judy and Donald:
  "In Those Good Old Days of Vaudeville"—Donald/"Nagasaki"—
  Donald/"Yacka Hula Hickey Dula"—Judy and Donald/"You Can Al-
  ways Find a Little Sunshine at the Y.M.C.A."—Donald/"At the Mov-
  ing-Picture Ball"—Judy and Donald/"The Old Soft Shoe"—Judy and
  Donald
"Born in a Trunk": **"Stagehand Caught in Curtain" story/"Chicago"**
  "Maybe I'll Come Back"

*taped but never broadcast: "Tea for Two"—Judy and Henry Fonda

THE JUDY GARLAND SHOW #8   Taped: 9/27/63

Guests: George Maharis, Jack Carter, The Dillards,   Aired: 10/20/63
Leo Durocher, Jerry Van Dyke

"Alexander's Ragtime Band"—Judy
"Be My Guest"—Judy, George, and Jack
"I Wish You Love"—Judy
"A Funny Thing Happened . . ." Jack Carter comedy routine (with
Dancers)
"Good-Bye"—George
"Side By Side"—Judy and George
"Tea for Two": Leo Durocher/"Take Me Out to the Ball Game"—Judy
and Leo
"Buckin' Mule"—The Dillards
"Country" medley—Judy, George, Jack, Jerry, Dancers, and Chorus:
"Y'all Come"—Judy and The Dillards/"Crawfishin' "—Jack and Jerry/
"Somebody Touched Me"—Judy (with The Dillards)/"Way Back
Home"—George/"Nobody's Business"—Jack/"Way, Way in the Middle
of the Air"—Entire Company/reprise: "Y'All Come (Y'All Go)"—En-
tire Company and Dancers
"Born in a Trunk": **"Feather Boa" story/"Swanee"**
"Maybe I'll Come Back"

THE JUDY GARLAND SHOW #9   Taped: 10/4/63

Guests: Barbra Streisand, The Smothers Brothers,   Aired: 10/6/63
Ethel Merman, Jerry Van Dyke

"Comes Once in a Lifetime"—Judy and Dancers
"Be My Guest"—Judy, Barbra, Jerry, and The Smothers Brothers
*"Just in Time"—Judy
The Smothers Brothers comedy-music routine:
"I Talk to the Trees"/"Dance, Boatman, Dance"
"Bewitched, Bothered and Bewildered"—Barbra
"Down with Love"—Barbra
Medley: **"Get Happy"/"Happy Days Are Here Again"**—Judy and Bar-
bra
"Tea for Two": Judy and Barbra (with "surprise" guest Ethel Mer-
man):
"There's No Business Like Show Business"—Judy, Ethel, Barbra
"Happy Harvest"—Judy and Dancers (Barbra appears at the end and
joins in last line of song)

"Hooray for Love" medley—Judy and Barbra:
   "After You've Gone"—Judy/"By Myself"—Barbra/" 'S Wonderful"—
   Judy/"How About You?"—Judy and Barbra/"Lover, Come Back to
   Me"—Barbra/"You and the Night and the Music"—Judy/"It All De-
   pends on You"—Judy and Barbra
"Born in a Trunk": Medley: **"You Made Me Love You"/"For Me and**
   My Gal"/"The Trolley Song"
   "Maybe I'll Come Back"

*replaced "The Days of Wine and Roses"

THE JUDY GARLAND SHOW #10   **Taped: 10/11/63**

Guests: Ray Bolger, Jane Powell, Jerry Van Dyke   **Aired: 3/1/64**

(*"I Feel a Song Comin' On"—Judy)
"A Lot of Livin' to Do"—Judy
"Be My Guest"—Judy, Ray, and Jane (an edited version aired)
"That's All"—Judy
"One for My Baby" (comedy version)—Judy, Jerry, and Dancers
***"Hello, Bluebird"**—Judy
***"If Love Were All"**—Judy
***"Zing! Went the Strings of My Heart"**—Judy
Ray Bolger song-and-dance routine:
   "Margie"/"Sweet Lorraine"/"Cecilia"/"The Lady in Red"/"Maria"/
   "When I'm Not Near the Girl I Love"/"Katie"
"Dear Friend"—Jane and Dancers
"Romantic Duets" medley—Judy, Jane, and Jerry:
   "Romantic Duets"—Judy and Jane/"I Remember It Well"—Judy and
   Jerry (lip-synching Maurice Chevalier)/"Make Believe"—Jane and Jerry
   (lip-synching Howard Keel)/"Will You Remember (Sweetheart)?"—
   Judy and Jerry (lip-synching Jane and Vic Damone)/"Finale"—Judy,
   Jane, and Jerry
"Tea for Two": Ray Bolger
   "If I Only Had a Brain"/"We're Off to See the Wizard"—Judy and
   Ray
"The Jitterbug"—Judy, Jane, Ray, and Dancers
"Born in a Trunk": **"When Your Lover Has Gone"**
   "Some People"
   "Maybe I'll Come Back"

*insert taped as the new opening for the Rooney show broadcast 12/8/63 (was originally to be shot in the course of the taping of show #9)
**deleted and inserted in final broadcast version of reedited show #5
***taped 12/19/63 as new opening for show #14; also included in air tape of this program. (This was Jerry Van Dyke's last episode.)

THE JUDY GARLAND SHOW #11   Taped: 10/18/63

Guests: Steve Allen, Mel Tormé, Jayne Meadows   Aired: 1/5/64

"This Could Be the Start of Something Big"—Judy, Singers, and Dancers
"Be My Guest"—Judy, Steve Allen, and Mel Tormé
  Comedy takeoff on school fight songs:
  "Cheer for Old Hyde Park"
  "We're from Old Metro (Are You from Dixie?)"
"Here's that Rainy Day"—Judy and Dancers
"One-Man Show" Steve Allen comedy routine
"Sophie" medley—Judy and Steve:
  "I Love You Today"—Judy and Steve/"When I'm in Love"—Judy and Steve/"I'll Show Them All"—Judy
"Comin' Home, Baby"—Mel Tormé
"The Party's Over"—Judy and Mel
"Tea for Two": Jayne Meadows
"Songwriter" sketch/medley—Judy, Steve, and Mel:
  "Ain't Misbehavin' "—Judy/"Makin' Whoopee"—Mel/"The Glory of Love"—Steve/"Way Back Home"—Judy/"Wrap Your Troubles in Dreams"—Mel/"You Took Advantage of Me"—Steve/"Mean to Me"—Judy/"The Girl Friend"—Steve and Mel/"Tip Toe Through the Tulips"—Judy/"Truckin' "—Mel/"Gypsy in My Soul"—Steve/"Nice Work If You Can Get It"—Steve and Mel/"The Glory of Love"—Steve and Mel/"My Heart Stood Still"—Judy/"Let's Do It"—All
"Born in a Trunk": **"Island in the West Indies"**
  "Through the Years"
  "Maybe I'll Come Back"

THE JUDY GARLAND SHOW #12   Taped: 11/1/63

Guests: Vic Damone, Zina Bethune   Aired: 11/3/63

"From This Moment On"—Judy
"Be My Guest"—Judy, Vic, and Zina (edited version aired)

"**Moon River**"—Judy
"**Crazy Rhythm**"—Zina and Boy Dancers
"**Getting to Know You**"—Judy and Zina
Medley: "**On the Street Where You Live**"/"**Let's Take an Old-Fashioned Walk**"—Vic and Girl Dancers
"**Porgy and Bess**" medley:
"Where Is My Bess?"—Vic/"Summertime"—Judy/"It Ain't Necessarily So"—Judy/"Summertime"—Vic/"I Got Plenty o' Nuttin' "—Judy/"There's a Boat That's Leavin' Soon for New York"—Vic/"Bess, You Is My Woman Now"—Judy and Vic
*"**Tea for Two**": George Jessel
"**All-Purpose Holiday**" medley—Judy, Vic, Zina, Dancers, and Chorus:
"Auld Lang Syne"—Judy/"Deck the Halls"—Judy, Vic, Zina/"Easter Parade"—Judy, Vic, Zina/"Dear Old Donegal"—Judy, Vic, Zina/"Brother, Can You Spare a Dime?"—Judy/"Yankee Doodle Boy" and "You're a Grand Old Flag"—Judy, Vic, Zina/"Thank Heaven for Little Girls"—Vic/"Happy Birthday to You"—Judy, Vic, Zina/"Me and My Shadow"—Judy/"M-O-T-H-E-R"—Judy, Vic, Zina/"Seasons Greetings"—Judy, Vic, Zina
**"Born in a Trunk": "What'll I Do?"
**"Puttin' On the Ritz"
"**Smile**"
"**Rock-a-Bye Your Baby (With a Dixie Melody)**"
"**Maybe I'll Come Back**"

* taped on 9/13/63 with show #6
** dropped from final rundown

THE JUDY GARLAND SHOW #13   Taped: 11/8/63

Guests: Peggy Lee, Jack Carter, Carl Reiner   Aired: 12/1/63

"**It's a Good Day**"—Judy and Boy Dancers
"**Never Will I Marry**"—Judy
"**Kids**"—Jack Carter and Dancers (production number leading into Carter's **comedy monologue**)
"**When the World Was Young**"—Peggy
Judy Garland–Peggy Lee duet:
"I Love Bein' Here with You"—Judy and Peggy (incorporates bits of "It's a Good Day"—Judy/"Over the Rainbow"—Peggy/"Under the Bamboo Tree"—Judy and Peggy/"Witch Doctor"—Judy and Peggy)
"**Broadway**" medley—Judy and Jack:
"My Defenses Are Down"—Jack/"They Say It's Wonderful"—Judy/

"This Nearly Was Mine"—Jack/"I'm Gonna Wash That Man Right Out of My Hair"—Judy/"I've Grown Accustomed to Her Face"—Jack/ "A Hymn to Him"—Jack/"Wouldn't It Be Loverly?"—Judy/"Too Close for Comfort"—Judy and Jack/"Mr. Wonderful"—Judy and Jack

*"Tea for Two": Carl Reiner

"I Like Men" medley—Judy and Peggy:
"I Like Men"—Judy and Peggy/"You Make Me Feel So Young"— Judy/"Tess's Torch Song"—Judy and Peggy/"Fever"—Peggy/"It's So Nice to Have a Man Around the House"—Judy and Peggy/"I'm Just Wild About Harry"—Peggy/"Charlie, My Boy"—Judy/"Oh, Johnny"— Peggy/"Big Bad Bill (Is Sweet William Now)"—Judy and Peggy/"Bill Bailey"—Judy and Peggy

"Born in a Trunk": **"How About Me?"**

"When You're Smiling"

"Maybe I'll Come Back"

*taped 11/1/63 during show #12

THE JUDY GARLAND SHOW #14   Taped: 11/30/63

Guests: Bobby Darin, Bob Newhart   Aired: 12/29/63

*"Football" medley—Judy and "The Mighty Mites":
"Buckle Down, Winsocki"/"You Gotta Be a Football Hero"—"The Mighty Mites"/"Jamboree Jones"—Judy and "The Mighty Mites"

"Sing, Sing, Sing"—Chorus

"Hello, Bluebird"—Judy

"If Love Were All"—Judy

"Zing! Went the Strings of My Heart"—Judy

Reprise: "Sing, Sing, Sing"—Judy, Bobby, and Bob

"The Twelve Days of Christmas" (comedy version)/monologue—Bob Newhart

"Michael, Row the Boat Ashore"—Bobby

"Canaan"—Bobby

Garland-Newhart comedy sketch

"More"—Judy

Garland-Darin "Train" medley:
"Sentimental Journey"—Judy and Bobby/"Goin' Home Train"—Judy/ "Blues in the Night"—Bobby/"Goin' Home"—Judy and Bobby/ "Chattanooga Choo-Choo"—Bobby/"On the Atchison, Topeka and the Santa Fe"—Judy/"River, Stay Away from My Door"—Judy/"Some of These Days"—Bobby/"Bye, Bye Blackbird"—Judy/"Toot, Toot, Tootsie"—Bobby/"Beyond the Blue Horizon"—Judy/"I Know That You

Know"—Bobby/"I've Been Working on the Railroad"—Judy and
Bobby/"Lonesome Road"—Judy and Bobby
"Take Five"—the Peter Gennaro Dancers
"Born in a Trunk": **"Do It Again"*****
  "Get Me to the Church on Time"
  "Maybe I'll Come Back"

*deleted ("Jamboree Jones" was included on the Capitol Records album *Just For Openers*.)
**taped 12/19/63 to replace "Football" medley; Garland's three solos were also seen on
the subsequent airing of show #10 on 3/1/64 to replace the deleted "That's All" and
"One for My Baby," which in turn were inserted into show #5. This was necessary
because the "Tea" segment with Steve Allen taped for show #5 was dropped due to his
later full-fledged guest appearance on show #11; it was cut so as not to "take the edge
off" that later program.
***Judy's story about "almost being electrocuted" during her 1961 Hollywood Bowl con-
cert was deleted; remaining only was a brief mention of selling "a million copies of the
Carnegie Hall album," which then cut into the opening of "Do It Again."
(A Rooney-Garland "Mickey-Judy" sketch/medley was taped on 11/29/63 for the revamped final broadcast version of show #1 to air 12/8/63.)

THE JUDY GARLAND SHOW #15
("THE CHRISTMAS SHOW")

                                                        Taped: 12/6/63

Guests: Jack Jones, Liza Minnelli, Lorna and   **Aired: 12/22/63**
  Joey Luft, Mel Tormé, Tracy Everitt

"Have Yourself a Merry Little Christmas"—Judy
"Consider Yourself"—Judy, Lorna, and Joey (immediately reprised with
  Liza)
"Where Is Love?"—Joey
"Steam Heat"—Liza and Tracy
"Little Drops of Rain"—Judy
"Wouldn't It Be Loverly?"—Jack
"Lollipops and Roses"—Jack
"Santa Claus Is Coming to Town"—Lorna
"Alice Blue Gown"—Liza
Garland-Minnelli-Jones "Holiday" medley:
  "Jingle Bells"—All/"Sleigh Ride"—All/ It Happened in Sun Valley"—
  Liza and Jack/"Winter Wonderland"—Judy/"Rudolph the Red-Nosed
  Reindeer" (no vocal)—Peter Gennaro Dancers/reprise: "Jingle Bells"—
  All
"Here We Come A-Caroling"—Mel and Chorus
"The Christmas Song"—Judy and Mel
Traditional Carol medley:
  "Caroling, Caroling"—Chorus/"What Child Is This?"—Judy/"God Rest

Ye, Merry Gentlemen"—Chorus/"Hark! The Herald Angels Sing"—Jack and Mel/"Good King Wenceslas"—Chorus/"It Came Upon a Midnight Clear"—Liza and Tracy/"Silent Night"—Lorna, Joey, and Chorus/"Deck the Halls"—All/reprise: "Here We Come A-Caroling"—Chorus/reprise: "Rudolph the Red-Nosed Reindeer"—Judy and the Peter Gennaro Dancers

"Over the Rainbow"—Judy (seated with Lorna and Joe)

THE JUDY GARLAND SHOW #16　　　　　Taped: 12/13/63

Guests: Ethel Merman, Shelley Berman,　　　Aired: 1/12/64
　Peter Gennaro

Medley: "Ev'rybody's Doin' It"/"Let's Do It"—Judy, Ethel, Shelley, Peter, and Dancers
Shelley Berman "Telephone" sketch—Shelley, Dancers, and Singers (as businessmen)
"Gee! But It's Good to Be Here"—Ethel
*"That Old Feeling"—Ethel
"I Get a Kick Out of You"—Ethel
"I Love a Parade"—Peter and Dancers
"Shenandoah"—Judy
**"Magazine" sketch—Judy and Shelley
"Makin' Whoopee"—Judy and Peter; joined by Shelley
Garland-Merman medley:
　"Friendship"/"Let's Be Buddies"/"You're the Top"/"You're Just in Love"/"It's De-lovely"/"Together (Wherever We Go)"—Judy and Ethel
"Born in a Trunk": **"A Pretty Girl Milking Her Cow"**
　"Puttin' On the Ritz"
***"The Battle Hymn of the Republic"**

*dropped from final rundown
**deleted
***"Maybe I'll Come Back" was scheduled, but Judy did not sing it; the orchestra played it alone.

THE JUDY GARLAND SHOW #17　　　　　Taped: 12/20/63

Guests: Vic Damone, Chita Rivera, Louis Nye,　Aired: 1/9/64
　Ken Murray

"They Can't Take That Away from Me"—Judy and Dancers

"I Believe in You"—Judy, Chita, and Louis (an abbreviated version of the routine done by Judy and Jerry Van Dyke in show #1)
Louis Nye comedy monologue
*"Adios"—Vic
"You're Nobody Till Somebody Loves You"—Vic
"I Got Plenty o' Nuttin' "—Chita and Dancers
"By Myself"—Judy
**"My Fair Lady"—introduction (Judy)/comedy sketch—Louis and Chita
Ken Murray and His Hollywood Home Movies—Judy and Ken
"West Side Story" medley: Judy and Vic (Chita's introduction was deleted)
"Maria"—Vic/"Something's Coming"—Judy/reprise: "Maria"—Vic/"Somewhere"—Judy and Vic/"Tonight"—Judy and Vic
"Born in a Trunk": **"Better Luck Next Time"**
"That's Entertainment"*
"Almost Like Being in Love"/"This Can't Be Love"
"Maybe I'll Come Back"

*dropped from final rundown
**deleted

THE JUDY GARLAND SHOW #18   Taped: 1/14/64

Guests: Martha Raye, Peter Lawford, Rich Little,   Aired: 1/26/64
Ken Murray

"76 Trombones"—Judy
Rich Little impressions segment—Judy and Rich
(Rich talks/sings "The Man That Got Away" as Judy calls out voices for him to impersonate)
"It's So Nice to Have a Man Around the House"—Peter (with Bert Mustin)/"I'm Old-Fashioned"—Judy
"Glenn Miller" medley—Judy and Martha
(Judy's introduction of segment as dress-rehearsal footage taped 1/17 during show #19):
"I've Heard That Song Before"—Judy and Martha/"Moonlight Cocktail"—Judy and Martha/"Pennsylvania 6-5000"—Judy and Martha/"Elmer's Tune"—Judy and Martha/*"Adios"—Martha/"At Last"—Judy/*"In the Mood"—Judy and Martha/"St. Louis Blues"—Judy and Martha
Ken Murray and His Hollywood Home Movies—Judy and Ken
"Hit Parade 1964" medley—Judy, Martha, and Peter:

"Be True to Your School"—Peter/"The Boy Next Door" ("rock version")—Judy/"Dumbhead"—Martha/"The Nitty-Gritty"—Dancers/ "That Wonderful Year"—All
"Born in a Trunk": "Just You, Just Me" **
   "All Alone"
   "Oh, Lord! I'm on My Way"
   "Maybe I'll Come Back" ***

*dropped from final rundown
**The number was spontaneously dropped (on camera) by Judy, who chose to begin with "All Alone" instead.
***Judy exited the stage and chose not to sing the song as planned, but it was played by orchestra.

THE JUDY GARLAND SHOW #19   Taped: 1/17/64

Guests: Louis Jourdan, The Kirby Stone Four,   Aired: 2/2/64
   Ken Murray

*"San Francisco"—Judy
"Baubles, Bangles and Beads"—The Kirby Stone Four
** " 'S Wonderful"—The Kirby Stone Four
"You Do Something to Me"—The Kirby Stone Four
"Whispering"—Judy and The Kirby Stone Four
"I Want a Girl Just Like the Girl That Married Dear Old Dad"—Louis Jourdan and Dancers
"Paris Is a Lonely Town"—Judy
"Smoke Gets in Your Eyes" (comedy version)—Judy and "Firemen"
"Shall We Dance?"—The Wally Seibert Dancers (Judy appears to ac- knowledge dancers)
Ken Murray and His Hollywood Home Movies—Judy and Ken
"Children's Songs" medley—Judy and Louis:
   "Popeye, the Sailor Man"—Judy and Louis/"Huckleberry Hound"— Louis/"Give a Little Whistle"—Judy and Louis/"Little Lulu"—Louis/ "When You Wish Upon a Star"—Judy and Louis/"Who's Afraid of the Big, Bad Wolf?"—Louis/"Zip-a-Dee Doo-Dah"—Judy and Louis/ "Some Day My Prince Will Come"—sung by Judy, danced by Judy and Louis
"Born in a Trunk": "Just You, Just Me" **
   "What'll I Do?"
   "Rock-a-Bye Your Baby (With a Dixie Melody)" **
   "The Battle Hymn of the Republic" *

*replaced original planned opening, "Great Day"
**dropped from final rundown
***Judy elected not to sing "Maybe I'll Come Back" as scheduled.

THE JUDY GARLAND SHOW #20   Taped: 1/24/64

"Judy Garland in Concert"   Aired: 2/9/64

Overture: "Give My Regards to Broadway"/"Swing Low, Sweet Char-
iot"/"Liza"/"Make Someone Happy"/"When Johnny Comes March-
ing Home"/"That's Entertainment"/"Over the Rainbow"/"The Man
That Got Away"/reprise: "Over the Rainbow"—Orchestra
Judy:
**Medley: "Swing Low, Sweet Chariot"/"He's Got the Whole World in
His Hands"**
"World War I" medley:
"When Johnny Comes Marching Home"/"There's a Long, Long Trail
A-Winding"/"Keep the Home Fires Burning"/"Give My Regards to
Broadway"/"Boy of Mine"/"Oh! How I Hate to Get Up in the Morn-
ing"/"Over There"
*"I Can't Give You Anything but Love (Baby)"
"That's Entertainment"
"Make Someone Happy"
"Liza"
"Happiness Is a Thing Called Joe"
"Lorna"
*reprise: "Make Someone Happy"
*"Just You, Just Me"
*"How Long Has This Been Going On?"
"Rock-a-Bye Your Baby (With a Dixie Melody)"
"A Couple of Swells"
"America, the Beautiful"

*deleted from final rundown; possibly not taped

THE JUDY GARLAND SHOW #21   Taped: 1/31/64

Guests: Diahann Carroll, Mel Tormé   Aired: 2/16/64

Overture: "I Can't Give You Anything but Love (Baby)"/"Just You, Just
Me"—Orchestra

Judy:
"Hey, Look Me Over"
"Smile"
*"Just You, Just Me"
"I Can't Give You Anything but Love (Baby)"
"After You've Gone"
"Alone Together"
"Come Rain or Come Shine"
"Quiet Nights"—Diahann
"Goody, Goody"—Diahann
"A Stranger in Town"—Judy (sings a few bars to introduce Mel Tormé)
"Blues in the Night"—Mel and Girl Dancers
"The Trolley Song"—Judy and Mel
"Richard Rodgers/Harold Arlen" medley—Judy and Diahann:
    "Let's Call the Whole Thing Off" (special material)—Judy and Di-
    ahann/"It's Only a Paper Moon"—Judy/"Dancing on the Ceiling"
    —Diahann/"That Old Black Magic"—Judy/"The Gentleman Is a
    Dope"—Diahann/"Ill Wind"—Judy/"It Might as Well Be Spring"—
    Diahann/"Hit the Road to Dreamland"—Judy/"The Surrey with the
    Fringe on Top"—Diahann/"It's a New World"—Judy**/"Stormy
    Weather"—Judy and Diahann/"Let's Take the Long Way Home"—
    Judy and Diahann/"Bali Ha'i"—Diahann/"Manhattan"—Diahann/"The
    Sweetest Sounds"—Diahann/"Any Place I Hang My Hat Is Home"—
    Judy and Diahann
"Born in a Trunk": **"Don't Ever Leave Me"**
    "Great Day"***

*deleted; possibly not taped
**dropped from final rundown
***"Great Day" taped on 2/14/64 during show #22 for insertion here

THE JUDY GARLAND SHOW #22   Taped: 2/14/64

Guests: Jack Jones, Ken Murray   Aired: 2/23/64

Judy:
"Swanee"
"Almost Like Being in Love"/"This Can't Be Love"
*"Just in Time"
*"A Foggy Day"
*"If Love Were All"
*"Just You, Just Me"
"Last Night When We Were Young"

"Judy at the Palace" medley:
"Unless You've Played the Palace"/"Shine On, Harvest Moon"/"Some
   of These Days"/"My Man"/"I Don't Care"/reprise: "Unless You've
   Played the Palace"
"Love with the Proper Stranger"—Jack Jones
"Wives and Lovers"—Jack Jones
**Ken Murray and His Hollywood Home Movies—Judy and Ken
"Jeanette MacDonald–Nelson Eddy" medley—Judy and Jack:
   "San Francisco" (Roger Edens's verse only)—Judy and Jack/"Will You
   Remember (Sweetheart)?"—Judy and Jack/"Rosalie"—Jack/"I'll See You
   Again"—Judy and Jack/"Lover, Come Back to Me"—Judy/"The Don-
   key Serenade"—Judy and Jack
*"Born in a Trunk": **"When the Sun Comes Out"**

*also telecast to complete show #26 on 3/29/64
**taped 1/31/64

THE JUDY GARLAND SHOW #23   Taped: 2/21/64

"Judy Garland in Concert": "Music from the Movies"   Aired: 3/8/64

Overture: "I'm Always Chasing Rainbows"/"Be a Clown"/"I'm No-
   body's Baby"/"Carolina in the Morning"/"On the Atchison, Topeka
   and the Santa Fe"/"The Boy Next Door"/"The Man That Got Away"/
   "Over the Rainbow"—Orchestra
Judy:
Medley: **"Once in a Lifetime"/"I Feel a Song Comin' On"**
Medley: **"If I Had a Talking Picture of You"/"Toot, Toot, Tootsie"**
"Dirty Hands, Dirty Face"
*"Carolina in the Morning"
"Love of My Life"
"The Boy Next Door"
"On the Atchison, Topeka and the Santa Fe"
"Alexander's Ragtime Band"
"You're Nearer"
*"How Long Has This Been Going On?"
"Steppin' Out with My Baby"
"I'm Always Chasing Rainbows"
"The Man That Got Away"
"Be a Clown"
Reprise: **"Once in a Lifetime"**

*deleted; possibly not taped

THE JUDY GARLAND SHOW #24

Guest: Vic Damone

Taped: 2/23/64

Aired: 3/15/64

Overture: "I Love You"/"When Your Lover Has Gone"/"Old Devil Moon"/"Do I Love You?"—Orchestra

Judy:

"**Lucky Day**"

"**Sweet Danger**"

"**Do I Love You?**"

"**I Love You**"

"**When Your Lover Has Gone**"

"**Down with Love**"

"**Old Devil Moon**"

"**Never Will I Marry**"

"**Any Place I Hang My Hat Is Home**"

"**Chicago**"

"**Who Are You Now?**"—Vic Damone

"**I'm Gonna Miss You**"—Vic Damone

"**Kismet**" medley:

"Night of My Nights"—Vic/"He's in Love"—Judy and Vic/"This Is My Beloved"—Judy and Vic

"Born in a Trunk": "**Lost in the Stars**"

THE JUDY GARLAND SHOW #25

Guest: Robert Cole

Taped: 3/6/64

Aired: 3/22/64

Overture: "Old Man River"/"Love"/"By Myself"/"Get Happy"—Orchestra

Judy:

"**Sail Away**"

"**Comes Once in a Lifetime**"

"**I Am Loved**"

"**Life Is Just a Bowl of Cherries**"

"**Why Can't I?**"

"**I Gotta Right to Sing the Blues**"

"**Joey, Joey, Joey**"

"**Love**"

*"By Myself"
"Get Happy"
"As Long as He Needs Me"
"From This Moment On"—Bobby Cole and His Trio
** "I Wonder What Became of Me?"—Bobby Cole and His Trio
"The Lady's in Love with You"—Bobby Cole and His Trio
"Poor Butterfly"—Judy, Bobby Cole and His Trio
"Born in a Trunk": "The Nearness of You"***
   "Old Man River"

* deleted and inserted into show #26
** deleted
*** dropped from final rundown; Judy performed the song on show #26

THE JUDY GARLAND SHOW #26   Taped: 3/13/64

"Judy Garland in Concert"   Aired: 3/29/64

Overture: "That Old Feeling"/"Here's to Us"/"Born in a Trunk"/"Love
  Walked In"/"Almost Like Being in Love"/"The Man That Got Away"/
  "Over the Rainbow"—Orchestra
Judy:
"After You've Gone"
"The Nearness of You"
"Time After Time"
"That Old Feeling"
"Carolina in the Morning"
"When You're Smiling"
"Almost Like Being in Love"/"This Can't Be Love"
*"By Myself"
"The Last Dance"
"Suppertime"
** "Just in Time"
** "A Foggy Day"
** "If Love Were All"
** "Just You, Just Me"
** "Born in a Trunk": **"When the Sun Comes Out"**

* deleted from show #25
** taken from show #22, used here as well
taped but not broadcast: "Here's To Us"/"Where Is the Clown?"
scheduled but not taped and/or completed: "Love Walked In"/special material "Travel"
medley/"Something Cool"/"I Stayed Too Long at the Fair"
("Born in a Trunk" one-woman concert version routine taped, but not completed, on
March 26.)

NOTE ON
SOURCES

Over seventy-five interviews were conducted for this book between 1988 and 1990. All first-person quotations are derived from these original-source interviews unless specified directly within the text or upon the insistence of anonymity. (The names of those interviewed appear in the acknowledgments.)

Whenever possible, origins of all source material—newspapers, magazines, column items, and interviews—are directly credited in the narrative. *TV Guide*, syndicated newspaper columnists, the trade papers *Variety*, *Daily Variety*, and *The Hollywood Reporter* were utilized for 1955 through 1964, as were various newspapers, including *The New York Times*, the *Los Angeles Times*, the *Washington Post*, and the *Chicago Tribune*.

A valuable source of information are the so-called Garland "fan" publications issued between 1962 and 1964. Designed for a rather specific audience, these magazines chronicled on almost a daily basis the singer's professional and personal activities. A good deal of the taping details of *The Judy Garland Show* were derived from articles published in these privately issued journals. These publications included Max Preeo's *Garland News*, the *Garland Gazette*, and the *Rainbow Review*, the latter the publication of the London-based Garland fan club that Judy recognized as the "official" of several such organizations.

Also greatly helpful were the newspaper-clippings files on Judy Garland at the Academy of Motion Picture Arts & Sciences Library in Los Angeles and the Lincoln Center Library in New York.

A bibliography appears on page 406.

BIBLIOGRAPHY

Bergreen, Laurence. *Look Now, Pay Later*. New York: Doubleday, 1980.

Brown, Joan Winmill. *No Longer Alone*. New York: Fleming H. Revell, 1975.

Finch, Christopher. *Rainbow*. New York: Grosset & Dunlap, 1975.

Frank, Gerold. *Judy*. New York: Harper & Row, 1975.

Merman, Ethel. *Merman: An Autobiography*. New York: Simon & Schuster, 1978.

Metz, Robert. *CBS: Reflections in a Bloodshot Eye*. Chicago: Playboy Press, 1976.

Paley, William S. *As It Happened: A Memoir*. New York: Doubleday, 1979.

St. Johns, Adela Rogers. *Some Are Born Great*. New York: Doubleday, 1974.

Slater, Robert. *This . . . Is CBS: A Chronicle of 60 Years*. Englewood, New Jersey: Prentice-Hall, 1988.

Spada, James. *Judy & Liza*. New York: Doubleday, 1983.

Tormé, Mel. *The Other Side of the Rainbow with Judy Garland on the Dawn Patrol*. New York: William Morrow, 1970.

ACKNOWLEDGMENTS

This book truly would not have been possible without the generosity of the uncommonly talented artists who created *The Judy Garland Show*. Many of them spoke publicly about the experience for the first time for this project, and all offered great insight, candor, and sensitivity. My sincere gratitude to: Norman Jewison, Gary Smith, Orval Paine, Marge Paine, Jerry Van Dyke, Johnny Bradford, Bob Wynn (for his unsparing candor and insight), Bobby Cole, Mel Tormé, George Sunga, Carl Jablonski, Frank Peppiatt, John Aylesworth, Frank Waldman (for his recollections *and* for trusting me with his irreplaceable scripts), Ernie Flatt, Ginny Mancini, Ray Aghayan, Bob Mackie, Bernie Rothman, Dee Dee Wood, Marc Breaux, Robert Kelly, Peter Gennaro, Danny Daniels, Bruce Hoy, Harvey Evans, Gene McAvoy, Jerry Leshay, Bea Busch, Sharon Shore Denoff, Jack Elliott, Bonnie Evans, Leard Davis, Bill Hobin, and Henry Vilardo. These outstanding people brought life and emotion to this book, far more so than any newspaper clipping, memoir, magazine or trade paper item could provide.

A special debt is owed three men for whom I have the utmost and profound respect: Mort Lindsey (a peerless musician and human being); Bill Colleran (who is as talented as he is extraordinary)—his love and respect for Judy can be found in every word quoted within; and George Schlatter, who was always *there*, always a fountain of unerring truth, integrity, and humor—he was, and remains, one of her greatest champions.

Top billing also to the performers who reminisced about working with Judy on the series: Jane Powell, Peggy Lee, Jack Jones, Vic Damone, Steve Allen (special thanks for allowing me to reprint the lyric to "I'll Show Them All"), Soupy Sales, Martha Raye, Rich Little, the late Ken Murray, Jack Carter, Zina Bethune, George Maharis, Louis Nye, Shelley Berman, and Billy Barnes. Particular thanks to Jayne Meadows and Tony Bennett for so abundantly, and eloquently, sharing memories of both their friendship and professional relationship with Judy.

Words cannot express my appreciation to Judy's children, Liza Minnelli, Lorna Luft, and Joe Luft. Their very personal, loving memories of their mother have added immeasurably to the telling of this story. I am completely in their debt for breaking a long-standing tradition of nearly two decades and becoming involved in this book. I admire these three extraordinarily warm, generous, and gifted people tremendously; I only hope that this book is worthy of their participation and, most of all, such trust.

Abundant thanks to Sid Luft, who single-handedly has gathered, preserved, and struggled (triumphantly) to maintain control "within the family" of Judy Garland's television programs. Aware of the enormous legacy that *The Judy Garland Show* represented to future generations, Mr. Luft had the foresight to carefully guard the videotapes through the years as well as produce superior-quality laser-film transfers to ensure the protection and preservation of Judy's television work. Without him, *The Judy Garland Show* might well have vanished without a trace upon its network demise; he was, and remains, an extraordinary influence in the continuing phenomenon of Judy Garland.

Inestimable gratitude to the brilliant Leigh Wiener. His spectacular photography inside these pages as well as his keen insights as an on-set observer are rich additions to this book. He is a man of great talent, intelligence, and generosity.

At CBS, Marty Silverstein (the anchor of the New York–based photo department) is in front of the line for his overwhelming kindness, patience, understanding, and generosity; this is not to exclude the indomitable Kris Slavik, the reigning queen of that department; Ann Nelson in Los Angeles; Ginny Frey in New York; and CBS's ace photographers, Gaby Rona and Tony Esparza—their work graces many of these pages, and their artistry, more often than not, elevated standard publicity pictures into masterpieces of portrait photography. My thanks also to former CBS executives Michael Dann, Sal Iannucci, Ethel Winant, and Alan Courtney—for their willingness to speak on the record and with remarkable candor. Special thanks to the amazing Joan Quick, who provided me with invaluable ratings information she painstakingly compiled by hand when she had far more pressing matters than gathering figures from a long-defunct series a quarter-century old!

At Capitol Records, I doff my hat to a man of singular style, Larry Hathaway, the guiding force who championed *Judy Garland Live!* and trusted me to fulfill his expectations—and we created a hit! Equal amounts of appreciation to Capitol's ace engineer, Larry Walsh, who put up with me *and* the killer daily doughnuts for three months while editing the album. Thanks to Mr. Hathaway for his particular kindness in providing me with several photographs included in this book; and to Mr. Walsh for his constant striving for perfection, his enthusiasm, and his astounding generosity.

At my alma mater, *The Hollywood Reporter*, I must thank my wonderful editor, Teri Ritzer; my star colleague Howard Burns; and the ever-amazing and ever-cheerful John Ginelli, who had patience and fortitude in allowing me to be crammed into his small work space while poring over microfilm (and jamming the machine) hour upon hour.

Personal (and wholehearted) notes of thanks to: Robert Osborne of *The Hollywood Reporter* and beyond; Karen Swenson, *the* Barbra Streisand authority; Randy Pursley; John Carlyle; Richard Jordan; Steve Young; Scott Schechter; Rick Sommers; Steve Paley; David Griffin; Rose Marie; Don Azars; Lily Tomlin; Judy Van Herpen; Kim Lundgreen (who generously sent to this complete stranger photographs from Denmark that he unearthed in London!); Marty Panzer; Eric Kulberg of Universal Media; Peter Jacobson; Beverly Mansfield; Joe Lauro of Archive Film Inc.; Bob and the other talented craftsmen at B & R Photo Graphics in Hollywood; and Army Archerd of *Daily Variety*.

Equal amounts of gratitude to the following for their assistance and encouragement in a myriad of ways: Tom Cooper; Lorna Smith, Gwen Potter, Ken Sephton and Billy Tweedie of the International Judy Garland Club; Patti Cavin; Pat McMath; Elly Oleson; Paul Chopak; Phyllis Bamberger; Dan Rathbone; Ron Paolillo; Joseph L. Gramm; Margo Slaughter; Ken Young; Max Preeo; Ed Jablonski; Stephen Spurgeon; Matthew West; Mark Herron; Robert Rosterman (for everything over the years); Marta Houske; Neal Hitchens; the one and only Sy Sher; Keith Riedell (who made this book tangible and—almost—on deadline by showing me how to work a computer!); Randy Henderson; the most generous and supportive Tom Brown and Wayne Kranick; the late Richard Connolly; and my very dearest Cherie Baker.

Special, special gratitude to John Edward Grasso, interview transcriber extraordinaire; he was tirelessly professional and thorough throughout. What was supposed to have been an eight-week assignment instead took up eight months of his life and without complaint. He was the model of patience, kindness, and accuracy.

Sincere appreciation to the many people who patiently accepted my persistent telephone calls and letters requesting interviews, photographs, and related materials. Unerringly professional and kind, they have my thanks: Henri Bollinger; Barry Landau; Joan Kramer; Michael Gennaro; Allan B. Goodrich (John F. Kennedy Library, Boston); Mrs. Gene Hibbs; Jake Hooker; Roni Gallion; the peerless Joseph Natalie of George Schlatter Productions; Sylvia Winer; Kelli of Yorktown Productions; and Joan Diegnan. Special thanks to: Al Da Silva; Al Kohn of Warner Bros. Music; Bruce Troy Sansing; and Les Perkins.

John Fricke deserves, and gets, a big, sustained round of applause. His generosity in friendship and willingness to share is unparalleled and I thank him, with great sincerity, for *everything;* it was he who introduced me to *The Judy Garland Show* many years ago and without such undaunting encouragement, then *and* now, this book might well never have been.

My debt to John Graham is no less profound. No one knows more about Judy Garland (or researching a book) than does Mr. Graham, and his support, enthusiasm, and outpouring of that incredible knowledge has been of inestimable value; Christopher Finch in *Rainbow* deemed him a "Garland scholar" without peer, and I wholeheartedly agree. Both Mr. Fricke (who also graciously provided me with information utilized in the show-listings appendix) and Mr. Graham have assisted me substantially in the research for the book, and I thank them for sharing their unrivaled friendship and expertise.

Special appreciation also to Tom Jones, a devoted Garland admirer and a wonderful friend; I thank him for his extraordinary generosity, kindness, and always "being there."

In a category all their own are my parents, Margaret and Richard O'Malley. My unwaveringly encouraging mother has not only been supportive of me but of my eternal fascination for all things Judy. For that alone, she deserves a special mention if not a Purple Heart.

And—listed at the end but really in the forefront—I must acknowledge my great debt and respect (and affection) to my incomparable editor at William Morrow, Lisa Drew, who so much believed in Judy and the series that she alone made this book a reality. Warm, sincere thanks as well to her indefatigable assistant, Robert Shuman, who was, and *is,* enormously patient, understanding, and sensitive. His singular kindness and long-distance friendship remain heartily appreciated.

INDEX